CHRONICLES OF AMERICAN INDIAN PROTEST

Compiled and edited with commentaries by

The Council on Interracial Books for Children

Published by

THE COUNCIL ON INTERRACIAL BOOKS FOR
CHILDREN

1841 Broadway, New York, N.Y. 10023

i

ACKNOWLEDGMENTS

The Council on Interracial Books for Children is grateful for permission to reprint the following:

Revolt of the Pueblo Indians of New Mexico, 1680-1682, copyright © 1942 by the University of New Mexico Press.

The newspaper article, "The Navajo and the New Deal," November 11, 1941, the *New York Times*: © 1941 by the *New York Times* Co. Reprinted by permission.

Land of the Spotted Eagle by Chief Luther Standing Bear. Copyright © 1933 by Chief Luther Standing Bear. Copyright © 1960 by May Jones.

"*The Denial of Legal Remedies to Indian Nations Under U.S. Law*," © 1977 by the Institute for the Development of Indian Law. Inc.

Cover Illustration: Poster available from *Akwesasne Notes* (address listed on p. 391)

CHRONICLES OF AMERICAN INDIAN PROTEST, Revised Edition

Library of Congress Cataloging in Publication Data
  Main entry under title:

  Chronicles of American Indian protest.
    Bibliography: p.
    SUMMARY: Includes a collection of documents, each prefaced by a brief historical introduction, mirroring the American Indians' struggle for survival from 1622 to 1978.
    1. Indians of North America—History—Addresses, essays, lectures. 2. Indians, Treatment of—United States—Addresses, essays, lectures. [1. Indians of North America—History—Addresses, essays, lectures]
  I. Council on Interracial Books for Children.
  E77.2.C5 1979   973'.04'97   78-26819
  ISBN 0-930040-30-9

Published by the Council on Interracial Books for Children
1841 Broadway, New York, N.Y. 10023

(Continued on the following page)

WHAT IS THE COUNCIL?

The Council on Interracial Books for Children, Inc. (CIBC) is a non-profit organization formed in 1965 by concerned editors, librarians, writers and historians. The CIBC was organized in order to initiate much needed change in the all-white world of children's book publishing and to promote a literature for children that better reflects the aspirations of a multiracial, multicultural society.

The Council publishes the *Interracial Books for Children Bulletin* eight times yearly. The *Bulletin* regularly reviews children's books for racism, sexism, ageism, handicapism and other anti-human values and provides a range of informative articles on the impact of these issues in children's books and learning materials.

The Council yearly sponsors a contest for previously unpublished minority writers of children's books. A number of the winners of the contest have had their works published by major publishers and have become well known and honored in the field.

The Council's Racism/Sexism Resource Center for Educators has prepared a variety of books, filmstrips, lesson plans and pamphlets to assist teachers, librarians, parents and students in the struggle against racism and sexism in education. Of particular note are a filmstrip and teacher's guide— *Unlearning "Indian" Stereotypes*— designed for use in elementary schools and public libraries to counteract commonly held stereotypes of Native people, as well as a book— *Stereotypes, Distortions and Omissions in U.S. History Textbooks*—which provides a section on the treatment of Native American/U.S. history. This book includes a content rating instrument, an analysis of a number of the new textbooks, plus supplemental information for classroom and discussion use.

For a free catalog listing all available materials as well as subscription information for the *Bulletin*, write to the Council on Interracial Books for Children, Inc., 1841 Broadway, New York, N.Y. 10023.

PREFACE TO SECOND EDITION

From the first resistance to the European invasion of the Americas up to and including the present, Native people have struggled to preserve their sovereign nations, their cultures and their very existence. For the most part, the history of this centuries-long struggle has been omitted and distorted by textbooks used in the U.S. educational system. These omissions and distortions of the textbooks—along with the biased reporting of the major news media—have had serious consequences. Most of the U.S. public have little awareness or understanding of the continuing struggle of Native peoples and thus exert little pressure on the U.S. government to end what has rightfully been called "America's longest war."

Chronicles of American Indian Protest has been updated and reprinted in the hope of countering some of the gross distortions perpetuated in the name of "American history" and to fill part of the enormous void created by the media's failure to provide full information on the current struggle. A volume this size can only scratch the surface of the multi-faceted and diverse histories of Native resistance first to European and later to U.S. aggression.

The resistance documents presented in *Chronicles* were selected because they represent Native voices. Yet, as the earlier edition noted, even materials considered authentically Indian can still reflect a white viewpoint; many of the documents themselves have been preserved in English translations prepared by non-Indian people.

This second edition of *Chronicles* has been revised and

expanded in order to present documents generated by the resurgence of the protest movement during the 1970's. This has been a period of intensifying struggle, brought about in large part because of increasing efforts by the U.S. government and multinational corporations to exploit the enormous energy-related resources on remaining Indian land—coal, uranium, oil, gas and water. As Third World countries gain independence and control of their own resources, the multinational corporations turn to the resources remaining in the U.S. This increases the oppression Native people face and the resistance they must mount to survive.

However, international recognition of the Native struggle is mounting as well—particularly from Third World nations. From its resurgence at Alcatraz, at the BIA occupation and at the liberation of Wounded Knee to the historic Geneva Conference of September, 1977, the struggle of Native people for sovereignty, independence and self-determination has been accorded recognition in the international arena. The recommendation of the Geneva Conference to "observe October 12, the day of so-called 'discovery' of America, as an International Day of Solidarity with the Indigenous Peoples of the Americas" will serve to strengthen awareness internationally and within the U.S.

This book can provide useful material for increasing understanding of the historical background which led to the present situation. The organizations listed at the back can provide additional materials and information. Though we cannot change the past, we are responsible for the present and for the future we leave to our children.

BUSINESS BEFORE . . . ANYTHING

1622

A Declaration of the State of the Colony and Affairs in Virginia

ABOUT THE DOCUMENT:

Jamestown, the first permanent white man's colony established in what is now the United States, was located within the territory of the Powhatan Confederacy of Algonquian nations, and it owed its survival to Algonquian hospitality. About two hundred towns were united in the Confederacy, with each separate nation and town enjoying a considerable autonomy. For example, during the first years of the English colony, when one or another town resented the increasing depredations of the colonists it could—and did—take action against the Englishmen without involving the whole confederacy in war. But though it might take longer, it was also possible for an enemy to rouse the collective anger and resistance of the whole Powhatan people. It took the Jamestown colonists fifteen years (from 1607 until 1622) to provoke massive attack by the Confederacy.

The colonists had been sent to America by an English joint-stock company: business men whose motive was financial profit. The colonists' conduct was ruled essentially by the ethics of trade. Weak at first and scarcely able to survive, the colonists were dependent on the Indians' crops. Survival as well as sound business policy dictated the need for friendly relations with a people from whom the London company directors expected sizable profits in trade. The generosity of the Powhatan was undeniable. According to Capt. John Smith, the colonists were given "corn and bread ready made." The corn was Indian corn—maize—and was unknown to Europeans. The Indians first taught them to eat it and then taught them how to plant and cultivate it. And the Indian corn made possible the Englishmen's survival. Still true to their traders' ethic, not even hunger could make them miss a sharp bargain. Two of those earliest settlers recorded how, when during the winter of 1608–1609 the colonists sought out the Powhatan to ask for corn, ". . . we wrangled out of the king 10 quarters of corn for a copper kettle; the which the President [Capt. John Smith] perceiving him much to effect, valued it at a much greater rate. . . ." Before long the colonists were trading at the rate of one bushel of corn per square inch of copper. And later, when time and sharp trading put the colonists in the position of having corn that the Indians needed desperately, the English colonists traded four hundred bushels of corn for a "mortgage on their whole countries."

The Indians' corn made it possible for the colonists to survive, and another Indian agricultural development created the profit for which the colonists had been sent. That crop was tobacco, for which a rich and ready market sprang up in Europe almost as soon as it had been introduced. Both corn and tobacco, of course, grow in the ground; naturally, then, the colonists wanted to get possession of the land. Nor was it just any land that they wanted; they wanted the fields that the Indians had already cleared for their own crops. Capt. John Smith described the tremendous efforts the colonists had to make in order to clear forty acres of land during their early days in America. The nearby Indian town of Kecoughtan had cornfields of more than two thousand acres. Now the same business ethic that had made peace profitable found aggression more profitable. Kecoughtan was seized and its inhabitants driven out. As the colonists increased in number, so did their depredations and provocations against the

Powhatan. William Brandon, in *The American Heritage Book of Indians*, gives an example of the way the colonists could provoke a situation that would end with the white people in possession of the Indian's fields. "Livestock introduced by the settlers damaged the unfenced Indian gardens, hogs being the worst offenders. But if you damaged the hog, the hog's owners would damage you, and if your friends damaged the hog's owner, the English would then burn an Indian town and put a dozen people to the sword (the second most common Algonquian name for Englishmen was 'cutthroats'). . . ." And another parcel of land would yield its fruit to white men rather than to the Indians who had labored to clear it—and, as often as not, to plant and cultivate it.

Wahunsonacock—called King Powhatan by the English and our history books—strove continually to maintain peace not only between the different Algonquian towns and nations in the Confederacy but also between them and the white intruders. The English claimed an urgent desire to live in peace and Wahunsonacock wanted to believe them. "I am not so simple," he said to Capt. John Smith, "as not to know that it is better to eat good meat, be well, and to sleep quietly with my women and children, to laugh and be merry with the English. . . ." Apparently unable to believe that the English could be "so simple," either, he patiently worked to resolve incident after incident (including the kidnaping of his own daughter, the famous Pocahontas) rather than declare a state of war between the colonists and the Confederacy. But Wahunsonacock was an old man, and in 1618 he died. He was succeeded in office by a brother, Opechancanough, whose attitude toward the colonists was much less optimistic—and, as history has proved, much more realistic. On March 22, 1962, Opechancanough led an attack by the Confederacy against the white settlements, and in the short space of a few hours a number of those settlements were wiped out and 347 colonists were dead. Four years earlier that had been the total number of white settlers within Confederacy territory, but in those four years the white population had quadrupled while the Powhatan suffered disastrous losses from European diseases. The Powhatan Confederacy had been patient four years too many.

An official of the London stock company wrote about the Powhatan attack and evaluated its meaning in terms of the business ethic by which the colony was governed. The document that follows is excerpted from that report. Note that in the first paragraph even the loss of 347 white colonists is seen as a blessing by this "gentleman" of the stock company, whose sole concern is with the profit to be made from "the Plantation." What value Indian lives have in this connection is all too clear.

THE DOCUMENT:

Excerpts from "A Declaration of The State of The Colony and Affairs in VIRGINIA with A Relation of The Barbarous Massacre in the time of peace and League, treacherously executed by the Native Infidels upon the English, the 22 of March last, 1622," by Edward Waterhouse. Published by Authoritie, London, 1622.

. . . Thus have you seene the particulars of this massacre . . . wherein treachery and cruelty have done their worst to us, or rather to themselves; for whose understanding is so shallow, as not to perceive that this must needs bee for the good of the Plantation after, and the losse of this blood to make the body more healthfull, as by these reasons may be manifest.

. . . Because our hands which before were tied with gentlenesse and faire usage, are now set at liberty by the treacherous violence of the Savages, not untying the knot, but cutting it: So that we, who hitherto have had possession of no more ground then their waste, and our purchase at a valuable consideration to their owne contentment, gained: may now by right of Warre, and law of Nations, invade the Country, and destroy them who sought to destroy us: whereby we shall enjoy their cultivated places, turning the laborious Mattocke into the victorious Sword (wherein there is more both ease, benefit, and glory) and possessing the fruits of others labours. Now their cleared grounds in all their villages (which are situate in the fruitfullest places of the land) shall be inhabited by us. . . .

. . . Because the way of conquering them is much more easie then of civilizing them by faire meanes, for they are a rude, barbarous, and naked people, . . . Besides that, a conquest may be of many, and at once; but civility is in particular, and slow, the effect of long time and great industry. Moreover, victorie of them may be gained many waies; by force, by surprise, by famine in burning their corne, by destroying and burning their Boats, Canoes, and Houses, by breaking their fishing Weares, by assailing them in their huntings, whereby they get the greatest part of their sustenance in Winter, by pursuing and chasing them with our horses, and blood-Hounds to draw after them, and Mastives to teare them, which take this naked, tanned, deformed Savages, for no other then wild beasts, and are so fierce and fell upon them, that they fear them worse then their old Devill. . . . By these and sundry other wayes, as by driving them (when they flye) upon their enemies, who are round about them, and by animating and abetting their enemies against them, may their ruine or subjection be soone effected. . . .

. . . Because the Indians who before were used as friends may now most justly be compelled to servitude and drugery, and supply the roome of men that labour, whereby even the meanest of the Plantation may imploy themselves more entirely in their Arts and Occupations, which are more generous, whilest Savages performe their inferiour workes digging in mynes, and the like, of whom also some may be sent for the service of the *Sommer Ilands*.

POSTSCRIPT TO THE DOCUMENT:

In the "Laws and Orders Concluded by the General Assembly of Virginia, March 5, 1623–1624," the following order is given:

That at the beginning of July next the inhabitants of every corporation shall fall upon their adjoyning salvages as we

did the last year, those that shall be hurte upon service to
be cured at the publique charge; in case any be lamed to be
maintained by the country according to his person and quality.

Thus, following the recommendations of persons such
as Waterhouse, the colonists made war upon the Indians,
carefully planned war, year after year. In 1641, Opechancanough, then well into his nineties and too feeble to even
walk on his own, coordinated a second major attack
against the oppressing colonists, killing hundreds of settlers in a single day. Eventually he was captured and shot,
and the uprising squelched.

By 1642, twenty years after the original Indian attack
of 1622, the white man had virtually exterminated the
Powhatan along the lower James and York rivers. Individual Powhatan tribes were forced to sign separate peace
treaties with the colonists, and those Indians who refused
to go to the reservations assigned them were either sold as
slaves, killed off, or fled to the less populated Chesapeake
Bay area. By the time of the American Revolution not
more than a thousand Indians remained of the Powhatan
Confederacy.

KING PHILIP CRIES OUT FOR REVENGE

1675

From the "Eulogy on King Philip," Delivered
by William Apes

ABOUT THE DOCUMENT:

While the Powhatan were defending themselves from
the white settlers of Jamestown, other Indian nations to

the north were also being invaded by colonial expeditions sent out by businessmen of England, Sweden, and the Netherlands. One such joint-stock company, the Plymouth Company of England, hired Capt. John Smith to explore to the north on their behalf; in 1614 he did so and on the coast of Massachusetts in the territory of the Wampanoag visited a town they called Patuxet. Captain Smith renamed the town Plymouth in honor of his employers. The town's inhabitants still called it Patuxet, however, when it was visited the next year by an English slaver, Captain Hunt, who kidnaped a number of Indians and, to round matters out, left smallpox behind him. Until 1619 the plague ravaged the Wampanoag and their immediate neighbors to the north, the Massachusett. It has been estimated that the Wampanoag lost two-thirds of their population and the Massachusett ninety percent. After the plague, came the Pilgrim Fathers, in 1620, a group of religious self-exiles from England financed as a joint-stock company by businessmen outside the Plymouth Company. Intending to settle just north of Jamestown, the pilgrims' shipmaster steered them too far north, and they landed in Wampanoag territory instead, at Plymouth, where they found no one left alive to dispute the town's name with them. They also found well-cleared fields, which they immediately claimed for their own. Their attitude toward the smallpox plague that had cleared the way for them was expressed by a Puritan colonist a few years later: he called the plague "the Wonderful Preparation the Lord Jesus Christ by His Providence for His People's Abode in the Western World" and gave the Lord an extra round of thanks because the plague had killed off "chiefly young men and children, the very seeds of increase." Other joint-stock companies, such as the Massachusetts Bay Company, soon followed the Pilgrims into Wampanoag territory. As had happened at Jamestown, the early colonists were received hospitably. Massassoit, chief sachem of the Wampanoag, formed a friendship with the Plymouth settlers which he honored as long as he had life. His visit to the colony with presents of food for their Thanksgiving Day feast is legendary and has become an often repeated incident in our history books, where it has come to symbolize a friendship between races that even then was much more fantasy than fact. Though Massassoit profited from the acquisition of guns and horses; though the friendship he honored so long must have owed much to his belief that his life had been saved in sickness by treatments prescribed by a Plymouth settler, Massassoit's own people had learned hatred of white people long before his death in 1622. They had cause.

Wampanoag lands, which in 1620 stretched from Narragansett Bay to Cape Cod, shrank under the white man's depredations until "the native proprietors were confined to a few tongues of land, jutting out into the sea, the chief of which is now Bristol, in Rhode Island . . . surrounded on three sides by the ocean, and, on the fourth, hemmed in by the ever-advancing tide of civilization."

That "civilization" passed laws that provided the death penalty for blasphemy—which included any Indian who refused to accept the colonists' religion—and that prohibited all Indian activity on the Puritan Sabbath. Its courts charged, tried, and jailed Indians for "trespassing" on lands that the colonists now claimed as their own—and not only when those lands were actually in use by colonists. Colonial "authority" threatened reprisal against any sachem who interfered with the eager efforts of white missionaries.

By the time that Massassoit died, his people were more than angry; they demanded that their new chief resist white abuses. This was Massassoit's son who had been given the English name of Alexander; his younger brother had in a similar way been named Philip. Alexander showed himself willing to resent the white man's highhanded treatment, and this made the colonists resentful in turn. Shortly after he assumed his chieftainship, he was ordered by the colonists to appear before them to give assurances of his "loyalty." When Alexander refused to run at their call, the colonists sent troops to fetch him. During the intensive interrogation that followed, Alexander fell ill of a fever. He died as his friends were carrying him back to his home.

Some of his people said he died of a broken heart caused by humiliation; others said he had been poisoned. His death sharpened the hatred his people already felt; his brother Philip never forgave it and, succeeding in his turn to the chieftainship, Philip began to prepare for revenge. For years Philip worked to unite the neighboring Indian nations for a war to the finish with the white intruders. He collected weapons and set up forest forges for gunsmithing. When in 1675 King Philip declared his war against the colonists, he had succeeded in attracting approximately twenty thousand Indians to his cause.

But by 1675 there were fifty thousand white colonists in New England. In spite of the odds, Philip's forces attacked fifty-two of the ninety settler towns, including Plymouth itself, where they burned sixteen houses. Twelve towns were totally destroyed, and nearly a thousand colonists were killed. Finally, the tide began to turn against the Indians as the white man's superiority in numbers and in weapons began to make itself felt. One by one, principal Indian war chiefs were killed in battle or betrayed by faint-hearted followers who lost hope in the face of white numbers. Philip's wife and son were captured and sold as slaves in the West Indies. By August of 1676 the Indian cause seemed lost, though Philip refused to accept defeat. When one of his companions suggested that perhaps they should surrender, Philip became so angry that he ordered the defeatist killed. This man's brother promptly deserted and in vengeance led the colonist soldiers to Philip's camp, where he was ambushed and killed.

With his death the remnants of his confederacy collapsed. Philip's head was cut off and taken to Plymouth where it was impaled on a pike and put up for public display: there it remained for twenty-five years. But the words that had so often found their echo within the hearts of Philip's Indian listeners have endured as the document that follows shows.

THE DOCUMENT:

Speech of King Philip as related in a speech by William

Apes, entitled "Eulogy on King Philip," delivered at the Odeon in Boston in 1836

Brothers,—You see this vast country before us, which the Great Spirit gave to our fathers and us; you see the buffalo and deer that now are our support.—Brothers, you see these little ones, our wives and children, who are looking to us for food and raiment; and you now see the foe before you, that they have grown insolent and bold; that all our ancient customs are disregarded; the treaties made by our fathers and us are broken, and all of us insulted; our council fires disregarded, and all the ancient customs of our fathers; our brothers murdered before our eyes, and their spirits cry to us for revenge. Brothers, these people from the unknown world will cut down our groves, spoil our hunting and planting grounds, and drive us and our children from the graves of our fathers, and our council fires, and enslave our women and children.

POSTSCRIPT TO THE DOCUMENT:

The above statement was quoted in a eulogy given by William Apes, an Indian, at the Odeon Club in Boston, one hundred and fifty years after King Philip's death. Apes' eulogy was a defense of the Indian and an attack on the white racist institutions of mid-nineteenth century America. After Apes delivered his eulogy, he left the Odeon Club on Federal Street and was never seen again.

PUEBLO WIPEOUT AT TAOS

1680

Declaration of Josephe, Spanish-speaking Indian

ABOUT THE DOCUMENTS:

Far to the west in what is now Arizona and New
Mexico, it seemed as if the white man from Spain would
have better luck than the white man from England and
the Netherlands. As far back as 1598 the Spanish conquerors claimed possession of those lands to which they
had come in search of the fabled golden city of Cibola.
When they found no gold, the Spaniards instituted the
cruel *encomienda* system they had developed in Hispanio-
la and Cuba, a system whereby huge estates of land were
parceled out to the conquerors, while the Indians who had
previously lived on them by free and natural right were
now bound to them as serfs and forced into brutal labor
and religious conformity. For eighty years the Spaniards
maintained their stern rule over the Pueblos without serious threat. In 1680, however, the Pueblo proved that
patience should not be confused with weakness or cowardice. Led principally by Popé, a medicine man from
the Taos Pueblo, the Indians rose up on August 11 in a
rebellion that had as its goal the reestablishment of ancient Indian worship. The uprising was marked by its fury
and by its almost unanimous support by the Indian people.
The Spaniards were defeated and everyone not killed in
battle was driven out of Pueblo territory. Within a few
weeks the Pueblo obliterated every trace of the white
man's oppression—a feat never before or since accomplished by the Indians of the New World. Attacking from
every part of the Pueblo territory, the Indians killed four

hundred Spaniards and drove twenty-five hundred soldiers and priests to seek refuge in Mexico.

Though the Pueblo victory was complete, it was not destined to endure. For twelve years the Pueblo lived without white rule, successfully defending themselves against repeated Spanish attempts to reconquer them. In 1692 the Spanish finally succeeded, and once more the Pueblo became a conquered people.

In the documents that follow, two Indian witnesses—referred to as "declarants"—describe the early stages of the extraordinary uprising. Particularly revealing in the testimony is the Indians' utter contempt for the Christian religion that the Spanish priests had tried to impose upon them.

The term "apostate" used in the testimony refers to the renegade Indians. It must be remembered that the actual testimony of the Indians is reinterpreted—often derogatorily to their cause—by the Spanish inquisitors who recorded the Indian statements.

THE DOCUMENTS:

From Revolt of the Pueblo Indians of New Mexico and Otermin's Attempted Reconquest, 1680–1682, introduced and annotated by Charles Wilson Hackett, translated from original documents by Charmion Clair Shelby. Coronado Cuarto Centennial Publications, 1540-1940, Vols. VIII and IX, Albuquerque, 1942.

DOCUMENT A:

Declaration of Josephe, Spanish-speaking Indian. [Place of the Rio del Norte, December 19, 1681.]

In this said place and plaza de armas of this army on the 19th day of the month of December, 1681, for the said judicial proceedings of this case, his lordship caused to appear before him an Indian prisoner named Josephe, able to speak the Castilian language, a servant of Sargento Mayor Sebastián de Herrera who fled from him and went among the apostates. The interpreters and assisting witnesses being present, his lordship received from the said Indian the oath in due legal form, in the name of God, our Lord, and a sign of the cross, under charge of which and having been absolved, he promised to tell the truth as to what he might know and as he might be questioned, he having been given to understand the seriousness of the oath. . . .

Asked what causes or motives the said Indian rebels had for renouncing the law of God and obedience to his Majesty, and for committing so many kinds of crimes, and who were the instigators of the rebellion, and what he had heard while he was among the apostates, he said that the prime movers of the rebellion were two Indians of San Juan, one named El Popé and the other El Taqu, and another from Taos named Saca, and another from San Ildefonso named Francisco. He knows that these were the principals, and the causes they gave were alleged ill treatment and injuries received from the present secretary, Francisco Xavier, and the maestre de campo, Alonso García, and from the sargentos mayores, Luis de Quintana and Diego López, because they beat them, took away what they had, and made them work without pay. Thus he replies.

Asked if he has learned or it has come to his notice during the time that he has been here the reason why the apostates burned the images, churches, and things pertaining to divine worship, making a mockery and a trophy of them, killing the priests and doing the other things they did, he said that he knows and has heard it generally stated that while they were besieging the villa the rebellious traitors burned the church and shouted in loud voices, "Now the God of the Spaniards, who was their father, is dead, and Santa María, who was their mother, and the saints, who were pieces of rotten wood," saying that only their own god lived. Thus they ordered all the temples and images, crosses and rosaries burned, and this function being over, they all went to bathe in the rivers, saying that they thereby washed away the water of baptism. For their churches, they placed on the four sides and in the center of the plaza some small circular enclosures of stone where they went to offer flour, feathers, and the seed of maguey, maize, and tobacco, and performed other superstitious rites, giving the children to understand that they must all do this in the future. The captains and chiefs ordered that the names of Jesus and of Mary should nowhere be uttered, and that they should discard their baptismal names, and abandon the wives whom God had given them in matrimony, and take the ones that they pleased. He saw that as soon as the remaining Spaniards had left, they ordered all the estufas erected, which are their houses of idolatry, and danced throughout the kingdom the dance of the cazina, making many masks for it in the image of the devil. Thus he replied to this question.

Asked what plans or information the said apostates communicated with regard to the possible return of the Spaniards and how they got along in the life they were living, he said that it is true that there were various opinions among them, most of them believing that they would have to fight to the death with the said Spaniards, keeping them out.

Asked why, since the said rebels had been of different minds, some believing that they should give themselves up peacefully and others opposing it, when the Spaniards arrived at the sierra of La Cieneguilla de Cochití, where the leaders of the uprising and people from all the nations were assembled, they had not attempted to give themselves up and return to the holy faith and to obedience to his Majesty—for while they had made some signs, they had done nothing definite—he said that although it is true that as soon as the Spaniards arrived some said that it was better to give up peaceably than to have war, the young men were unwilling to agree, saying that they wished to fight. In particular one Spanish-speaking Indian or coyote named Francisco, commonly called El Ollita, said that no one should surrender in peace, that all must fight, and that although some of his brothers were coming with the Spaniards, if they fought on the side of the Spaniards he would kill them, and if they came over to the side of the Indians he would not harm them. Whereupon everyone was disturbed, and there having arrived at this juncture Don Luis Tupatú, governor of the pueblo of Los Pecuríes, while they were thus consulting, news came to the place where the junta was being held from another Indian named Alonso Catití, a leader of the uprising, believed to be a coyote, in which he sent to notify the people that he had already planned to deceive the Spaniards with feigned peace. He had arranged to send to the pueblo of Cochití all the prettiest, most pleasing, and neatest Indian women so that, under pretense of coming down to prepare food for the Spaniards, they could provoke them to lewdness, and that night while they were with them, the said coyote Catití would come down with all the men of the Queres and Jemez nations, only the said Catití attempting to speak with the said Spaniards, and at a shout from him they would all rush down to kill the said Spaniards; and he gave orders that all the rest who were in the other junta where the said Don Luis and El Ollita were present, should at the same time attack the horse drove, so as to finish that too. This declarant being present during all these proceedings, and feeling compassion because of the treason they were plotting, he determined to come to warn the Spaniards, as he did, whereupon they put themselves under arms and the said Indians again went up to the heights of the sierra, and the Spanish withdrew. Thus he replies to the question.

DOCUMENT B:

Declaration of Pedro Naranjo of the Queres Nation. [Place of the Rio del Norte, December 19, 1681.]

In the said plaza de armas on the said day, month, and year, for the prosecution of the judicial proceedings of this case his lordship caused to appear before him an Indian prisoner named Pedro Naranjo, a native of the pueblo of San Felipe, of the Queres nation, who was captured in the advance and attack upon the pueblo of La Isleta. He makes himself understood very well in the Castilian language and speaks his mother tongue and the Tegua. He took the oath in due legal form in the name of God, our Lord, and a sign of the cross, under charge of which he promised to tell the truth concerning what he knows and as he might be questioned, and having understood the seriousness of the oath and so signified through the interpreters, he spoke as indicated by the contents of the *autos*.

Asked whether he knows the reason or motives which the Indians of this kingdom had for rebelling, forsaking the law of God and obedience to his Majesty, and committing such grave and atrocious crimes, and who were the leaders and principal movers, and by whom and how it was ordered; and why they burned the images, temples, crosses, rosaries, and things of divine worship, committing such atrocities. . . , he said that since the government of Señor General Hernando Ugarte y la Concha they have planned to rebel on various occasions through conspiracies of the Indian sorcerers, and that although in some pueblos the messages were accepted, in other parts they would not agree to it; and that it is true that during the government of the said señor general seven or eight Indians were hanged for this same cause, whereupon the unrest subsided. Some time thereafter they [the conspirators] sent from the pueblo of Los Taos through the pueblos of the custodia two deerskins with some pictures on them signifying conspiracy after their manner, in order to convoke the people to a new rebellion, and the said deerskins passed to the province of Moqui, where they refused to accept them. The pact which they had been forming ceased for the time being, but they always kept in their hearts the desire to carry it out, so as to live as they are living to-day. Finally, in the past years, at the summons of an Indian named Popé who is said to have communication with the devil, it happened that in an estufa of the pueblo of Los Taos there appeared to the said Popé three figures of Indians who never came out of the estufa. They gave the said Popé to understand that they were going underground to the lake of Copala. He saw these figures emit fire from all the extremities of their bodies, and that one of them was called Caudi, another Tilini, and the other Tleume; and these three beings spoke to the said

Popé, who was in hiding from the secretary, Francisco Xavier, who wished to punish him as a sorcerer. They told him to make a cord of maguey fiber and tie some knots in it which would signify the number of days that they must wait before the rebellion. He said that the cord was passed through all the pueblos of the kingdom so that the ones which agreed to it [the rebellion] might untie one knot in sign of obedience, and by the other knots they would know the days which were lacking; and this was to be done on pain of death to those who refused to agree to it. As a sign of agreement and notice of having concurred in the treason and perfidy they were to send up smoke signals to that effect in each one of the pueblos singly. The said cord was taken from pueblo to pueblo by the swiftest youths under the penalty of death if they revealed the secret. Everything being thus arranged, two days before the time set for its execution, because his lordship had learned of it and had imprisoned two Indian accomplices from the pueblo of Tesuque, it was carried out prematurely that night, because it seemed to them that they were now discovered. . . .

Finally the senor governor and those who were with him escaped from the siege, and later this declarant saw that as soon as the Spaniards had left the kingdom an order came from the said Indian, Popé, in which he commanded all the Indians to break the lands and enlarge their cultivated fields, saying that now they were as they had been in ancient times, free from the labor they had performed for the religious and the Spaniards, who could not now be alive. He said that this is the legitimate cause and the reason they had for rebelling, because they had always desired to live as they had when they came out of the lake of Copala. Thus he replies to the question.

Asked for what reason they so blindly burned the images, temples, crosses, and other things of divine worship, he stated that the said Indian, Popé, came down in person, and with him El Saca and El Chato from the pueblo of Los Taos, and other captains and leaders and many people who were in his train, and he ordered in all the pueblos through which he passed that they instantly

break up and burn the images of the holy Christ, the
Virgin Mary and the other saints, the crosses, and everything pertaining to Christianity, and that they burn the
temples, break up the bells, and separate from the wives
whom God had given them in marriage and take those
whom they desired. In order to take away their baptismal
names, the water, and the holy oils, they were to plunge
into the rivers and wash themselves with amole, which is a
root native to the country, washing even their clothing,
with the understanding that there would thus be taken
from them the character of the holy sacraments. They did
this, and also many other things which he does not recall,
given to understand that this mandate had come from the
Caydi and the other two who emitted fire from their
extremities in the said estufa of Taos, and that they thereby returned to the state of their antiquity, as when they
came from the lake of Copala; that this was the better life
and the one they desired, because the God of the Spaniards was worth nothing and theirs was very strong, the
Spaniard's God being rotten wood.

BETWEEN TWO FIRES

1684

Garangula's Speech to the Governor of Canada

ABOUT THE DOCUMENT:

By the year 1608 when the French founded their first
permanent colony (Quebec) in present-day Canada, they
already had behind them some seventy years of profitable
business experience in the New World. The profits came
from furs, especially beaver, obtained in trade with the
Indians. Unlike the English colonists south of them who

destroyed the Indian cultures they came in contact with as fast as they could, the French found it more profitable to take advantage of trade systems already developed between the Indian nations. French traders also had to depend on the Indian woodscraft, on their knowledge of waterways and the ways of beaver, and on such tools as snowshoes and birch-bark canoes—Indian inventions enabling them to move freely within the world they inhabited. In return, the French supplied European manufactures: hatchets, guns, kettles, and cloth. The resulting fur trade was essentially a partnership between French and Indian, and each side felt it had cause to preserve and foster friendship. To the French the Huron were the most important of the Indian peoples with whom they traded. These were a confederacy of four northern Iroquois nations, through whose agency the French reaped a rich harvest of furs from the country north and west of the Great Lakes.

South of the Huron in what is now New York was another group of Iroquois nations. Known as the Five Nations, the Mohawk, Oneida, Onondaga, Cayuga, and Seneca were leagued together in what is generally recognized as "the best organized of any of the many confederacies north of Mexico." They were also tough fighters and able politicians: because of these qualities they were to ingrain themselves so deeply in the consciousness of European intruders that the name Iroquois when used even today usually refers to the Five Nations.

The Five Nations and the Huron were traditional enemies, and since the Huron met with white men before the Five Nations did, it was a Huron war party that first introduced the Five Nations to gunfire. The guns were actually fired by a French trading-ally of the Huron, however, and the Five Nations generously extended their animosity for the one to include the other. From Dutch fur traders who set up a post on the Hudson River near Albany, the Five Nations first acquired guns of their own. They began to compete with the Huron for control of the fur trade, dealing with the Dutch and then later with the English. In the process they became virtual masters of the surrounding Indian nations: in 1649 they destroyed

the Huron as a coherent force and defeated the important
Tobacco nation on the west. In 1651 they defeated the
Neutrals' Confederacy; in 1655 the powerful Erie nation;
in the 1670s they gained the upper hand in a long struggle
with the Susquehanna to the south.

Meanwhile, as the French and the English presence in
America grew stronger, the Five Nations managed to
balance between the two and retain their independence of
either. Though more often than not siding with the British
in their conflicts with the French, they never became a
vassal ally. For their part the French tried unsuccessfully
time and again to smash the Iroquois and so regain their
old ascendancy in the European market for furs. In between attempts to conquer the Five Nations uneasy peace
would be established. The English, of course, were more
than glad to have the Five Nations fight their French
business competitors and did their best to keep up tensions
between the two. They also tried to maneuver the Five
Nations into acknowledging subservience to the English
king.

The document that follows relates to one such period of
peace and intrigue. About the year 1684 the French took
advantage of a peace with the Five Nations to build a
series of forts in the north and tried to increase their
influence among the northern and western tribes whose
furs were being channeled through the Five Nations and
into English hands. Opposed particularly by the Seneca,
the French finally collected the whole armed force of
Canada at Fort Cadarqui. This was a mistake on the part
of the French, for the summer heat combined with illness
to make their troops militarily useless against the Five
Nations. Hoping to accomplish by bluff what they knew
they could not by bullets, the French asked the Five
Nations to send emissaries to negotiate.

At this point the English officer in command at Albany
took a hand in matters and did his best to stop the Five
Nations from negotiating with the French. Two of the
Five Nations—the Seneca and the Mohawk—refused to
talk with the French, but the remaining three would not
listen to the English commander. "You say we are subjects

of the King of England and the Duke of York," was their answer. "We say we are brethren, and take care of ourselves."

At the council that took place between the French and the representatives of the Five Nations, the Canadian governor demanded reparations from the Indians for past wrongs as well as guarantees of security for the future. Not only did the governor threaten war if his demands were not met, but he also claimed that the English would join with the French to "burn the castles of the Five Nations, and destroy you."

The reply was delivered to the Canadian governor by Garangula (a corruption of his French-given name La Grande Guele, or "Big Mouth"), an orator of the Onondaga. In the document that follows, Garangula expressed a spirit and independence that the Five Nations' whole history of dealings with white men proved sincere.

THE DOCUMENT:

From B. B. Thatcher, *Indian Biography*, 1837

Yonondio! [the title always given to the Canadian governor by the Five Nations]—I honor you, and the warriors that are with me all likewise honor you. Your interpreter has finished your speech; I now begin mine. My words make haste to reach your ears. Hearken to them.

Yonondio!—You must have believed when you left Quebec, that the sun had burnt up all the forests, which render our country inaccessible to the French, or that the lakes had so far overflown the banks, that they had surrounded our castles, and that it was impossible for us to get out of them. Yes, surely you must have dreamed so, and the curiosity of seeing so great a wonder, has brought you so far. *Now* you are undeceived. I and the warriors here present, are come to assure you, that the Senecas, Cayugas, Onondagas, Oneidas and Mohawks are yet alive. I thank you in their name, for bringing back into their country the calumet, which your predecessor received from their hands. It was happy for you, that you left under ground that murdering hatchet, so often dyed in the blood of the French.

Hear, Yonondio!—I do not sleep. I have my eyes open. The sun, which enlightens me, discovers to me a great captain at the head of a company of soldiers, who speaks as if he were dreaming. He says, that he only came to the lake to smoke on the great calumet with the Onondagas. But *Garangula* says, that he sees the contrary; that it was to knock them on the head, if sickness had not weakened the arms of the French. I see Yonondio raving in a camp of sick men, whose lives the Great Spirit has saved by inflicting this sickness on them.

Hear, Yonondio!—Our women had taken their clubs, our children and old men had carried their bows and arrows into the heart of your camp, if our warriors had not disarmed them, and kept them back, when your messenger came to our castles. It is done and I have said it.

Hear, Yonondio!—We plundered none of the French, but those that carried guns, powder and balls to the Twightwies and Chictaghicks, because those arms might have cost us our lives. Herein we follow the example of the Jesuits, who break all the kegs of rum brought to our castles, lest the drunken Indians should knock them on the head. Our warriors have not beaver enough to pay for all the arms they have taken, and our old men are not afraid of the war. This belt preserves my words.

We carried the English into our lakes, to trade there with the Utawawas and Quatoghies, as the Adirondacks brought the French to our castles, to carry on a trade, which the English say is theirs. We are born free. We neither depend on Yonondio nor Corlear. [The name given the governors of New York.] We may go where we please, and carry with us whom we please, and buy and sell what we please. If your allies be your slaves, use them as such, command them to receive no other but your people. This belt preserves my words.

We knock the Twightwies and Chictaghicks on the head, because they had cut down the trees of peace, which were the limits of our country. They have hunted beaver on our lands. They have acted contrary to the customs of all Indians, for they left none of the beavers alive,—they killed both male and female. They brought the Satanas into their country, to take part with them, after they had concerted ill designs against us. We have done less than either the English or French, that have usurped the lands of so many Indian nations, and chased them from their own country. This belt preserves my words.

Hear, Yonondio!—What I say is the voice of all the Five Nations. Hear what they answer. Open your ears to what they speak. The Senecas, Cayugas, Onondagas, Oneidas and Mohawks say, that when they buried the hatchet at Cadarackui, in the presence of your predecessor, in the middle of the fort, they planted the tree of peace in the same place, to be there carefully preserved: That in the place of a retreat for soldiers, that fort might be a rendezvous for merchants: that in place of arms and ammunition of war, beavers and merchandize should only enter there.

Hear, Yonondio!—Take care for the future that so great a number of soldiers as appear there, do not choke the tree of peace planted in so small a fort. It will be a great loss, if, after it had so easily taken root, you should stop its growth, and prevent its covering your country and ours with its branches. I assure you, in the name of the Five Nations, that our warriors shall dance to the calumet of peace under its leaves. They shall remain quiet on their mats, and shall never dig up the hatchet, till their brother Yonondio, or Corlear, shall either jointly or separately endeavor to attack the country, which the Great Spirit has given to our ancestors. This belt preserves my words, and this other the authority which the Five Nations have given me.

[Here the orator paused for a moment, and then addressed himself to Monsieur Le Maine, who stood near him, acting as interpreter.]

Take courage, Ohguesse! You have spirit—Speak! Explain my words. Forget nothing. Tell all that your brethren and friends say to Yonondio, your Governor, by the mouth of Garangule, who loves you, and desires you to accept of this present of beaver, and take part with me in my feast, to which I invite you. This present of beaver is sent to Yonondio, on the part of the Five Nations.

". . . A STATE OF DAMNATION?"

c. 1710

A Conestoga Chief Answers a Swedish Missionary

ABOUT THE DOCUMENT:

South of the Five Nations, the Susquehanna—also called Conestoga—occupied most of what is now inland Pennsylvania. They were a powerful nation; at the beginning of their struggle with the Five Nations for control of the fur trade in the middle 1600s, the Susquehanna badly defeated the Seneca and Cayuga. Then the Susquehanna were swept by a fierce epidemic which weakened them beyond hope of competing with the Five Nations, so that by the 1670s they had become subordinate allies.

It was with the Susquehanna, as well as their coastal neighbors the Delaware, that William Penn made his famous treaties of friendship forever. It was through the Susquehanna that William Penn also sought the Five Nations' permission to settle on lands over which he recognized their supremacy. For a time it seemed as if, indeed, there were white men in the world who could live in peace with neighbors of another race. But genuine peace is not possible between peoples unless accompanied by respect, and though Pennsylvania settlers were often forced to respect Indians as individual human beings, their own racial and religious prejudices would not permit them to respect the Indians as a people. Even during the times of greatest professed peace white missionaries were continually going among the Indians and seeking to persuade them to give up their religion: seeking always to change the Indian into a kind of imitation white person. The first document is the reply of a Susquehanna (Conestoga) chief to a Swedish missionary who, about 1710, tried to persuade the Indians that they were guilty of original sin and could not escape its consequences unless they accepted Christianity. The following reply by the chief was preserved for us because the missionary found himself unable to refute its logic; he felt compelled to write it down and forward it to his theological superiors along with a request for arguments to refute it.

THE DOCUMENT:

From *A Century of Dishonor*, H. H. Jackson, New York, 1881

Our forefathers were under a strong persuasion (as we are) that those who act well in this life will be rewarded in the next according to the degrees of their virtues; and, on the other hand, that those who behave wickedly here will undergo such punishments hereafter as were proportionate to the crimes they were guilty of. This has been constantly and invariably received and acknowledged for a truth through every successive generation of our ancestors. It could not, then, have taken its rise from fable; for human fiction, however artfully and plausibly contrived, can never gain credit long among people where free inquiry is allowed, which was never denied by our ancestors. . . . Now we desire to propose some questions. Does he believe that our forefathers, men eminent for their piety, constant and warm in their pursuit of virtue, hoping thereby to merit eternal happiness, were all damned? Does he think that we who are zealous imitators in good works, and influenced by the same motives as we are, earnestly endeavoring with the greatest circumspection to tread the path of integrity, are in a state of damnation? If that be his sentiment, it is surely as impious as it is bold and daring. . . . Let us suppose that some heinous crimes were committed by some of our ancestors, like to that we are told of another race of people. In such a case God would certainly punish the criminal, but would never involve us that are innocent in the guilt. Those who think otherwise must make the Almighty a very whimsical, evil-natured being. . . . Once more: are the Christians more virtuous, or, rather, are they not more vicious than we are? If so, how came it to pass that they are the objects of God's beneficence, while we are neglected? Does he daily confer his favors without reason and with so much partiality? In a word, we find the Christians much more depraved in their morals than we are; and we judge from their doctrine by the badness of their lives.

POSTSCRIPT TO THE DOCUMENT:

White missionaries' work did produce some converts among the Indians, however, especially as the ever-encroaching white culture corroded that of those Indians who tried to remain on their lands near white settlements, rather than move far away. Over and over such Indians discovered that the white man's racial disrespect was only increased by Indian meekness; the more genuinely Christian any Indian became, the more he was likely to be regarded as a target for vicious abuse by white racial bigotry—often justified by the very Christian teachings the Indian had been told he must espouse. The foregoing describes the experience of the few Indians who in 1763 still lived at Conestoga, once the principal town of the Susquehanna and the place where white commissioners used to come for council talks with the Susquehanna and with emissaries of the Five Nations. (In 1712, it had become the Six Nations with the addition of the Tuscarora to the Iroquois League.) By 1763, however, the Conestoga village was within Lancaster County and surrounded by white settlers. During the French-Indian War which had just ended, these Conestoga had remained at peace, refusing to take up arms against their "Christian Brothers." And on December 14 a group of white bounty scalp hunters from a Pennsylvania town called Paxton attacked the Conestoga village and earned some fifteen hundred dollars by killing and scalping three old men, two women, and a boy.

This action upset some of the residents of Lancaster Town, and fearing for the lives of Indians in their employ, they rounded them up with their families and held them, for safety, in the town jail. Two weeks later the Paxton Boys rode into town, broke into the jail, and killed every Conestoga there. A regiment of English soldiers were in the town at the time but did nothing to stop the massacre. An eyewitness described the brutality of the murders:

> Near the back door of the prison lay an old Indian and his squaw, particularly well known and esteemed by the people of the town . . . His name was Will Soc. Around him and his squaw lay two children, about the age of three years, whose heads were split with the tomahawk and their scalps taken off . . . along the west side of the wall, lay a stout Indian, whom I particularly noticed to have been shot in the breast. His legs were chopped with the tomahawk, his hands cut off, and finally a rifle-ball discharged in his mouth so that his head was blown to atoms, and the brains were splashed against and yet hanging to the wall for three or four feet around.

There were white Pennsylvanians (Quakers) who protested the Paxton Massacre, and reaction to that protest produced the document which follows. Written by a "Gentleman of Lancaster," the document is taken from a pamphlet justifying the massacre and attacking anyone who would take the Indians' part. The NARRATIVE referred to in the document's first paragraph was a pamphlet deploring the murders. The pamphlet with the original footnotes follows.

A pamphlet titled The Conduct of the Paxton-Men, impartially represented, with some remarks on the narrative, Thomas Barton, Philadelphia, 1764

A mighty Noise and Hubbub has been made about killing a Few Indians in Lancaster-County; and even

*Philosopher*s and *Legislators* have been employed to raise
the Holloo upon those that killed them; and to ransack
*Tome*s and *Systems,* Writers ancient and modern, for
Proofs of their Guilt and Condemnation! And what
have they proved at last? Why, that the WHITE SAV-
AGES of *Paxton* and *Donnegall* have violated the Laws
of Hospitality! I can sincerely assure the ingenious and
worthy Author of the NARRATIVE, that a shock of
electricity would have had a much more sensible Effect
upon these People than all the Arguments and Quotations
he has produced.

For my own Part, I utterly abhor and disclaim every
Act and Species of Cruelty, and I solemnly declare that I
disapprove of the Manner of killing the Indians in *Lancaster*, as it was a Kind of Insult to the Civil Magistrates,
and an Encroachment upon the Peace and Quiet of that
Town; and I wish that the *Women* and *little ones* at least,
could have been spared.—But no doubt the Actors in that
Affair, thought with *Friend Bishop,* whom I quoted before, that the best Way was, while their Hands were in, to
kill all, "lest out of the SERPENT'S EGG, there should
come a COCKATRICE, and his Fruit should be a Fiery
Flying SERPENT."

Would the Limits I have prescribed to myself in this
Letter allow me, I could easily shew you, that every one
of those Nations have, in a Thousand Instances, violated
the Laws of Hospitality, and Faith too, in a much higher
Degree than those People could possibly have been guilty
of.—But without carrying you through *Homer,* old *Leg-
ends*, and *Fabulous Travels* and *Voyages*—if you look
into your *Bible,* you will find a very notable Instance,
which will set this Matter right.—

And the Lord discomfited Sisera, and all *his* chariots, and
all *his* host, with the edge of the sword before Barak; so
that Sisera lighted down off his chariot, and fled away on
his feet.

   But Barak pursued after the chariots, and after the host,
unto Harosheth of the Gentiles: and all the host of Sisera
fell upon the edge of the sword; *and* there was not a man
left.

Howbeit Sisera fled away on his feet to the tent of Jael the wife of Heber the Kenite: for *there was* peace between Jabin the king of Hazor and the house of Heber the Kenite.

And Jael went out to meet Sisera, and said unto him, Turn in, my lord, turn in to me; fear not. And when he had turned in unto her into the tent, she covered him with a mantle.

And he said unto her, Give me, I pray thee, a little water to drink; for I am thirsty. And she opened a bottle of milk, and gave him drink, and covered him.

Again he said unto her, Stand in the door of the tent, and it shall be, when any man doth come and inquire of thee, and say, Is there any man here? that thou shalt say No.

Then Jael Heber's wife took a nail of the tent, and took a hammer in her hand, and went softly unto him, and smote the nail into his temples, and fastened it into the ground: for he was fast asleep and weary. So he died.

And, behold, as Barak pursued Sisera, Jael came out to meet him, and said unto him, Come, and I will show thee the man who thou seekest. And when he came into her *tent,* behold, Sisera lay dead, and the nail *was* in his temples. [Judges 4: 15-22]

I shall now conclude, Sir, with this Request to you, that you will advise your visionary QUAKERS and DON QUIXOTES to consider these Things—And, that . . . they will suffer the Complaints of the People to be heard, their Grievances redress'd, and their Country rescued from total *Ruin*—That they will immediately remove the INDIANS, or whatever else may create their JEALOUSY, and give them Cause to murmur.—And then we may expect to feel the happy effects resulting from LIBERTY and LAW.

> *Dated from my* FARM-HOUSE, March 17, 1764
> A Day dedicated to LIBERTY and ST. PATRICK

Footnotes written by Thomas Barton and contained in the pamphlet quoted above.

ABRAHAM NEWCOMER, of the County of *Lancaster,* one of the People called *Menonists,* and by Trade a Gun-smith, hath personally appeared before the Chief-Burgess of Lancaster, and upon his solemn Affirmation hath declared, "That divers Times within these few years, BILL SOC and INDIAN JOHN, two of the *Conenstogoe Indians,* threatened to *scalp* him, the *Affirmant,* as soon as they would a Dog."

He further affirms, that a few Days before the Indians were killed in the *Manner, Bill Soc,* aforesaid, brought a Tomahawk to him to be steel'd, which the *Affirmant* refusing to do, the said *Bill Soc* threatened, and said, *"You will not! You will not!—I'll have it mended to your sorrow!"*—From which Expressions this *Affirmant* hath declared, that he apprehended Danger from said *Soc.*

Mrs. T—p—n, a Lady of Character, of the Borough of *Lancaster,* also personally appear'd before the Chief-Burgess, and upon her solemn Oath on the Holy Evangelists, hath declared, "That sometime in the Summer of the Year 1761, *Bill Soc* came to her Apartment, and threatened her Life, saying, *'I kill you, and all Lancaster cannot catch me;'* which put her into great Terror. And this Lady hath further depos'd, that said *Bill Soc,* added, *'This Place* [meaning *Lancaster*] *is mine and I will have it yet.'*

"THAT THE CALAMITIES MAY BE AVERTED"

1756

Scarroyada's Reply to the Quaker Peace Emissaries

Governor Morris's Declaration of War against
the Delaware Indians

ABOUT THE DOCUMENTS:

The French-Indian war that began in 1754 was the
final contest between the French and English for control
of North America. It was also a struggle of many Indian
nations against the English, whose colonizing and trading
methods the Indians found much more destructive than
those of the French. The French were content to trade and
were willing to allow even relatively weak Indian nations to
keep their lands and their culture, while the English sought
to swallow everything in their way.

The Six Nations refused to be committed to either side,
preferring to let the two different sorts of white men fight
their own quarrel. But such nations as the Delaware were
forced by the pressure of events to join one side or the
other or else be caught in the middle. Already the Delaware had been pushed out of their original territory in
eastern Pennsylvania, and under the tutelage of the Six
Nations had found a new home on the upper Ohio west of
the Alleghenies. Unfortunately for them, it was precisely a
fight between the French and the colonists of Virginia for
control of the forks of the Ohio (at present day Pitts-
burgh) that set off the French-Indian War. Twice, in
1754 and in 1755 Indian forces allied with the French
defeated major English expeditions into the Ohio Valley.
George Washington commanded troops against the Indians on both those expeditions. After the 1755 defeat

31

the Indians went from defensive to offensive and began to strike back at English frontier settlements. For the Delaware, who had already experienced the results of English settlement, English penetration of their new Ohio Valley home was a threat to resist at all costs.

In the colony of Pennsylvania, of course, Delaware retaliation was denounced widely as another "provocation" by the "brutal savage," and a cry went up for colonial government to declare war against the Delaware.

It is often said when past atrocities are brought to light, that "times were different then" and that "people of those days didn't think the way we do." In the light of such arguments it is interesting to note that there *were* people in Pennsylvania in the 1750s who thought the way most of us at least claim to think today. In 1756 the Quakers of Pennsylvania sent a petition to the Pennsylvania government headed by Lt. Gov. Robert Hunter Morris in an attempt to stave off a declaration of war against the Delaware, since they believed the Delaware, not the English, to be the aggrieved. In part the appeal read:

> We therefore, with Sincerity and Ardency, pray that the Calamities may be averted, . . . some of the melancholy effects of which the Annals of a neighboring Province, full of the most warlike People, have testifyed; and as the fear of God, Honour of the King, Love of our Brethren and Fellow Christians, are the Motives which have engaged us to make this Address, we hope to demonstrate by our Conduct that every Occasion of assisting and relieving the Distressed (the Delawares) and contributing towards obtaining Peace, in a Manner consistent with our peaceable Profession, will be cheerfully improved by us, and even though a much larger Part of our Estates should be necessary than the heaviest Taxes of a War can be expected to require, we shall cheerfully, by voluntary Grant, evidence our Sincerity therein.

The petition did not go unnoticed by Governor Morris; he replied that ". . . the Council advised him to proceed immediately to a Declaration of War, which being agreeable to his own sentiments, he should accordingly do . . ."

The Quakers did not yet give up, however. Following the logic that if the aggressor will not respond to a moral appeal, then perhaps the victim might, the Quaker gentlemen held council with emissaries of the Six Nations, asking them to intervene with the Delaware and convince them to surrender. If the Delaware would "stop from doing further Mischief," the Quakers said, then they would be "ready to stand betwixt them and the Government that they may be forgiven."

The Six Nations replied through their emissaries that they would communicate the Quaker offer to the Delaware, but they held out little hope. Indian response to the offer was expressed by Chief Scarroyada, from whose speech Document A is taken.

Governor Morris did in fact proceed immediately to declare war on the Delaware. Document B is an excerpt from that declaration which sheds light on recurring incidents such as the Paxton Massacre.

DOCUMENT A:

Conferences between the Pennsylvania government and the Six Nations in alliance with Britain, New Castle upon Tyne, 1756

SCARROYADA: Brethren, We are glad to hear what you have said to us, and to understand by the Belt you gave us, that you offer to stand up as *William Penn's* Children, and that the old Principles of Peace and Love are yet in being. Your Fathers declared they had nothing but Love and good Will in their Hearts to all Men—We thought that the People of that Profession had been all dead, or buried in the Bushes, or in the Ashes; but we are very glad that there are some of the same Men living: And that you offer to stand as Mediators between our Cousins the *Delawares* and this Government now at Variance.

We are glad to hear there are some People left of your peaceable Principle. We wish you had told us sooner, and that you had always spoke and acted agreeable to this Principle; for we are sure that tho' our Cousins the *Delawares* have struck the Blow, they would not have hurt any of you, if they knew you as such; for if you had kept them constantly under your *Eyes,* they would still have been your Children: But they are now grown stiff, like a great Tree, not to be easily bowed.

DOCUMENT B:

From Governor Morris's Declaration of War against the Delaware Indians, Philadelphia, April 14, 1756

"I DO hereby declare and promise that there shall be paid ... to all and every Person and Persons, as well *Indian*s as *Christians,* not in the Pay of the Province, the several and respective Premiums and Bounties following; that is to say: FOR every Male *Indian* Enemy, above Twelve Years old, who shall be taken Prisoner, and delivered at any Forts garrisoned by the Troops in the Pay of this Province, or at any of the County Towns, to the Keepers of the Common Jails there, the *Sum of One Hundred and Fifty Spanish Dollars of Pieces of Eight.* FOR the Scalp of every Male *Indian* Enemy, above the Age of Twelve Years, Produced as Evidence of their being killed, the *Sum of One Hundred and thirty Pieces of Eight.* For every Female Indian, taken Prisoner and brought in as aforesaid; and for every Male *Indian* Prisoner, under the Age of Twelve Years, taken and brought in as aforesaid, *One Hundred and Thirty Pieces of Eight.* FOR the Scalp of every *Indian* Woman, produced as evidence of their being killed, the Sum of *Fifty Pieces of Eight.* AND for every *English* Subject, that has been taken and carried from this Province in Captivity, that shall be recovered and brought in, and delivered at the City of *Philadelphia* to the Governor of this Province, the Sum of *One Hundred and Fifty Pieces of Eight, but* nothing *for their scalps.*[1] AND that there shall be paid to every Officer or Soldier as are, or shall be; in the Pay of

[1] *English* Prisoners are adopted by the *Indians,* and have *Indian* Names immediately given them, and if killed by our friendly *Indians,* they would claim the same rewards as for *Indian* scalps.

this Province, who shall redeem and deliver any *English* Subject, carried into Captivity as aforesaid; or shall take, being in, and produce, an Enemy Prisoner or Scalp, as aforesaid, One Half of the said several and respective Premiums and Bounties.

GIVEN under my Hand, and the Great Seal of the Province, at *Philadelphia,* the Fourteenth Day of *April,* in the Twenty-ninth Year of His Majesty's Reign, and in the Year of our Lord One Thousand Seven Hundred and Fifty-six.

PONTIAC'S REBELLION

1763

Minavavana Challenges the English Trader

Pontiac Speaks—April 27

Pontiac Speaks—May 5

ABOUT THE DOCUMENTS:

Defeat of the French by the British did not yield the automatic control of the entire fur trade that had been anticipated. Although the French gave up the struggle following the fall of Quebec in 1760, many of their Indian allies were not so quick to yield. Even though it seemed to the Indians that the French were pulling up stakes and leaving their allies to do the best that they could with unseemly haste, many Indians felt certain that French troops would return. After all, were they not partners with the Indians in a lucrative trade?

The British were not conciliatory. Under Lord Jeffrey

Amherst, who administered the lands "acquired" from the French, the inland trading nations (the Shawnee, Miami, Kickapoo, Sauk, Potawatomie, Fox, Chippewa, Illinois, Ottawa, and Delaware) were expected to accept a painful relationship to the English, who clearly felt they were not the Indians' partners but rather, their masters. This was an especially galling presumption in the eyes of the Indians since they well knew that the only major defeats suffered on their side during the French-Indian War were by wholly French armies attacked by the English far to the east of Indian territories.

Yet Amherst expected them to meekly accept the presence of English trading posts and English soldiers within their lands. He expected them to deal with traders who cheated them much more than the French had dared; who refused them credit in goods to get them through the long winters, as the French had realized that they must; who served as beachheads for the white settlement, unlike the French traders, who tended to become practically indistinguishable from the Indians they lived among. The Indians resisted. They listened to the words of a new Prophet who rose up among them preaching that they must return to the ways of their forefathers and shun all traffic with the whites. Amherst responded by asking Colonel Henry Boquet of Pennsylvania: "Could it not be contrived to send the small pox among the disaffected tribes of Indians? We must on this occasion use every stratagem in our power to reduce them." He also discussed the feasibility of using large numbers of dogs to hunt Indians down but decided that the right breed of dog was not available.

In 1763 the troubles between the English and the Indian nations broke out in a major war led by an Ottawa chief named Pontiac. Known in our history books as Pontiac's Rebellion, Pontiac's Conspiracy, or Pontiac's War, it was actually a war brought on by English policy which was resented and resisted by a confederation of eighteen Indian nations. The war had far reaching effects, not the least of which was to drive a strong wedge between American colonists and their British rulers.

Evidence that this war against the English reflected much more than the disaffection of a few Indians is contained in the first of the documents which follow. It is an address made by a Chippewa chief named Minavavana to an English trader who sought to establish a post in territory previously allied with the French. After first remarking that "the English were brave men, and not afraid of death, since they dared to come thus fearlessly among their enemies," Minavavana spoke as is recorded in the document.

As to Pontiac himself, from the little that is known of his early life, it is calculated that he was born around 1720 in a village on the north side of the Detroit River. It is probable, but not documented, that he fought during the French-Indian War. It is also recorded that he was an extremely shrewd leader, grandly eloquent, and a great warrior and military tactician.

By 1762 Pontiac has risen to prominence. Whereas he had agitated for the continuance of warfare against the British even after the French capitulated in 1760 and found little support, now, for the reasons mentioned above, he found his people receptive to his ideas. In 1762 he sent messengers to all the tribes in the old Northwest urging them to a final action to oust the British.

Almost all the tribes in the area met with Pontiac in secret councils on April 27 and on May 5, 1763. Document B contains statements recorded at these two councils. In the first Pontiac uses a parable to urge his people to fight the British, and in the second he sums up the grievances of his people against the British.

DOCUMENT A:

From B. B. Thatcher, *Indian Biography*, 1837

Englishman!— It is to you that I speak, and I demand your attention!

Englishman!—You know that the French King is our father. He promised to be such; and we, in return, promised to be his children. This promise we have kept.

Englishman!—It is you that have made war with this our father. You are his enemy; and how then could you have the boldness to venture among us, his children? You know that his enemies are ours.

Englishman!—We are informed that our father, the king of France, is old and infirm; and that being fatigued with making war upon your nation, he is fallen asleep. During his sleep, you have taken advantage of him, and possessed yourselves of Canada. But his nap is almost at an end. I think I hear him already stirring, and inquiring for his children the Indians;—and, when he does awake, what must become of you? He will destroy you utterly!

Englishman!—Although you have conquered the French, you have not yet conquered us! We are not your slaves. These lakes, these woods and mountains, were left to us by our ancestors. They are our inheritance, and we will part with them to none. Your nation supposes that we, like the white people, cannot live without bread, and pork, and beef! But, you ought to know, that He—the Great Spirit and Master of Life—has provided food for us, in these broad lakes, and upon these mountains.

Englishman!—Our father, the king of France, employed our young men to make war upon your nation. In this warfare, many of them have been killed; and it is our custom to retaliate, until such time as the spirits of the slain are satisfied. Now the spirits of the slain are to be satisfied in either of two ways. The first is by the spilling of the blood of the nation by which they fell; the other, by *covering the bodies of the dead,* and thus allaying the resentment of their relations. This is done by making presents.

Englishman!—Your king has never sent us any presents, nor entered into any treaty with us. Wherefore he and we are still at war; and, until he does these things, we must consider that we have no other father, nor friend, among the white men, than the king of France. But, for you, we have taken into consideration, that you have ventured your life among us, in the expectation that we should not molest you. You do not come armed, with an intention to make war. You come in peace, to trade with

us, and supply us with necessaries, of which we are much
in want. We shall regard you, therefore, as a brother; and
you may sleep tranquilly, without fear of the Chippewas.
As a token of our friendship, we present you with this
pipe, to smoke.

DOCUMENT B:

From journal or history of "A Conspiracy by the Indians against the English and of the Siege of the Fort Detroit, by Four Different Nations Beginning on the 7th of May, 1763." Written by an unknown French author, possibly Robert Navarre. (The Pontiac manuscript translated.) In Michigan Pioneer and Historical Society Collections, Vol. 8, 1886.

Pontiac's speech of April 27, 1763.
The words of the Master of Life to the Wolf—from a parable told by Pontiac to the assembled council

I am the Master of Life, whom thou desirest to know
and to whom thou wouldst speak. Listen well to what I
am going to say to thee and all thy red brethren. I am He
who made heaven and earth, the trees, lakes, rivers, all
men, and all that thou seest, and all that thou hast seen
on earth. Because [I have done this and because] I love
you, you must do what I say and [leave undone] what I
hate. I do not like that you drink until you lose your
reason, as you do; or that you fight with each other; or
that you take two wives, or run after the wives of others;
you do not well; I hate that. You must have but one wife,
and keep her until death. When you are going to war, you
juggle, join the medicine dance, and believe that I am
speaking. You are mistaken, it is to Manitou to whom you
speak; it is a bad spirit who whispers to you nothing but
evil, and to whom you listen because you do not know me
well. This land, where you live, I have made for you and
not for others. How comes it that you suffer the whites on
your lands? Can't you do without them? I know that those
whom you call the children of your Great Father supply

your wants, but if you were not bad, as you are, you would well do without them. You might live wholly as you did before you knew them. Before those whom you call your brothers came on your lands, did you not live by bow and arrow? You had no need of gun nor powder, nor the rest of their things, and nevertheless you caught animals to live and clothe yourselves with their skins, but when I saw that you went to the bad, I called back the animals into the depths of the woods, so that you had need of your brothers to have your wants supplied and cover you. You have only to become good and do what I want, and I shall send back to you the animals to live on. I do not forbid you, for all that, to suffer amongst you the children of your father [the French]. I love them, they know me and pray to me, and I give them their necessities and all that they bring to you, but as regards those who have come to trouble your country [the British], drive them out, make war to them! I love them not, they know me not, they are my enemies and the enemies of your brothers! Send them back to the country which I made for them! There let them remain.

Pontiac's speech of May 5, 1763

It is important for us, my brothers, that we exterminate from our land this nation which only seeks to kill us. You see, as well as I do, that we cannot longer get our supplies as we had them from our brothers, the French. The English sell us the merchandise twice dearer than the French sold them to us, and their wares [are worth] nothing. Hardly have we bought a blanket, or something else to cover us, than we must think of having another of the kind. When we want to start for our winter quarters they will give us no credit, as our brothers, the French, did. When I go to the English chief to tell him that some of our comrades are dead, instead of weeping for the dead, as our brothers, the French, used to do, he makes fun of me and of you. When I ask him for something for our sick, he refuses, and tells me that he has no need of us. You can well see by that that he seeks our ruin. Well, my brothers, we must all swear to ruin them! Nor will we wait any longer, nothing impedes us. There are very few of them, and we can easily overcome them. All the nations who are our brothers strike a blow at them; why should we not do the same? Are we not men like them? Have I not shown you the war-belts which I have received from our great father, the Frenchman? He tells us to strike; why should we not listen to his words? Whom fear we? It is time. Are we afraid that our brothers, the French, who are here amongst us, would hinder us? They know not our designs, and could not if they wanted to. You know as well as I do, that when the English came to our country to drive out our father, Belleestre, they have taken away all the guns of the Frenchmen, and that they have no weapons to defend themselves. Thus it is. Let us strike all together! If there are any French who take up for them, we shall strike them as we do the English. Remember what the Master of Life has said to our brother, the Wolf. That regards us all as well as them. I have sent war-belts and word to our brothers, the Sauteux, of the Saginaw, and to our brothers, the Ottawas, of Michelimakinak, and to those of the river's mouth to join them with us, and they will not tarry to come. While waiting for them, let us commence the attack. There is no more time to lose, and when the English shall be defeated, we shall see what to do, and we shall cut off the passage so that they cannot come back to our country.

POSTSCRIPT TO THE DOCUMENTS:

The confederacy of eighteen tribes that Pontiac organized and led enjoyed outstanding military success. Within months they seized and occupied every British post in the Northwest Territory except Forts Detroit and Pitt. They didn't seize Detroit, due to the treachery of an informer. But they did lay siege to Detroit—and kept it up for eight months—one of the longest sieges in American military history.

The consequences of Pontiac's Rebellion on the course of American history were profound. The British Crown, in a hasty effort to stop the rebellion and prevent new rebellions from breaking out, set an official line of demarcation between the Indian and the colonists. This line ran along the crest of the Appalachian Mountains from north to south and prohibited white settlement west of this line. Designed to root out the cause of Indian uprisings— white men encroaching on their lands—the proclamation also outlawed private purchase of Indian property.

This was the famous Proclamation of October, 1763. It infuriated the colonists, especially the colonists on the western frontiers. They had assumed that victory over the French in the French-Indian War would enable them to expand even further westward and settle wherever they chose. Land speculators who had invested money in the territory west of the Appalachians were particularly incensed because the Proclamation of 1763 demanded that white settlements already in that area were to "forthwith . . . remove themselves."

It is probable that the line of demarcation was drawn not only to stop new Indian outbreaks, but to protect British pocketbooks by cramping the colonists. Confine the colonists to the eastern seaboard, and they would be unable to expand westward in such a way that they would start manufacturing their own goods and be less dependent on British finished goods. In addition the colonists were becoming increasingly restive in general, and a confined land area was more easily controllable.

No adequate measure has ever been made to weigh the Crown Proclamation of 1763 as a precipitating cause of the "American" Revolution against the Crown taxes on tea and other things. The proclamation line lay very, very heavy, and the frontier west became vocally and actively seditious within a very short time after the Crown proclaimed it.

At the time of the American Revolution George Washington and Patrick Henry were leading landowners among the colonists. Most of their extensive holdings were in Indian territory, and it is known that they regarded the British Proclamation of 1763 as a serious infringement of their right to make profits.

Records show that just prior to the Proclamation of 1763 George Washington bought shares in the Indian land speculation scheme of the Mississippi Company. That scheme involved 2.5 million acres of Indian territory in the Ohio Valley, and after the scheme was outlawed by the British proclamation, Washington secretly employed a surveyor to locate "valuable land" in the prohibited area for him.

The following letter to the surveyor William Crawford appears in the thirty-nine volume *The Writings of George Washington* (edited by John C. Fitzpatrick, Washington, D.C., 1931–1944):

> I can never look upon that proclamation in any other light (but this I say among ourselves) than as a temporary expedient to quiet the minds of the Indians which must fall; of course, in a few years. . . . I would recommend to you to keep this whole matter a profound secret . . . because I might be censured for the opinion I have given in respect to the King's proclamation, and then, if the scheme I am now proposing to you was known, it might give the alarm to others and, by putting them upon a plan of the same nature (before we could lay a proper foundation for success ourselves) set the different interests aclashing, and probably in the end overturn the whole; all of which may be avoided by silent management and the [operation] snugly carried on by you under the pretence of hunting other game.

Patrick Henry was another active speculator in Indian lands. A shareholder in the Ohio Company, he was involved in a wide variety of other land schemes (particularly in Indian territory of West Virginia) which clearly violated the Proclamation of 1763 and which placed his own financial interests solidly against the British.

Benjamin Franklin, as a representative of the American colonies to the Crown, used his office during the years 1767 to 1775 to push through the plan of the Walpole Company to take over a staggering twenty million acres of Indian land. The scheme was in direct competition with the Ohio and Mississippi companies, and it menaced the financial interests of George Washington and Patrick Henry.

In exchange for his influence with the British government, Franklin received seventy-two shares in the Walpole Company, and he stood to gain incredible profits. Lord Hillsborough, the King's minister of American affairs, steadfastly opposed the scheme on the grounds that it would abrogate the Proclamation of 1763 to protect the Indians and that it would foment new Indian rebellions.

With Franklin's connivance scores of high British officials were bribed by the offer of company shares. These officials included the secretary of the British treasury, the lord chamberlain, the lord chancellor, and the president and other members of the king's Privy Council. Over Lord Hillsborough's objections the Privy Council sanctioned the scheme a year before the outbreak of the "American" Revolution interrupted it.

LOGAN'S REVENGE

1774

Speech at the Conclusion of Lord Dunmore's War

ABOUT THE DOCUMENT:

He was born Tah-ha-yu-ta, which means "His Eyelashes Stick Out." He was the second son of an Iroquois chief, and his mother was the daughter of an Indian and a white man. He was still a teenager when he befriended the English settler, James Logan, who was the mayor of Philadelphia. Out of regard for James Logan he discarded his Indian name and took Logan's name.

As the Indian Logan grew to adulthood, he became noted for his friendliness and for the generosities he extended to white settlers. Of all the Iroquois leaders Logan was one of the most outspoken advocates of peaceful accommodations with the white man.

The document below is a speech Logan delivered to tell why he had finally taken up arms against the white man. It was of this speech that Thomas Jefferson said: "I challenge the whole orations of Demosthenes and Cicero, and of any more eminent, to produce a single passage, superior to the speech of Logan."

While Logan's birthplace was in central Pennsylvania, by the 1770s he had settled near Sandusky, Ohio, on the banks of Lake Erie. His enforced westward wandering was typical of the fate of thousands of Indians forced by white expansion to move even further west.

Despite British Crown efforts to protect the Indian territory, colonial land speculators and anxious settlers refused to be stopped. The Crown Proclamation in the Indians' behalf was announced in 1763 right after the outbreak of Pontiac's Rebellion. But when Pontiac capitulated two years later, there was nothing to really stop the settlers from defying the Crown by crossing the Alleghenies to settle in Ohio, West Virginia, and Kentucky. As a result, clashes between the settlers and a number of Indian tribes kept up almost continuously for the next eight years. Logan, now in the geographic area of conflict, still preached peace and friendship with the whites.

Then in 1774 the colonial governor of Virginia, the Earl of Dunmore, suddenly laid territorial claim to the whole of the southern portion of the Northwest Territory— "guaranteed" Indian land by the Proclamation of 1763.

To make good his land claim, Dunmore sent two military expeditions of Virginia colonists into Kentucky and Ohio to drive the Indians out. One force was led by Michael Cresap, a colonel who figures in Logan's speech. These expeditions marked the opening of the war referred to in our history books as Lord Dunmore's War. (It is refreshing for a change to come across a war with the Indians that was named after the true aggressor.)

When the two armies invaded Indian territories under the pretext of Lord Dunmore's land claim, a settler by the name of Daniel Greathouse initiated a war of his own against the Indians. At Yellowcreek, Ohio, Greathouse and his men attacked an unarmed party of Indians. This Indian party consisted of women, children, and one man. Greathouse killed them all, and among those killed (according to most sources) were the wife of Logan, the children of Logan, and Logan's one brother.

As Logan would say in his speech, "This called on me for revenge." His embitterment found its first expression in the retaliatory campaign he led against the white settlements at the headwaters of the Monongahela River in Pennsylvania. These were the campaigns used by Dunmore to justify a new full-scale military offensive with close to three thousand men. In fact history books often place the cause of Lord Dunmore's War on Logan's attacks rather than on the aggressive actions of Dunmore and Greathouse.

Against Dunmore's forces Logan joined an alliance with some Iroquois, the Delaware, the Shawnee, and the Wyandotte, under the leadership of the Shawnee chief Cornstalk. (The Shawnee leader Tecumtha was six years of age at the time of the war, but his father and older brother fought in the war.)

At Point Pleasant, Ohio—near modern day Cincinnatti—the Indians were defeated and forced into a peace council with Lord Dunmore. The ensuing treaty forced the Indians to surrender the old Kentucky hunting grounds and with these all the lands south of the Ohio River.

Chief Logan refused to attend the peace council, whereupon Lord Dunmore sent to him an emissary named John Gibson. Logan's speech was recorded by Gibson, who in turn relayed it to Dunmore.

THE DOCUMENT:

From Samuel G. Goodrich, Lives of Celebrated American Indians, Boston: 1853

I appeal to any white man to say, if ever he entered Logan's cabin hungry, and he gave him not meat; if ever he came cold and naked, and he clothed him not. During the course of the last long and bloody war, Logan remained idle in his cabin, an advocate of peace. Such was my love for the whites, that my countrymen pointed as they passed, and said, "Logan is the friend of white man." I had even thought to have lived with you but for the injuries of one man. Colonel Cresap[1], the last spring, in cold blood and unprovoked, murdered all the relations of Logan[2], not even sparing my women and children. There runs not a drop of my blood in the veins of any living creature. This called on me for revenge. I have sought it; I have killed many; I have fully glutted my vengeance. For my country, I rejoice at the beams of peace. But do not harbor a thought that this is the joy of *fear*. Logan never felt fear. He will not turn on his heel to save his life. Who is there to mourn for Logan?—Not one!

POSTSCRIPT TO THE DOCUMENT:

Chief Logan never again participated in any action against the white man. In 1780 on his return home from a trip to Detroit Chief Logan was killed by a party of white men.

Perhaps the greatest beneficiary from Dunmore's War was George Washington. In payment for his service as an Indian fighter in Virginia during the French-Indian War, Washington was given thousands of acres of land beyond the Appalachians. In addition he purchased the smaller tracts of men who had served under him. These good lands on the south bank of the Ohio River, southwestern

[1] This is an error on Logan's part. He apparently never knew that the murderer of his people was Greathouse, not the colonel in Dunmore's army.
[2] There is some controversy over exactly who was killed in the massacre. Some sources say Logan's sister was killed, that he had neither wife nor children. Others say Logan had a wife, but she wasn't killed in the massacre.

Pennsylvania and northwestern Virginia mounted in value
after the Revolutionary War. When he died in 1799
Washington possessed more than forty thousand acres of
land, most beyond the mountains.

WHOSE INDEPENDENCE?

1781

Pachgantschilas Speaks

Chief Hopocan Speaks

ABOUT THE DOCUMENTS:

The year 1776 was late to make up for two hundred
years of injustice to the Indians. The question asks itself:
could the "American" Revolutionary patriots have ended
the oppression and established justice for the Indians?
Conceivably, they could have, but after all, many of the
Revolutionary patriots were themselves great landowners
and business men deeply implicated in schemes to exploit
the Indians. On the Indian issue the patriots wanted freedom from England to do their own exploiting.

With all the fiery rhetoric from the great "American"
Revolutionaries, nowhere was there a voice questioning
the right of the colonists to be in lands not legitimately
theirs. Nowhere even was there a voice demanding a new
deal for the American Indians. We can seriously question
the motives of the patriots of 1776, considering also the
absence of revolutionary sentiment to end the oppression
of blacks or for that matter, the oppression of women. By
1776 white male supremacy was an integral part of every
American institution. White males might agree in theory

that other people had rights, but if they did, those rights were for dispensation by white males only.

Had the founding fathers really believed what they professed—liberty and equality for all—they would have used their powers to bring to a halt the land grabbing of the western settlers and an end to the gross, profiteering schemes of the Ohio Company and other land speculators. It is not too much to project that had the Revolutionary patriots been truly revolutionary, the Indians would have known it and sided with the colonists against the British Crown.

As it was, not a single Indian tribe of consequence joined the colonists in the "American" Revolution of 1776.

Even before the "American" Revolution began the colonists knew perfectly well that they had long since lost the friendship of the Indians and that they would be unable to count on active Indian support. The most they could hope for was to keep some of the Indians neutral.

The first recorded treaty of the new "American" nation was a desperate bid by the Second Continental Congress to keep as many Indians as possible from siding against them. The Treaty of 1775 recognized the right of Indians to lands they occupied.

Yet in that very same year (1775) Daniel Boone acquired for the Transylvania Company practically all the land that is today Kentucky—land well beyond the crest of the Appalachians and very definitely guaranteed to the Indians against white encroachment.

In 1778, three years into the "American" Revolutionary War, the "American" government went as far as to offer equality and statehood to some Indians tribes to entice them away from the British. The following excerpt is from the treaty signed with the Delaware at Fort Pitt on September 17, 1778:

> . . . the United States do engage to guarantee to the aforesaid nation of Delawares, and their heirs, all their territorial rights in the fullest and most ample manner as it hath been

bound by former treaties, as long as they the said Delaware nation shall abide by and hold fast the chain of friendship now entered into. And it is further agreed on between the contracting parties should it for the future be found conducive for the mutual interest of both parties to invite any other tribes who have been friends to the interest of the United States, to join the present confederation, and to form a state whereof the Delaware nation shall be the head, and have a representation in Congress: Provided nothing contained in this article to be considered as conclusive until it meets with the approbation of Congress.

Had this inducement been credible to the Delaware, many would probably have signed it, but only a few did; most of the Delaware chiefs (among them, Pachgantschilas and Hopocan whose speeches appear below) stayed with the British.

The documents below reveal two viewpoints for the Indians joining the British. Document A is an example of a chief who fought against the "Americans" because he saw them as the enemy—the land stealer and the killer.

Document B, a more sophisticated analysis of the situation, shows that economic necessity was often a strong factor in chosing sides. The document also reveals that many Indians saw the American-British struggle as just one more power play by white men for the control of Indian lands. In the past Indians had allied themselves with various factions of white people, sometimes with the French, sometimes with the British, only to have their interest sold out in the end, no matter which side they took.

The "father" in Document A refers to the British, while the "sone" or "children" refers to the colonists. The "Long-Knives" in Document B represent the "American" colonists who often fought with sabers and dirks during this period.

DOCUMEN A:

Speech of Pachgantschilas as recorded by John Hekewelder, Narrative of the Mission of the United Brethren Among the Delaware and Mohegan Indians, . . . Philadelphia, 1820

Friends and kinsmen!—Listen to what I say to you! You see a great and powerful nation divided! You see the father fighting against the son, and the son against the father!—The father has called on his Indian children, to assist him in punishing his children, the Americans, who have become refractory!—I took time to consider what I should do—whether or not I should receive the hatchet of my father, to assist him!—At first I looked upon it as a family quarrel, in which I was not interested—However, at length it appeared to me, that the father was in the right; and his children deserved to be punished a little!— That this must be the case, I concluded from the many cruel acts his offspring had committed from time to time, on his Indian children; in encroaching on our land, stealing their men, women and children—Yes! even murdering those, who at times had been friendly to them, and were placed for protection under the roof of their father's house—The father himself standing centry at the door, at the time.

Friends! Often has the father been obliged to settle, and make amends for the wrongs and mischiefs done to us, by his refractory children, yet these do not grow better! No! they remain the same, and will continue to be so, as long as we have any land left us! Look back at the murders committed by the Long Knives on many of our relations, who lived peaceable neighbors to them on the Ohio! Did they not kill them without the least provocation?—Are they, do you think, better now than they were then?—No, indeed not; and many days are not elapsed since you had a number of these very men at your doors, who panted to kill you, but fortunately were prevented from doing so by the *Great Sun,* [the name the Indians had given to Col.

Daniel Broadhead] who, at that time, had been ordained by the Great Spirit to protect you!

Friends and relatives!—Now listen to me, and hear what I have to say to you.—I am myself come to bid you rise and go with me to the secure place! Do not, my friends, covet the land you now hold under cultivation. I will conduct you to a country [the Miami country] equally good, where your cattle shall find sufficient pasture; where there is plenty of game; where your women and children, together with yourselves, will live in peace and safety; where no Long Knife shall ever molest you!— Nay! I will live between you and them, and not even suffer them to frighten you!—There, you can worship your God without fear!—Here, where you are, you cannot do this!—Think on what I have now said to you, and believe, that if you stay where you now are, one day or another the Long Knives will, in their usual way, speak fine words to you, and at the same time murder you!

DOCUMENT B:

Speech of Chief Hopocan (Captain Pipe) as taken from Samuel Drake, Biography and History of the Indians of North America, Book V, Boston, 1834

Father [then he stopped a little, and, turning towards the audience, with a countenance full of great expression, and a sarcastic look, said, in a lower tone of voice,] I have said FATHER, although, indeed, I do not know WHY I am to call HIM so, having never known any other father than the French, and considering the English only as BROTHERS. But as this name is also imposed upon us, I shall make use of it, and say, [at the same time fixing his eyes upon the commandant,] Father, some time ago you put a war hatchet into my hands, saying, "Take this weapon and try it on the heads of my enemies, the Long-Knives, and let me afterwards know if it was sharp and good." Father, at the time you gave me this weapon, I had neither cause nor inclination to go to war against a people who had done me no injury; yet in obedience to you, who say you are my father, and call me your child, I received the hatchet; well knowing that if I did not obey, you would withhold from me the necessaries of life, without which I could not subsist, and which are not elsewhere to be procured, but at the house of my father—You may perhaps think me a fool, for risking my life at your bidding, in a cause too, by which I have no prospect of gaining any thing; for it is *your* cause and not *mine*. It is *your* concern to fight the Long-Knives; *you* have raised a quarrel amongst yourselves, and *you* ought yourselves to fight it out. You should not compel your children, the Indians, to expose themselves to danger, for *your* sake.— Father, many lives have already been lost on your account!—Nations have suffered, and been weakened!— children have lost parents, brothers, and relatives!—wives have lost husbands!—It is not known how many more may perish before *your* war will be at an end!—Father, I have said, that you may, perhaps, think me a fool, for thus thoughtlessly rushing on *your* enemy!—Do not believe this, father: Think not that I want sense to convince me, that although you *now* pretend to keep up a perpetual enmity to the Long-Knives, you may before long conclude a peace with them.—Father, you say you love your children, the Indians.—This you have often told them, and indeed it is your interest to say so to them, that you may have them at your service. But, father, who of us can believe that you can love a people of a different color from your own, better than those who have a white skin like yourselves? Father, pay attention to what I am going to say. While you, father, are setting me on your enemy, much in the same manner as a hunter sets his dog on the game; while I am in the act of rushing on that enemy of yours, with the bloody destructive weapon you gave me, I may, perchance, happen to look back to the place from whence you started me; and what shall I see? Perhaps I may see my father shaking hands with the Long-Knives; yes, with these very people he now calls his enemies. I may then see him laugh at my folly for having obeyed his

orders; and yet I am now risking my life at his command!
Father, keep what I have said in remembrance.—Now,
father, here is what has been done with the hatchet you
gave me. [With these words he handed the stick to the
commandant, with the scalp upon it, . . .] I have done
with the hatchet what you ordered me to do, and found it
sharp. Nevertheless, I did not do *all* that I *might* have
done. No, I did not. My heart failed within me. I felt
compassion for *your* enemy. Innocence [helpless women
and children] had no part in your quarrels; there I distinguished—I spared. I took some *live flesh,* which, while I
was bringing to you, I spied one of your large canoes, on
which I put it for you. In a few days you will recover this
flesh, and find that the skin is of the same color with your
own. Father, I hope you will not destroy *what* I have
saved. You, father, have the means of preserving that
which with me would perish for want. The warrior is
poor, and his cabin is always empty; but your house,
father, is always full.

A LINE BETWEEN US

1793

An Address by the Council of Indians

ABOUT THE DOCUMENT:

From the viewpoint of the Indian nations their involve-
ment in the "revolutionary" war fought between England
and the newly declared United States was simply a contin-
uation of the long struggle in which the French-Indian
War, Pontiac's War and Lord Dunmore's War had been
merely phases: that is, their struggle for sovereignty and
freedom in their own land. That Indian nation after Indian nation chose to side with the British clearly shows that
it was the "Americans" from the colonies that they regard-

ed as their worst enemy and as their most real threat. So, fighting for their own territorial integrity, the Indian nations refused to accept the separate peace made by their English allies, just as they had refused to accept automatic defeat when the French gave up and withdrew during the French-Indian War. They defined the boundary as the line recognized by England in the Declaration of 1763 and by the US in the treaties of 1768 and 1775.

On the "American" side the Continental Congress declared that the victory over England left the Indian nations a defeated enemy with no more rights than their "conquerors" might please to grant them—that by siding with the English the Indians had lost all right to expect recognition of the territorial treaties. This completely disregarded, of course, that the white settlements pushing into Kentucky and Ohio constituted armed aggression against Indian territorial integrity—an aggression much older than the Indians' "siding with the British." From the Indian point of view, in fact, it could well be argued that it was the British who had sided with them—and then pulled out when the going got too hot.

With British support gone the Indians continued their resistance in Ohio and Kentucky, fighting a guerrilla-style war against a steadily increasing flow of white intruders. And those intruders kept up a continual demand that the Congress use the Army to protect them. This demand was joined to political pressures exerted by big-time eastern land speculators to the personal ambitions of political leaders, and to pressures from state governments (some states had promised Indian lands to veterans to recruit them for the fight against England.)

One June 15, 1789, Secretary of War Henry Knox made a report on the "Indian problem."

In examining the question how the disturbances on the frontiers are to be quieted, two modes present themselves, by which the object might perhaps be effected; the first of which is by raising an army, and extirpating the refractory tribes entirely, or secondly by forming treaties of peace with them, in which their rights and limits should be explicitly defined, and the treaties observed on the part of the United

States with the most rigid justice, by punishing the whites, who should violate the same. In considering the first mode an inquiry would arise, whether, under the existing circumstance of affairs, the United States have a clear right, consistently with the principles of justice and the laws of nature, to proceed to the destruction or expulsion of the savages. . . . [Presumably] a nation solicitous of establishing its character on the broad basis of justice, would not only hesitate at, but reject every proposition to benefit itself, by the injury of any neighboring community. . . . The Indians being the prior occupants, possess the right of the soil. It cannot be taken from them unless by their free consent, or by the right of conquest in case of a just war. To dispossess them on any other principle, would be a gross violation of the fundamental laws of nature. . . .

The moral issue recognized so clearly by the Secretary of War was not the only consideration, however, for he went on to say that if, ". . . it should be decided, on an abstract view of the situation, to be just, to remove by force the Wabash Indians [those nations fighting to force white people back to the Demarcation Line] from the territory they occupy, the finances of the United States would not at present admit of the operation . . ."

Such arguments, plus a series of defeats by the Indians, led the US to try to make peace with the Indian nations, but it insisted that peace must be based on Indian recognition of the white man's right to the Ohio and Kentucky territory already encroached on and occupied.

THE DOCUMENT:

From an address sent from the Council of Indians at Miami Rapids, August 13, 1793, to the Commissioners appointed by the President of the United States

Brothers: Money to us is of no value, and to most of us unknown; and as no consideration whatever can induce us to sell the lands on which we get sustenance for our women and children, we hope we may be allowed to point out a mode by which your settlers may be easily removed, and peace thereby obtained.

We know that these settlers are poor, or they would never have ventured to live in a country which has been in continual trouble ever since they crossed the Ohio. Divide, therefore, this large sum of money which you have offered us among these people; give to each, also, a proportion of what you say you would give to us annually, over and above this very large sum of money, and we are persuaded they would most readily accept of it in lieu of the lands you sold them. If you add, also, the great sums you must expend in raising and paying armies with a view to force us to yield you our country, you will certainly have more than sufficient for the purpose of repaying these settlers for all their labor and their improvements.

You have talked to us about concessions. It appears strange that you should expect any from us, who have only been defending our just rights against your invasions. We want peace. Restore to us our country, and we shall be enemies no longer.

Brothers: You make one concession by offering to us your money, and another by having agreed to do us justice, after having long and injuriously withheld it; we mean, in the acknowledgement you have now made that the King of England never did, nor ever had a right to give you our country by the treaty of peace. And you want to make this act of common justice a great part of your concession, and seem to expect, that because you have at last acknowledged our independence, we should for such a favor surrender to you our country.

Brothers: You have also talked a great deal about pre-emption, and your exclusive right to purchase the Indian lands, as ceded to you by the King at the treaty of peace.

Brothers: We never made any agreement with the King, nor with any other nation, that we would give to either the exclusive right to purchase our lands; and we declare to you, that we consider ourselves free to make any bargain or cession of lands whenever and to whomsoever we please. If the white people, as you say, made a treaty that none of them but the King should purchase of us, and he has given that right to the United States, it is an affair that

concerns you and him, and not us. We have never parted
with such a power.

Brothers: At our general council held at the Glaize last
Fall, we agreed to meet Commissioners from the United
States, for the purpose of restoring peace, provided they
consented to acknowledge and confirm our boundary line
to be the Ohio; and we determined not to meet you until
you gave us satisfaction on that point. That is the reason
we have never met.

Brothers: We desire you to consider that your only demand is the peaceable possession of a small part of our
once great country. Look back and view the lands from
whence we have been driven to this spot. We can retreat
no farther, because the country behind hardly affords food
for its present inhabitants; and we have therefore resolved
to leave our bones in this small space, to which we are
now consigned.

Brothers: We shall be persuaded that you mean to do us
justice, if you agree that the Ohio shall remain the boundary line between us. If you will not consent thereto, our
meeting will be altogether unnecessary. This is the great
point, which we hoped would have been explained before
you left your houses; as our message last Autumn was
principally directed to obtain that information.

Done in General Council at the foot of the Miami
Rapids, on the 13th day of August, 1793.

POSTSCRIPT TO THE DOCUMENT:

The assurances given over and over by the US government that its people wanted "only this one little piece and
will never again ask for more" fell on deaf ears. The
Indians knew better from experience, for one thing. They
also knew that in spite of a secretary of war's ability to
recognize a moral responsibility (though not necessarily to
feel bound to act on it), the real white man's attitude
was much closer to that expressed by an important Pitts-
burgh resident in 1782, who wrote "some observations
with regard to the animals, vulgarly called Indians. . . ."

This writer's opinion on Indian land rights was crystal clear.

> On what is their claim founded?—Occupancy. A wild Indian with his skin painted red, and a feather through his nose, has set his foot on the broad continent of North and South America; a second wild Indian with his ears cut in ringlets, or his nose slit like a swine or a malefactor, also sets his foot on the same extensive tract of soil. . . . What use do these ringed, streaked, spotty and speckled cattle make of the soil? Do they till it? Revelation said to man, "Thou shalt till the ground." This alone is human life. . . . What would you think of . . . addressing yourself to a great buffalo to grant you land?

It is immaterial to the above writer, of course, that he is wrong even on the basic premise which he claims gives the white person a better right than the Indian to the land. After all, who taught the white man to plant corn, squash, tobacco, and so on? But he was not the first—not the last —white man whose racism and greed would deny him the direct testimony of his eyes.

A BASIS FOR UNITY

1805

Red Jacket Replies to the Missionary

ABOUT THE DOCUMENT:

The idea of Indian unity against a many-faced white oppressor expressed by Pontiac in his appeal to the various nations—and at least partially fulfilled in the confederacy he led to war—did not die with his defeat. During the years that followed the "American" Revolution, the idea grew. Nations such as the Shawnee, Delaware and Wyandot (who had moved often under a complexity of pressures since the white man's arrival) grew more and more keenly aware that the white man was the same threat to Indian life wherever the two races met. The white man scarcely distinguished between one Indian nation or people and another, as the nearly incredible confusion of names and references in white history books all too clearly shows. Also, the specific boundary line of the Declaration of 1763 was an issue that the Indian nations—on both sides of that line—found themselves in almost unanimous agreement about. Further, with the decrease of competition for Indian trade between different European groups, a major force that had worked to set nation against nation was weakened. The sum of these factors was that Indian unity became more of a reality and the white policy of divide and conquer became less effective.

In the Ohio territory being defended by the Indians, Shawnee and other nations' warriors joined with the Miami led by Little Turtle in 1790 to defeat a 1400-man army commanded by Gen. Josiah Harmar. Among the warriors who forced Harmar's retreat that day was a Shawnee youth named Tecumtha (Tecumseh in many

books) who would prove in time to be the most powerful
voice raised in the cry for Indian unity. In the year
following Harmar's defeat it was again a united Indian
force of Miami, Shawnee, and Delaware[1] that completely destroyed Gen. Arthur St. Clair's army of over two
thousand men in a fierce battle fought November 4, 1791.
More than six ·hundred "American" soldiers were killed
that day in what has been described as "one of the worst
routs ever suffered by an American army." And among
the Shawnee who distinguished themselves in that day's
fight was once again young Tecumtha.

But in 1794, maddened by successive defeats at the
hands of the Indians and despairing of ever bringing the
Indian nations to agree to a peace not based on the
original Ohio boundary, the United States staged a massive, new armed attack into Indian territory. Under the
command of Gen. Anthony Wayne, more than 3600
Army regulars invaded Indian land. They advanced slowly in a kind of leap-frog tactic, stopping to build forts, and
then continuing on to a further site and repeating the
operation. Tecumtha, who had been heading a Shawnee
war party that had gone to the aid of their Creek and
Cherokee allies fighting Tennessee settlers, returned to
the Northwest and joined the confederated forces now
under the command of another Shawnee chief, Blue Jacket. And on August 20, 1794, at a place along the Mau-
mee River known as Fallen Timbers, Blue Jacket led his
1400 warriors against General Wayne's army. A fierce
battle ended with the Indians' defeat. General Wayne
celebrated by burning every Indian village he could find
and then returned to the fort he had built at Greenville,
Ohio.

The next spring, chiefs of the defeated nations were
invited to a peace council at Greenville. After two months
of heavy pressure aided by free-flowing liquor provided by
the "Americans" and conscious of their people's hunger,[2]

[1] They were led by Pachgantschilas, whose reasons for joining the British
during the "Revolutionary" War are expressed in WHOSE INDEPEN-
DENCE?, Pachgantschilas Speaks.
[2] Along with the villages that General Wayne burned the previous summer
he also destroyed cornfields, which he described as the most extensive he had
ever seen.

the chiefs signed the Treaty of Greenville, ceding nearly two-thirds of Ohio, a piece of Indiana, and sixteen sites in the Northwest, including the sites of Detroit, Chicago and Toledo. For this cession the Indians received $20,000 worth of goods and the promise of $9500 in annuities. It is worth noting that Tecumtha refused to attend the council and repudiated the treaty signed there.

Following the Greenville Treaty, white men established themselves on the ceded lands and, of course, began almost immediately to push beyond them. Missionaries went to work among the nations, preaching the white man's religion, the life style that the white man seemed to consider inseparable from Christ's teachings. Whiskey flowed in rivers in what can only have been a deliberate attempt to destroy Indian morale and self-respect; prostitution and disease accompanied the white man once more into Indian territory and once more became a weakening force in Indian life. White depredations, white crowding, white cheating in trade reduced Indian wealth; poverty made many Indians more vulnerable to vice and despair; vice made Indians easier prey for white depredation, crowding, and cheating.

But during these years, on both sides of the old Demarcation Line an answering force of regeneration and of Indian unity made itself felt in the teachings of Indian prophets who preached that the Indians must forsake the white man's teachings and his influence—that they must return to the religion and the teachings they had known before the white man's coming. In these teachings of religious revival there was an insistence on reasserting a clear division between the ways of the white man and the ways of the Indian. And this way of seeing, which put all white men on one side and all Indians on the other, enhanced the Indian sense of brotherhood with others of his race but not of his nation. In the Northwest the most famous of the prophets was Tecumtha's brother, of whom we shall hear more later. To the east in the land of the once mighty Six Nations, Handsome Lake of the Seneca nation preached this Indian gospel with great effect.

The chief of the Seneca was Sagu-yu-what-hah ("Keeper Awake"), more commonly called Red Jacket. He reportedly once asked a young Indian returning from a white school where he had been "educated": "What have we here? You are neither a white man nor an Indian; for heaven's sake tell us; what are you?" And to a white missionary who tried to point out the error of the Indian way, Red Jacket once responded: "If you white people murdered 'the Savior,' make it up among yourselves. We had nothing to do with it. If he had come among us we should have treated him better."

In the document that follows, Red Jacket answers more fully a missionary of the Boston Missionary Society who had asked the Indians for a council and came to it accompanied by a US agent for Indian Affairs. Of the agent the missionary said that he himself would "inform you what his business is, and it is my request that you would listen with attention to his words." The missionary went on to assure his listeners that he was not interested in Indian lands or money, that his sole concern was for their souls, and that they should not continue to worship "in great errors and darkness."

After the missionary closed his speech, the Indians met in council together for two hours over their reply. It was expressed by Red Jacket in a speech notable for the beauty of its oratory as well as its brilliant logic in refuting the missionary's offers. It also reflects the suspicion that anything white would turn out bad for the Indian—not a new attitude, but one that shaped the new Indian drive for unity then gathering its strength among Red Jacket's brothers to the west.

It is also perhaps worth noting that Red Jacket and the other chiefs were capable of expressing the strongest disagreement with their white visitors without the slightest breach of courtesy or good manners, offering their hands and commending the white men to the care of the Great Spirit for their journey home. The civilized missionary, Mr. Cram, refused to shake their hands, saying there was "no fellowship between the religion of God and the devil."

THE DOCUMENT:

Red Jacket to the Missionary: From a pamphlet, Indian Speeches; delivered by Farmer's Brother and Red Jacket, Two Seneca Chiefs, Canandaigua, New York, 1809

Friend and Brother! It was the will of the Great Spirit that we should meet together this day. He orders all things, and he has given us a fine day for our council. He has taken his garment from before the sun, and caused it to shine with brightness upon us. Our eyes are opened that we see clearly. Our ears are unstopped that we have been able to hear distinctly the words you have spoken. For all these favors we thank the Great Spirit, and him only.

Brother! This council fire was kindled by you. It was at your request that we came together at this time. We have listened with attention to what you have said. You requested us to speak our minds freely. This gives us great joy, for we now consider that we stand upright before you, and can speak what we think. All have heard your voice, and all speak to you as one man. Our minds are agreed.

Brother! You say you want an answer to your talk before you leave this place. It is right you should have one, for you are a great distance from home, and we do not wish to detain you. But we will first look back a little, and tell you what our fathers have told us, and what we have heard from the white people.

Brother! Listen to what we say. There was a time when our forefathers owned this great island. Their seats extended from the rising to the setting sun. The Great Spirit had made it for the use of Indians. He had created the buffalo, the deer, and other animals for food. He made the bear and the beaver, and their skins served us for clothing. He had scattered them over the country, and taught us how to take them. He had caused the earth to produce corn for bread. All this he had done for his red children because he loved them. If we had any disputes about hunting grounds, they were generally settled without the shedding of much blood. But an evil day came upon us. Your forefathers crossed the great waters, and landed on this island. Their numbers were small. They found friends and not enemies. They told us they had fled from their own country for fear of wicked men, and come here to enjoy their religion. They asked for a small seat. We took pity on them, granted their request, and they sat down amongst us. We gave them corn and meat. They gave us poison in return. The white people had now found our country. Tidings were carried back, and more came amongst us. Yet we did not fear them. We took them to be friends. They called us brothers. We believed them, and gave them a larger seat. At length their numbers had greatly increased. They wanted more land. They wanted our country. Our eyes were opened, and our minds became uneasy. Wars took place. Indians were hired to fight against Indians, and many of our people were destroyed. They also brought strong liquors among us. It was strong and powerful, and has slain thousands.

Brother! Our seats were once large, and yours were very small. You have now become a great people, and we have scarcely a place left to spread our blankets. You have got our country, but are not satisfied. *You want to force your religion upon us.*

Brother! *Continue to listen.* You say that you are sent to instruct us how to worship the Great Spirit agreeably to his mind; and if we do not take hold of the religion which you white people teach, we shall be unhappy hereafter. You say that you are right and we are lost. How do we know this to be true? We understand that your religion is written in a book. If it was intended for us as well as for you, why had not the Great Spirit given it to us; and not only to us, but why did he not give to our forefathers the knowledge of that book, with the means of understanding it rightly? We only know what you tell us about it. How shall we know when to believe, being so often deceived by the white people?

Brother! You say there is but one way to worship and serve the Great Spirit. If there is but one religion, why do you white people differ so much about it? Why not all agree, as you can all read the book?

Brother! We do not understand these things. We are told that your religion was given to your forefathers, and has been handed down from father to son. We also have a religion which was given to our forefathers, and has been handed down to us their children. We worship that way. It teacheth *us to be thankful for all the favors we receive, to love each other, and to be united. We never quarrel about religion.*

Brother! The Great Spirit has made us all; but he has made a great difference between his white and red children. But he has given us a different complexion and different customs. To you he has given the arts; to these he has not opened our eyes. We know these things to be true. Since he has made so great a difference between us in other things, why may we not conclude that he has given us a different religion, according to our understanding? The Great Spirit does right. He knows what is best for his children. We are satisfied.

Brother! We do not wish to destroy your religion, or take it from you. We only want to enjoy our own.

Brother! You say you have not come to get our land or our money, but to enlighten our minds. I will now tell you that I have been at your meetings and saw you collecting money from the meeting. I cannot tell what this money was intended for, but suppose it was for your minister; and if we should conform to your way of thinking, perhaps you may want some from us.

Brother! We are told that you have been preaching to white people in this place. These people are our neighbors. We are acquainted with them. We will wait a little while, and see what effect your preaching has upon them. If we find that it does them good and makes them honest and less disposed to cheat Indians, we will then consider again what you have said.

Brother! You have now heard our answer to your talk, and this is all we have to say at present. As we are going to part, we will come and take you by the hand, and hope the Great Spirit will protect you on your journey, and return you safe to your friends.

THE FIGHT FOR A NATION

1810

Tecumtha Answers Governor Harrison

Tecumtha Speaks to the Osage

ABOUT THE DOCUMENTS:

"He yelled like a tiger, and urged his braves to the attack," recalled a Kentucky soldier who had faced him in battle.

An Indiana newspaper said of him that he "was truly great—and his greatness was his own, unassisted by science or the aids of education. As a statesman, a warrior and a patriot, take him all in all, we shall not look upon his like again."

Gen. William Henry Harrison spoke of him as one of the "uncommon geniuses, which spring up occasionally to produce revolutions and overturn the established order of things."

And a modern writer, Alvin M. Josephy, Jr. (*The Patriot Chiefs*) has written that "he looked beyond the mere resistance by a tribe or group of tribes to white encroachments. He was a Shawnee, but he considered himself first an Indian, and fought to give all Indians a national rather than a tribal consciousness, and to unite them in defense of a common homeland where they might all continue to dwell under their own laws and leaders."

All these men were talking or writing about Tecumtha, the great Shawnee born in 1768 and killed in 1813. No other voice was ever more loudly raised or widely heard in North America among the countless expressions of anger at white treachery and greed. No one ever explained more clearly the meaning of the white men's presence and civilization to the people whose continent they invaded. No one ever brought closer to reality the Indian dream that somewhere the white advance would halt—or would be halted.

Tecumtha means "Panther Lying in Wait." White men fumbled the name and turned it into Tecumseh, meaning "Shooting Star." He was born in March, 1768, near present-day Dayton, Ohio. His father was a Shawnee war chief who, reflecting the nomadic experience of the Shawnee, was born in Florida, moved north to Pennsylvania, retreated from there on the bloody crest of the advancing white frontier, got married in Alabama, and settled near the Mad River in Ohio shortly before Tecumtha was born.

At the time of Tecumtha's birth Pontiac had just been defeated. During the first few years of his childhood settlers began to move west of the mountains into Kentucky and Ohio, and the long struggle for that territory was begun. Lord Dunmore's War, in which both Tecumtha's father and elder brother fought, broke out when he was six years old. He was not much older when he and his mother went searching one night for his father, who had not come home; they found him dying but still able to tell them how white men had called to him and then shot him without provocation. When he was ten he saw the famous Daniel Boone, captured with twenty-six other white men during an Indian raid into Kentucky, brought back to Ohio. Two years later a US army burned the Shawnee town where Tecumtha lived; he went with the other Shawnee to build a new town which they named Piqua, the "town that rises from the ashes." At about fourteen he took part for the first time in a battle: beside his brother Cheeseekau he fought against white intruders in Kentucky. Still a teenager, he joined other young Shawnee in guerrilla raids designed to prevent white settlers from moving freely down the Ohio river. Then later he became the leader of his own warrior band and continued the guerrilla struggle for Ohio. His part in the defeats of

Generals Harmar and St. Clair has been noted; he commanded a group of scouts against Gen. Anthony Wayne at the disaster of Fallen Timbers, and on that day his brother was killed.

After Tecumtha refused to attend the Greenville peace council or to accept the treaty signed there, he rejected Blue Jacket, war chief of the Shawnee. Rather than remain near the white people who now moved into the newly ceded territory, he and his followers moved further west to Indiana. Increasing numbers of angry warriors joined him there, eager to bind their loyalty to a chief who had not given up the struggle against the white man.

One of the stories about Tecumtha's life during this period is that while visiting a sister in Ohio, he met a white girl who seems to have been unusually well educated for a "wilderness" settler's daughter. In any event she is said to have read to him from classical history, Shakespeare, and the Bible. Their relationship became romantic; he asked her to marry; she answered that she would, but only if he would abandon his Indian life and take up that of the white man. He never saw her again.

The demoralizing effect of white settlements (symptomized by drunkenness, poverty, and disease) took its toll, often weakening the Indian population as the white population increased. With the growing white population came, once again, a swelling of white voices demanding access to new Indian lands. As if anticipating the inevitable, the government began to prepare a new territorial administration for the Territory of Indiana, though all but a small piece of Indiana, where Tecumtha and his Shawnee lived, had been recognized as belonging to the Indians forever by the Treaty of Greenville.

Living far removed from white traders, Tecumtha's Shawnee kept their strength and their morale and were less susceptible to plague of whiskey and disease. Tecumtha denounced the use of liquor and was himself a teetotaler, but despite his opposition unscrupulous traders did sell whiskey to the Shawnee, and one of its best known victims was Tecumtha's younger brother. But then something happened; in 1805 (the same year that Red

Jacket told the white missionary that he would wait and see if Christian preaching improved the lives and characters of his white neighbors) Tecumtha's brother fell into a trance from which he emerged a changed man. He began to preach against alcohol with such conviction and eloquence that he began to attract followers. Soon, as did the Seneca prophet, Handsome Lake, he was preaching abstinence from all of the white man's ways. Allying himself with his brother, he elaborated a spiritual code that complemented Tecumtha's political one. Together they became a force that on the one hand appealed to Indian spiritual pride and self-respect and on the other, demanded strength and unity for the struggle against the white advance. Leaving their remote home in Indiana, Tecumtha and his brother the Prophet (as he was beginning to be called) returned to Greenville, site of the despised treaty of 1795, and established a settlement for their followers and converts. Response to the brothers was wide; followers came to them from every tribe in the Northwest.

This development was not wasted on General Harrison, the territorial governor with his headquarters at Vincennes. It made no difference that the principles of simplicity, honesty, brotherhood and reverence preached by the Prophet—and being lived by his followers—were much closer to the teachings of the religion Harrison professed to believe in than to the example of white traders, settlers, soldiers, and even missionaries. Harrison scoffed at the Prophet and did his best to discredit him. The attempt backfired badly on him, for he suggested to a group of Indians that they ask the Prophet for proof of his divine inspiration—such as causing the sun to stand still. The Prophet accepted the challenge and announced that on June 16, 1806, he would cause the sun to darken. On the appointed day, as he commanded the sun to darken, a total eclipse began, and Harrison lost his gamble.

The message of Tecumtha and his brother the Prophet gained ground among the Indians of the Northwest, inspiring them with pride and unity. Young warriors loyal to Tecumtha's principles ousted old chiefs and chiefs who had sold out to the white man. Tecumtha's dream defined itself more clearly, and he rested it on a solid, basic principle: all Indian land belonged to all Indians, and no one had the right to sell any of it to anyone. He preached this as the basis of an Indian unity which alone could unite all the nations to fight together in common defense of their common land. His following grew, more nations pledged their support to his idea, and tensions among the white "Americans" mounted—increased by the suspicion that this Indian activity was connected to the new war with England that everyone feared. Tecumtha became convinced that the "Americans" would attack the Indians, partly from fear of the English and partly as an excuse to take more Indian lands "by conquest in a just war." To prevent conflict before he was sure of the forces required for an Indian victory, Tecumtha and the Prophet moved from Greenville to a remote place near the fork of the Wabash and Tippecanoe rivers. There they built a new Prophet Town in 1808; to it came more than a thousand Shawnee, Ojibwa, Kickapoo, Delaware, Wyandot, and Ottawa to live as the Prophet taught them. (In that year also, Thomas Jefferson wrote to Governor Harrison that "to promote this disposition [among the Indians] to exchange lands . . . we shall push our trading houses, and be glad to see the good and influential among them run into debt, because we observe that when these debts get beyond what the individuals can pay, they become willing to lop them off by cession of lands . . .")

In 1808, almost as soon as Prophet Town was built, Tecumtha set out to take his message personally to all the Indian nations. First in the Northwest he won declarations of support from Potawatomi, Menominee and Winnebagoe. He was opposed by the Sauk and Fox—except for a war chief named Black Hawk, for whom one day an entire war would be named. Kicapoo and Ottawa pledged support, as did many groups of Illinois, Delaware, Wea, Chippewa, Piankasaw, and Wyandot. The Missisinewa and the Miami turned him down, as did many chiefs who had signed the Greenville Treaty.

Tecumtha did not stop with the Northwest. He went as

far south as Seminole land; west into Missouri where the
Osage made their famous bows and even tried, without
success, to arouse the Iroquois of the Six Nations.

But he returned to Tippecanoe to find that in his absence Governor Harrison had carefully selected a council
of old and weak chiefs, gotten them drunk, and pressured
them into signing a new cession. For $7000 in cash and an
annuity of $1750 Harrison "bought" three million acres of
Indiana, including some of the Shawnee's finest hunting
grounds. Tecumtha's response was to announce that Indian land belonged to all Indians and that he would not
recognize the cession Harrison had swindled. Frightened,
Harrison asked Tecumtha to parley; Tecumtha agreed.
Followed by several hundred armed warriors, he appeared
at Vincennes and for two days met with Harrison and told
him exactly what he planned. "The way, the only way to
stop this evil is for all the red men to unite in claiming a
common and equal right in the land, as it was at first, and
should be now—for it was never divided, but belongs to
all." The first of the two documents below is a portion of
the speech made by Tecumtha on that occasion. Other
than an exchange of views, however, nothing was accomplished there; Harrison made no concessions, and it was
clear that he meant to keep pressing for more Indian
lands. Tecumtha certainly made it clear that he meant to
prevent any such thing.

Tensions grew even greater among western settlers who
feared a joint war by the British and Indians against the
Ohio Valley. Determined to forestall the event, Harrison looked for an excuse to move against Prophet Town
while Tecumtha was once more away urging the Indian
alliance. An incident in 1811 in which some white men in
Illinois were killed by Potawatomi gave Harrison the excuse he wanted, and blaming the deaths on Tecumtha and
the Prophet, he led an army of a thousand men against the
Prophet Town. The Prophet allowed a much smaller band
of over-eager Winnebago to attack Harrison's army,
camped and fortified at Tippecanoe; in the battle that followed white casualties were more than double those of the
Indians, but in the end the Prophet's men withdrew, leav-

ing the town to Harrison. Though militarily of little importance, the victory of Harrison's force had a tremendous
psychological effect. To the "Americans" the victory
seemed so important that twenty-nine years later Harrison
won a presidential election with the slogan "Tippecanoe
and Tyler, too." Tyler was included because he was the
vice-presidential candidate.

The consequences of the Prophet's bungling were enormous for the Indians. Tecumtha, realizing that it would
set off the kind of uncoordinated border war he had tried
to avoid, came very near to killing his brother in his
anger. Thoroughly discredited, the Prophet was driven
from the town and became a wandering preacher whose
influence steadily declined.

Tecumtha's prediction of undisciplined warfare proved
a true one. Here and there on the white-Indian frontier,
war parties attacked white settlers in search of revenge for
Tippecanoe. Settlers' fears of British-Indian attacks increased and pressured the government for war with England. That war was declared on June 18, 1812. Now
Tecumtha could only try to rouse as many Indian nations
as possible to ally themselves with the British. He hoped
that perhaps the common ally would become the focal
point of a unity he had worked so hard and long to
achieve. So now he could only fight and hope that his message to the Indian nations might bear fruit. The second
document records Tecumtha's speech made to the Osage
during his mission to Missouri.

DOCUMENT A:

*From Samuel Gardner Drake, Biography and History
of the Indians of North America; Comprising a General
Account of Man, and Details in the Lives of All the Most
Distinguished Chiefs . . . Boston, 1834*

It is true I am a Shawnee. My forefathers were warriors. Their son is a warrior. From them I only take my
existence; from my tribe I take nothing. I am the maker
of my own fortune; and oh! that I could make that of my

red people, and of my country, as great as the conceptions of my mind, when I think of the Spirit that rules the universe. I would not then come to Gov. *Harrison,* to ask him to tear the treaty, and to obliterate the landmark; but I would say to him, Sir, you have liberty to return to your own country. The being within, communing with past ages, tells me, that once, nor until lately, there was no white man on this continent. That it then all belonged to red men, children of the same parents, placed on it by the Great Spirit that made them, to keep it, to traverse it, to enjoy its productions, and to fill it with the same race. Once a happy race. Since made miserable by the white people, who are never contented, but always encroaching. The way, and the only way, to check and to stop this evil, is, for all the red men to unite in claiming a common and equal right in the land, as it was at first, and should be yet; for it never was divided, but belongs to all, for the use of each. That no part has a right to sell, even to each other, much less to strangers; those who want all, and will not do with less. The white people have no right to take the land from the Indians, because they had it first; it is theirs. They may sell, but all must join. Any sale not made by all is not valid. The late sale is bad. It requires a few to make a bargain for all. All red men have equal rights to the unoccupied land. The right of occupancy is as good in one place as in another. There cannot be two occupations in the same place. The first excludes all others. It is not so in hunting or travelling; for there the same ground will serve many, as they may follow each other all day; but the camp is stationary, and that is occupancy. It belongs to the first who sits down on his blanket or skins, which he has thrown upon the ground, and till he leaves it no other has a right.

DOCUMENT B:

From John D. Hunter, *Memoirs of a Captivity Among the Indians of North America,* London, 1824

Brothers,—We all belong to one family; we are all

children of the Great Spirit; we walk in the same path; slake our thirst at the same spring; and now affairs of the greatest concern lead us to smoke the pipe around the same council fire!

Brothers,—We are friends; we must assist each other to bear our burdens. The blood of many of our fathers and brothers has run like water on the ground, to satisfy the avarice of the white men. We, ourselves, are threatened with a great evil; nothing will pacify them but the destruction of all the red men.

Brothers,—When the white men first set foot on our grounds, they were hungry; they had no place on which to spread their blankets, or to kindle their fires. They were feeble; they could do nothing for themselves. Our fathers commiserated their distress, and shared freely with them whatever the Great Spirit had given his red children. They gave them food when hungry, medicine when sick, spread skins for them to sleep on, and gave them grounds, that they might hunt and raise corn.

Brothers—the white people are like poisonous serpents: when chilled, they are feeble, and harmless, but invigorate them with warmth, and they sting their benefactors to death.

The white people came among us feeble; and now we have made them strong, they wish to kill us, or drive us back, as they would wolves and panthers.

Brothers,—The white men are not friends to the Indians: at first, they only asked for land sufficient for a wigwam; now, nothing will satisfy them but the whole of our hunting grounds, from the rising to the setting sun.

Brothers,—The white men want more than our hunting grounds; they wish to kill our warriors; they would even kill our old men, women and little ones.

Brothers,—Many winters ago, there was no land; the sun did not rise and set: all was darkness. The Great Spirit made all things. He gave the white people a home beyond the great waters. He supplied these grounds with game, and gave them to his red children; and he gave them strength and courage to defend them.

Brothers,—My people wish for peace; the red men all

wish for peace; but where the white people are, there is no peace for them, except it be on the bosom of our mother.

Brothers,—The white men despise and cheat the Indians; they abuse and insult them; they do not think the red men sufficiently good to live.

The red men have borne many and great injuries; they ought to suffer them no longer. My people will not; they are determined on vengeance; they have taken up the tomahawk; they will make it fat with blood; they will drink the blood of the white people.

Brothers,—My people are brave and numerous; but the white people are too strong for them alone. I wish you to take up the tomahawk with them. If we all unite, we will cause the rivers to stain the great waters with their blood.

Brothers,—If you do not unite with us, they will first destroy us, and then you will fall an easy prey to them. They have destroyed many nations of red men because they were not united, because they were not friends to each other.

Brothers,—The white people send runners amongst us; they wish to make us enemies, that they may sweep over and desolate our hunting grounds, like devastating winds, or rushing waters.

Brothers,—Our Great Father, over the great waters, is angry with the white people, our enemies. He will send his brave warriors against them; he will send us rifles, and whatever else we want—he is our friend, and we are his children.

Brothers,—Who are the white people that we should fear them? They cannot run fast, and are good marks to shoot at: they are only men; our fathers have killed many of them; we are not squaws, and we will stain the earth red with their blood.

Brothers,—The Great Spirit is angry with our enemies; he speaks in thunder, and the earth swallows up villages, and drinks up the Mississippi. The great waters will cover their lowlands; their corn cannot grow; and the Great Spirit will sweep those who escape to the hills from the earth with his terrible breath.

Brothers,—We must be united; we must smoke the same pipe; we must fight each other's battles; and more than all, we must love the Great Spirit; he is for us; he will destroy our enemies, and make all his red children happy.

THE WAR OF 1812

Walk-in-the-Water Addresses the Malden Council

Black Hawk's Account

Tecumtha Shames Colonel Procter

ABOUT THE DOCUMENTS:

With the outbreak of the War of 1812 both English and "American" agents courted the Indian nations' support or, failing that, at least their neutrality, just as they had in the Revolutionary War. In spite of the success Tecumtha had achieved in spreading the gospel of Indian unity, Indian response was neither unanimous nor automatic. Tecumtha himself, when approached by "American" agents, broke the pipes of peace they handed to him and told them that the opportunity at hand was

. . . a chance such as will never occur again—for us Indians of North America to form ourselves into one great combination and cast our lot with the British in this war. And should they conquer and again get the mastery of all North America, our rights to at least a portion of the land of our fathers would be respected by the King. If they should not win and the whole country should pass into the hands of the Long Knives—we see this plainly—it will not be many years before our last place of abode and our last hunting ground will be taken from us, and the remnants of the different tribes between the Mississippi, the Lakes, and the Ohio River will all be driven toward the setting sun.

Then, followed by a party that included Shawnee, Delaware, Kickapoo, and Potawatomi, he marched to declare his support of the British. Though the massive united uprising he had hoped and worked for did not occur, in the days that followed, war parties from many of the nations he had visited came to join him. Black Hawk led in a party of Sauk, Fox, and Winnebago; Wyandot, Chippewa, and Sioux remembered his message and came to give him support. In the South, on the upper Mississippi, and in the Northwest bands of warriors followed his lead—if not his directions—and rose up against the settlers.

But there were Indians who fought against the US too, though they were few. Many more remained neutral, unable to see why they should take sides in a white man's war. The first document records the speech of Walk-in-the-Water, a Wyandot chief who argued the neutralist case at a meeting between the Indians and the British commanding officer at Fort Malden. It is interesting to note, however, that in spite of the Wyandot's desire to remain neutral, circumstances of the war did force him to fight—and when he did, he chose to fight with Tecumtha and the British.

The second document is from Black Hawk's autobiography, and in it he describes the events and motives that led him to choose the British side. When he did decide, he remembered his meeting with Tecumtha and led a combined war party all the way from the Mississippi River to unite with the Indians at Fort Malden.

For the Indian-British forces the war began well. After frustrating Gen. William Hull's attempted invasion of Canada, Tecumtha and the British Maj. Gen. Isaac Brock agreed on an attack at Detroit—an attack proposal that only one other British officer supported. Tecumtha maneuvered his warriors before the fort so skillfully that General Hull was convinced five thousand Indians had descended on him; and with scarcely a show of resistance General Hull surrendered.

The victory at Detroit raised Indian nationalist hopes and more tribes entered the war against the "Americans." Potawatomi captured Fort Dearborn. Miami, who had always rejected Tecumtha's appeals, besieged Fort Wayne. And after another lightning tour of the southern nations by Tecumtha during the fall of 1812, the great Creek Confederation began to war against the white men in the South. Tecumtha's forces in the Northwest swelled until they numbered three thousand warriors—just about the largest Indian army ever put together.

Then the tide of war turned, demonstrating once again that although battles are fought by soldiers, they can be won or lost by their leaders. On the "American" side command of troops passed from the weak-kneed General Brush to Gen. William Henry Harrison who, whatever else might be said of him, was no coward. On the British side the general who had supported Tecumtha's successful attack of Detroit, General Brock, was killed in battle, and his command was taken over by Col. Henry Procter. Procter was cowardly, vain, and contemptuous of Indians. After a major victory by British-Indian troops over an army of Kentuckians at River Basin, Procter encouraged angry, whiskey-goaded Indians to take revenge against unarmed prisoners—an action for which Tecumtha severely criticized the British commander's weakness. When a similar incident was encouraged by Procter in Tecumtha's absence, the Shawnee chief hurried to the scene and with sword in hand forced the warriors to stop the massacre. "Are there no men here?" he challenged; the killing stopped. Again he criticized Procter, whose only reply was that the "Indians cannot be controlled."

"You are unfit to command," Tecumtha answered and added, "I conquer to save, and you to murder."

Procter was a coward. When he withdrew the siege of Fort Miegs, Tecumtha forced him to resume it, but before long Procter again abandoned that contest. One after another, the British commander let all opportunities to strike the US army slip away until, following a US naval victory on Lake Erie, he made up his mind to pull the British troops out of the area and abandon his Indian allies altogether. He tried to conceal this plan from Tecumtha, but his preparations for flight could not be hidden. Tecumtha gathered his warriors at Fort Malden and in front of them and the other British officers publicly accused Procter of cowardice. The third document that follows records the words with which Tecumtha tried to shame the British commander into fighting.

Procter preferred to swallow his shame; that same day he began the withdrawal from Fort Malden. Tecumtha reluctantly agreed to follow on the strength of Procter's promise that the retreat would be only as far as the Thames River, where they would turn and fight. Harrison's forces naturally came in pursuit, and all the way from Fort Malden to the Thames the Indian forces fought a rearguard action while Procter rode at the head of his retreating forces, as far away from the US forces as he could get. During one of those rearguard fights Tecumtha was wounded, though not seriously.

Once more Tecumtha tried to shame the British general into fighting after the Thames was reached. Finally Tecumtha himself took practical command of the British-Indian forces and disposed them in battle form to face Harrison's army of 3500 troops, including a Kentucky cavalry force of 1500 men. To oppose them, Tecumtha had 700 British troops and 1000 Indian warriors, for the British commander's lack of will to fight had weakened Indian unity and many groups had gone their own way, to fight "Americans" as they saw fit. In the battle that followed, the British troops fled almost at once from the Kentucky cavalry—they were still led by Procter. Jumping into a carriage, he had run from the battle and abandoned even his own troops before they abandoned the Indians. Left alone, the Indians fought furiously and held the US soldiers at bay until after dark. It was of this battle that a Kentuckian later told how Tecumtha "yelled like a tiger, and urged his braves to the attack." Others recalled seeing the Shawnee chief hit again and again but with blood pouring from his mouth and covering his body, still moving about the battle field and encouraging his warriors to hold out.

With their British allies gone and their principal leader killed, united Indian resistance in the Northwest came to an end. There would be further fighting, but what Tecumtha had described as their last chance to "form ourselves into one great combination" that would force white men to respect the Indians' right to a nation had been lost.

DOCUMENT A:

From B. B. Thatcher, *Indian Biography*, 1837

WALK-IN-THE-WATER OF THE WYANDOT: We have no wish to be involved in a war with our father, the Long-Knife, for we know by experience that we have nothing to gain by it, and we beg our father, the British, not to force us to war. We remember, in the former war between our fathers, the British and the Long-Knife, we were both defeated, and we the red men lost our country; and you, our father, the British, made peace with the Long-Knife, without our knowledge, and you gave our country to him. You still said to us, "my children, you must fight for your country, for the Long-Knife will take it from you." We did as you advised us, and we were defeated with the loss of our best chiefs and warriors, and of our land. And we still remember your conduct towards us, when we were defeated at the foot of the rapids of the Miami. We sought safety for our wounded in your fort. But what was your conduct? You closed your gates against us, and we had to retreat the best way we could. And then we made peace with the Americans, and have enjoyed peace with them ever since. And now you wish us, your red children, again to take up the hatchet against our father, the Long-Knife. We say again, we do not wish to have anything to do with the war. Fight your own battles, but let us, your red children, enjoy peace.

DOCUMENT B:

From the autobiography of Black Hawk, Life of Ma-ka-tai-me-she-kia-kiak or Black Hawk, Dictated by Himself. Boston, 1834

Runners continued to arrive from different tribes, all confirming the report of the expected war. The British agent, Col. Dixon, was holding *talks* with, and making presents to, the different tribes. I had not made up my mind whether to join the British or remain neutral. *I had not discovered one good trait in the character of the Americans that had come to the country!* They made *fair promises,* but *never fulfilled them!* Whilst the *British* made but few—but we could always *rely upon their word!*

One of our people having killed a Frenchman at Prairie du Chien, the British took him prisoner, and said they would *shoot him* the next day! His family were encamped a short distance below the mouth of the Ouisconsin. He begged for permission to go and see them that night, as he was *to die the next day!* They permitted him to go, after promising to return the next morning by sunrise. He visited his family, which consisted of a wife and six children. I cannot describe their *meeting* and *parting,* to be understood by the whites; as it appears that their feelings are acted upon by certain rules laid down by their *preachers!*—whilst ours are governed only by the monitor within us. He parted from his wife and children, hurried through the prairie to the fort, and arrived in time! The soldiers were ready, and immediately marched out *and shot him down!* I visited his family, and by hunting and fishing, provided for them until they reached their relations.

Why did the Great Spirit ever send the whites to this island, to drive us from our homes, and introduce among us *poisonous liquors, disease and death?* They should have remained on the island where the Great Spirit first placed them. But I will proceed with my story. My memory, however, is not very good, since my late visit to the white people. I have still a buzzing in my ears, from the noise—

and may give some parts of my story out of place; but I will endeavor to be correct.

Several of our chiefs and head men were called upon to go to Washington, to see their Great Father. They started; and during their absence, I went to Peoria, on the Illinois river, to see an old friend, a trader, to get his advice. He was a man that always told us the truth, and knew every thing that was going on. When I arrived at Peoria, he was not there, but had gone to Chicago. I visited the Pottawatomie villages, and then returned to Rock river. Soon after which, our friends returned from their visit to our Great Father—and related what had been said and done. Their Great Father (they said) wished us, in the event of a war taking place with England, not to interfere on either side— but to remain neutral. He did not want our help—but wished us to hunt and support our families, and live in peace. He said that British traders would not be permitted to come on the Mississippi, to furnish us with goods—but we would be well supplied by an American trader. Our chiefs then told him that the *British traders* always gave us *credits* in the fall, for guns, powder and goods, to enable us to hunt, and clothe our families. He replied that the trader at fort Madison would have plenty of goods— that we should go there in the fall, and he would supply us *on credit,* as the *British traders had done.* The party gave a good account of what they had seen, and the kind treatment they received.

This information pleased us all very much. We all agreed to follow our Great Father's advice, and not inter- fere with the war. Our women were much pleased at this good news. Every thing went on cheerfully in our village. We resumed our pastimes of playing ball, horse racing, and dancing, which had been laid aside when this great war was first talked about.

We had fine crops of corn, which were now ripe—and our women were engaged in gathering it, and making *cashes* to contain it. In a short time we were ready to start to fort Madison, to get our supply of goods, that we might proceed to our hunting grounds. We passed merrily down the river—all in high spirits. I had determined to spend the winter at my old favorite hunting ground, on Skunk river, and left part of my corn and mats at its mouth, to take up when I returned: others did the same. Next morning we arrived at the fort, and made our encampment. Myself and principal men paid a visit to the war chief at the fort. He received us kindly, and gave us some tobacco, pipes and provision. The trader came in, and we all rose and shook hands with him—for on him all our dependence was placed, to enable us to hunt, and thereby support our families. We waited a long time, expecting the trader would tell us that he had orders from our Great Father to supply us with goods—but he said nothing on the subject. I got up, and told him, in a short speech, what we had come for—and hoped he had plenty of goods to supply us—and told him that he should be well paid in the spring—and concluded, by informing him, that we had determined to follow our Great Father's advice, and not go to war.

He said that he was happy to hear that we intended to remain at peace. That he had a large quantity of goods; and that, if we made a good hunt, we would be well supplied: but remarked, that *he had received no instructions to furnish us any thing on credit!—nor could he give us any without receiving the pay for them on the spot!*

We informed him what our Great Father had told our chiefs at Washington—and contended that he could supply us if he would—believing that our *Great Father always spoke the truth!* But the war chief said that the trader could not furnish us on credit—and that *he had received no instructions from our Great Father at Washington!* We left the fort dissatisfied, and went to our camp. What was now to be done, we knew not. We questioned the party that brought us the news from our Great Father, that we would get credit for our winter's supplies, at this place. They still told the same story, and insisted upon its truth. Few of us slept that night—all was gloom and discontent!

In the morning, a canoe was seen descending the river— it soon arrived, bearing an express, who brought intelligence that La Gutrie, a *British trader,* had landed at Rock Island, with *two boats* loaded with goods—and requested us to come up immediately—because he had *good news* for us, and a *variety of presents*. The express presented us with tobacco, pipes and wampum.

The news run through our camp like *fire in the prairie*. Our lodges were soon taken down, and all started for Rock Island. Here ended all hopes of our remaining at peace—having been *forced into* WAR *by being* DECEIVED!

Our party were not long in getting to Rock Island. When we came in sight, and saw tents pitched, we yelled, fired our guns, and commenced beating our drums. Guns were immediately fired at the island, returning our salute, and a *British flag hoisted!* We landed, and were cordially received by La Gutrie—and then smoked the pipe with him! After which he made a speech to us, that had been sent by Colonel Dixon, and gave us a number of handsome presents—a large silk flag, and a keg of rum, and told us to retire—take some refreshments and rest ourselves, as he would have more to say to us on the next day.

We accordingly, retired to our lodges, (which had been put up in the mean time,) and spent the night. The next morning we called upon him, and told him that we wanted his two boats' load of goods to divide among our people—for which he should be well paid in the spring with furs and peltries. He consented—told us to take them—and do as we pleased with them. Whilst our people were dividing the goods, he took me aside, and informed me that Col. Dixon was at Green Bay, with twelve boats, loaded with goods, guns, and ammunition—and wished me to raise a party immediately and go to him. He said that our friend, the trader at Peoria, was collecting the Pottawatomies, and would be there before us. I communicated this information to my braves, and a party of two hundred warriors were soon collected and ready to depart.

DOCUMENT C:

Father! Listen to your children.

The war before this [Revolutionary War], our British

father gave the hatchet to his red children, when our old chiefs were alive. They are now dead. In that war our father was thrown flat on his back by the Americans, and our father took them by the hand without our knowledge. We are afraid that our father will do so again this time.

The summer before last, when I came forward with my red brethren, and was ready to take up the hatchet in favor of our British father, we were told not to be in a hurry—that he had not yet determined to fight the Americans.

Listen! When war was declared, our father stood up and gave us the tomahawk, and told us that he was then ready to strike the Americans—that he wanted our assistance—and that he would certainly get us our lands back which the Americans had taken from us.

Listen! You told us, at that time, to bring forward our families to this place, and we did so. You also promised to take care of them—they should want for nothing, while the men would go and fight the enemy—that we need not trouble ourselves about the enemy's garrison—that we knew nothing about them—and that our father would attend to that part of the business. You also told your red children that you would take good care of your garrison here, which made our hearts glad.

Father, listen! Our fleet has gone. We know they have fought. We have heard the great guns. But we know nothing of what has happened. Our ships have gone one way, and we are much astonished to see our father tying up everything and preparing to run away the other, without letting his red children know what his intentions are. You always told us to remain here, and take care of our lands. It made our hearts glad to hear that was your wish. Our great father, the king, is the head, and you represent him. You always told us that you would never draw your foot off British ground. But now, father, we see you are drawing back, and we are sorry to see our father doing so without seeing the enemy. We must compare our father's conduct to a fat dog, that carries its tail upon its back, but when affrighted, it drops it between its legs and runs off.

Father, listen! The Americans have not yet defeated us

by land. Neither are we sure that they have done so by water. We therefore wish to remain here, and fight our enemy, should they make their appearance. If they defeat us, we will then retreat with our father.

At the battle of the rapids, last war, the Americans certainly defeated us. And when we returned to our father's fort, at that place the gates were shut against us. We were afraid that it would now be the case; but instead of that, we now see our British father preparing to march out of his garrison.

Father! You have got the arms and ammunition which our great father sent for his red children. If you have an idea of going away, give them to us, and you may go and welcome for us. Our lives are in the hands of the Great Spirit. We are determined to defend our lands, and if it be his will, we wish to leave our bones upon them.

LAST STAND IN THE OLD NORTHWEST

1816–1832

From: Black Hawk's Autobiography

ABOUT THE DOCUMENT:

One of the most remarkable records of the white man's use of the divide-and-conquer technique is contained in the autobiography of Tecumtha's western ally, Black Hawk, war chief of the Sauk-Fox. From the time of this nation's first formal dealings with Indians until Black Hawk's final humiliation, white men exploited every opportunity to set Indian against Indian.

The Sauk-Fox Nation,[1] occupied all of present day

---

[1] It resulted from the merger of two distant Indian peoples driven from their original lands during troubles that were the western echoes of seventeenth and eighteenth century conflicts between whites and Indians further east.

Illinois above the Illinois River, part of Wisconsin, and part of Missouri. Saukenuk, their principal town, was at the fork of the Mississippi and Rock rivers and was surrounded by fields of corn, beans, squash, and pumpkins. These fields were planted in the spring, tended during the summer, and harvested in the fall; and during that time the Indians lived in their town houses. But after harvest time they left their towns and went to the hunting grounds, returning the next spring to plant their fields again.

Before the Revolutionary War, the Sauk-Fox had little contact with "Americans." They traded with Frenchmen who came down the Mississippi, and with the Spanish who controlled the lands west of the Mississippi from their headquarters at St. Louis. But after the Revolutionary War the westward thrust that followed the Indian defeat at Fallen Timbers and the Treaty of Greenville was felt as far as the Mississippi. And when the 1803 Louisiana Purchase substituted United States for Spanish possession of the Mississippi's west flanks, it became certain that the "American" tide would find the Sauk-Fox Nation a rock in its path. The conflict began nearly at once.

In 1804 US soldiers took over St. Louis from the Spanish in the month of March. In June of that year the US Secretary of War wrote to William Harrison of the Indiana Territory authorizing him to negotiate with the Sauk-Fox in order to "procure from the Sacs, such cessions on both sides of the Illinois, as may entitle them to an annual compensation of five or six hundred dollars."

In the mind of a William Henry Harrison there was no end to how much land such a sum could be expected to purchase from Indians. Taking advantage of an incident in which three white men were reported killed by a Sauk party, Harrison went to St. Louis and called the Sauk-Fox chiefs to council. He said nothing about wanting to buy land, but he did order the chiefs to bring "the murderers" along with them. The Indians sent a deputation of chiefs to St. Louis with one of the accused men, giving them instructions to make payment—in the Indian fashion—to the aggrieved to remove the offense between them. Seizing on that, Harrison said the payment would have to be in land. He also followed his usual tactic for Indian dealings by lavishing whiskey on the chiefs; when they left St. Louis, they had signed a treaty ceding all Sauk-Fox lands to the US. Harrison agreed to ask for a presidential pardon for the surrendered Indian (though it appeared that he had killed in self-defense). But while still imprisoned, the warrior had his head blown off by a charge of buckshot from a guard's shotgun.

Such were the beginnings of relations between the US and the Sauk-Fox. The Indians, of course, denied that they had agreed to the terms written in the treaty—for which they were paid $2234.50 This was the sum Harrison had "advanced" for their "entertainment," and it was he who received the money from the government. The Indians were made to give up the money for their lands to pay for the whiskey that had been pressed on them to get them to sell their land. Perhaps that seemed a bit much even for Harrison, for he further promised that they would receive an additional annuity of $1000—to be paid in trade goods.

For a few more years, however, the "Americans" were not strong enough in the area to force the Sauk-Fox off their land. They were content to keep up what harassment they were strong enough for and to save the treaty for a better day. Then came the War of 1812. Black Fox led his warriors off to fight with Tecumtha, weakening the home strength of the Sauk-Fox, who were caught between the British and the US forces. Influenced by elderly civil chiefs who feared the power of the white man, many of the Sauk-Fox wanted peace and neutrality and were susceptible to the arguments of "American" agents who wanted them to move west of the Mississippi where the US Army could protect them.

After Tecumtha's defeat Black Hawk returned to find his nation divided and the "pro-British" band that still lived in Sauk-Fox territory greatly diminished. And here there was a further division, for this band's fears of a US attack had caused them to elect an unknown upstart—not even a full warrior when Black Hawk left—

as war chief. This man, named Keokuk, soon became the darling of the US agents, who discovered that he liked presents—and liked them even better when the "Americans" gave him preference over the other Sauk-Fox chiefs. During the last years of the War of 1812 when Black Hawk tried to carry on the war along the Mississippi, Keokuk shifted his allegiance to the "Americans" and increased his arguments that the Sauk-Fox should do what the white man wanted.

In the document that follows Black Hawk takes up the narrative in 1816, following the St. Louis council held with the "Americans" in the wake of the peace treaty between England and the US. From that time on the white men increased pressure on the Sauk-Fox to abandon their lands in conformity to the fraudulent Treaty of 1804. The effects of Keokuk's sell-out are apparent in the document, as is the determination to resist that was held by Black Hawk and his followers—a determination that ended in the Black Hawk War: the last stand in the Northwest.

THE DOCUMENT:

From the autobiography of Black Hawk, Life of Ma-ka-tai-me-she-kia-kiak or Black Hawk, Dictated by Himself. Boston, 1834

The great chief at St. Louis having sent word for us to go down and confirm the treaty of peace, we did not hesitate, but started immediately, that we might smoke the *peace-pipe* with him. On our arrival, we met the great chiefs in council. They explained to us the words of our Great Father at Washington, accusing us of heinous crimes and divers misdemeanors, particularly in not coming down when first invited. We knew very well that *our Great Father had deceived us,* and thereby *forced* us to join the British, and could not believe that he had put this speech into the mouths of these chiefs to deliver to us. I was not a civil chief, and consequently made no reply: but our chiefs told the commissioners that "what they had said was a *lie!*—that our Great Father had sent no such speech, he knowing the situation in which we had been placed had been *caused by him!*" The white chiefs appeared very angry at this reply, and said they "would break off the treaty with us, and *go to war,* as they would not be insulted."

Our chiefs had no intention of insulting them, and told them so—"that they merely wished to explain to them that *they had told a lie,* without making them angry; in the same manner that the whites do, when they do not believe what is told them!" The council then proceeded, and the pipe of peace was smoked.

Here, for the first time, I touched the goose quill to the treaty—not knowing, however, that, by that act, I consented to give away my village. Had that been explained to me, I should have opposed it, and never would have signed their treaty, as my recent conduct will clearly prove.

What do we know of the manner of the laws and customs of the white people? They might buy our bodies for dissection, and we would touch the goose quill to confirm it, without knowing what we are doing. This was the case with myself and people in touching the goose quill the first time.

We can only judge of what is proper and right by our standard of right and wrong, which differs widely from the whites, if I have been correctly informed. The whites *may do bad* all their lives, and then, if they are *sorry for it* when about to die, *all is well!* But with us it is different: we must continue throughout our lives to do what we conceive to be good. If we have corn and meat, and know of a family that have none, we divide with them. If we have more blankets than sufficient, and others have not enough, we must give to them that want. But I will presently explain our customs and the manner we live.

We were friendly treated by the white chiefs, and started back to our village on Rock river. Here we found that troops had arrived to build a fort at Rock Island. This, in our opinion, was a contradiction to what we had done—"to prepare for war in time of peace." We did not, however, object to their building the fort on the island, but we were very sorry, as this was the best island on the Mississippi, and had long been the resort of our young people during the summer. It was our garden (like the white people have near to their big villages) which supplied us with strawberries, blackberries, gooseberries, plums, apples, and nuts of different kinds; and its waters supplied us with fine fish, being situated in the rapids of the river. In my early life, I spent many happy days on this island. A good spirit had care of it, who lived in a cave in the rocks immediately under the place where the fort now stands, and has often been seen by our people. He was white, with large wings like a *swan's,* but ten times larger. We were particular not to make much noise in that part of the island which he inhabited, for fear of disturbing him. But the noise of the fort has since driven him away, and no doubt a *bad spirit* has taken his place!

Our village was situated on the north side of Rock river, at the foot of its rapids, and on the point of land between Rock river and the Mississippi. In its front, a prairie extended to the bank of the Mississippi; and in our rear, a continued bluff, gently ascending from the prairie. On the side of this bluff we had our cornfields, extending about two miles up, running parallel with the Mississippi; where we joined those of the Foxes, whose village was on the bank of the Mississippi, opposite the lower end of Rock island, and three miles distant from ours. We had about eight hundred acres in cultivation, including what we had on the islands of Rock river. The land around our village, uncultivated, was covered with blue-grass, which made excellent pasture for our horses. Several fine springs broke out of the bluff, near by, from which we were supplied with good water. The rapids of Rock river furnished us with an abundance of excellent fish, and the land, being good, never failed to produce good crops of corn, beans, pumpkins, and squashes. We always had plenty—our children never cried with hunger, nor our people were never in want. Here our village had stood for more than a hundred years, during all which time we were the undisputed possessors of the valley of the Mississippi, from the

Ouisconsin to the Portage des Sioux, near the mouth of the Missouri, being about seven hundred miles in length.

At this time we had very little intercourse with the whites, except our traders. Our village was healthy, and there was no place in the country possessing such advantages, nor no hunting grounds better than those we had in possession. If another prophet had come to our village in those days, and told us what has since taken place, none of our people would have believed him! What! to be driven from our village and hunting grounds, and not even permitted to visit the graves of our forefathers, our relations and friends? ...

The whites were now selling the country fast. I was out one day hunting in a bottom, and met three white men. They accused me of killing their hogs; I denied it; but they would not listen to me. One of them took my gun out of my hand and fired it off—then took out the flint, gave back my gun, and commenced beating me with sticks, and ordered me off. I was so much bruised that I could not sleep for several nights.

Some time after this occurrence, one of my camp cut a bee-tree, and carried the honey to his lodge. A party of white men soon followed, and told him that the bee-tree was theirs, and that he had no right to cut it. He pointed to the honey, and told them to take it; they were not satisfied with this, but took all the packs of skins that he had collected during the winter, to pay his trader and clothe his family with in the spring, and carried them off!

How could we like such people, who treated us so unjustly? We determined to break up our camp, for fear that they would do worse—and when we joined our people in the spring, a great many of them complained of similar treatment.

This summer our agent came to live at Rock Island. He treated us well, and gave us good advice. I visited him and the trader very often during the summer, and, for the first time, heard talk of our having to leave my village. The trader explained to me the terms of the treaty that had Illinois side of the Mississippi, and advised us to select a been made, and said we would be obliged to leave the good place for our village, and remove to it in the spring. He pointed out the difficulties we would have to encounter, if we remained at our village on Rock river. He had great influence with the principal Fox chief, [his adopted brother] and persuaded him to leave his village, and go to the west side of the Mississippi river, and build another—which he did the spring following.

Nothing was now talked of but leaving our village. Ke-o-kuck had been persuaded to consent to go; and was using all his influence, backed by the war chief at fort Armstrong, and our agent and trader at Rock Island, to induce others to go with him. He sent the crier through the village to inform our people that it was the wish of our Great Father that we should remove to the west side of the Mississippi—and recommended the Ioway river as a good place for the new village—and wished his party to make such arrangements, before they started out on their winter's hunt, as to preclude the necessity of their returning to the village in the spring.

The party opposed to removing, called upon me for my opinion. I gave it freely—and after questioning Quàsh-quà-me about the sale of the lands, he assured me that he "never had consented to the sale of our village." I now promised this party to be their leader, and raised the standard of opposition to Ke-o-kuck, with a full determination not to leave my village. I had an interview with Ke-o-kuck, to see if this difficulty could not be settled with our Great Father—and told him to propose to give other land, (any that our Great Father might choose, even our *lead mines*,) to be peaceably permitted to keep the small point of land on which our village and fields were situate. I was of opinion that the white people had plenty of land, and would never take our village from us. Ke-o-kuck promised to make an exchange if possible; and applied to our agent, and the great chief at St. Louis, (who has charge of all the agents,) for permission to go to Washington to see our Great Father for that purpose. This satisfied us for some time. We started to our hunting grounds, in good hopes that something would be done for us. During the winter, I received information that three families of whites had arrived at our village and destroyed some of our lodges, and were making fences and dividing our corn-fields for their own use—*and were quarrelling among themselves about their lines, in the division!* I immediately started for Rock river, a distance of ten days' travel, and on my arrival, found the report to be true. I went to my lodge, and saw a family occupying it. I wished to talk with them, but they could not understand me. I then went to Rock Island, and (the agent being absent,) told the interpreter what I wanted to say to those people, viz: "Not to settle on our lands—nor trouble our lodges or fences— that there was plenty of land in the country for them to settle upon—and they must leave our village, as we were coming back to it in the spring." The interpreter wrote me a paper, and I went back to the village, and showed it to the intruders, but could not understand their reply. I expected, however, that they would remove, as I requested them. I returned to Rock Island, passed the night there, and had a long conversation with the trader. He again advised me to give up, and make my village with Ke-o-kuck, on the Ioway river. I told him that I would not. The next morning I crossed the Mississippi, on very bad ice— but the Great Spirit made it strong, that I might pass over safe. I travelled three days farther to see the Winnebago sub-agent, and converse with him on the subject of our difficulties. He gave me no better news than the trader had done. I started then, by way of Rock river, to see the prophet, believing that he was a man of great knowledge. When we met, I explained to him every thing as it was. He at once agreed that I was right, and advised me never to give up our village, for the whites to plough up the bones of our people. He said, that if we remained at our village, the whites would not trouble us—and advised me to get Ke-o-kuck, and the party that had consented to go with him to the Ioway in the spring, to return, and remain at our village.

I returned to my hunting ground, after an absence of one moon, and related what I had done. In a short time we came up to our village, and found that the whites had not left it—but that others had come, and that the greater

part of our corn-fields had been enclosed. When we landed, the whites appeared displeased because we had come
back. We repaired the lodges that had been left standing,
and built others. Ke-o-kuck came to the village; but his
object was to persuade others to follow him to the Ioway.
He had accomplished nothing towards making arrangements for us to remain, or to exchange other lands for our
village. There was no more friendship existing between us.
I looked upon him as a coward, and no brave, to abandon
his village to be occupied by strangers. What *right* had
these people to our village, and our fields, which the Great
Spirit had given us to live upon?

My reason teaches me that *land cannot be sold*. The
Great Spirit gave it to his children to live upon, and
cultivate, as far as is necessary for their subsistence; and
so long as they occupy and cultivate it, they have the right
to the soil—but if they voluntarily leave it, then any other
people have a right to settle upon it. Nothing can be sold,
but such things as can be carried away.

In consequence of the improvements of the intruders on
our fields, we found considerable difficulty to get ground
to plant a little corn. Some of the whites permitted us to
plant small patches in the fields they had fenced, keeping
all the best ground for themselves. Our women had great
difficulty in climbing their fences, (being unaccustomed to
the kind,) and were ill-treated if they left a rail down.

One of my old friends thought he was safe. His corn-
field was on a small island of Rock river. He planted his
corn; it came up well—but the white man saw it!—he
wanted the island, and took his team over, ploughed up
the corn, and re-planted it for himself! The old man shed
tears; not for himself, but the distress his family would be
in if they raised no corn.

The white people brought whisky into our village, made
our people drunk, and cheated them out of their horses,
guns, and traps! This fraudulent system was carried to
such an extent that I apprehended serious difficulties
might take place, unless a stop was put to it. Consequently, I visited all the whites and begged them not to sell
whisky to my people. One of them continued the practice

openly. I took a party of my young men, went to his house, and took out his barrel and broke in the head and turned out the whisky. I did this for fear some of the whites might be killed by my people when drunk.

Our people were treated badly by the whites on many occasions. At one time, a white man beat one of our women cruelly, for pulling a few suckers of corn out of his field, to suck, when hungry! At another time, one of our young men was beat with clubs by two white men for opening a fence which crossed our road, to take his horse through. His shoulder blade was broken, and his body badly bruised, from which he soon after *died!*

Bad, and cruel, as our people were treated by the whites, not one of them was hurt or molested by any of my band. I hope this will prove that we are a peaceable people—having permitted ten men to take possession of our corn-fields; prevent us from planting corn; burn and destroy our lodges; ill-treat our women; and *beat to death* our men, without offering resistance to their barbarous cruelties. This is a lesson worthy for the white man to learn: to use forbearance when injured.

We acquainted our agent daily with our situation, and through him, the great chief at St. Louis—and hoped that something would be done for us. The whites were *complaining* at the same time that *we* were *intruding* upon *their rights!* THEY made themselves out the *injured* party, and *we* the *intruders!* and called loudly to the great war chief to protect *their* property!

How smooth must be the language of the whites, when they can make right look like wrong, and wrong like right.

During this summer, I happened at Rock Island, when a great chief arrived, (whom I had known as the great chief of Illinois, [governor Cole,] in company with another chief, who, I have been told, is a great writer, [judge Jas. Hall.] I called upon them and begged to explain to them the grievances under which me and my people were laboring, hoping that they could do something for us. The great chief, however, did not seem disposed to counsel with me. He said he was no longer the great chief of Illinois—that his children had selected another father in his stead, and that he now only ranked as they did. I was surprised at this talk, as I had always heard that he was a good, brave, and great chief. But the white people never appear to be satisfied. When they get a good father, they hold councils, (at the suggestion of some bad, ambitious man, who wants the place himself,) and conclude, among themselves, that this man, or some other equally ambitious, would make a better father than they have, and nine times out of ten they don't get as good a one again.

I insisted on explaining to these two chiefs the true situation of my people. They gave their assent: I rose and made a speech, in which I explained to them the treaty made by Quásh-quá-me, and three of our braves, according to the manner the trader and others had explained it to me. I then told them that Quásh-quá-me and his party *denied* positively, having ever sold my village; and that, as I had never known them to *lie,* I was determined to keep it in possession.

I told them that the white people had already entered our village, *burnt our lodges, destroyed our fences, ploughed up our corn, and beat our people:* that they had brought *whisky* into our country, *made our people drunk,* and taken from them their *horses, guns,* and *traps;* and that I had borne all this injury, without suffering any of my braves to raise a hand against the whites.

My object in holding this council, was to get the opinion of these two chiefs, as to the best course for me to pursue. I had appealed in vain, time after time, to our agent, who regularly represented our situation to the great chief at St. Louis, whose duty it was to call upon our Great Father to have justice done to us; but instead of this, we are told *that the white people want our country, and we must leave it to them!*

I did not think it possible that our Great Father wished us to leave our village, where we had lived so long, and where the bones of so many of our people had been laid. The great chief said that, as he was no longer a chief, he could do nothing for us; and felt sorry that it was not in his power to aid us—nor did he know how to advise us. Neither of them could do any thing for us; but both evidently appeared very sorry. It would give me great pleasure, at all times, to take these two chiefs by the hand.

That fall I paid a visit to the agent, before we started to our hunting grounds, to hear if he had any good news for me. He had news! He said that the land on which our village stood was now ordered to be sold to individuals; and that, when sold, *our right* to remain, by treaty, would be at an end, and that if we returned next spring, we would be *forced* to remove!

We learned during the winter, that *part* of the lands where our village stood had been sold to individuals, and that the *trader* at Rock Island had bought the greater part that had been sold. The reason was now plain to me, why *he* urged us to remove. His object, we thought, was to get our lands. We held several councils that winter to determine what we should do, and resolved, in one of them, to return to our village in the spring, as usual; and concluded, that if we were removed by force, that the *trader,* agent, and others, must be the cause; and that, if found guilty of having us driven from our village, they should be *killed!* The trader stood foremost on this list. He had purchased the land on which my lodge stood, and that of our *grave yard* also! Ne-a-pope promised to kill him, the agent, interpreter, the great chief at St. Louis, the war chief at fort Armstrong, Rock Island, and Ke-o-kuck— these being the principal persons to blame for endeavoring to remove us.

Our women received bad accounts from the women that had been raising corn at the new village—the difficulty of breaking the new prairie with hoes—and the small quantity of corn raised. We were nearly in the same situation in regard to the latter, it being the first time I ever knew our people to be in want of provision.

I prevailed upon some of Ke-o-kuck's band to return this spring to the Rock river village. Ke-o-kuck would not return with us. I hoped that we would get permission to go to Washington to settle our affairs with our Great Father. I visited the agent at Rock Island. He was displeased because we had returned to our village, and told me that we *must* remove to the west of the Mississippi. I told him plainly that we *would not!* I visited the interpreter at his house, who advised me to do as the agent had directed me. I then went to see the trader, and upbraided him for buying our lands. He said that if he had not purchased them, some person else would, and that if our Great Father would make an exchange with us, he would willingly give up the land he had purchased to the government. This I thought was fair, and began to think that he had not acted as badly as I had suspected: We again repaired our lodges, and built others, as most of our village had been burnt and destroyed. Our women selected small patches to plant corn, (where the whites had not taken them within their fences,) and worked hard to raise something for our children to subsist upon.

I was told that, according to the treaty, we had no *right* to remain upon the lands *sold,* and that the government would *force* us to leave them. There was but a small portion, however, that *had been sold;* the balance remaining in the hands of the government, we claimed the right (if we had no other) to "live and hunt upon, as long as it remained the property of the government," by a stipulation in the same treaty that required us to evacuate it *after* it had been sold. This was the land that we wished to inhabit, and thought we had the best right to occupy.

I heard that there was a great chief on the Wabash, and sent a party to get his advice. They informed him that we had not sold our village. He assured them, then, that if we had not sold the land on which our village stood, our Great Father would not take it from us.

I started early to Malden to see the chief of my British Father, and told him my story. He gave the same reply that the chief on the Wabash had given; and in justice to him, I must say, that he never gave me any bad advice: but advised me to apply to our American Father, who, he said, would do us justice. I next called on the great chief at Detroit, and made the same statement to him that I had to the chief of our British Father. He gave the same reply. He said, if we had not sold our lands, and would remain peaceably on them, that we would not be disturbed. This assured me that I was right, and determined me to hold out, as I had promised my people.

I returned from Malden late in the fall. My people were gone to their hunting ground, whither I followed. Here I learned that they had been badly treated all summer by the whites; and that a treaty had been held at Prairie du Chien. Ke-o-kuck and some of our people attended it, and found out that our Great Father had exchanged a small strip of the land that was ceded by Quásh-quá-me and his party, with the Pottowatomies, for a portion of their land, near Chicago; and that the object of this treaty was to get it back again; and that the United States had agreed to give them *sixteen thousand dollars a year, forever,* for this small strip of land—it being less than the twentieth part of that taken from our nation, for *one thousand dollars a year!* This bears evidence of something I cannot explain. This land, they say, belonged to the United States. What reason, then, could have induced them to exchange it with the Pottowatomies, if it was so valuable? Why not keep it? Or, if they found that they had made a bad bargain with the Pottowatomies, why not take back their land at a fair proportion of what they gave our nation for it? If this small portion of the land that they took from us for *one thousand dollars* a year, be worth *sixteen thousand dollars a year forever,* to the Pottowatomies, then the whole tract of country taken from us ought to be worth, to our nation, *twenty times* as much as this small fraction.

Here I was again puzzled to find out how the white people reasoned; and began to doubt whether they had any standard of right and wrong!

Communication was kept up between myself and the Prophet. Runners were sent to the Arkansas, Red river and Texas—not on the subject of our lands, but a secret mission, which I am not, at present, permitted to explain.

It was related to me, that the chiefs and headmen of the Foxes had been invited to Prairie du Chien, to hold a council to settle the differences existing between them and the Sioux. That the chiefs and headmen, amounting to *nine,* started for the place designated, taking with them one woman—and were met by the Menomonees and

Sioux, near the Ouisconsin, and all *killed,* except one man. Having understood that the whole matter was published shortly after it occurred, and is known to the white people, I will say no more about it.

I would here remark, that our pastimes and sports had been laid aside for the last two years. We were a divided people, forming two parties. Ke-o-kuck being at the head of one, willing to barter our rights merely for the good opinion of the whites; and cowardly enough to desert our village to them. I was at the head of the other party, and was determined to hold on to my village, although I had been *ordered* to leave it. But, I considered, as myself and band had no agency in selling our country—and that as provision had been made in the treaty, for us all to remain on it as long as it belonged to the United States, that we could not be *forced* away. I refused, therefore, to quit my village. It was here, that I was born—and here lie the bones of many friends and relations. For this spot I felt a sacred reverence, and never could consent to leave it without being forced therefrom.

When I called to mind the scenes of my youth, and those of later days—and reflected that the theatre on which these were acted, had been so long the home of my fathers, who now slept on the hills around it, I could not bring my mind to consent to leave this country to the whites, for any earthly consideration.

The winter passed off in gloom. We made a bad hunt, for want of the guns, traps, &c. that the whites had taken from our people for whisky! The prospect before us was a bad one. I fasted, and called upon the Great Spirit to direct my steps to the right path. I was in great sorrow—because all the whites with whom I was acquainted, and had been on terms of friendship, advised me so contrary to my wishes, that I began to doubt whether I had a *friend* among them.

Ke-o-kuck, who has a smooth tongue, and is a great speaker, was busy in persuading my band that I was wrong—and thereby making many of them dissatisfied with me. I had one consolation—for all the women were on my side, on account of their corn-fields.

On my arrival again at my village, with my band increased, I found it worse than before. I visited Rock Island. The agent again ordered me to quit my village. He said, that if we did not, troops would be sent to drive us off. He reasoned with me, and told me, it would be better for us to be with the rest of our people, so that we might avoid difficulty, and live in peace. The *interpreter* joined him, and gave me so many good reasons, that I almost wished I had not undertaken the difficult task that I had pledged myself to my brave band to perform. In this mood, I called upon the *trader,* who is fond of talking, and had long been my friend, but now amongst those advising me to give up my village. He received me very friendly, and went on to defend Ke-o-kuck in what he had done, and endeavored to show me that I was bringing distress on our women and children. He inquired, if some terms could not be made, that would be honorable to me, and satisfactory to my braves, for us to remove to the west side of the Mississippi? I replied, that if our Great Father would do us justice, and would make the proposition, I could then give up honorably. He asked me, "if the great chief at St. Louis would give us six thousand dollars to purchase provisions and other articles, if I would give up peaceably, and remove to the west side of the Mississippi?" After thinking some time, I agreed, that I could honorably give up, by being paid for it, according to our customs; but told him, that I could not make the proposal myself, even if I wished, because it would be dishonorable in me to do so. He said he would do it, by sending word to the great chief at St. Louis, that he could remove us peaceably, for the amount stated, to the west side of the Mississippi. A steam-boat arrived at the island during my stay. After its departure, the *trader* told me that he had "requested a war chief, who is stationed at Galena, and was on board of the steam-boat, to make the offer to the great chief at St. Louis, and that he could soon be back, and bring his answer." I did not let my people know what had taken place, for fear they would be displeased. I did not much like what had been done myself, and tried to banish it from my mind.

After a few days had passed, the war chief returned, and brought for answer, that "the great chief at St. Louis would give us *nothing!*—and said if we did not remove immediately, we should be *drove off!*"

I was not much displeased with the answer brought by the war chief, because I would rather have laid my bones with my forefathers, than remove for any consideration. Yet if a friendly offer had been made, as I expected, I would, for the sake of my women and children, have removed peaceably.

I now resolved to remain in my village, and make no resistance, if the military came, but submit to my fate! I impressed the importance of this course on all my band, and directed them, in case the military came, not to raise an arm against them.

About this time, our agent was put out of office—for what reason, I never could ascertain. I then thought, if it was for wanting to make us leave our village, it was right—because I was tired of hearing him talk about it. The interpreter, who had been equally as bad in trying to persuade us to leave our village, was retained in office—and the young man who took the place of our agent, told the same old story over about removing us. I was then satisfied, that this could not have been the cause.

Our women had planted a few patches of corn, which was growing finely, and promised a subsistence for our children—but the *white people again commenced ploughing it up!* I now determined to put a stop to it, by clearing our country of the *intruders.* I went to the principal men and told them, that they must and should leave our country—and gave them until the middle of the next day, to remove in. The worst left within the time appointed—but the one who remained, represented, that his family, (which was large,) would be in a starving condition, if he went and left his crop—and promised to behave well, if I would consent to let him remain until fall, in order to secure his crop. He spoke reasonably, and I consented.

We now resumed some of our games and pastimes—having been assured by the prophet that we would not be removed. But in a little while it was ascertained, that a great war chief, [Gen. Gaines,] with a large number of soldiers, was on his way to Rock river. I again called upon the prophet, who requested a little time to see into the matter. Early next morning he came to me, and said he had been *dreaming!* "That he saw nothing bad in this great war chief, [Gen. Gaines,] who was now near Rock river. That the *object* of his mission was to *frighten* us from our village, that the white people might get our land for *nothing!*" He assured us that this "great war chief dare not, and would not, hurt any of us. That the Americans were at peace with the British, and when they made peace, the British required, (which the Americans agreed to,) that they should never interrupt any nation of Indians that was at peace—and that all we had to do to retain our village, was to *refuse* any, and every offer that might be made by this war chief."

The war chief arrived, and convened a council at the agency. Ke-o-kuck and Wà-pel-lo were sent for, and came with a number of their band. The council house was opened, and they were all admitted. Myself and band were then sent for to attend the council. When we arrived at the door, singing a *war song,* and armed with lances, spears, war clubs and bows and arrows, as if going to battle, I halted, and refused to enter—as I could see no necessity or propriety in having the room crowded with those who were already there. If the council was convened for us, why have others there in our room? The war chief having sent all out, except Ke-o-kuck, Wà-pel-lo, and a few of their chiefs and braves, we entered the council house, in this war-like appearance, being desirous to show the war chief that we were *not afraid!* He then rose and made a speech.

He said:

"The president is very sorry to be put to the trouble and expense of sending a large body of soldiers here, to remove you from the lands you have long since ceded to the United States. Your Great Father has already warned you repeatedly, through your agent, to leave the country; and he is very sorry to find that you have disobeyed his orders. Your Great Father wishes you well: and asks nothing from you but what is reasonable and right. I hope you will consult your own interest, and leave the country you are occupying, and go to the other side of the Mississippi."

I replied: "That *we* had never sold our country. *We* never received any annuities from our American father! And *we* are determined to hold on to our village!"

The war chief, apparently angry, rose and said:—"Who is *Black Hawk?* Who is *Black Hawk?*"

I responded:

"I am a *Sac!* my forefather was a SAC! and all the nations call me a SAC!!"

The war chief said:

"I came here, neither to *beg* nor *hire* you to leave your village. My business is to remove you, peaceably if I can, but *forcibly* if I must! I will now give you two days to remove in—and if you do not cross the Mississippi within that time, I will adopt measures to *force* you away!"

I told him that I never could consent to leave my village, and was determined not to leave it!

BLACK HAWK'S FAREWELL

1832

Black Hawk's Surrender

ABOUT THE DOCUMENTS:

Black Hawk and his band were driven from Saukenuk by a force of federal troops reinforced by 1500 militiamen recruited among the "American" residents. Their job was made easier by Keokuk who incessantly urged Black Hawk's followers to desert their chief; this had enough effect to weaken his forces. Then, in order to win Black

Hawk's acceptance of defeat and thereby keep to the west bank of the Mississippi, the "American" agent promised him corn for the winter equal to what he and his followers would have harvested from the fields they had already planted. When that promise was reneged upon, Black Hawk—believing he could arouse support from surrounding nations for a renewed attack on the white man—took once more to war. At this time he was about sixty-five years old.

The war was short lived. He was not able to gain the active support he needed, and though he won several minor skirmishes with white soldiers, Black Hawk's War was more of a rebellious flight during which his Sauk-Fox (accompanied by wives and children) were pursued by several armies. These were both federal and militia troops; among the latter was a company of Illinois volunteers led by Capt. Abraham Lincoln.

The principal "battle" of the Black Hawk War took place between Gen. Henry Atkinson's troops and several hundred worn-out Sauk-Foxes whom he found trying to cross over the Mississippi and escape the war. In the "battle" that took place almost all of the Indians were killed—a large number were women and children.

Black Hawk continued his resistance a while longer but was finally persuaded by a group of Winnebago that he should surrender.

The moving speech he made at the time of his surrender is recorded in the document that follows; it should be noted that this defiant speech was addressed directly to the white soldiers in whose power he found himself.

Black Hawk went to prison, then was freed by the President of the United States, and ordered on a tour of United States cities in the hope that he would be overawed by "American" strength. When he was returned to his people, the "American" officials told him that from that time on they would not recognize him as a chief among the Sauk-Fox but instead would recognize only Keokuk. And with Keokuk they signed a new treaty that cost the Sauk six million acres on the west side of the Mississippi.

Black Hawk died in 1838, poor and without position,

but believing he would be buried on Sauk-Fox land. His grave was robbed, and his skeleton was displayed as an object for white curiosity in an Iowa museum.

Keokuk died in 1848, rich and important. He died in Kansas, where he had gone after selling the last Sauk-Fox lands in Iowa. "Americans"—proving they know how to be grateful after all—had a bronze bust made of Keokuk and placed it in the Capitol in Washington.

THE DOCUMENT:

From Samuel G. Drake, *Biography and History of the Indians of North America*, Book V, 1834

You have taken me prisoner with all my warriors. I am much grieved, for I expected, if I did not defeat you, to hold out much longer, and give you more trouble before I surrendered. I tried hard to bring you into ambush, but your last general understands Indian fighting. The first one was not so wise. When I saw that I could not beat you by Indian fighting, I determined to rush on you, and fight you face to face. I fought hard. But your guns were well aimed. The bullets flew like birds in the air, and whizzed by our ears like the wind through the trees in winter. My warriors fell around me; it began to look dismal. I saw my evil day at hand. The sun rose dim on us in the morning, and at night it sank in a dark cloud, and looked like a ball of fire. That was the last sun that shone on Black Hawk. His heart is dead, and no longer beats quick in his bosom. He is now a prisoner to the white men; they will do with him as they wish. But he can stand torture, and is not afraid of death. He is no coward. Black Hawk is an Indian.

He has done nothing for which an Indian ought to be ashamed. He has fought for his countrymen, the squaws and papooses, against white men, who came, year after year, to cheat them and take away their lands. You know the cause of our making war. It is known to all white men. They ought to be ashamed of it. The white men despise the Indians, and drive them from their homes. But the Indians are not deceitful. The white men speak bad of the Indian, and look at him spitefully. But the Indian does not tell lies; Indians do not steal.

An Indian who is as bad as the white men, could not live in our nation; he would be put to death, and eaten up by the wolves. The white men are bad schoolmasters; they carry false looks and deal in false actions; they smile in the face of the poor Indian to cheat him; they shake them by the hand to gain their confidence, to make them drunk, to deceive them, and ruin our wives. We told them to let us alone, and keep away from us; but they followed on and beset our paths, and they coiled themselves among us like the snake. They poisoned us by their touch. We were not safe. We lived in danger. We were becoming like them, hypocrites and liars, adulterers, lazy drones, all talkers, and no workers.

We looked up to the Great Spirit. We went to our great father. We were encouraged. His great council gave us fair words and big promises; but we got no satisfaction. Things were growing worse. There were no deer in the forest. The opossum and beaver were fled; the springs were drying up, and our squaws and papooses without victuals to keep them from starving; we called a great council and built a large fire. The spirit of our fathers arose and spoke to us to avenge our wrongs or die. We all spoke before the council fire. It was warm and pleasant. We set up the war-whoop, and dug up the tomahawk; our knives were ready, and the heart of Black Hawk swelled high in his bosom when he led his warriors to battle. He is satisfied. He will go to the world of spirits contented. He has done his duty. His father will meet him there, and commend him.

Black Hawk is a true Indian, and disdains to cry like a woman. He feels for his wife, his children and friends. But he does not care for himself. He cares for his nation and the Indians. They will suffer. He laments their fate. The white men do scalp the head; but they do worse—they poison the heart; it is not pure with them. His countrymen will not be scalped, but they will, in a few years, become like white men, so that you can't trust them, and there must be, as in the white settlements, nearly as many officers as men, to take care of them and keep them in order.

Farewell, my nation! Black Hawk tried to save you, and avenge your wrongs. He drank the blood of some of the whites. He has been taken prisoner, and his plans are stopped. He can do no more. He is near his end. His sun is setting, and he will rise no more. Farewell to Black Hawk.

"THE BLESSINGS OF LIBERTY"

1823–1838

Cherokee Council Addresses the United States Commissioners

Memorial and Protest of the Cherokee Nation

Letter to a Gentleman

ABOUT THE DOCUMENTS:

On July 4, 1827, a convention of duly elected delegates met at their nation's capitol; three weeks later they adopted a document and declared its purpose in a preamble that stated:

We, the Representatives of the people, of the Cherokee Nation, in Convention assembled, in order to establish justice, ensure tranquility, promote our common welfare, and secure to ourselves and our posterity the blessings of liberty; acknowledge with humility and gratitude the goodness of the sovereign Ruler of the Universe, in offering us an opportunity so favorable to the design, and imploring His aid and direction in its accomplishment, do ordain and establish this Constitution for the Government of the Cherokee Nation.

In Article I, Section 1, the Cherokee Constitution defined itself as the supreme law of the land "solemnly guaranteed and reserved forever to the Cherokee Nation by the Treaties concluded with the United States."

The Cherokee, along with the Choctaw, Creek, Chickasaw, and Seminole, were one of what "Americans" called the Five Civilized Tribes originally occupying most of the southeastern part of the United States. To the "Americans" "civilized," of course, meant that these nations saw benefit in learning the white man's technical skills. So, as the pressures and aggressions of the white population forced the Indian nations to live within continually shrinking boundaries increasingly manipulated by the white man's economic and political systems, the "civilized" Indians found themselves competing with the white man on his own terms. The Cherokee Constitution was not an instrument that *gave* the Cherokee Nation its existence; it was instrument that *defined* the Cherokee Nation in terms that the white man claimed to respect.

But if the Cherokee were willing to learn *from* the white man, they were not willing to learn to *be* white people— with a few personal exceptions. One clear proof of this is an 1820 Cherokee law that made it a crime punishable by death for a Cherokee to agree to a land sale or cession not authorized by his people. For in dealings with the Cherokee, as with other Indian nations, a favorite ploy of the white land thieves was to find an Indian who succumbed to greed, ambition, threat, or alcohol—or, probably more often, to his reliance on the honesty of a white man he believed a friend. These factors would lead him to sign a paper which would soon reappear in the hands of armed white men claiming they had bought—"in good faith"— another chunk of Indian land.

Further evidence of Cherokee determination to remain Cherokee can be seen in the monumental accomplishment of Sequoyah, one of their artists and warriors with a strong aversion toward white men and white ways. Sequoyah recognized the advantages the white people gained in reading and writing a language to communicate elaborately with each other and preserve complex bodies of knowledge in books. But he could not believe that the Cherokee needed to learn an alien language and risk the influence of alien ideas to enjoy the advantages of this tool. So Sequoyah invented an alphabet for the Cherokee language—a language so complex that the professional etymologists of New England and the Moravian missionary society had been completely baffled for years in their attempts to put it into written form. When Sequoya was finished in 1821, he had an alphabet of eighty-five characters so accurately expressing the roots of the Cherokee language that any Cherokee could learn to read and write in a few days. Within three years the rate of Cherokee literacy in their language was probably higher than the literacy rate among the white settlers busily encroaching on Cherokee land. And material evidence of the Cherokee decision to force the white man's respect in his own terms was revealed in an 1826 survey which showed that the Cherokee people (somewhat more than 13,000) owned 22,000 head of cattle, 7600 horses, 46,000 pigs, 726 looms, 2488 spinning wheels, 172 wagons, 2943 plows, 10 sawmills, 31 grain mills, 62 blacksmith shops, 8 cotton machines, 18 schools, and 18 ferries. The next year after the adoption of their Constitution, Cherokee publishers started a bilingual newspaper, the *Cherokee Phoenix,* with the support of the Cherokee Legislative Council.

A statement of editorial policy contained in the *Cherokee Phoenix'* first issue (February 21, 1828) gives insight into their success in winning the kind of respect that would force the US to be honorable in its dealings with the Cherokee: "We will invariably state the will of the majority of our people on the subject of the present controversy with Georgia, and the present removal policy of the United States Government."

The controversy with Georgia and the removal policy of the United States government were linked together. In 1828 they represented two facets of a history of "Ameri-

can" aggression which was on the brink of fulfilling itself
by the forcible expulsion of all Indian nations from their
lands east of the Mississippi River. This had been decided
on by the US government as the best solution to the
"Indian problem"—in spite of treaty after treaty in which
the United States pledged to guarantee forever the lands
of the Cherokee and, by similar treaties, the lands of the
Chocktaw, Chickasaw, Creek, and Seminole.

But in 1802 the US had entered into an agreement with
the state of Georgia, whose original charter boundaries
included large parts of the Creek and Cherokee nations.
Under the 1802 agreement the US was to encourage the
Indians to sell their lands to the federal government so
that it could make those lands available to Georgia.
The trouble was that the Indians did not want to sell. The
Cherokee law of 1820, already referred to and the first of
the documents that follows, makes very clear their determination "never again to cede *one foot* more of land."
This determination left the United States with a dilemma;
it would either have to force the Indians off their land or
send troops to protect the Cherokee from white Georgians
who cared little about treaties. Rather than earning white
respect by what the "Americans" called Cherokee "progress," the Cherokee were further stimulating white greed.
White settlers and land speculators were being driven almost crazy by the spectacle of Indians who could afford to
ride in carriages, build stone houses, and read and write in
two languages. As was the case with white men everywhere, the sight of a well-tended field or prosperous farm
in Indian hands was enough to literally drive Georgia
settlers to murder. Then, to top it all off, the Cherokee
discovered gold in their nation, and they actually had the
effrontery to expect to mine and keep it for *themselves!*
The state of Georgia got tired of waiting for the US to
move the Indians off their land. In 1829 the Georgia
legislature passed a law that:

1. Confiscated all Cherokee land to be distributed to
   white owners.

2. Abolished all authority of the Cherokee government and nullified all Cherokee laws.
3. Prohibited any gathering of Cherokee people, even for religious purposes.
4. Made it a crime, punishable by imprisonment, for any Cherokee to advise another not to emigrate.
5. Declared void any contract between Indians and whites unless witnessed by two white men.
6. Refused the right of any Cherokee to testify in court against any white man.
7. Specifically prohibited any Cherokee to dig gold in the Cherokee gold fields.

In 1830 the United States Congress passed and made into law the Removal Bill, which authorized Congress to negotiate a new treaty with the Indians to provide them with lands west of the Mississippi in exchange for their removal from their present and ancient lands. The western lands, of course, would be "guaranteed to them forever."

The documents which follow reveal another sordid page of "American" history as Georgia and the United States tried to force a removal treaty on the Cherokee Nation.

DOCUMENT A:

Statement of Cherokee Council to US Commissioners Duncan G. Campbell and James Meriwether from US Congress, American State Papers, *Class II, Indian Affairs, Vol. II, 1815-27*

In General Council   New Town, October 20, 1823
    ... Brothers: We have fully deliberated on your communication. The application which you have made, under the authority of your mission from the President of the United States, for the extinguishment of the Cherokee title to the *whole* or a *part* of the lands now occupied by them, and lying within the chartered limits of Georgia, either by exchange for lands west of the Mississippi river, or by

purchase, we have to state, that the unfortunate part of our nation who have emigrated to the west have suffered severely since their separation from this nation and settlement in their new country: Sickness, wars, and other fatalities have visited them and lessened their numbers; and many of them, no doubt, would willingly return to the land of their nativity, if it were practicable for them to do so, without undergoing various difficulties, which would be almost insurmountable in so fatiguing and so long a journey by men, women, and children, without friends and without money to perform it. When we call to recollection the period which separated our countrymen, acquaintances, friends, and relatives from us, and look to [the] circumstances and means which caused our separation, we are grieved; the tears flow in our eyes, and we weep. Had it been the desire of the remaining part of this nation to have left this country, they would have embraced the opportunity, and emigrated with their fellow-countrymen; but this was not their desire. They loved the so[il] which gave them birth, and they have continued thereon. The limits of this nation are small, and embrace mountains, hills, and poor lands, which can never be settled. The Cherokees once possessed an extensive country, and they have made cession after cession to our father the President, to gratify the wishes of our neighboring brethren, until our limits have become circumscribed; and it appears, from the eager desire of our brethren to obtain our lands, that it would be unreasonable for us to presume that a small cession at any time would ever satisfy them.

Brothers: The improving situation of this nation is visible, and has been acknowledged; and it would be reproachful and degrading to our character did we not look to its interest, prosperity, and future happiness. You give us one reason why a cession is urged: that is, "from the crowded settlements of the people of Georgia." We presume, if Georgia were in possession of the whole extent of her chartered limits, that it would not remedy the inconvenience complained of.

Brothers: From the comparative view which you have

taken of the population of Georgia and the Cherokee nation, you say "that the difference is too great ever to have been intended by the Great Father of the Universe, who must have given the earth equally as the inheritance of his white and red children." We do not know the intention of the Supreme Father in this particular, but it is evident that this principle has never been observed or respected by nations or by individuals. If your assertion be a correct idea of His intention, why do the laws of civilized and enlightened nations allow a man to monopolize more land than he can cultivate, to the exclusion of others?

Brothers: We cannot accede to your application for a cession. It is the fixed and unalterable determination of this nation never again to cede *one foot* more of land. We will make known to you, as coming from our father the President, that the boundary line from the Unicoy turnpike, on the Blue Ridge, and the source of the Chestatee, has not been run by the United States surveyor, agreeably to the stipulation or intention of the treaty of 1819; but it has been run so as to include a larger tract of land than was admitted by said treaty, to the great inconvenience and injury of this nation, particularly those of our citizens who have lived in that quarter, and have been compelled to *remove*. As this fact has been reported to the President, we trust that he has given you some instructions relative to the investigation of the subject.

With the brightness of the sun, we renew our assurances of respect and brotherly friendship.

> PATH KILLER, his *X* mark,
> *Principal Chief*
> MAJOR RIDGE, his *X* mark,
> *Speaker of Council*
> JOHN ROSS, *President of National Committee*

A. McCoy, *Clerk of National Committee*
Elijah Hicks, *Clerk of National Council*

DOCUMENT B:

MEMORIAL AND PROTEST OF THE CHEROKEE NATION.

June 22, 1836

Submitting the protest of the Cherokee nation against the ratification, execution, and enforcement of the treaty negotiated at New Echota, in December, 1835.

To the honorable Senate and House of Representatives of the United States of North America in Congress assembled:

The undersigned representatives of the Cherokee nation, east of the river Mississippi, impelled by duty, would respectfully submit, for the consideration of your honorable body, the following statement of facts: It will be seen, from the numerous subsisting treaties between the Cherokee nation and the United States, that from the earliest existence of this Government, the United States, in Congress assembled, received the Cherokees and their nation into favor and protection; and that the chiefs and warriors, for themselves and all parts of the Cherokee nation, acknowledged themselves and the said Cherokee nation to be under the protection of the United States of America, and of no other sovereign whatsoever: they also stipulated, that the said Cherokee nation will not hold any treaty with any foreign power, individual State, or with individuals of any State: that for, and in consideration of, valuable concessions made by the Cherokee nation, the United States solemnly guaranteed to said nation all their lands not ceded, and pledged the faith of the Government, that "all white people who have intruded, or may hereafter intrude, on the lands reserved for the Cherokees, shall be removed by the United States, and proceeded against, according to the provisions of the act, passed 30th March, 1802," entitled "An act to regulate trade and intercourse with the Indian tribes, and to preserve peace on the frontiers." It would be useless to recapitulate the numerous provisions for the security and protection of the rights of the Cherokees, to be found in the various treaties between their nation and the United States. The Cherokees were happy and prosperous under a scrupulous observance of treaty stipulations by the Government of the United States, and from the fostering hand extended over them, they made rapid advances in civilization, morals, and in the arts and sciences. Little did they anticipate, that when taught to think and feel as the American citizen, and to have with him a common interest, they were to be *despoiled by their guardian*, to become strangers and wanderers in the land of their fathers, forced to return to the savage life, and to seek a new home in the wilds of the far west, and that without their consent. An instrument purporting to be a treaty with the Cherokee people, has recently been made public by the President of the United States, that will have such an operation, if carried into effect. This instrument, the delegation aver before the civilized world, and in the presence of Almighty God, is fraudulent, false upon its face, made by unauthorized individuals, without the sanction, and against the wishes, of the great body of the Cherokee people. Upwards of fifteen thousand of these people have protested against it, solemnly declaring they will never acquiesce. The delegation would respectfully call the attention of your honorable body to their memorial and protest, with the accompanying documents, submitted to the Senate of the United States, on the subject of the alleged treaty, which are herewith transmitted. . . .

That the Cherokees are a distinct people, sovereign to some extent, have a separate political existence as a society, or body politic, and a capability of being contracted with in a national capacity, stands admitted by the uniform practice of the United States from 1785, down to the present day. With them have treaties been made through their chiefs, and distinguished representatives. That they have not the right to manage their own internal affairs, and to regulate, by treaty, their intercourse with other nations, is a doctrine of modern date. In 1793, Mr. Jefferson said, ". . . . That the Indians *have the full, undivided, and independent sovereignty as long as they choose to keep it, and that this may be forever."* This opinion was recognised and practised upon, by the Government of the United States, through several successive administrations, also recognised by the Supreme Court of the United States, and the several States, when the question has arisen. It has not been the opinion only of jurists, but of politicians, as may be seen from various reports of Secretaries of War—beginning with Gen. Knox, also the correspondence between the British and American ministers at Ghent in the year 1814. If the Cherokees have power to judge of their own interests, and to make treaties, which, it is presumed, will be denied by none, then to make a contract valid, the assent of a majority must be had, expressed by themselves or through their representatives, and the President and Senate have no power to say what their will shall be, for from the laws of nations we learn that "though a nation be obliged to promote, as far as lies in its power, the perfection of others, it is not entitled forcibly to obtrude these good offices on them." Such an attempt would be to violate their natural liberty. Those ambitious Europeans who attacked the American nations and subjected them to their insatiable avidity of dominion, in order, as they pretended, for civilizing them, and causing them to be instructed in the true religion (as in the present instance to preserve the Cherokees as a distinct people,) these usurpers grounded themselves on a pretence equally unjust and ridiculous." It is the expressed wish of the Government of the United States to remove the Cherokees to a place west of the Mississippi. That wish is said to be founded in humanity to the Indians. To make their situation more comfortable, and to preserve them as a distinct people. Let facts show how this *benevolent* design has been prosecuted, and how faithful to the spirit and letter has the promise of the President of the United States to the Cherokee been fufilled—that *"those who remain may be assured of our patronage, our aid, and good neighborhood."* The delegation are not deceived by empty professions, and fear their race is to be destroyed by the mercenary policy of the present day, and their lands wrested from them by physical force; as proof, they will refer to the preamble of an act of the General Assembly of Georgia, in reference to the Cherokees, passed the 2nd of December, 1835, where it is said, "from a knowledge of the Indian character, and from the present feelings of these Indians, it is confidently believed, that the right of occupancy of the lands in their possession should be withdrawn, *that it would be a strong inducement to them to treat with the General Government, and consent to a removal to the west*; and whereas, the present Legislature openly avow that their primary object in the measures intended to be pursued, *are founded on real humanity to these Indians,* and with a view, in a distant region, to perpetuate them with their old identity of character, *under the paternal care of the Government of the United States;* at the same time frankly disavowing *any selfish or sinister motives towards them in their present legislation.*" This is the profession. Let us turn to the practice of *humanity,* to the Cherokees, by the State of Georgia. In violation of the treaties between the United States and the Cherokee nation, that State passed a law requiring all white men, residing in that part of the Cherokee country, in her limits, to take an oath of allegiance to the State of Georgia. For a violation of this law, some of the ministers of Christ, missionaries among the Cherokees, were tried, convicted, and sentenced to hard labor in the penitentiary. Their case may be seen by reference to the records of the Supreme Court of the United States.

Valuable gold mines were discovered upon Cherokee lands, within the chartered limits of Georgia, and the Cherokees commenced working them, and the Legislature of that State interfered by passing an act, making it penal for an Indian to dig for gold within Georgia, no doubt *"frankly disavowing any selfish or sinister motives towards them."* Under this law many Cherokees were arrested, tried, imprisoned, and otherwise abused. Some were even shot in attempting to avoid an arrest; yet the Cherokee people used no violence, but humbly petitioned the Government of the United States for a fulfilment of treaty engagements, to protect them, which was not done, and the answer given that the United States could not interfere. Georgia discovered she was not to be obstructed in carrying out her measures, *"founded on real humanity to these Indians,"* she passed an act directing the Indian country to be surveyed into districts. This excited some alarm, but the Cherokees were quieted with the assurance it would do no harm to survey the country. Another act was shortly after passed, to lay off the country into lots. As yet there was no authority to take possession, but it was not long before a law was made, authorizing a lottery for the lands laid off into lots. In this act the Indians were secured in possession of all the lots touched by their improvements, and the balance of the country allowed to be occupied by white men. This was a direct violation of the 5th article of the treaty of the 27th of February, 1819. The Cherokee made no resistance, still petitioned the United States for protection, and received the same answer that the President could not interpose. After the country was parcelled out by lottery, a horde of speculators made their appearance, and purchased of the "fortunate drawers," lots touched by Indian improvements, at reduced prices, declaring it was uncertain when the Cherokees would surrender their rights, and that the lots were encumbered by their claims. The consequence of this speculation was that, at the next session of the Legislature, an act was passed limiting the Indian right of occupancy to the lot upon which he resided, and his actual improvements adjoining. Many of the Cherokees filed bills, and obtained injunctions against dispossession, and would have found relief in the courts of the country, if the judiciary had not been prostrated at the feet of legislative power. For the opinion of a judge, on this subject, there was an attempt to impeach him, then to limit his circuit to one county, and when all this failed, equity jurisdiction was taken from the courts, in Cherokee cases, by acts passed in the years 1833 and 1834. The Cherokees were then left at the mercy of an interested agent. This agent, under the act of 1834, was the notorious William N. Bishop, the captain of the Georgia Guard, aid to the Governor, clerk of a court, postmaster, &c. and his mode of trying Indian rights is here submitted:

"Murray county, Georgia, *January* 20, 1835.

"Mr. John Martin:

"Sir: The legal representative of lots of land,

No. 95	25 district	2d section.
86	25 "	2 "
93	25 "	2 "
89	25 "	2 "
57	25 "	2 "

has called on me, as States agent, to give him possession of the above described lots of land, and informs me that you are the occupant upon them. Under the laws of the State of Georgia, passed in the years 1833 and 1834, it is made my duty to comply with his request, you will, therefore, prepare, yourself to give entire possession of said premises, on or before the 20th day of February next, fail not under the penalty of the law.

"WM. N. BISHOP, *States Agent.*"

Mr. Martin, a Cherokee, was a man of wealth, had an extensive farm; large fields of wheat growing; and was turned out of house and home, and compelled, in the month of February, to seek a new residence within the limits of Tennessee. Thus Mr. Bishop settled his rights according to the notice he had given. The same summary process was used towards Mr. John Ross, the principal chief of the Cherokee nation. He was at Washington city, on the business of his nation. When he returned, he travelled till about 10 o'clock at night, to reach his family; rode up to the gate; saw a servant, believed to be his own; dismounted, ordered his horse taken; went in, and to his utter astonishment, found himself a stranger in his own house, his family having been, some days before, driven out to seek a new home. A thought then flitted across his mind, that he could not, under all the circumstances of his situation, reconcile it to himself to tarry all night under the roof of his own house as a stranger, the new host of that house being the tenant of that mercenary band of Georgia speculators, at whose instance his helpless family had been turned out and made homeless.

Upon reflecting, however, that "man is born unto trouble," Mr. Ross at once concluded to take up lodgings there for the night, and to console himself under the conviction of having met his afflictions and trials in a manner consistent with every principle of moral obligation towards himself and family, his country and his God. On the next morning he arose early, and went out into the yard, and saw some straggling herds of his cattle and sheep browsing about the place. His crop of corn undisposed of. In casting a look up into the wide spread branches of a majestic oak, standing within the enclosure of the garden, and which overshadows the spot where lies the remains of his dear babe, and most beloved and affectionate father, he there saw, perched upon its boughs, that flock of beautiful pea-fowls, once the matron's care and delight, but now left to destruction and never more to be seen. He ordered his horse, paid his bill, and departed in search of his family, after travelling amid heavy rains, had the happiness of overtaking them on the road, bound for some place of refuge within the limits of Tennessee. Thus had his houses, farm, public ferries and other property, been seized and wrested from him. Mr. Richard Taylor was, also, at Washington, and in his absence, his family was threatened with expulsion, and compelled to give two hundred dollars for leave to remain at home for a few months only. This is the *"real humanity"* the Cherokees were shown by the real or pretended authorities of Georgia, "disavowing any selfish or sinister motives towards them."

Mr. Joseph Vann, also, a native Cherokee, was a man of great wealth, had about eight hundred acres of land in cultivation; had made extensive improvements, consisting, in part, of a brick house, costing about ten thousand dollars, mills, kitchens, negro houses, and other buildings. He had fine gardens, and extensive apple and peach orchards. His business was so extensive, he was compelled to employ an overseer and other agents. In the fall of 1833, he was called from home, but before leaving, made a conditional contract with a Mr. Howell, a white man, to oversee for him in the year 1834, to commence on the first of January of that year. He returned about the 28th or 29th of December 1833, and learning Georgia had prohibited any Cherokee from hiring a white man, told Mr. Howell he did not want his services. Yet Mr. Bishop, the State's agent, represented to the authorities of Georgia, that Mr. Vann had violated the laws of that State, by hiring a white man, had forfeited his right of occupancy, and that a grant ought to issue for his lands. There were conflicting claims under Georgia for his possessions. A Mr. Riley pretended a claim, and took possession of the upper part of the dwelling house, armed for battle. Mr. Bishop, the State's agent, and his party, came to take possession, and between them and Riley, a fight commenced, and from twenty to fifty guns were fired in the house. While this was going on, Mr. Vann gathered his trembling wife and children into a room for safety. Riley could not be dislodged from his position up stairs, even after being wounded, and Bishop's party finally set fire to the house. Riley surrendered and the fire was extinguished.

Mr. Vann and his family were then driven out, unprepared, in the dead of winter, and snow upon the ground, through which they were compelled to wade, and to take shelter within the limits of Tennessee, in an open log cabbin, upon a dirt floor, and Bishop put his brother Absalom in possession of Mr. Vann's house. This Mr. Vann is the same, who, when a boy, volunteered as a private soldier in the Cherokee regiment, in the service of the United States, in the Creek war, periled his life in crossing the river at the battle of the Horse Shoe. What has been his reward?

Hundreds of other cases might be added. In fact, near all the Cherokees in Georgia, who had improvements of any value, except the favorites of the United States agents, under one pretext or other, have been driven from their homes. Amid the process of expulsion, the Rev. John F. Schermerhorn, the United States commissioner, visited the legislatures of Tennessee and Alabama, and importuned those bodies to pass laws, prohibiting the Cherokees who might be turned out of their possessions from within the Georgia limits, taking up a residence in the limits of those States.

In the month of May, 1835, the general council of the Cherokee nation passed a resolution, appointing agents to ascertain the value of improvements, taken by white men, and also the amount of all claims against the United States for spoliations upon the Cherokees. It was believed full justice could not be done in a treaty, otherwise than by ascertaining the injuries they had sustained. This resolution looked to a treaty with the United States, so soon as arrangements therefor could be made. Numbers of Cherokees had been forced from their houses and farms, particularly by the authorities of Georgia, and the citizens of the United States being in possession of the improvements, if they were not valued in a short time, daily undergoing alterations and additions, they could not be identified as Cherokee improvements. These agents were required to register all claims for improvements and spoliations, in books to be kept for that purpose. To proceed forthwith and to report to the principal chief, to be submitted to the next general council of the nation, which was to commence in October following, when the commissioner of the United States was to appear for the purpose of making a treaty. Messrs. J. J. Trott, Robert Rogers, Elijah Hicks, Walter S. Adair, and Thomas F. Taylor, were appointed as agents, and in the latter part of July proceeded to the duties assigned them. After having made some progress, Messrs. Trott and Hicks were arrested by a part of the Georgia guard. The officer commanding deprived them of all their books and papers, marched them off sixty miles, tied with ropes, to Spring Place, the station of the guard, and there kept them, with Messrs. Taylor and Adair, who had also been arrested, in close confinement, in a guard-house, built to keep Indians in, for nine or ten days. A writ of *habeas corpus* was obtained, to bring the prisoners before a judge, but the guard evaded the service of the writ, by running the prisoners from place to place. The prisoners were finally required by Bishop, the captain

of the guard, to give bond and surety to the State of
Georgia, in the sum of one thousand dollars each, to
appear at court, and to desist from valuing Cherokee
improvements. They appeared at court, but no further
steps were taken against them. Their books and papers
have never been returned. This arrest was stated to be at
the instance of Messrs. Schermerhorn and Currey, agents
for the United States, who, it is said, corresponded with
the Governor of Georgia and the Secretary of War on the
subject, and that a part of this correspondence may be
seen in the War Department.

Joseph M. Lynch, an officer of the Cherokee nation,
for executing the laws of the nation, was arrested by the
Georgia guard, lodged in jail, and bail for his appearance
at a court of justice refused. His negroes were also seized
and committed to jail, and there continued until they
broke jail and made their escape. Not less barbarity has
been practised towards the Cherokees, by Benjamin F.
Curry, the agent of the United States for Cherokee emigration, openly alleging it to be the policy of the United
States to make the situation of the Indians so miserable as
to drive them into a treaty, or an abandonment of their
country, as may be seen by his letter to Messrs. Brazleton
and Kennedy, of 14th September, 1835. A few instances
will be given as illustration of his mode of operation and
general conduct.

Wahka and his wife were natives of, and residents in,
the Cherokee nation east of the Mississippi. The agents of
the United States prevailed upon the wife to enrol for
emigration, against the remonstrances of the husband, and
they afterwards, by force, separated her from her husband, and took her and the children to Arkansas, leaving
the husband and father behind, because he would not
enrol. The improvements upon which he resided, were
valued in the name of the wife, and he turned out of
possession.

Atalah Anosta was prevailed upon to enrol when drunk,
contrary to the wish and will of his wife and children;
when the time arrived for him to leave for Arkansas, he
absconded. A guard was sent after him by B. F. Cur-

rey, which arrested the woman and children, and brought them to the agency about dark, in a cold rain, shivering and hungry. They were detained under guard all night, and part of the next day, and until the woman agreed to enrol her name as an emigrant. The husband then came in, and he and his wife and their children were put on board a boat and taken to Arkansas. There they soon lost two or three of their children, and then returned on foot to the Cherokee nation east of the Mississippi.

Sconatachee, when drunk, was enrolled by Benjamin F. Currey: when the emigrants were collecting, he did not appear, and Currey and John Miller, the interpreter, went after him. Currey drew a pistol, and attempted to drive the old man to the agency, who presented his gun and refused to go. Currey and Miller returned without him. He made the facts known to Hugh Montgomery, the Cherokee agent, who gave him a certificate that he should not be forced away against his will. So the matter rested till the emigrants were collected the next year, and then Currey sent a wagon and guard for him. He was arrested, tied, and hauled to the agency, leaving some of his children behind in the woods, where they had fled on the approach of the guard. Richard Cheek enrolled for emigration, but before the time of departure, he hired to work on the Tuscumbia rail-road, in Alabama. When the emigrants started, Currey had Cheek's wife taken, put on board a boat, and started to Arkansas. She was even denied the privilege of visiting her husband as she descended the river. He was left behind, and never saw her more. She died on the way.

Such outrages, and violations of treaty stipulations, have been the subject of complaint to the Government of the United States, on the part of the Cherokees, for years past; and the delegation are not surprised, that the American people are not now startled at those wrongs, so long continued, for by habit men are brought to look with indifference upon death itself. If the Government of the United States have determined to take the Cherokee lands without their consent, the power is with them; and the American people can "reap the field that is not their own, and gather the vintage of his vineyard whom by violence they have oppressed."

There is no ground for the pretended necessity under which the authorities of the United States have acted, for at the time of the formation and ratification of the pretended treaty, the Cherokee people had their delegation and representatives in Washington city, with instructions and full powers to negotiate a treaty. This delegation were importuning the Government for an opportunity to do so, as their correspondence with the War Department will show. It will further show, they were at first received and recognised as the proper party with which to make a treaty, and then rejected, unless they would adopt the act of the faction at New Echota, which, in them, would have been a violation of the express will of their constituents. They were willing to act under their authority for the Cherokee people, but the opportunity to do so was refused. Then there is no force in the argument for the ratification of a fraudulent treaty, that it was necessary something should be done. There is as little in the assertion, that the Cherokees were in a distressed and starving condition, and that it was therefore necessary to ratify the New Echota instrument, as a treaty for their benefit and preservation, as the best that could be done. This position denies to the Cherokees the right to think for themselves.

Their distresses have not been denied, but the argument comes with a bad grace from the agents of the United States, who have produced them avowedly for the purpose of forcing a treaty. The Cherokees have not asked, but refused the proffered relief, and are surely the best judges of their own true situation, can properly appreciate the motives for the offer, as also the expressed sympathy for their misfortunes, and the avowed benevolence towards the Indian race, all of which amounts simply to this: "we want, and intend to take your lands, and are sorry you are unwilling for us to do so in our own way." . . .

The Cherokee delegation have thus considered it their duty to exhibit before your honorable body a brief view of the Cherokee case, by a short statement of facts. A detailed narrative would form a history too voluminous to

be presented, in a memorial and protest. They have, therefore, contented themselves with a brief recital, and will
add, that in reviewing the past, they have done it alone for
the purpose of showing what glaring oppressions and
sufferings the peaceful and unoffending Cherokees have
been doomed to witness and endure. Also, to tell your
honorable body, in sincerity, that owing to the intelligence
of the Cherokee people, they have a correct knowledge of
their own rights, and they well know the illegality of those
oppressive measures which have been adopted for their
expulsion, by State authority. Their devoted attachment to
their native country has not been, nor ever can be, eradi-
cated from their breast. This, together with the implicit
confidence, they have been taught to cherish, in the *justice, good faith, and magnanimity of the United States,*
also, their firm reliance on the generosity and friendship of
the American people, have formed the anchor of their
hope and upon which alone they have been induced and
influenced to shape their peaceful and manly course, under some of the most trying circumstances any people ever
have been called to witness and endure. For more than
seven long years have the Cherokee people been driven
into the necessity of contending for their just rights, and
they have struggled against fearful odds. Their means of
defence being altogether within the grasp and control of
their competitors, they have at last been trampled under
foot. Their resources and means of defence, have been
seized and withheld. The treaties, laws, and constitution of
the United States, their bulwark, and only citadel of refuge: put beyond their reach; unfortunately for them, the
protecting arm of the commander-in-chief of these for-
tresses has been withdrawn from them. The judgments of
the judiciary branch of the government, in support of their
rights, have been disregarded and prostrated; and their
petitions for relief, from time to time before Congress,
been unheeded. Their annuities withheld; their printing
press, affording the only clarion through which to proclaim their wrongs before the American people and the
civilized world, has been seized and detained, at the instance of an agent of the United States.

An attorney at law, employed by them to defend the rights of the suffering Cherokees, before the courts of Georgia, has been induced to desert his clients' cause, under expectations of being better paid, at their expense, by taking sides against them. Some of their own citizens, seduced and prompted by officers of the United States Government to assume upon themselves the powers of the nation, unconferred, have been brought to negotiate a treaty, over the heads and remonstrances of the nation. Is there to be found in the annals of history, a parallel case to this? By this treaty all the lands, right, interests, and claims, of whatsoever nature, of the Cherokee people east of the Mississippi, are pretended to be ceded to the United States for the pittance of $5,600,000. Let us take a cursory view of the country and other rights of the Cherokees professed to be surrendered to the United States, under the provisions of this fraudulent treaty. The Cherokee Territory, within the limits of North Carolina, Georgia, Tennessee and Alabama, is estimated to contain *ten millions of acres.* It embraces a large portion of the finest lands to be found in any of the States; and a salubrity of climate unsurpassed by any; possessing superior advantages in reference to water power; owing to the numerous rills, brooks and rivers, which flow from and through it; some of these streams afford good navigation, others are susceptible of being easily improved and made navigable. On the routes where roads have been opened by the Cherokees, through this country, there must necessarily pass some of the most important public roads and other internal improvements, which at no distant day will be constructed.

The entire country is covered with a dense forest of valuable timber, also abounding in inexhaustible quarries of marble and lime stone. Above all, it possesses the most extensive regions of the precious metal known in the United States. The riches of the gold mines are incalculable, some of the lots of *forty acres* of land, embracing gold mines, which have been surveyed and disposed of by lottery, under the authority of Georgia, (with the encumbrance of the Indian title) have been sold for *upwards of thirty thousand dollars!* . . .

For the surrender then of a territory containing about ten millions of acres; together with the various interests and claims spoken of, and the amount that will be required to cover these claims, no man, without data, can form any estimate. The sum of five millions, six hundred thousand dollars only, is proposed to be paid: the price given for the lands at this rate would not exceed thirty cents per acre. Will Georgia accept the whole amount, for that portion within her limits?

The faith of the United States being solemnly pledged to the Cherokee nation for the guarantee of the quiet and uninterrupted protection of their territorial possessions forever; and it being an unquestionable fact, that the Cherokees love their country; that no amount of money could induce them voluntarily to yield their assent to a cession of the same. But, when under all the circumstances of their peculiar situation and unhappy condition, the nation see the necessity of negotiating a treaty for their security and future welfare, and having appointed a delegation with full powers for that purpose, is it liberal, humane, or just, that a fraudulent treaty, containing principles and stipulations altogether objectionable, and obnoxious to their own sense of propriety and justice, should be enforced upon them? The basis of the instrument, the sum fixed upon, the commutation of annuities, and the general provisions of the various articles it contains, are all objectionable. Justice and equity demand, that in any final treaty for the adjustment of the Cherokee difficulties, that their rights, interests, and wishes should be consulted; and that the individual rights of the Cherokee citizens, in their possessions and claims, should be amply secured; and as freemen, they should be left at liberty to stay or remove where they please. Also, that the territory to be ceded by the United States to the Cherokee nation west of the Mississippi, should be granted to them by a patent in fee simple, and not clogged with the conditions of the act of 1830; and the national funds of the Cherokees should be placed under the control of their national council.

The delegation must repeat, the instrument entered into at New Echota, purporting to be a treaty, is deceptive to the world, and a fraud upon the Cherokee people. If a doubt exist as to the truth of their statement, a committee of investigation can learn the facts, and it may also learn that if the Cherokees are removed under that instrument, it will be by force. This declaration they make in sincerity, with hearts sickening at the scenes they may be doomed to witness; they have toiled to avert such a calamity; it is now with Congress, and beyond their control; they hope they are mistaken, but it is hope against a sad and almost certain reality. It would be uncandid to conceal their opinions, and they have no motive for expressing them but a solemn sense of duty. The Cherokees cannot resist the power of the United States, and should they be driven from their native land, then will they look in melancholy sadness upon the golden chains presented by President Washington to the Cherokee people as emblematical of the brightness and purity of the friendship between the United States and the Cherokee nation.

> JNO. ROSS,
> JOHN MARTIN,
> JAMES BROWN,
> JOSEPH VANN,
> JOHN BENGE,
> LEWIS ROSS,
> ELIJAH HICKS,
> RICH'D FIELDS,
> *Representatives*
> *of the Cherokee nation.*

WASHINGTON CITY, 21*st June,* 1836.

DOCUMENT C:

LETTER FROM JOHN ROSS,

The Principal Chief of the Cherokee Nation, to a Gentleman of Philadelphia, 1837

. . . The friendly intercourse between the United States and the Cherokees, commenced at a very early period of your national history. The treaty of Hopewell, by which our nation was received into the favour and protection of the United States, was dated in 1785. This instrument fixed the boundary which was then agreed upon. It will be remarked that the line which it indicates, was designed merely as a demarcation between the parties to it, and is consequently exclusively confined to the eastern limits of the Cherokee nation. It begins at the mouth of the Duck river, in what is now the state of Tennessee, and, running through portions of both Carolinas and Georgia, terminates at the head of the south fork of the Oconee, in the last named state. The country which we then owned, comprehends what is now a fertile and densely populated portion of the Union.

At a very early period after the organisation of your present form of government, the illegal encroachments upon our lands, and the outrages perpetrated upon our rights, attracted the notice of President Washington. With a view to adjust all the difficulties growing out of these fruitful sources of discord, another treaty was negotiated in 1791, at Holston. A different boundary was established, and the Cherokees placed themselves under the protection of the United States. A reference to this treaty will show that we had yielded to our neighbours a large portion of our territory, but by the seventh article we obtained the solemn guarantee of the United States to all our lands not then ceded.

In the year 1798, a further treaty was concluded between the parties, at Tellico, by which another large cession was made, and again by the express provisions of the instrument, the remainder of their country was for ever guaranteed to the Cherokees. This was, however, soon followed by another treaty of cession in 1804, two treaties in 1805, and early in 1806, another. By each of these treaties important and valuable districts were ceded. A temporary suspension of these proceedings now occurred, but in 1816 three several treaties were made, in 1817 another, and these were followed up by that of February

1819. Each of these instruments contributed to narrow our limits and to curtail our territory. A peace of permanent policy was avowed, and the treaty of 1819 was regarded as a final measure. Such of the nation as were disposed to emigrate beyond the Mississippi, and to retain their original hunter habits, were provided for; those who preferred remaining, and to pursue the arts of civilisation, were to remain; property which had been held in common, was to be enjoyed in severalty; the limits of individual rights were to be fixed and permanent interests to be held in land.

The Cherokees, who had already made considerable progress in the pursuits of agriculture, &c., continued rapidly to advance under this system. Education became more widely diffused, a new alphabet invented by one of them, became the vehicle for disseminating useful information in their own language. A newspaper was established, a code of laws framed, and political institutions, adapted to their circumstances, were organised. With this change of manners their numbers increased, and wealth began to accumulate. Such were some of the blessings which the Cherokees had derived from their intercourse with the whites. They were contented, prosperous, and happy, and looked forward with confidence to an augmentation of all their sources of prosperity. They realised, to a considerable extent, the benefits which had been promised them. They had parted with nineteen twentieths of their original possessions, but the rest was secured to them by sanctions, guarantees, and pledges, which professed to be sacred and inviolable.

These anticipations were however not to be wholly fulfilled. Notwithstanding the understanding of all parties that the arrangements of 1819 were to be permanent and final, that no further cessions of territory were to be required or made, that we were to be suffered to retain as private property, the comparatively small remnant of our original territory which had not been disposed of, it soon appeared that while one acre remained in our hands it would be viewed with the eyes of cupidity. Although one of the conditions upon which we had given so much was that the residue should be guaranteed to us for ever, although the treaty of 1819 was declared to be a final adjustment, although the United States had stipulated to remove all intruders from our lands, and to protect us against similar outrages in future, yet none of these provisions in our favour have for years been of any practical value.

In our memorial to the senate, in March, 1836, you will find a summary statement of the wrongs under which we laboured. We then stated that "the Cherokees were happy and prosperous till the year 1828, when the United States entered into a treaty with the Cherokees west of the Mississippi, in which, though the Cherokee nation east was no party, or consulted, certain stipulations were introduced affecting their interests. From this date the agents of the United States commenced their interference with the internal affairs of the Cherokee people. A system was devised and prosecuted to force them to emigrate by rendering them unhappy where they were."

In June, 1834, a paper, purporting to be an agreement, was executed between John H. Eaton, a commissioner, on the part of the United States, and Andrew Ross, Thomas J. Park, John West, and James Starr. These individuals were members of the Cherokee community, but were never authorised to act on behalf of the nation, nor did they hold any appointment or office which would carry with it a presumption that they had authority so to act. Yet with these men an instrument purporting to be a treaty, was signed. As soon as it came to the ears of the nation, decisive steps were taken, a protest from about thirteen thousand Cherokees was submitted to the government, disclaiming the proceeding. It was submitted to the senate for ratification as a treaty properly and duly negotiated, but in consequence of the representations made to that honourable body, and the evidence exhibited before it, it was rejected. Upon what ground it could ever be claimed to be an authoritative national act, is yet to be learned.

By direction of the President this repudiated instrument was, in November, 1834, submitted to the general council of the nation for its approval. It was, however, again most deliberately and solemnly rejected.

During the ensuing winter a delegation from the nation was at Washington for the purpose of arranging the existing difficulties. Before terms were agreed upon, and shortly after the conferences had begun, a few individuals of the nation, equally without authority as those who had been before prevailed upon to assume such powers, arrived in the city, and within a few days the regularly appointed delegation was again passed by, and new negotiations opened with these parties. On the 14th of March, 1835, an instrument purporting to be a treaty was signed by these parties and transmitted by the president to the nation for its approval. Every effort was made to extort this approbation. The annuities due to the nation were withheld—the fears of some were excited by threats of personal violence, made by the United States agents,—others were arrested by the military and placed in confinement,—their press was seized. At one of the meetings of the nation, the reverend Mr. Schermerhorn, who has performed a conspicuous part in these transactions, distinctly apprised the Cherokees that if they remained on this side of the Mississippi, their difficulties would increase, "that the screws would be turned upon them till they would be ground into powder."

Notwithstanding all these efforts to intimidate the nation into an approval of this instrument, it was rejected with great unanimity. A delegation, however, was again appointed to negotiate with the United States commissioner upon all the subjects of difference. It appeared, however, that his powers were limited, and in consequence of this and other causes it was deemed advisable that the delegation should proceed to Washington, and this determination was announced to the commissioner.

During the interval between the adoption and execution of this plan, the principal chief of the nation, who was also the chairman of the delegation, was arrested and imprisoned, his papers seized and examined, without any cause being assigned and without any legal process. This act of outrage, followed by no judicial investigation, was, according to the avowal of one of the actors in it, perpetrated by the orders of B. F. Curry, a United States agent.

Mr. Curry himself hastened to Washington, procured an order from the department forbidding the delegation to proceed to that place. They notwithstanding did proceed, and on their arrival at the seat of government apprised the department in the customary mode of the fact; and that they were ready to proceed in the business which had brought them on. They were received as usual; propositions were invited from them with assurances that these propositions should be acted upon.

Within a few days, however, information reached Washington that the commissioners who remained behind had negotiated another treaty with a body of unauthorised individuals, and was bringing on with him a delegation. This instrument, to which less than one hundred of the nation ever gave their sanction, directly or indirectly, was in its terms unacceptable to the president: it was again varied in Washington in some important features; and, notwithstanding every remonstrance and opposition on the part of the regularly authorised representatives of the nation, was submitted to the senate, and finally obtained the ratification of that body by a bare constitutional majority.

I have thus given you a rapid sketch of the proceedings which terminated in the so called treaty of December, 1835. The details may be found at large in the congressional documents. This instrument we consider as the consummation of our wrongs. By its provisions all the benefits which we deemed secured to us by valid and effective treaties are in substance annihilated,—all the territory remaining in the hands of the nation or of individuals, is ceded. This instrument, to which so small a portion of our people as less than one hundred have ever been induced, by all the appliances used, to give their sanction, is, we are told, a solemn and sacred treaty, and its stipulations will be fully and rigidly enforced.

It was to have been expected that a measure so monstrous and so glaring, would be followed by acts and misrepresentations of all sorts for the purpose of sustaining it. Paragraphs, calculated to produce alarm and consternation, were insidiously thrown into the public papers the moment this spurious treaty was signed, and some of them before the news of its ratification by the senate could have reached the nation. Rumours of an armed opposition to its enforcement were fabricated, and one of these publications was headed, "The Cherokees are up!!!"

For myself, I had calls of too serious and pressing import to allow of my wasting time in hunting down these calumnies or exposing these prophecies, which had no other prospect of being verified than by themselves producing the effects they affected to foretell. The principal agent in getting up this spurious treaty was the reverend Mr. Schermerhorn, the same individual who by similar means involved the country in a war with the Seminolians, by which millions of money, and lives still more valuable, have been lost. I was persuaded that however the cases and the people might differ, it would be attempted to confound the Cherokees with the Seminolians, and to take alarm at and to exaggerate the slightest expression of discontent. I knew that the perpetrator of a wrong never forgives his victim; and that there were some who would excite our people to open indications of resentment as a pretext for violence and a justification of themselves. It was therefore made my earnest business, by a calm and direct course, to endeavour to confirm the often expressed resolution of the Cherokees, to rely entirely upon remonstrance, and to pursue such a course as would satisfy the people of the United States and their representatives, that we had been the victims of injustice. Our people were assured that when the treaty-making power should discover the real truth he could not fail to be just.

The agents of the United States seem to be aware that the Cherokee nation had never sanctioned this pretended treaty. No sooner had it been hurried through the forms of ratification than they obtained a military force to overawe the Cherokees and to oppose every attempt to pursue a faithful and honest enquiry into the real facts of the case. On my return to my constituents, having been detained some time by business, I arrived at Athens, in Tennessee, where I met General Wool, the commander of the troops, who had actually reached our country before me. The general expressed great satisfaction that I had come, and informed me that my presence had been much wanted, as he had already been in the valley towns, and found there a feeling so decidedly hostile to the treaty as to require the operation of the most powerful counteracting influences. I assured him that I considered his admission of that fact very important, as it proved that I had been guilty of no misrepresentation, and that his own experience would now enable him to show General Jackson that the impression under which he professed to act in making this arrangement with the Cherokees was a mistaken one,—he had made a compact to which only one side, and what was still worse only the interested one, had consented, when to ratify a bargain requires the free consent of two. General Wool, in reply, dwelt on the impossibility of changing the determination of the present, and hoped I would advise the people accordingly, and thus prevent such scenes as had taken place in Florida. I assured him that I would pledge my life that the Cherokees would never assert their rights by bloodshed, but that I could not as an honest man advise their assent to a spurious treaty. They might be persuaded to remove, and to remove without resistance, and would be better reconciled to their fate, if the United States would only show them the fairness formally to recognise the removal as the compelled submission of the weaker to the stronger, but they would not in the face of heaven, put their hands and seals to a falsehood. They would not say that arrangements were brought about by honest treaty which were really brought about by deliberate and steadily resisted and exposed craft and duplicity.

General Wool appeared chagrined at his reception in the valley towns. After our interview I discovered the cause. On reaching my destination I learned that various efforts had been made on the arrival of the army in the valley towns, and in various ways, to obtain an acknowledgment of the spurious treaty, but without effect. Even the arms of the people had been demanded, and, although they were actually required by the farmers for the protection of their fields and stock from birds and beasts of prey, in order to remove the smallest pretext for suspicion they were forthwith given up. Some of our people were unable to understand why an army should be sent among us while we were at perfect peace, to enforce the stipulations of a treaty, which, if even obligatory, was not to be executed for two years. Several arrests of men and women, as afterwards appeared, were attributed to expressions of natural surprise upon this head. None of these annoyances, however, produced any unfortunate result. The Cherokees, though unwavering in their objections to the pretended treaty, remained and will remain inoffensive and unresisting.

About four weeks after my return, the nation was convened to receive the report of the delegation. The general was invited to be present, with the troops under his command,—about five hundred of the army attended. Just before the commencement of the proceedings, while upon the platform, a package was placed in my hands, addressed on the envelope to me, and on the inside to the Cherokee people. It was a notice from General Wool communicating in substance the determination of President Jackson that no alteration in the treaty would be made by him, but that its stipulations should be scrupulously fulfilled.

This communication from General Wool was publicly read and interpreted, and afterwards the paper called the treaty was in like manner read and interpreted. The people were entirely silent in relation to the former. They were then asked if they were disposed to give their assent to the latter. They unanimously answered, No! and insisted upon a new arrangement, alleging that the one exhibited to them had been made with irresponsible, unauthorised individuals, and contained terms and conditions distinctly at variance with their often and publicly proclaimed instructions.

The nation having thus spontaneously and without advice from their rulers, rejected this spurious treaty, and disclaimed it as their act, it appeared to me the most prudent course to encourage them in hoping for better things. It also occurred to me that if those of our brethren who were already in the west, were to unite with us in endeavouring to make the truth of the case known, our prospects of ultimately obtaining justice would be improved. I also knew that this portion of the nation considered the provisions of the treaty, under which they had emigrated and received lands beyond the Mississippi in lieu of what was ceded in the east, as seriously infringed by the document in question. I was further persuaded that the reason assigned for our opposition to the arrangement, viz., our distaste for Arkansas, could not be attributed to those who actually resided there. With these impressions, I recommended the appointment of a delegation to confer with our brethren in the west, upon the propriety of sending a joint embassy to Washington for the purpose of satisfying the government how much they had been misinformed and deceived, and of making a definitive arrangement upon terms acceptable to the nation. At the same time, I assured the people that the treaties already recognised by both parties as existing between them and the United States, would not be broken, and they might confidently trust to that security for obtaining a fair and honest adjustment of controversies, which was all they had ever desired.

The principal resolutions consequent upon these explanations are the following:—

"Whereas, an instrument has been read and interpreted to us, purporting to be a treaty made at New Echota, on the 29th of December, 1835, by the Reverend John F. Schermerhorn, commissioner of the United States, and the chiefs, head men, and people of the Cherokee tribe of Indians, ratified by the senate and approved by the president of the United States;—and whereas, by the provisions of this instrument all the lands of the Cherokees are ceded to the United States; the private improvements and possessions of individuals unjustly alienated from their rightful owners; the rights of the Cherokees as freemen wrested from the guardianship of their legitimate representatives; and the management of their affairs placed in the hands of individuals without responsibility, and under the control of officers of the United States government:—and whereas the makers of said compact, who are represented as acting on the part of the Cherokees, and who assume the style of chiefs and head men, hold no such title or designation from the Cherokees, nor have they received authority from the nation to form said instrument.

"Resolved, therefore, by the chiefs, national committee, and council, and the people of the Cherokee nation in general council assembled, that the said instrument is null and void, and can never in justice be enforced upon our nation; and we do hereby solemnly disclaim and utterly reject said instrument, in its principles and all its provisions.

"Resolved, That a respectful memorial to the government of the United States, be prepared on behalf of the Cherokee people, praying that the said instrument be set aside as a fraud upon the government of the United States, and an act of oppression on the Cherokee people.

"Resolved, That a delegation be invested with full powers to represent the Cherokee people before the government of the United States, to enter into arrangements for the final adjustment of all their existing difficulties: and be it further resolved, that the said delegation be, and they are hereby instructed to confer with the Cherokees west of the Mississippi, on the subject of their acting in concert with us, in efforts to procure the rescinding of said instrument, which in its provisions is calculated to affect injuriously the interests and happiness of both parts of the Cherokee family.

"Resolved, That any irresponsible individuals, assuming to themselves the power to act in the name of our nation, without the authority of the same first legitimately obtained, will be deemed guilty of infringing the prerogatives of the government and violating the rights of the Cherokee people, who will assuredly never sanction such usurpation, nor acquiesce in the doings of such people.

"Resolved, That in the course we have adopted in reference to the instrument in question, no departure from the most respectful and friendly feelings towards the president, the government, and the people of the United States is contemplated; but, on the contrary, our determination is to maintain and cultivate those friendly relations which have long subsisted between the government and people of the United States and our own nation."

In addition to the resolutions as here quoted, it was at the same time determined, as no public business remained to be transacted, to waive the general annual council, which in course would have taken place a few days subsequently, (the second Monday in October,) and thus avoid all pretence for charges of a disposition to keep up agitation by public meetings. The paper from which I have made the foregoing extract was signed by the chiefs, committee and council, and people to the number of about two thousand two hundred and fifty-five male adults.

On the 22d of September, 1836, the chiefs, members of the national committee and council, wrote to General Wool, officially communicating the proceedings of the meeting. They returned their thanks to him for the gentlemanly deportment of himself and the troops under his command on the council ground; and they respectfully asked for the restoration of the guns previously surrendered under the impression that sufficient evidence must have been afforded him that no reasonable grounds for their detention existed. I have not learned that the guns have even yet been returned to the owners.

According to their instructions, the delegation proceeded to Arkansas. The principal chief and authorities of the western Cherokees, convened a council to assemble to eighteen days, at the council house at Tollunteeskey. On calling at Fort Gibson we made known the objects of our visit to the agent, Governor Stokes. After passing a few days with some of my friends, I returned to fort Gibson, and was there privately apprised that an order had been received for the arrest of myself and the other members of the delegation. It was said that we were to be prosecuted under the intercourse act of 1834, an act in no manner applicable to us, as Cherokees visiting Cherokees, its object being confined to intruding citizens of the United States. Nevertheless, I was advised not to appear at the council. To his intimation I replied, that I could not allow myself to be deterred from the plain course of duty, and that as I had nothing to conceal, I had nothing to fear. The council met on the 8th of December, 1836, and we attended. No impediment was thrown in our way, and we heard no more of the order. Among the resolutions adopted at this council were the following:—

"That the course adopted by the general council of the Cherokee nation east, in regard to the instrument aforesaid (the pretended treaty) is hereby approved, and inasmuch as said instrument is equally objectionable to us, and will in its enforcement also effect our best interests and happiness,

"Resolved; That a delegation be and hereby are appointed to represent the Cherokee nation west, before the government of the United States, and to co-operate with the delegation from the east of the Mississippi, in their exertions to procure the rescinding of the aforesaid instrument; and also with full powers to unite with the delegation aforesaid in any treaty arrangement which they may enter into with the government of the United States for the final adjustment of the Cherokee difficulties, and to promote the advancement of the best interests and happiness of the whole Cherokee people, and to do all things touching the affairs of the Cherokees west for their welfare."

We departed with the members appointed to serve upon this delegation, but the severity of the winter and the obstruction of our route by the ice in the rivers, prevented our arrival at Washington until the 9th of February, 1837, within a month of the close of General Jackson's presidency. We attempted to obtain access to the president, but we were denied an official interview with the president or the secretary. We then memorialised the senate, which memorial was presented, but owing to the press of business, no opportunity occurred for presenting that which we addressed to the house. Copies of our correspondence with the department, and of our memorial, will be attached to this communication, as will also other documents, which shall be presently alluded to. In this memorial we exhibited an account of the treatment we had experienced, and urged our claims in the most earnest and respectful manner. We selected what we considered the strongest arguments in support of our application. We adverted to the extraordinary and inexplicable change which had taken place in the mode of receiving us and our appeals. Among other things we said, "we have asked and we will reiterate the question—how have we offended? Show us in what manner we have, however unwittingly, inflicted upon you a wrong, you shall yourselves be the judges of the extent and manner of compensation; show us the offence which has awakened your feelings of justice against us, and we will submit to that measure of punishment which you shall tell us we have merited. We cannot bring to our recollection any thing we have done or any thing we have omitted, calculated to awaken your resentment against us."

All, however, was in vain. It may be observed that our appeal to the senate was necessarily presented so late in the session that we could not have been fully heard, whatever disposition may have existed in that honourable body to give their full attention to our case.

On the 4th of March Mr. Van Buren assumed the presidential chair. On the 16th of March we addressed the new president, stating to him fully our position and wishes, reviewing the circumstances which had occurred, and the hopes we entertained of receiving redress at his hands. We entreated the president to examine for himself into the grounds upon which we rested our charge, that the document called a treaty was fraudulent and equally an imposition upon the United States and upon ourselves. We asked, "Will the government of the United States claim the right to enforce a contract thus assailed by the other nominal party to it? Will they refuse to examine into charges of such grave import? Will they act in matters so momentous, involving consequences so awful, without enquiry?" Such an enquiry we earnestly courted, saying to the president, "We do not arrogate to ourselves so high a standing in your estimation as to authorise us to ask that you will rely implicitly upon our statements; but we have deceived ourselves most egregiously, if we have not presented to the consideration of the government sufficient grounds to induce hesitation and enquiry. You have at your command hundreds of individuals to whom you may confide the duty of making the investigation which we solicit. Select such as you can implicitly believe, associate with them but a single individual to be appointed by us to direct to the sources of information, and if we fail to establish the truth of our allegations, we shall no longer ask you to delay exercising your power in the enforcement of your rights. Should it, however, appear from such investigation that this instrument has been made without authority, that it meets with the almost unanimous reprobation of our nation, that you have been deceived by false information, we cannot and we will not believe, that under its colour, and under the sanction of those principles of justice which impose an obligation faithfully to perform our contracts and our promises, we shall be forced to submit to its iniquitous provisions.

We concluded our earnest supplication with three specific propositions,—

First. That the president would enter into a negotiation with us, as the duly authorised and regularly accredited representatives of the Cherokees in reference to every matter mutually interesting to the United States and the Cherokee nation.

Second. To have a full and impartial examination of all means of information, for the purpose of ascertaining whether the Cherokee nation, in conformity with its political institutions and forms, long recognised by the United States, ever authorised the execution of the instrument signed at New Echota, and the additional articles signed at Washington, or ever gave them their sanction and ratification; or,

Third. That the instrument in question be now submitted for approval or rejection to the free and unbiased choice of the Cherokee nation.

To this communication we received for answer, from Mr. Secretary Poinsett, on the 24th of March, that the president regarded himself as bound to carry into effect all the stipulations of the document in question, because it had been ratified according to the forms prescribed by the constitution, under a full knowledge of the considerations now urged against it, and must therefore be considered as the supreme law of the land. This being the case, he added that the second and third propositions could not be entertained, because they would involve an admission that the treaty was incomplete. In answer to the first proposition, we were promised a candid examination of any measure we should suggest, if not inconsistent with, or in contravention of, the determination to enforce the treaty against which we had protested.

It is due to Mr. Secretary Poinsett to say, that in accordance with his professions, every courtesy was extended to us in our intercourse with him. It may not be amiss, however, at this time to make one or two observations, upon the grounds taken by the government, and upon which it appears to have finally resolved to act.

In the first place it appears to us an extraordinary ground, that because a treaty has actually been made which the one party deems to be of perfect obligation upon both, that therefore no further official intercourse shall take place between the parties. It is obvious that the instrument in question is ambiguous, and of doubtful construction, and it is well known that objections have been made to it on behalf of the Western Cherokees, who think, and we think justly, that it most seriously impairs their rights, although we believe it has not *yet* been assumed that they are bound by its provisions, having not, thus far, at least, been considered as parties to it. There are questions still open between the parties, which, under any view of the case, it appears to us, can only be settled by negotiation and further treaty.

Secondly. It strikes us as equally extraordinary that because our avowed object was to make a treaty which should annul the provisions of this spurious compact, no negotiations would be opened with us. Had such a ground ever been presumed to present an obstacle to negotiation, why was it not discovered when the treaty of Holston, and every succeeding treaty ever formed with us, was under consideration. The stipulations of each and every of them, abrogate to a greater or less extent those which preceded it. How insuperably might it have been urged against the pretended treaty itself which professes to annul and abrogate pre-existing treaties, to annihilate public and private rights held under its sanction.

Thirdly. The idea that the ratification of the senate, under the circumstances, had at all impaired the rights of either party, is equally incomprehensible. It was the act of one party alone. It was an act required by the constitution of the United States to give legal effect to a compact, which, until that was consummated, was inchoate and imperfect. But if no treaty had in fact ever been signed, if the instrument was in truth fraudulent or unauthorised, we are not aware that the action of the senate could make that valid which before was void, could impose any obligation upon us who were not previously bound. Indeed, if this doctrine be true to the extent it has been pressed, the Cherokee nation, or even their self-constituted representatives, need never have been consulted or their signatures obtained. The president himself might, of his own mere motion, dictate the terms of a treaty to the senate, and by the ratification of that body it becomes binding upon all who never saw or assented to it.

Fourth. But this doctrine, which we candidly confess to be beyond our comprehension, does not seem to our feeble intellects to have any bearing upon the question. For surely, if the president and senate are empowered to negotiate and make our treaties for us, without our assent or knowledge, it does not seem very clear how this power, in this particular so unlimited, can be prevented from at least listening to our objections, and at their good pleasure substituting one less offensive, if they please.

Fifth. In what we asked, we considered ourselves as calling upon the executive to do what it had once done under similar circumstances, and what, had it been prevailed upon to do in another, would have saved the expenditure of blood and treasure recently lavished in Florida. We do not pretend to be very profoundly versed in constitutional law, or in the diplomatic history of the Union, but we well know, that on the 12th of February,

1825, a treaty was executed between the United States and our neighbours, the Creeks, at the Indian Springs, which was duly ratified by the senate. We know that this treaty was disavowed by the Creek nation, and that circumstances occurred which produced bloodshed and threatened the most serious consequences. We know that that instrument was signed by individuals actually holding the situations among the Indians which they professed to hold, but that upon the allegation that they had acted without competent authority, and after the ratification by the senate, the then executive received and listened to the remonstrances of the nation, opened a new negotiation, executed a new treaty, which was submitted to the senate and received the ratification of that body. This last treaty, which may be found in the seventh volume of the laws of the United States . . . , contains this remarkable preamble.

"Whereas a treaty was concluded at the Indian Springs, on the 12th day of February last, between commissioners on the part of the United States and a portion of the Creek nation, by which an extensive district of country was ceded to the United States:—

"And whereas a great majority of the chiefs and warriors of the said nation have protested against the execution of the said treaty, and have represented that the same was signed on their part by persons having no sufficient authority to form treaties or to make cessions, and that the stipulations in said treaty are therefore wholly void:—

"And whereas the United States are unwilling that difficulties should exist in the said nation which may eventually lead to an intestine war, and are still more unwilling that any cessions of land should be made to them, unless with the fair understanding and full extent of the tribe making such cession, and for a just and adequate consideration, it being the policy of the United States in all their intercourse with the Indians, to treat them justly and liberally, as becomes the relative situation of the parties."

Such was the preamble of the treaty of January 24th, 1826: the first article of which declared the previous treaty to be "null and void to every intent and purpose whatever, and every right and claim arising from the same is hereby cancelled and surrendered."

These were historical facts with which we were familiar, and we had not been informed what had occurred since that period to prevent a similar action, under circumstances not similar only, because the case more imperatively demanded such action. We could not understand why the Creeks should be relieved from the burthen of an unjust and illegal because unauthorised compact, and we should be held to one even more destitute of any semblance of authority. We could not understand why if President Adams possessed the constitutional power to negotiate such an arrangement as we have just adverted to, how or why President Jackson or President Van Buren would transcend their legitimate functions by instituting an enquiry into the truth of our allegations, and laying the result of such investigation before the congress of the United States. Nor could we comprehend what there was so irregular or improper in our requests as to furnish a reason for debarring us from our accustomed official intercourse with the president or war department.

Here, therefore, rests our case at present. You will perceive that our only object has been to obtain a fair arrangement upon terms which our nation can approve, to be negotiated with persons whom they have authorised to act on their behalf. Our object has been an honest one and sincerely expressed. We had hoped that the government of the United States would listen to our representations. We know that they had been led by similar false suggestions and fraudulent devices into the expenditure of four times the amount of money in attempting to settle their differences with the Indians by force of arms, which would have sufficed to accomplish all their desires without exasperation of feeling and without bloodshed. We asked that an instrument should not be called a treaty obligatory upon us, to which we never yielded directly or by implication, any assent. We asked that if we were to be driven from our homes and our native country, we should not also be denounced as treaty breakers, but have at least the consolation of being recognised as the unoffending, unresisting Indian, despoiled of his property, driven from his domestic fireside, exiled from his home, by the mere dint of superior power. We ask that deeds shall be called by their right names.

We distinctly disavow all thoughts, all desire, to gratify any feelings of resentment. That possessions acquired, and objects attained by unjust and unrighteous means, will, sooner or later, prove a curse to those who have thus sought them, is a truth we have been taught by that holy religion which was brought to us by our white brethren. Years, nay, centuries may elapse before the punishment may follow the offence, but the volume of history and the sacred Bible assure us, that the period will certainly arrive. We would with Christian sympathy labour to avert the wrath of Heaven from the United States, by imploring your government to be just. The first of your ancestors who visited as strangers the land of the Indian, professed to be apostles of Christ, and to be attracted by a desire to extend the blessings of his religion to the ignorant native. Thousands among you still proclaim the same noble and generous interest in our welfare; but will the untutored savage believe the white man's professions, when he feels that by his practices he has become an outcast and an exile? Can he repose with confidence in the declarations of philanthropy and universal charity, when he sees the professors of the religion which he is invited to embrace, the foremost in acts of oppression and of outrage?

Most sincerely and ardently do we pray that the noble example of William Penn may be more generally followed, and that the rich rewards which attended his exertions may be showered upon the heads of those who, like him, never outraged the rights or despoiled the property of the Indian. To such, among their highest earthly comforts, and among the assurances of still higher enjoyments hereafter, will be the blessing and prayer of the friendless native.

I have the honour to be, sir, most respectfully,
Your very obedient servant,
JNO. ROSS

To J. R. Tyson

POSTSCRIPT TO THE DOCUMENT:

All Cherokee efforts to make the United States honor its own laws failed; in May 1838, Gen. Winfield Scott arrived at the Cherokee Nation with an army of seven thousand men (to deal with a total Cherokee population of about fourteen thousand, including women, children, and the aged) and began rounding up the Cherokee people. Family by family, the Cherokee were taken at gunpoint from their homes and packed into concentration camps from which they were to be shipped to Indian Territory (Oklahoma). A few made the trip by river boat; most went overland on the Trail of Tears and left approximately four thousand along the way, dead from starvation, exhaustion, exposure, and disease. This did not prevent US President Van Buren from bragging to Congress that "the measures [for Cherokee removal] authorized by Congress . . . have had the happiest effects. . . . The Cherokees have emigrated without any apparent reluctance . . ."

In 1839, now "settled" in Oklahoma, Cherokees assassinated the few chiefs who had signed the obnoxious—and to the Cherokee, illegal—treaty of 1835. Suddenly moral, the US government responded to the "murders" by cutting off the payments it had agreed to by that very treaty. It ignored that it itself had guaranteed the Cherokee right to self-government if they would move west (the Cherokee law of 1820 that the nation took with it explicitly provided the death penalty for any Cherokee who sold Indian land without authorization from the Cherokee people).

"AN APPARENT RELUCTANCE"

1816–1837

Wildcat's Account

Cherokee Protest

ABOUT THE DOCUMENTS:

Cherokee, Creek, Choctaw, Chickasaw, and Seminole—
the Five Civilized Tribes: for all of them the Removal Act
of 1830 was a hypocritically worded statement of the US
government's real commitment to expel them to lands
west of the Mississippi which "Americans" then considered unfit for white habitation. The Choctaw were the first
to go, forced on foot in the middle of the winter of 1832
from Mississippi to Oklahoma. Then in 1836 the Creek
were forced out after some fancy treaty shuffling and a
fake Creek War that even the white *Montgomery Adver-
tiser* called "a base and diabolical scheme, devised by
interested men, to keep an ignorant race of people from
maintaining their just rights." The "war" involved approximately one hundred Creek warriors and eleven thousand
US soldiers; it provided the United States with what it
considered just cause for taking Creek land by "conquest"
and giving up even the pretense of paying compensation.

The Chickasaw—traditional enemies of the "Americans" and never beaten by them in battle—estimated the
odds and decided that with the French gone from Louisiana and the Spanish from Florida, they could not successfully sustain war against the "Americans." Nor did they
have any illusions that the whites might be moved by
reason. They elected instead to drive the best bargain they
could for their lands and to take charge themselves of

153

their migration. They did, in fact, manage a less unequal settlement than most Indians ever did; they began their migration in 1838. In *Disinherited* Dale Van Every wrote of them:

> It might have been expected that were removal ever to be conducted under acceptable conditions it might prove so in their case. But it did not. Their relative prosperity became one of the major causes of their undoing. Sensing unusual profits, contractors gathered stock piles along the way in such quantities that the food spoiled before it could be eaten. The travelers were charged exorbitantly for transportation and their every other requirement. They picked up smallpox en route . . . they were soon as hungry as their poorer fellow colonists. The move west had made plaintive beggars of the once proud and warlike Chickasaw.

The year 1838 marked the end of the long moral and legal struggle of the Cherokee (as has been recounted), and they started on their Trail of Tears. That year also saw the end of another struggle against expulsion: that of the Seminole, most southerly of the Civilized Tribes. But unlike the legal protest the Cherokee made in Congress and in the courts, the Seminole struggle was guerrilla warfare, and it was made in the swamps and forests of Florida.

It was called the Second Seminole War, and Andrew Jackson (who had much to do with precipitating it, as he did with the whole removal policy) described it as "disgraceful" for the United States because of its long series of "American" defeats and humiliations. Over two thousand "American" soldiers died; about sixty million dollars were spent; and it was never truly won. Or lost—depending on the point of view.

The First Seminole War had began in 1817 while Florida still belonged to Spain. It had started with a US Army raid against Seminole accused of giving refuge to runaway Black slaves. That war had seemed successful for the United States: in 1819 Spain had ceded Florida, and in 1823 some Seminole chiefs had agreed to a treaty by which they would remain within a reservation. But in the years that followed, black slaves continued to seek freedom among the Seminole, white slave raiders continued to chase them; Seminole (black, red, and mixed) continued to defend themselves. Then the Removal Act of 1830 was passed; in 1832 the War Department began to move seriously against the Seminole.

True to form, the "Americans" first trumped up a treaty with which they could lie to themselves. Deliberately misleading the Seminole chiefs, Col. James Gadsden (who would later make his name famous in dealings with the Mexican government) got them to sign what they thought was an agreement to send a delegation to report on the Oklahoma lands the "Americans" were telling them about. In reality it proved to be a document agreeing to the Seminole removal. The Seminole refused to honor the fraud; led by Micanopy, Jumper, Osceola, and other *tustenuggees,* or "war chiefs," the largest part of the Seminole people chose to fight, rather than leave their homeland.

In the first months of the fighting the Seminole killed several hundred settlers and a number of soldiers. In 1834 Osceola led a successful attack on the reservation agency headquarters while at almost the same time another Seminole band completely wiped out a hundred-man force led by Maj. Francis L. Dade. More soldiers came. Eight hundred of them led by General Clinch were driven back from an attempted river crossing by a Seminole force of 250 warriors.

By 1836 the war was going so badly that the War Department raised a new, bigger army for the campaign and put Maj. Gen. Winfield Scott in command. The Seminole made such fools of this new army that after two months in the field General Scott was transferred to Alabama. Scott's successor, Florida Gov. Robert Call, did no better. After being forced to abandon Fort Drane, Call was relieved by Gen. Thomas S. Jesup.

Jesup had an army of eight thousand regulars, plus volunteers, but he won no victories, either. He did, however, profit from the toll of hunger, exhaustion, and privation that the lengthening war was beginning to take from the Seminole. In a truce meeting with Micanopy and

Jumper he arranged a peace in return for migration to Oklahoma. Since Micanopy was the principal chief of all the Seminole, it seemed for a little while that Jesup had won the war even if the "Americans" had lost all the battles. But as the Seminole groups began to come in to surrender, they heard news of the treatment they could expect while migrating and of the slave traders waiting at the Army posts to claim any dark-skinned Seminole as an escaped slave. They rebelled again. Led by Osceola, the Seminole refused to migrate and once more took up their guerrilla war. But not all Seminole; in 1837 war-weary bands began to make separate peace and to accept migration.

The US, angered and humiliated by Seminole resistance, redoubled its efforts. The fighting continued, and the Seminole began to have losses. Gen. Joseph M. Hernandez succeeded in making a series of almost bloodless captures, and from his prisoners he learned of the growing illness and fatigue among the Seminole. Thinking peace might be arranged by treaty, Hernandez succeeded in arranging a truce talk with Osceola, who allowed the "Americans" to come to his camp. Hernandez, under orders from Jesup, violated the white flag of truce and, while pretending to parley, suddenly called on two hundred mounted soldiers who had come up secretly. Osceola, along with eleven other chiefs and a number of warriors, was taken prisoner. Osceola was taken to Fort Marion, then moved to Fort Moultrie, where he died of malaria, an infected throat, and—some said—of a broken heart. He was attended by an "American" doctor, though he would not actually allow himself to be treated. After his death, this doctor cut off his head and kept it as a personal trophy.

Meanwhile, the US was giving more attention to trying to achieve by negotiation what it had not been able to achieve by force. Among other attempts was one in which the mediation of Cherokee chiefs, led by John Ross, was enlisted. This delegation was able to talk a group of Seminole chiefs into a truce talk in December, 1837. When the chiefs appeared, Jesup again violated a truce, made the chiefs prisoners, and sent them to Fort Moultrie. This treachery aroused strong protest from the Cherokee, as is expressed in the second of the two documents that follow.

More effective protest, however, to such duplicity was arranged by a group of Seminole themselves who had been captured via another truce violation. Led by Wildcat, twelve chiefs broke out of Fort Marion and returned to their people to continue the struggle. Wildcat's account of his jailbreak is contained in the first of the two documents which follow.

In 1838 the majority of the Seminole were forced to accept removal to the west, but a remnant band led by Wildcat and Alligator held on. In 1842, still unable to bring these Seminole chiefs and their more than three hundred followers to defeat, the US finally gave up. Descendants of their undefeated enemies still live proudly in Florida.

DOCUMENT A:

From The origin, progress and conclusion of the Florida War, by John T. Sprague, 1848

We had been growing sickly from day to day, and we resolved to make our escape, or die in the attempt. We were in a small room, eighteen or twenty feet square. All the light admitted, was through a hole (embrasure) about eighteen feet from the floor. Through this we must effect our escape, or remain and die with sickness. A sentinel was constantly posted at the door. As we looked at it from our bed, we thought it small, but believed that, could we get our heads through, we should have no further or serious difficulty. To reach the hole was the first object. In order to effect this, we from time to time cut up the forage-bags allowed us to sleep on, and made them into ropes. The hole I could not reach when upon the shoulder of my companion; but while standing upon his shoulder, I worked a knife into a crevice of the stonework, as far up as I could reach, and upon this I raised myself to the aperture, when I found, that with some reduction of person, I could get through. In order to reduce ourselves as much as possible, we took medicine five days. Under the pretext of being very sick, we were permitted to obtain the roots we required. For some weeks we watched the moon, in order that the night of our attempt it should be as dark as possible. At the proper time we commenced the medicine, calculating upon the entire disappearance of the moon. The keeper of this prison, on the night determined upon to make the effort, annoyed us by frequently coming into the room, and talking and singing. At first we thought of tying him and putting his head in a bag; so that, should he call for assistance, he could not be heard. We first, however, tried the experiment of pretending to be asleep, and when he returned to pay no regard to him. This accomplished our object. He came in, and went immediately out; and we could hear him snore in the immediate vicinity of the door. I then took the rope, which we had secreted under our bed, and mounting upon the shoulder of my comrade, raised myself upon the knife worked into the crevices of the stone, and succeeded in reaching the embrasure. Here I made fast the rope, that my friend might follow me. I then passed through the hole a sufficient length of it to reach the ground upon the outside (about fifty feet) in the ditch. I had calculated the distance when going for roots. With much difficulty I succeeded in getting my head through; for the sharp stones took the skin off my breast and back. Putting my head through first, I was obliged to go down head-foremost, until my feet were through, fearing every moment the rope would break. At last, safely on the ground, I awaited with anxiety the arrival of my comrade. I had passed another rope through the hole, which, in the event of discovery, Talmus Hadjo was to pull, as a signal to me upon the outside, that he was discovered, and could not come. As soon as I struck the ground, I took hold of the signal, for intelligence from my friend. The night was very dark. Two men passed near me, talking earnestly, and I could see them distinctly. Soon I heard the struggle of my companion far above me. He had succeeded in getting his head through, but his body would come no farther. In the lowest tone of voice, I urged him to throw out his breath, and then try; soon after, he came tumbling down the whole distance. For a few moments I thought him dead. I dragged him to some water close by, which restored him; but his leg was so lame, he was unable to walk. I took him upon my shoulder to a *scrub* near the town. Daylight was just breaking; it was evident we must move rapidly. I caught a mule in the adjoining field, and making a bridle out of my sash, mounted my companion and started for the St. John's river. The mule we used one day, but fearing the whites would track us, we felt more secure on foot in the hammock, though moving very slow. Thus we continued our journey five days, subsisting upon roots and berries, when I joined my band, then assembled on the head waters of the Tomoka river, near the Atlantic coast. I gave my warriors the history of my capture and escape, and assured them that they should be satisfied that my capture was no trick of my own, and that I would not deceive them. When I came in to St. Augustine, to see my father, I took the word of friends; they said I should return, but they cheated me. When I was taken prisoner, my band was inclined to leave the country, but upon my return, they said, let us all die in Florida. This caused great suffering among our women and children. I was in hopes I should be killed in battle, but a bullet would never touch me. I had rather be killed by a white man in Florida, than die in Arkansas.

DOCUMENT B:

Letter from John Ross to Hon. Joel R. Poinsett, Secretary of War, January 2, 1838

Sir:

The Cherokee deputation who were charged with the duty of endeavouring to restore peace between the Seminole Indians and the United States, in the character of mediators . . . penetrated the deep swamps and hammocks of Florida, under the escort of Coahachee, one of the captive chiefs; . . . they met the Seminole and Mickasucky chiefs and warriors in council, and there delivered to them the talk which I, with your approbation, had sent them. After reading and fully explaining its import through the interpreter, the assembled chiefs and warriors at once agreed to receive it in friendship, as coming through their red brethren the Cherokees, with the utmost sincerity and good feelings, from their elder brother the Secretary of War, who represents their father, the President of the United States. When the usual Indian ceremonies on this occasion, in smoking the pipe of peace &c., were concluded, Micanopy, the principal chief, with twelve others of his chieftains, and a number of their warriors, agreed to accompany the Cherokee deputation, and accordingly went with them, under a flag of truce, into the headquarters of the United States army, at Fort Mellon. After this successful meeting, further steps were taken for inviting all the people to go in; and whilst some were coming in, the escape of Wild-cat from the fort of St. Augustine, and other events altogether beyond the control of the Cherokee deputation, produced a sudden and unexpected distrust and change of determination in the minds of the chiefs and warriors of the nation who were still out in their fastnesses. Upon being informed of this fact, it is reported that General Jesup immediately ordered his troops to be put in motion for hostile operations, and also caused all the chiefs and warriors who had come in under the Cherokee flag to be forthwith made prisoners of war; they were then placed in the hold of a steamboat, and shipped to the fort at St. Augustine, and there imprisoned . . . Under this extraordinary state of the affair, (1) it has become my imperious though painful duty, for the defence of my own reputation, as well as that of the deputation who acted under my instructions, for carrying out the humane objects of this mediation, also, in justice to the suffering chiefs and warriors, whose confidence in the purity of our motives, as well as in the sincerity of the Government, by the assurances held out to them under your authority in my talk, had thus placed themselves under the flag of truce before the American army, and I do hereby, most solemnly protest against this unprecedented violation of that sacred rule which has ever been recognised by every nation, civilized and uncivilized, of treating with all due respect those who had ever presented themselves under a flag of truce before their enemy, for the purpose of proposing the termination of a warfare. Moreover, I respectfully appeal to and submit for your decision, whether justice and policy do not require at your hands that these captives should be forthwith liberated, that they may go and confer with their people, and that whatever obstacles may have been thrown in the way of their coming in to make peace may be removed. In a word, under all the circumstances of the case, so far as the particular captives alluded to are concerned, I feel myself called upon, by every sense of justice and honor, to ask that they may be released and placed at liberty, to determine with their people what to do under all the circumstances of their affairs, as freely and untrammelled as they were previous to the council held with them by the Cherokee mediation, as it was through the influence of the Cherokee talk they had consented to go under the flag of truce into General Jesup's headquarters ...

> John Ross. (Koo-we-skoo-we)

FROM SEA TO SHINING SEA

1855

Chief Sealth Speaks

ABOUT THE DOCUMENT:

Protected by distance, the Indians of the Pacific Northwest Coast probably first met white men in 1774, when an expedition sent from Mexico anchored at Vancouver Island. In the following year another Mexican expedition sent a landing party ashore on the coast of present day Washington, where they were killed by Indians who took offense at their presence. After the Mexicans came the English and the Russians. Originally, the motive for these explorations was the hope of finding the mythical Northwest Passage. What the explorers found instead was a source of profits in furs, particularly the sea otter, which was soon the basis of a trade that reached its peak around 1790. But thirty years later the wholesale slaughter of the sea otter (encouraged by the white trading companies) had nearly caused its extinction; the trade fell off; and with the trade decline there came also a decline in the presence of foreign ships.

In the early 1800s, however, the Pacific Northwest had begun to be reached by "Americans" who came overland, also in search of furs. Lewis and Clark's famous expedition reached the Pacific in 1805; they had been preceded not long before by the Canadian, McKenzie. Soon the "American" Astoria Company and the Canadian North West Company were in competition for the Indian fur trade. During the War of 1812 the Astoria Company sold out and left—but in 1824 "American" fur traders returned. By then the United States had reached agreements with Spain, Russia, and England about their respective rights to the Oregon country, and the US Congress had begun to press vigorously for these powers to recognize US claims to the Pacific Coast. The dispute with Russia was a principal factor in the US formulation of the famous (and famously misunderstood) Monroe Doctrine. Neither Russia, Spain, Mexico, nor England included the Indians in their discussions or considered them contenders for title to their lands.

Still, the Pacific Coast was a long way from the "American" settlements. The southern part (California) belonged to the Mexicans, and the British in Canada were a strong presence in the Northwest; both these circumstances, added to the distance, did nothing to encourage settler migration. That migration was not prevented, however; it was only postponed. By 1844 "American" attention was strongly enough focused on the Northwest that Polk was elected to the presidency on the basis of his promise to settle the boundary problem with the English. Two years later President Polk plunged the United States into a trumped-up war with Mexico and so managed (though not as easily as he had expected) to remove the Mexican presence in California. In 1848 the US Congress established the Oregon Territory, and the Pacific Northwest Indians began to experience in earnest the problems of white encroachment they had already tasted at the hands of white traders, missionaries, and occasional settlers.

In 1850 the US Oregon Donation Land Act provided that each adult US citizen could be given 320 acres in the Oregon Territory. A man and his wife could receive 640 acres (a section) of free land, which is an area one mile square. No agreements had yet been made with the Indians when the Donation Law was made public, but the United States hurried to set that matter right. With many years' experience to draw on, it had no fears that it might not succeed in negotiating with the Indians. In 1851 Anson Dart was appointed to negotiate with the Indians of the Willamette Valley—with all too familiar results. The government wanted the Indians to give up their lands altogether; the Indians would not agree. While Congress was debating what should be done, white settlers moved onto the lands and harassed the Indians. Indians retaliated; white settlers screamed for vengeance, and Army troops were sent on "punitive expeditions." Harassed, weakened by epidemics of white diseases, and facing overwhelming military strength, band after band of Indians was forced to settle where they were told.

In 1853 the present state of Washington became a territory of the United States—again with no reference to Indian wishes. Isaac Ingalls Stevens was appointed both governor and superintendent of Indian affairs. He also was given the job of surveying for possible railroad routes. Governor Stevens met head on the task of "negotiating" the Indian claim to their lands. In hurried council after council he forced treaty after treaty with Indian bands, compelling them to accept (or at least claiming that they had accepted) whatever piece of ground he thought fit to put them on. In less than a year he had treaties by which he claimed more than one hundred thousand square miles of land. A number of chiefs later claimed that they had never signed treaties, that their signatures had been forged. Others said that they had not had the treaty honestly explained. This is very likely, since Stevens refused to allow the English of the treaties translated into the Indians' own languages, insisting instead that translation be made into Chinook, a kind of *lingua franca* made up of words from a variety of Indian languages plus some French and English, and containing only three hundred words. Chinook was merely a traders' jargon for people from different Indian nations to carry on the most basic communications required in casual trade and travel. As white settlers began to press in on the lands that Governor Stevens claimed the Indians had sold, protests flared again and again, followed as usual by "punitive expeditions" against the Indians. One Indian tried to communicate the Indians' concept of their relationship to their land—a concept which clearly was at odds with the "Americans" and which made agreement on the meanings of treaties almost impossible. Impossible certainly, as long as the "Americans" insisted there could be no other concept than theirs. This spokesman said, "My friends, I wish to show you my mind, interpret right for me. How is it I have been troubled in mind? If your mothers were here in this country who gave you birth, and suckled you, and while you were suckling some person came and took away your mother and left you alone and sold your mother, how would you feel then? This is our mother, this country, as if we drew our living from her." Probably the Indian spokesman had not heard about the "American" customs being practiced against Black mothers and their suckling children, or else he might have sought another example.

In the Pacific Northwest most Indians felt that to struggle against the white man would accomplish nothing. They did struggle again and again but not with the hope of driving the white man away. They sensed that he was there to stay. They saw the white man; they went much farther than the white man in trying to understand the conflict between the cultures—in trying to understand their own tragedy. The white man did not see himself as being involved in tragedy but rather, in a kind of triumph that was his natural right by some mysterious kind of divine favor; he felt little need to understand anything—or perhaps he was simply too busy taking.

In the document that follows, Sealth (Seattle), chief of the Duwamish, speaks to Governor Stevens at the council that produced the Treaty of Point Elliott. He attempted to reach across the gulf that separates the white people and the Indians. Chief Sealth's words now seem laden with prophecy that suggests he knew then something the white man is only now beginning to suspect: that the tragedy of the Indians was not their tragedy alone.

THE DOCUMENT:

From the *Washington Historical Quarterly*, Vol. 22, October, 1931

CHIEF SEALTH (SEATTLE): Yonder sky that has wept tears of compassion upon my people for centuries untold, and which to us appears changeless and eternal, may change. Today is fair. Tomorrow it may be overcast with clouds. My words are like the stars that never change. Whatever Seattle says the great chief at Washington can rely upon with as much certainty as he can upon the return of the sun or the seasons. The White Chief says that Big Chief at Washington sends us greetings of friendship and good will. This is kind of him for we know he has little need of our friendship in return. His people are many. They are like the grass that covers vast prairies. My people are few. They resemble the scattering trees of a storm-swept plain. The Great—and I presume—good White Chief sends us word that he wishes to buy our lands but is willing to allow us enough to live comfortably. This indeed appears just, even generous, for the Red Man no longer has rights that he need respect, and the offer may be wise also, as we are no longer in need of an extensive country. . . . I will not dwell, nor mourn over, our untimely decay, nor reproach our paleface brothers with hastening it, as we too may have been somewhat to blame.

Youth is impulsive. When our young men grow angry at some real or imaginary wrong, and disfigure their faces with black paint, it denotes that their hearts are black, and then they are often cruel and relentless, and our old men and old women are unable to restrain them. Thus it has ever been. Thus it was when the white men first began to push our forefathers further westward. But let us hope that the hostilities between us never return. We would have everything to lose and nothing to gain. Revenge by young braves is considered gain, even at the cost of their own lives, but old men who stay at home in times of war, and mothers who have sons to lose, know better.

Our good father at Washington—for I presume he is now our father as well as yours, since King George has moved his boundaries further north—our great and good father, I say, sends us word that if we do as he desires he will protect us. His brave warriors will be to us a bristling wall of strength, and his wonderful ships of war will fill our harbors so that our ancient enemies far to the north-ward—the Hidas and Timpsions, will cease to frighten our women, children and old men. Then in reality will he be our father and we his children. But can that ever be? Your God is not our God! Your God loves your people and hates mine. He folds his strong protecting arms lovingly about the pale face and leads him by the hand as a father leads his infant son—but He has forsaken His red children—if they are really His. Our God, the Great Spirit, seems also to have forsaken us. Your God makes your people wax strong every day. Soon they will fill all the land. Our people are ebbing away like a rapidly receding tide that will never return. The white man's God can not love our people or He would protect them. They seem to be orphans who can look nowhere for help. How then can we be brothers? How can your God become our God and renew our prosperity and awaken in us dreams of returning greatness. If we have a common Heavenly Father He must be partial—for He came to his paleface children. We never saw Him. He gave you laws but had no words for His red children whose teeming multitudes once filled this vast continent as stars fill the firmament. No. We are two distinct races with separate origins and separate destinies. There is little in common between us.

To us the ashes of our ancestors are sacred and their resting place is hallowed ground. You wander far from the graves of your ancestors and seemingly without regret. Your religion was written upon tables of stone by the iron finger of your God so that you could not forget. The Red Man could never comprehend nor remember it. Our religion is the traditions of our ancestors—the dreams of our old men, given them in solemn hours of night by the Great Spirit; and the visions of our sachems; and it is written in the hearts of our people.

Your dead cease to love you and the land of their nativity as soon as they pass the portals of the tomb and wander beyond the stars. They soon are forgotten and never return. Our dead never forget the beautiful world that gave them being. . . .

Day and night cannot dwell together. The Red Man has ever fled the approach of the White Man as morning mist flees before the rising sun.

However, your proposition seems fair, and I think that my people will accept it and will retire to the reservation you offer them. Then we will dwell apart in peace for the words of the Great White Chief seem to be the voice of Nature speaking to my people out of dense darkness.

It matters little where we pass the remnant of our days. They will not be many. . . .

A few more moons. A few more winters—and not one of the descendants of the mighty hosts that once moved over this broad land or lived in happy homes, protected by the Great Spirit, will remain to mourn over the graves of a people—once more powerful and hopeful than yours. But why should I mourn at the untimely fate of my people? Tribe follows tribe, and nation follows nation, like the waves of the sea. It is the order of nature, and regret is useless. Your time of decay may be distant—but it will surely come, for even the White Man whose God walked and talked with him as friend with friend, can not be exempt from the common destiny. We may be brothers after all. We will see.

We will ponder your proposition, and when we decide we will let you know. But should we accept it, I here and now make this condition—that we will not be denied the privilege without molestation of visiting at any time the tombs of our ancestors, friends and children. Every part of this soil is sacred in the estimation of my people. Every hillside, every valley, every plain and grove, has been hallowed by some sad or happy event in days long vanished ... the very dust upon which you now stand responds more lovingly to their footsteps than to yours, because it is rich with the dust of our ancestors and our bare feet are conscious of the sympathetic touch ... even the little children who lived here and rejoiced here for a brief season, still love these sombre solitudes and at eventide they grow shadowy of returning spirits. And when the last Red Man shall have perished, the memory of my tribe shall have become a myth among the white man, these shores will swarm with the invisible dead of my tribe, and when your children's children think themselves alone in the field, the store, the shop, upon the highway, or in the silence of the pathless woods, they will not be alone.... At night when the streets of your cities and villages are silent and you think them deserted, they will throng with the returning hosts that once filled them and still love this beautiful land. The White Man will never be alone.

Let him be just and deal kindly with my people, for the dead are not powerless. Dead—I say? There is no death. Only a change of worlds.

EAST IS EAST AND WEST IS WEST

1862

Big Eagle Describes a War

ABOUT THE DOCUMENT:

The "Americans" argued that Indian Removal was not only just but benevolent because it would accomplish exactly what Indian leaders such as Tecumtha had fought for—a permanent Indian frontier that would run from north to south and eternally separate the land of the white man from that of the Indian. Of course, Tecumtha and such "benevolent" white men had radically different ideas about where that line should be. When white men finally established the line and forced some ninety thousand Eastern Indians[1] to move beyond it, the Permanent Boundary ran north from the Gulf of Mexico along the eastern border of Texas, then on north along the western boundaries of Arkansas and Missouri. At the top of Missouri the line turned to the east toward the Mississippi River. But Keokuk's last treacherous cession of Sauk-Fox land after the Black Hawk War stopped the line fifty miles west of the river and turned it north again to the upper limit of that cession before it could again turn east and finally reach the Missssippi. The line then followed the Mississippi deep into Minnesota before turning east once more until it reached the shores of Lake Michigan. By 1840 this Permanent Boundary was established. With one line the white man thought he had separated white from Indian, civilized from uncivilized, and useful land from the Great American Desert (as he called it).

[1] This left only about twelve thousand Indians in small and scattered groups isolated among the sea of white settlement in the east.

It was not a desert by any means. It was the Great Plains, home of the Sioux in their three major divisions and many subdivisions; of the Cheyenne, Arapaho, Pawnee, Crow, and others; home for great herds of elk and antelope; of prairie dog colonies that covered hundreds of square miles; of buffalo herds that a man could ride through all day long and still find himself surrounded by when the sun went down. Fifteen million buffalo, at least, were on the short-grass section of the Great Plains in the early 1800s. And though the white man thought the land unfit for cultivation, in the northeast there were Indians who tended extensive fields of corn (a few years later the white man wanted to send farming instructors to teach them white "civilization"). But the "Americans" were convinced that this land was desert, so they felt willing to let the Indians have it "forever." To the south in the most arid part of the region the Five Civilized Tribes settled at the end of the Trail of Tears. North of them the "Horse Indians" lived. For a while it seemed as if finally the white man had taken all the Indian land he would want.

It is instructive to consider for a moment just what this "idyllic interlude" was really like—this brief period when the white man was "leaving the Indian alone." All along the boundary, traders and whiskey-peddlers, soldiers and ministers, worked their corruption as they had always done in the east. Smallpox, cholera, measles, and venereal diseases raged through the Indian nations in devastating epidemics; they were among the most effective of all the white man's tools of destruction against the Indians. Army troops "policed" the country, often attacking the next group of Indians they met in punishment for what they had been told the last group of Indians had done. But even this "idyll" was to be very shortlived.

The pressure of white settlement against the Indian Boundary developed much more slowly than it had in other areas, but it did increase and in time would prove to be the most destructive of the forces mobilized against the Indian peoples. But in 1842 another event occurred that produced more immediate consequences: the opening of the Oregon Trail by settlers who had heard of the lush lands and easy pickings in the Pacific Northwest. It seemed that the tide of settlers was skipping the Great Plains in favor of better spoils beyond—but the Plains had to be crossed. In 1842 only a hundred settlers followed the Oregon Trail, but the next year a thousand of them came and with them were five thousand head of cattle. Soon the Trail was a highway for thousands of settlers whose livestock consumed the grass, whose wagons rutted the plains in a mile-wide swath, whose garbage and debris befouled the countryside, and whose presence interrupted the great buffalo migrations. It was the beginning of real aggression against the Indians within their own lands, and it provoked retaliations. With the white presence also came an increase in white disease and white corruption; Sioux on the western Plains believed that cholera had been brought to them deliberately. And remembering Lord Amherst's proposal during Pontiac's War, who can dismiss the suspicion as preposterous?

In 1851 a council with the Indians was held at Traverse des Sioux on the Minnesota River. There the Santee Sioux were tricked into signing away all their lands in Minnesota, Iowa, and the Dakota Territory, keeping only a twenty-mile wide reservation along the upper Minnesota River. In return they were to get a cash annuity for fifty years. They didn't get it; immediately, traders and other white men appeared with huge claims against the Santee, and their annuity funds were signed over to repay those "debts." In the same year a council deep within the Plains country resulted in Indian agreement not to molest travelers on the Oregon Trail. The white commissioners also insisted that the various Indian nations attending the council agree on their respective land boundaries, a move that would make it possible for the white man to deal with individual nations in isolation. Treaty terms included a fifty-thousand-dollar annuity to the Indians for a period of fifty years, but when the treaty came before Congress, someone simply reduced the time-span to ten years. The amended treaty was not resubmitted to the Indian nations for their consideration.

Of all the Sioux the Santee were closest to the Permanent Boundary and so were the first to see it violated by the "Americans." During the 1850s more than 150,000 white settlers crossed the line into Santee territory, and government pressure to take away Indian lands resumed—resumed, because that pressure had a long history. In 1837 the Santee had been forced to give up all their lands east of the Mississippi; in the 1851 cession at Traverse des Sioux (already described) they lost more; and then in 1858 by simple Senate decree they were deprived of half their remaining land and left with only the portion of it that lay along the south bank of the Minnesota River. Again money was appropriated to compensate them for their loss, and again their money found its way into the pockets of white men who presented claims for vague services rendered in behalf of the Indians.

By 1862 the Santee were on the way to ruin. Factionalism had developed between prowhite and antiwhite Indians as the "Americans" did their best to encourage division, showing favoritism to those Indians who might trade their people's interests for personal gain. Centered around two trading agencies, a small Indian faction began to dress like the white man, accept stone houses built by the white man, cut their hair, and generally become "good Indians." They were resented by their people almost as much as the thieving traders were. Tensions increased as white contempt mounted and white pressures became more limiting. Finally, in 1862 the Santee Sioux struck back. It is perhaps significant that their principal war chief, Little Crow, had been with the prowhite party and had even been instrumental in arranging the land cession at Traverse des Sioux. As much as anything, Little Crow's War (as it was called) demonstrated the barriers to an Indian's maintaining a cordial relationship with the white man and keeping his own and his people's respect, too.

This point is further illustrated in the document, which is a Santee chief's account of that war. Big Eagle also was inclined to find some way to get along with the white man but found it impossible. Big Eagle's account was written down years after the war. It is remarkable that the document barely reveals that defeat had taken its toll on Big

Eagle's spirit—it *is* remarkable that so much of his spirit and his vision survived the ordeals of his life.

THE DOCUMENT:

From Minnesota Historical Society *Collections*, Vol. 6, 1894

BIG EAGLE: Of the causes that led to the outbreak of August, 1862, much has been said. Of course it was wrong, as we all know now, but there were not many Christians among the Indians then, and they did not understand things as they should. There was great dissatisfaction among the Indians over many things the whites did. The whites would not let them go to war against their enemies. This was right, but the Indians did not then know it. Then the whites were always trying to make the Indians give up their life and live like white men—go to farming, work hard and do as they did—and the Indians did not know how to do that, and did not want to anyway. It seemed too sudden to make such a change. If the Indians had tried to make the whites live like them, the whites would have resisted, and it was the same way with many Indians. The Indians wanted to live as they did before the treaty of Traverse des Sioux—go where they pleased and when they pleased: hunt game wherever they could find it, sell their furs to the traders and live as they could.

Then the Indians did not think the traders had done right. The Indians bought goods of them on credit and when the government payments came the traders were on hand with their books, which showed that the Indians owed so much and so much, and as the Indians kept no books they could not deny their accounts, but had to pay them, and sometimes the traders got all their money. I do not say that the traders always cheated and lied about these accounts. I know many of them were honest men and kind and accommodating, but since I have been a citizen I kow that many white men, when they go to pay their accounts, often think them too large and refuse to pay them, and they go to law about them and there is

much bad feeling. The Indians could not go to law, but
there was always trouble over their credits. Under the
treaty of Traverse des Sioux the Indians had to pay a very
large sum of money to the traders for old debts, some of
which ran back fifteen years, and many of those who had
got the goods were dead and others were not present, and
the traders' books had to be received as to the amounts,
and the money was taken from the tribe to pay them. Of
course the traders often were of great service to the Indians in letting them have goods on credit, but the Indians
seemed to think the traders ought not to be too hard on
them about the payments, but do as the Indians did
among one another, and put off the payment until they
were better able to make it.

Then many of the white men often abused the Indians
and treated them unkindly. Perhaps they had excuse, but
the Indians did not think so. Many of the whites always
seemed to say by their manner when they saw an Indian,
'I am much better than you,' and the Indians did not like
this. There was excuse for this, but the Dakotas did not
believe there were better men in the world than they.
Then some of the white men abused the Indian women in
a certain way and disgraced them, and surely there was no
excuse for that.

All these things made many Indians dislike the whites.
Then a little while before the outbreak there was trouble
among the Indians themselves. Some of the Indians took a
sensible course and began to live like white men. The
government built them houses, furnished them tools, seed,
etc., and taught them to farm. At the two agencies, Yellow
Medicine and Redwood, there were several hundred acres
of land in cultivation that summer. Others staid in their
tepees. There was a white man's party and an Indian
party. We had politics among us and there was much
feeling. A new chief speaker for the tribe was to be
elected. There were three candidates—Little Crow, myself
and Wa-sui-hi-ya-ye-dan ("Traveling Hail"). After an ex-
citing contest Traveling Hail was elected. Little Crow felt
sore over his defeat. Many of our tribe believed him
responsible for the sale of the north ten-mile strip, and I

think this was why he was defeated. I did not care much about it. Many whites think that Little Crow was the principal chief of the Dakotas at this time, but he was not. Wabasha was the principal chief, and he was of the white man's party; so was I; so was old Shakopee, whose band was very large. Many think if old Shakopee had lived there would have been no war, for he was for the white men and had great influence. But he died that summer, and was succeeded by his son, whose real name was Ea-to-ka ("Another Language"), but when he became chief he took his father's name, and was afterwards called 'Little Shakopee,' or 'Little Six,' for in the Sioux language 'Shakopee' means six. This Shakopee was against the white men. He took part in the outbreak, murdering women and children, but I never saw him in a battle, and he was caught in Manitoba and hanged in 1864. My brother, Medicine Bottle, was hanged with him.

As the summer advanced, there was great trouble among the Sioux—troubles among themselves, troubles with the whites, and one thing and another. The war with the South was going on then, and a great many men had left the state and gone down there to fight. A few weeks before the outbreak the president called for many more men, and a great many of the white men of Minnesota and some half-breeds enlisted and went to Fort Snelling to be sent South. We understood that the South was getting the best of the fight, and it was said that the North would be whipped. The year before the new president had turned out Maj. Brown and Maj. Cullen, the Indian agents, and put in their places Maj. Galbraith and Mr. Clark Thompson, and they had turned out the men under them and put in others of their own party. There were a great many changes. An Indian named Shonka-sha ("White Dog"), who had been hired to teach the Indians to farm, was removed and another Indian named Ta-opi ("The Wounded Man"), a son of old Betsy, of St. Paul, put in his place. Nearly all of the men who were turned out were dissatisfied, and the most of the Indians did not like the new men. At last Maj. Galbraith went to work about the agencies and recruited a company of soldiers to go South.

His men were nearly all half-breeds. This was the company called the Renville Rangers, for they were mostly from Renville county. The Indians now thought the whites must be pretty hard up for men to fight the South, or they would not come so far out on the frontier and take half-breeds or anything to help them.

It began to be whispered about that now would be a good time to go to war with the whites and get back the lands. It was believed that the men who had enlisted last had all left the state and that before help could be sent the Indians could clean out the country, and that the Winnebagoes, and even the Chippewas, would assist the Sioux. It was also thought that a war with the whites would cause the Sioux to forget the troubles among themselves and enable many of them to pay off some old scores. Though I took part in the war, I was against it. I knew there was no good cause for it, and I had been to Washington and knew the power of the whites and that they would finally conquer us. We might succeed for a time, but we would be overpowered and defeated at last. I said all this and many more things to my people, but many of my own bands were against me, and some of the other chiefs put words in their mouths to say to me. When the outbreak came Little Crow told some of my band that if I refused to lead them to shoot me as a traitor who would not stand up for his nation, and then select another leader in my place.

But after the first talk of war the counsels of the peace Indians prevailed, and many of us thought the danger had all blown over. The time of the government payment was near at hand, and this may have had something to do with it. There was another thing that helped to stop the war talk. The crops that had been put in by the "farmer" Indians were looking well, and there seemed to be a good prospect for a plentiful supply of provisions for them the coming winter without having to depend on the game of the country or without going far out to the west on the plains for buffalo. It seemed as if the white men's way was certainly the best. Many of the Indians had been short of provisions that summer and had exhausted their credits and were in bad condition. "Now," said the farmer Indians, "if you had worked last season you would not be starving now and begging for food." The "farmers" were favored by the government in every way. They had houses built for them, some of them even had brick houses, and they were not allowed to suffer. The other Indians did not like this. They were envious of them and jealous, and disliked them because they had gone back on the customs of the tribe and because they were favored. They called them "farmers," as if it was disgraceful to be a farmer. They called them "cut-hairs," because they had given up the Indian fashion of wearing the hair, and "breeches men," because they wore pantaloons, and "Dutchmen," because so many of the settlers on the north side of the river and elsewhere in the country were Germans. I have heard that there was a secret organization of the Indians called the "Soldiers' Lodge," whose object was to declare war against the whites, but I knew nothing of it.

At last the time for the payment came and the Indians came in to the agencies to get their money. But the paymaster did not come, and week after week went by and still he did not come. The payment was to be in gold. Somebody told the Indians that the payment would never be made. The government was in a great war, and gold was scarce, and paper money had taken its place, and it was said the gold could not be had to pay us. Then the trouble began again and the war talk started up. Many of the Indians who had gathered about the agencies were out of provisions and were easily made angry. Still, most of us thought the trouble would pass, and we said nothing about it. I thought there might be trouble, but I had no idea there would be such a war. Little Crow and other chiefs did not think so. But it seems some of the tribe were getting ready for it.

You know how the war started—by the killing of some white people near Acton, in Meeker county. I will tell you how this was done, as it was told me by all of the four young men who did the killing. These young fellows all belonged to Shakopee's band. Their names were Sungigidan ("Brown Wing"), Ka-om-de-i-ye-ye-dan ("Breaking Up"), Nagi-wi-cak-te ("Killing Ghost"), and Pa-zo-i-yo-pa

("Runs against Something when Crawling"). I do not
think their names have ever before been printed. One of
them is yet living. They told me they did not go out to kill
white people. They said they went over into the Big
Woods to hunt; that on Sunday, Aug. 17, they came to a
settler's fence, and here they found a hen's nest with some
eggs in it. One of them took the eggs, when another said:
"Don't take them, for they belong to a white man and we
may get into trouble." The other was angry, for he was
very hungry and wanted to eat the eggs, and he dashed
them to the ground and replied: "You are a coward. You
are afraid of the white man. You are afraid to take even
an egg from him, though you are half-starved. Yes, you
are a coward, and I will tell everybody so." The other
replied: "I am not a coward. I am not afraid of the white
man, and to show you that I am not I will go to the house
and shoot him. Are you brave enough to go with me?"
The one who had called him a coward said: "Yes, I will go
with you, and we will see who is the braver of us two."
Their two companions then said: "We will go with you,
and we will be brave, too." They all went to the house of
the white man (Mr. Robinson Jones), but he got alarmed
and went to another house (that of his son-in-law, Howard
Baker), where were some other white men and women.
The four Indians followed them and killed three men and
two women (Jones, Baker, a Mr. Webster, Mrs. Jones and
a girl of fourteen). Then they hitched up a team belonging
to another settler and drove to Shakopee's camp six miles
above Redwood agency), which they reached late that
night and told what they had done, as I have related.

The tale told by the young men created the greatest
excitement. Everybody was waked up and heard it.
Shakopee took the young men to Little Crow's house (two
miles above the agency), and he sat up in bed and listened
to their story. He said war was now declared. Blood had
been shed, the payment would be stopped, and the whites
would take a dreadful vengeance because women had
been killed. Wabasha, Wacouta, myself and others still
talked for peace, but nobody would listen to us, and soon
the cry was "Kill the whites and kill all these cut-hairs

who will not join us." A council was held and war was declared. Parties formed and dashed away in the darkness to kill settlers. The women began to run bullets and the men to clean their guns. Little Crow gave orders to attack the agency early next morning and to kill all the traders. When the Indians first came to him for counsel and advice he said to them, tauntingly: "Why do you come to me for advice? Go to the man you elected speaker (Traveling Hail) and let him tell you what to do"; but he soon came around all right and somehow took the lead in everything, though he was not head chief, as I have said.

At this time my village was up on Crow creek, near Little Crow's. I did not have a very large band—not more than thirty or forty fighting men. Most of them were not for the war at first, but nearly all got into it at last. A great many members of the other bands were like my men; they took no part in the first movements, but afterward did. The next morning, when the force started down to attack the agency, I went along. I did not lead my band, and I took no part in the killing. I went to save the lives of two particular friends if I could. I think others went for the same reason, for nearly every Indian had a friend that he did not want killed; of course he did not care about anybody's else friend. The killing was nearly all done when I got there. Little Crow was on the ground directing operations. The day before, he had attended church there and listened closely to the sermon and had shaken hands with everybody. So many Indians have lied about their saving the lives of white people that I dislike to speak of what I did. But I did save the life of George H. Spencer at the time of the massacre. I know that his friend, Chaska, has always had the credit of that, but Spencer would have been a dead man in spite of Chaska if it had not been for me. I asked Spencer about this once, but he said he was wounded at the time and so excited that he could not remember what I did. Once after that I kept a half-breed family from being murdered; these are all the people whose lives I claim to have saved. I was never present when the white people were willfully murdered. I saw all the dead bodies at the agency. Mr.

Andrew Myrick, a trader, with an Indian wife, had refused some hungry Indians credit a short time before when they asked him for some provisions. He said to them: "Go and eat grass." Now he was lying on the ground dead, with his mouth stuffed full of grass, and the Indians were saying tauntingly: "Myrick is eating grass himself."

When I returned to my village that day I found that many of my band had changed their minds about the war, and wanted to go into it. All the other villages were the same way. I was still of the belief that it was not best, but I thought I must go with my band and my nation, and I said to my men that I would lead them into the war, and we would all act like brave Dakotas and do the best we could. All my men were with me; none had gone off on raids, but we did not have guns for all at first.

That afternoon word came to my village that soldiers were coming to the agency from Fort Snelling. (These were Capt. Marsh and his men.) At once I mounted the best horse I had, and, with some of my men, rode as fast as I could to meet them at the ferry. But when I got there the fight was over, and I well remember that a cloud of powder smoke was rising slowly from the low, wet ground where the firing had been. I heard a few scattering shots down the river, where the Indians were still pursuing the soldiers, but I took no part. I crossed the river and saw the bodies of the soldiers that had been killed. I think Mr. Quinn, the interpreter, was shot several times after he had been killed. The Indians told me that the most of them who fired on Capt. Marsh and his men were on the same side of the river; that only a few shots came from the opposite or south side. They said that White Dog did not tell Mr. Quinn to come over, but told him to go back. Of course I do not know what the truth is about this. White Dog was the Indian head farmer who had been replaced by Taopi and who was hanged at Mankato.

I was not in the first fight at New Ulm nor the first attack on Fort Ridgely. Here let me say that the Indian names of these and other places in Minnesota are different from the English names. St. Paul is the 'White Rock;' Minneapolis is 'the Place Where the Water Falls;' New Ulm is 'the Place Where There Is a Cottonwood Grove on the River;' Fort Ridgely was 'the Soldiers' House;' Birch Coulie was called 'Birch Creek,' etc. I was in the second fight at New Ulm and in the second attack on Fort Ridgely. At New Ulm I had but a few of my band with me. We lost none of them. We had but few, if any, of the Indians killed; at least I did not hear of but a few. A half-breed named George Le Blanc, who was with us, was killed. There was no one in chief command of the Indians at New Ulm. A few sub-chiefs, like myself, and the head soldiers led them, and the leaders agreed among themselves what was to be done. I do not think there was a chief present at the first fight. I think that attack was made by marauding Indians from several bands, every man for himself, but when we heard they were fighting we went down to help them. I think it probable that the first attack on Fort Ridgely was made in the same way; at any rate, I do not remember that there was a chief there.

The second fight at Fort Ridgely was made a grand affair. Little Crow was with us. Mr. Good Thunder, now at Birch Coulie agency, was with us. He counted the Indians as they filed past him on the march to the attack, and reported that there were 800 of us. He acted very bravely in the fight, and distinguished himself by running close up to the fort and bringing away a horse. He is now married to the former widow of White Dog, and both he and his wife are good Christian citizens. We went down determined to take the fort, for we knew it was of the greatest importance to us to have it. If we could take it we would soon have the whole Minnesota valley. But we failed, and of course it was best that we did fail.

Though Little Crow was present, he did not take a very active part in the fight. As I remember, the chief leaders in the fight were "The Thief," who was the head soldier of Mankato's band, and Mankato ("Blue Earth") himself. This Mankato was not the old chief for whom the town was named, but a sub-chief, the son of old Good Road. He was a very brave man and a good leader. He was killed at the battle of Wood lake by a cannon ball. We went down to the attack on both sides of the river. I went down on the south side with my men, and we crossed the river in front of the fort and went up through the timber and fought on that side next the river. The fight commenced about noon on Friday after the outbreak. We had a few Sissetons and Wakpatons with us, and some Winnebagoes, under the "Little Priest," were in this fight and at New Ulm. I saw them myself. But for the cannon I think we would have taken the fort. The soldiers fought us so bravely we thought there were more of them than there were. The cannons disturbed us greatly, but did not hurt many. We did not have many Indians killed. I think the whites put the number too large, and I think they overestimated the number killed in every battle. We seldom carried off our dead. We usually buried them in a secluded place on the battle-field when we could. We always tried to carry away the wounded. When we retreated from Ridgely I recrossed the river opposite the fort and went up on the south side. All our army but the scouts fell back up the river to our villages near Redwood agency, and then on up to the Yellow Medicine and the mouth of the Chippewa.

Our scouts brought word that our old friend Wapetonhonska ('The Long Trader'), as we called Gen. Sibley, was coming up against us, and in a few days we learned that he had come to Fort Ridgely with a large number of soldiers. Little Crow, with a strong party, went over into the Big Woods, towards Forest City and Hutchinson. After he had gone, I and the other sub-chiefs concluded to go down and attack New Ulm again and take the town and cross the river to the east, or in the rear of Fort Ridgely, where Sibley was, and then our movements were to be governed by circumstances. We had left our village near the Redwood in some haste and alarm, expecting to be followed after the defeat at Ridgely, and had not taken all our property away. So we took many of our women with us to gather up the property and some other things, and we brought along some wagons to haul them off.

We came down the main road on the south side of the river, and were several hundred strong. We left our camps in the morning and got to our old villages in the afternoon. When the men in advance reached Little Crow's village—which was on the high bluff on the south side of the Minnesota, below the mouth of the Redwood—they looked to the north across the valley, and up on the high bluff on the north side, and out on the prairie some miles away, they saw a column of mounted men and some wagons coming out of the Beaver creek timber on the prairie and going eastward. We also saw signs in Little Crow's village that white men had been there only a few hours before, and judging from the trail they had made when they left, these were the men we now saw to the northward. There was, of course, a little excitement, and the column halted. Four or five of our best scouts were sent across the valley to follow the movements of the soldiers, creeping across the prairie like so many ants. It was near sundown, and we knew they would soon go into camp, and we thought the camping ground would be somewhere on the Birch Coulie, where there was wood and water. The women went to work to load the wagons. The scouts followed the soldiers carefully, and a little after sundown returned with the information that they had gone into camp near the head of Birch Coulie. At this time we did not know there were two companies there. We thought the company of mounted men (Capt. Anderson's) was all, and that there were not more than seventy-five men.

It was concluded to surround the camp that night and attack it at daylight. We felt sure we could capture it, and that 200 men would be enough for the undertaking. So about that number was selected. There were four bands— my own, Hu-sha-sha's ("Red Legs"), Gray Bird's and Mankato's. I had about thirty men. Nearly all the Indians had double-barreled shotguns, and we loaded them with buckshot and large bullets called "traders' balls." After dark we started, crossed the river and valley, went up the bluffs and on the prairie, and soon we saw the white tents and the wagons of the camp. We had no difficulty in surrounding the camp. The pickets were only a little way from it. I led my men up from the west through the grass and took up a position 200 yards from the camp, behind a small knoll or elevation. Red Legs took his men into the coulie east of the camp. Mankato ("Blue Earth") had some of his men in the coulie and some on the prairie. Gray Bird and his men were mostly on the prairie.

Just at dawn the fight began. It continued all day and the following night until late the next morning. Both sides fought well. Owing to the white men's way of fighting they lost many men. Owing to the Indians' way of fighting they lost but few. The white men stood up and exposed themselves at first, but at last they learned to keep quiet. The Indians always took care of themselves. We had an easy time of it. We could crawl through the grass and into the coulie and get water when we wanted it, and after a few hours our women crossed the river and came up near the bluff and cooked for us, and we could go back and eat and then return to the fight. We did not lose many men. Indeed, I only saw two dead Indians, and I never heard that any more were killed. The two I saw were in the coulie and belonged to Red Legs' band. One was a Wakpaton named Ho-ton-na ("Animal's Voice") and the other was a Sisseton. Their bodies were taken down the coulie and buried during the fight. I did not see a man killed on the prairie. We had several men wounded, but none very badly. I did not see the incident which is related of an Indian, a brother of Little Crow, who, it is said, rode up on a white horse near the camp with a white flag and held a parley and had his horse killed as he rode away. That must have happened while I was absent from the field eating my dinner. Little Crow had no brother there. The White Spider was not there. I think Little Crow's brothers were with him in the Big Woods at this time. The only Indian horse I saw killed that I remember was a bay. Buffalo Ghost succeeded in capturing a horse from the camp. Late in the day some of the men who had been left in the villages came over on their horses to see what the trouble was that the camp had not been taken, and they rode about the prairie for a time, but I don't think many of them got into the fight. I do not remember that we got many re-enforcements that day. If we got any, they must have come up the coulie and I did not see them. Perhaps some horsemen came up on the east side of the coulie, but I knew nothing about it. I am sure no re-enforcements came to me. I did not need any. Our circle about the camp was rather small and we could only use a certain number of men.

About the middle of the afternoon our men became much dissatisfied at the slowness of the fight, and the stubbornness of the whites, and the word was passed around the lines to get ready to charge the camp. The brave Mankato wanted to charge after the first hour. There were some half-breeds with the whites who could speak Sioux well, and they heard us arranging to assault them. Jack Frazer told me afterward that he heard us talking about it very plainly. Alex Faribault was there and heard the talk and called out to us: "You do very wrong to fire on us. We did not come out to fight; we only came out to bury the bodies of the white people you killed." I have heard that Faribault, Frazer and another half-breed dug a rifle pit for themselves with bayonets, and that Faribault worked so hard with his bayonet in digging that he wore the flesh from the inside of his hand. One half-breed named Louis Bourier attempted to desert to us, but as he was running towards us some of our men shot and killed him. We could have taken the camp, I think. During the fight the whites had thrown up breastworks, but they were not very high and we could easily have jumped over them. We did not know that Maj. Joe Brown was there; if we had, I think some of our men would have charged anyhow, for they wanted him out of the way. Some years ago I saw Capt. Grant in St. Paul and he told me he was in command of the camp at Birch Coulie.

Just as we were about to charge word came that a large number of mounted soldiers were coming up from the east toward Fort Ridgely. This stopped the charge and created some excitement. Mankato at once took some men from the coulie and went out to meet them. He told me he did not take more than fifty, but he scattered them out and they all yelled and made such a noise that the whites must have thought there were a great many more, and they stopped on the prairie and began fighting. They had a

cannon and used it, but it did no harm. If the Indians had
any men killed in the fight I never heard of it. Mankato
flourished his men around so, and all the Indians in the
coulie kept up a noise, and at last the whites began to fall
back, and they retreated about two miles and began to dig
breastworks. Mankato followed them and left about thirty
men to watch them, and returned to the fight at the coulie
with the rest. The Indians were laughing when they came
back at the way they had deceived the white men, and we
were all glad that the whites had not pushed forward and
driven us away. If any more Indians went against this
force than the fifty or possibly seventy-five that I have
told you of I never heard of it. I was not with them and
cannot say positively, but I do not think there were. I
went out to near the fortified camp during the night, and
there was no large force of Indians over there, and I know
there were not more than thirty of our men watching the
camp. When the men of this force began to fall back, the
whites in the camp hallooed and made a great commo-
tion, as if they were begging them to return and relieve
them, and seemed much distressed that they did not.

The next morning Gen. Sibley came with a very large
force and drove us away from the field. We took our time
about getting away. Some of our men said they remained
till Sibley got up and that they fired at some of his men as
they were shaking hands with some of the men of the
camp. Those of us who were on the prairie went back to
the westward and on down the valley. Those in the coulie
went down back southward to where their horses were,
and then mounted and rode westward across the prairie
about a mile south of the battle-field. There was no pursuit. The whites fired their cannons at us as we were
leaving the field, but they might as well have beaten a big
drum for all the harm they did. They only made a noise.
We went back across the river to our camps in the old
villages, and then on up the river to the Yellow Medicine
and the mouth of the Chippewa, where Little Crow joined
us.

For some time after the fight at Birch Coulie the greater
part of the Indians remained in the camps about the

Yellow Medicine and the mouth of the Chippewa. At last
the word came that Sibley with his army was again on the
move against us. Our scouts were very active and vigilant,
and we heard from him nearly every hour. He had left a
letter for Little Crow in a split stick on the battle-field of
Birch Coulie, and some of our men found it and brought
it in, and correspondence had been going on between us
ever since. Tom Robinson and Joe Campbell, half-breed
prisoners, wrote the letters for Little Crow. It seems that
some letters were written to Gen. Sibley by the half-breeds
which Little Crow never saw. I and others understood
from the half-breeds that Gen. Sibley would treat with all
of us who had only been soldiers and would surrender as
prisoners of war, and that only those who had murdered
people in cold blood, the settlers and others, would be
punished in any way. There was great dissatisfaction
among us at our condition. Many wanted to surrender;
others left us for the West. But Sibley came on and on,
and at last came the battle of Wood lake.

When we learned that Sibley had gone into camp at the
Wood lake, a council of the sub-chiefs and others was
held and it was determined to give him a battle near there.
I think the lake now called Battle lake was the old-time
Wood lake. As I understand it, there once were some
cottonwoods about it, and the Indians called it "M'da-
chan"—Wood lake. The larger lake, two miles west, now
called Wood lake, was always known to me by the Indian
name of "Hinta hauk-pay-an wo-ju," meaning literally,
"the Planting Place of the Man who ties his Moccasins
with Basswood Bark." We soon learned that Sibley had
thrown up breastworks and it was not deemed safe to
attack him at the lake. We concluded that the fight should
be about a mile or more to the northwest of the lake, on
the road along which the troops would march. This was
the road leading to the upper country, and of course
Sibley would travel it. At the point determined on we
planned to hide a large number of men on the side of the
road. Near the lake, in a ravine formed by the outlet, we
were to place another strong body. Behind a hill to the
west were to be some more men. We thought that when

Sibley marched out along the road and when the head of
his column had reached the farther end of the line of our
first division, our men would open fire. The men in the
ravine would then be in the rear of the whites and would
begin firing on that end of the column. The men from
behind the hill would rush out and attack the flank, and
then we had horsemen far out on the right and left who
would come up. We expected to throw the whole white
force into confusion by the sudden and unexpected attack
and defeat them before they could rally.

I think this was a good plan of battle. Our concealed
men would not have been discovered. The grass was tall
and the place by the road and the ravine were good hiding
places. We had learned that Sibley was not particular
about sending out scouts and examining the country before he passed it. He had a number of mounted men, but
they always rode together, at the head of the column,
when on a march, and did not examine the ground at the
sides of the road. The night he lay at Wood lake his
pickets were only a short distance from camp—less than
half a mile. When we were putting our men into position
that night we often saw them plainly. I worked hard that
night fixing the men. Little Crow was on the field, too.
Mankato was there. Indeed, all our fighting chiefs were
present and all our best fighting Indians. We felt that this
would be the deciding fight of the war. The whites were
unconscious. We could hear them laughing and singing.
When all our preparations were made Little Crow and I
and some other chiefs went to the mound or hill to the
west so as to watch the fight better when it should commence. There were numbers of other Indians there.

The morning came and an accident spoiled all our
plans. For some reason Sibley did not move early as we
expected he would. Our men were lying hidden waiting
patiently. Some were very near the camp lines in the
ravine, but the whites did not see a man of all our men. I
do not think they would have discovered our ambuscade.
It seemed a considerable time after sun-up when some
four or five wagons with a number of soldiers started out
from the camp in the direction of the old Yellow Medicine

agency. We learned afterwards that they were going without orders to dig potatoes over at the agency, five miles away. They came on over the prairie, right where part of our line was. Some of the wagons were not in the road, and if they had kept straight on would have driven right over our men as they lay in the grass. At last they came so close that our men had to rise up and fire. This brought on the fight, of course, but not according to the way we had planned it. Little Crow saw it and felt very badly.

Of course you know how the battle was fought. The Indians that were in the fight did well, but hundreds of our men did not get into it and did not fire a shot. They were out too far. The men in the ravine and the line connecting them with those on the road did the most of the fighting. Those of us on the hill did our best, but we were soon driven off. Mankato was killed here, and we lost a very good and brave war chief. He was killed by a cannon ball that was so nearly spent that he was not afraid of it, and it struck him in the back, as he lay on the ground, and killed him. The whites drove our men out of the ravine by a charge and that ended the battle. We retreated in some disorder, though the whites did not offer to pursue us. We crossed a wide prairie, but their horsemen did not follow us. We lost fourteen or fifteen men killed and quite a number wounded. Some of the wounded died afterwards, but I do not know how many. We carried off no dead bodies, but took away all our wounded. The whites scalped all our dead men—so I have heard.

Soon after the battle I, with many others who had taken part in the war, surrendered to Gen. Sibley. Robinson and the other half-breeds assured us that if we would do this we would only be held as prisoners of war a short time, but as soon as I surrendered I was thrown into prison. Afterward I was tried and served three years in the prison at Davenport and the penitentiary at Rock Island for taking part in the war. On my trial a great number of the white prisoners, women and others, were called up, but not one of them could testify that I had murdered any one or had done anything to deserve death, or else I would have been hanged. If I had known that I would be sent to the penitentiary I would not have surrendered, but when I had been in the penitentiary three years and they were about to turn me out, I told them they might keep me another year if they wished, and I meant what I said. I did not like the way I had been treated. I surrendered in good faith, knowing that many of the whites were acquainted with me and that I had not been a murderer, or present when a murder had been committed, and if I had killed or wounded a man it had been in fair, open fight. But all feeling on my part about this has long since passed away. For years I have been a Christian and I hope to die one. My white neighbors and friends know my character as a citizen and a man. I am at peace with every one, whites and Indians. I am getting to be an old man, but I am still able to work. I am poor, but I manage to get along. This is my second wife, and this little girl is our adopted daughter. I will come and see you when I come to St. Paul. Good-bye.

POSTSCRIPT TO THE DOCUMENT:

The split between prowhite and antiwhite factions among the Santee that is revealed in Big Eagle's account had further consequences. First of all it was the prowhite Wabasha (whom Big Eagle names as the most important civil chief) who negotiated with General Sibley and encouraged the Santee surrender. Little Crow and his followers would not surrender; instead, they escaped to Canada, where Little Crow reminded the British of the Indian aid they had received in the War of 1812. Now, he said, was the time for the British to help the Sioux. The British issued a ration of food, but would not even provide the Sioux with ammunition for their hunting rifles. Little Crow decided to return to Minnesota with a raiding party to steal horses, leaving most of his followers camped at Devil's Lake in present-day North Dakota. While in Minnesota Little Crow and his sixteen-year-old son went to pick berries one day; they were surprised by two white hunters who immediately gunned Little Crow down, though his son managed to escape. Minnesota was paying

a scalpbounty of twenty-five dollars then, but when the
authorities found whose scalp they had, the two hunters
received an added five hundred dollars. Little Crow's
scalp—as well as his skull—was preserved and exhibited
in St. Paul.

As for the Santee in Minnesota: following the war, more
than three hundred were sentenced to hang. Of these,
however, President Lincoln commuted the sentence for all
but thirty-eight, who were hanged on one scaffold. Nine
years later officials admitted that two of the men hanged
had not been on Lincoln's list.

As was usual in such cases, the US claimed that the
Indians' aggression absolved the US of all treaty obligations. The Santee Nation was removed to a reservation
on the Missouri River—a place so barren and the water so
bad that nearly a third died during the first winter, while
their remaining lands along the Minnesota were seized by
white men who didn't even pretend they should pay for
them.

"THE WORLD WAS NOT ALWAYS THIS WAY"

1858–1871

Geronimo Speaks

Cochise Speaks

ABOUT THE DOCUMENTS:

The rebellion of the Santee Sioux in 1862 took place
near the northern limit of the Indian Territory. In the
same year in the south a different war between white
man and Indian broke out far to the west of the Perma-

nent Boundary. As with the Little Crow War the one in the south was preceded by a long history of white abuse and Indian retaliation. It became a ten year war to exterminate Apache bands in Arizona and New Mexico; before it was over it would cost the "Americans" a thousand lives, more than forty million dollars, and result in total failure of its objectives. Not only were the Apache not eliminated, not a single band was subjugated.

The Apache had learned to deal with attempts at their extermination and in the process earned a place among the world's masters of guerrilla warfare. Certainly, they were the most successful guerrilla fighters within the present-day United States.

First they lived for two centuries on the frontier of Spanish conquest, successfully defying the aggression of soldiers who had brought down the mightiest civilizations that America had known. Then the newly independent Mexican government sent its soldiers against them, as well as its settlers, and in raid and counterraid, theft and countertheft, the Apache more than held their own. The Mexicans raided the Apache for slaves, and the government paid as much as $250 for an Apache scalp. The Apache raided the Mexicans for horses and cattle and children and made scalp-bounty hunters work for their money. Sometimes the scalp hunters were "Americans," even before the US took the Southwest away from Mexico. One example of "American" ingenuity and resourcefulness in turning a profit took place in 1840, when a band of seventeen white trappers led by a man named Johnson went to trap beaver in the mountain headwaters of the Gila River. This was Apache country, but the Apache had not yet learned to hate "Americans" the way they hated Spaniards and Mexicans, and they made the trappers welcome. After some time spent at their trapping, the white men went into Sonora to drink. The governor of Sonora acquainted them with the going rate for Apache scalps—one ounce of gold per scalp at that time. When Johnson and his men returned to the Apache mountains this time, they took a mountain howitzer with them. In camp they and the neighboring Apaches celebrated with roast bear and venison. With the Indians, including women and children, gathered comfortably around the campfire, Johnson and his men suddenly opened fire with rifles, pistols, and the howitzer which had been charged with bullets. The improvised shrapnel was most effective; only a very few Apache escaped to tell the tale. In retaliation Apache warriors sought out the camp of another white trapper group—this one made up of about thirty men—and killed almost every one in a surprise attack.

The war between the United States and Mexico gave the US possession of the Southwest, which resulted in more white settlers, trappers, and miners invading Apache lands. It became the US Army's turn to try to "discipline" the Apache. The Apache were no more willing to be disciplined by "American" soldiers than by Mexican or Spanish. In proving that, they made some of their names well known to "Americans" and created a symbol of resistance for all time. Geronimo, Cochise, Nana, Victorio—these are a few of the Apache chiefs who made fools of years-long efforts to wipe them out in a war that allowed any means. The kind of truce violations that had roused some protest when practiced against the Seminoles (though not enough protest to prevent them) went unrebuked when practiced against the Apache. Nor were the US officials' efforts limited to Apaches proper: led by the famous Kit Carson, "American" soldiers trapped the Apache cousins, the Navajo, in their Canyon de Chelley stronghold in 1863. There the Navajo had peach orchards of some five thousand trees, gardens, herds, and houses. All this was utterly destroyed, and the Navajo removed. In a white-arranged truce talk in 1863 under a white flag Mangas Coloradas, chief of Geronimo's band of the Bedonkohe Apache, was killed. Mangas Coloradas had hated the white man since the day that trappers bound him and whipped his back raw for sport; his death by treachery did little to make Geronimo challenge his chief's attitude.

It was a similar incident of white treachery that had much to do with precipitating the war that began in 1862. In February, 1861, a company of white soldiers came into Chiricahua Apache country to recover some cattle and a mixed-blood boy supposedly stolen from a white rancher. Word was sent to the Chiricahua chief, Cochise, to come to the stage coach station at Apache Pass for a parley. Suspecting nothing (the stage route through Chiricahua country had been agreed upon amicably by Cochise and the US Army), Cochise went to the meeting with five members of his family, including a woman and a child. At the station Cochise and his party were immediately surrounded by armed soldiers. Cochise denied that the Chiricahua had either the cattle or the boy, though he thought he knew who did have them and offered to see if he could arrange a ransom. The white officer refused to believe him and demanded the return of boy and cattle. Cochise refused to take the accusation seriously, whereupon the officer ordered his arrest. The soldiers moved into the tent where the talk was being held; Cochise ripped the tent with his knife and escaped from the stage station under a volley of rifle fire that wounded him three times. But the white soldiers still held his relatives prisoner. Chochise knew the white man well enough by then to know that it was better to bargain than to reason, so he captured three white men and offered them in exchange for his family. If the white officer had not been so blindly convinced that Indians always lied, the exchange might have been possible. But the officer would agree to no deal until the cattle and the boy were returned. Cochise did not have either the cattle or the boy to return, so instead he laid siege to the station. Finally, after repeated offers to exchange prisoners, Cochise executed the three white men he held, and the white officer retaliated by hanging three of Cochise's relatives. Raid and counterraid followed, and by 1862 General Carleton was in the territory with thousands of US soldiers, bent on the extermination of the Apache.

The first of the documents that follow is taken from the autobiography of Geronimo, dictated in 1906. It deals with the period of the Apache wars until 1871, when the "Americans" gave up their extermination campaign and decided instead to pacify them. The Apache were tired of war and hoped peace would be possible; when the US government offered them peace and quiet on reservations suitable to the Apache, agreements were reached. The second document is a speech made by Cochise in 1871 at the time of his pledge to remain at peace.

DOCUMENT A:

From Geronimo's autobiography, Geronimo's Story of His Life, edited by S. M. Barrett, New York, 1906

About the time of the massacre of "Kaskiyeh" (1858) we heard that some white men were measuring land to the south of us. In company with a number of other warriors I went to visit them. We could not understand them very well, for we had no interpreter, but we made a treaty with them by shaking hands and promising to be brothers. Then we made our camp near their camp, and they came to trade with us. We gave them buckskin, blankets, and ponies in exchange for shirts and provisions. We also brought them game, for which they gave us some money. We did not know the value of this money, but we kept it and later learned from the Navajo Indians that it was very valuable.

Every day they measured land with curious instruments and put down marks which we could not understand. They were good men, and we were sorry when they had gone on into the west. They were not soldiers. These were the first white men I ever saw.

About ten years later some more white men came. These were all warriors. They made their camp on the Gila River south of Hot Springs. At first they were friendly and we did not dislike them, but they were not as good as those who came first.

After about a year some trouble arose between them and the Indians, and I took the warpath as a warrior, not as a chief.[1] I had not been wronged, but some of my people had been, and I fought with my tribe; for the soldiers and not the Indians were at fault.

---

[1] As a tribe they would fight under their tribal chief, Mangus-Colorado. If several tribes had been called out, the war chief, Geronimo, would have commanded.

Not long after this some of the officers of the United States troops invited our leaders to hold a conference at Apache Pass (Fort Bowie). Just before noon the Indians were shown into a tent and told that they would be given something to eat. When in the tent they were[2] attacked by soldiers. Our chief, Mangus-Colorado, and several other warriors, by cutting through the tent, escaped; but most of the warriors were killed or captured. Among the Bedonkohe Apaches killed at this time were Sanza, Kladetahe, Niyokahe, and Gopi. After this treachery the Indians went back to the mountains and left the fort entirely alone. I do not think that the agent had anything to do with planning this, for he had always treated us well. I believe it was entirely planned by the soldiers.

From the very first the soldiers sent out to our western country, and the officers in charge of them, did not hesitate to wrong the Indians. They never explained to the Government when an Indian was wronged, but always reported the misdeeds of the Indians. Much that was done by mean white men was reported at Washington as the deeds of my people.

The Indians always tried to live peaceably with the white soldiers and settlers. One day during the time that the soldiers were stationed at Apache Pass I made a treaty with the post. This was done by shaking hands and promising to be brothers. Cochise and Mangus-Colorado did likewise. I do not know the name of the officer in command, but this was the first regiment that ever came to Apache Pass. This treaty was made about a year before we were attacked in a tent, as above related. In a few days after the attack at Apache Pass we organized in the mountains and returned to fight the soldiers. There were two tribes—the Bedonkohe and the Chokonen Apaches, both commanded by Cochise. After a few days' skirmishing we

[2] Regarding this attack, Mr. L. C. Hughes, editor of *The Star*, Tucson, Arizona, to whom I was referred by General Miles, writes as follows:

"It appears that Cochise and his tribe had been on the warpath for some time and he with a number of subordinate chiefs was brought into the military camp at Bowie under the promise that a treaty of peace was to be held, when they were taken into a large tent where handcuffs were put upon them. Cochise, seeing this, cut his way through the tent and fled to the mountains; and in less than six hours had surrounded the camp with from three to five hundred warriors; but the soldiers refused to make fight."

attacked a freight train that was coming in with supplies for the Fort. We killed some of the men and captured the others. These prisoners our chief offered to trade for the Indians whom the soldiers had captured at the massacre in the tent. This the officers refused, so we killed our prisoners, disbanded, and went into hiding in the mountains. Of those who took part in this affair I am the only one now living.

In a few days troops were sent out to search for us, but as we were disbanded, it was, of course, impossible for them to locate any hostile camp. During the time they were searching for us many of our warriors (who were thought by the soldiers to be peaceable Indians) talked to the officers and men, advising them where they might find the camp they sought, and while they searched we watched them from our hiding places and laughed at their failures.

After this trouble all of the Indians agreed not to be friendly with the white men any more. There was no general engagement, but a long struggle followed. Sometimes we attacked the white men—sometimes they attacked us. First a few Indians would be killed and then a few soldiers. I think the killing was about equal on each side. The number killed in these troubles did not amount to much, but this treachery on the part of the soldiers had angered the Indians and revived memories of other wrongs, so that we never again trusted the United States troops.

Perhaps the greatest wrong ever done to the Indians was the treatment received by our tribe from the United States troops about 1863. The chief of our tribe, Mangus-Colorado, went to make a treaty of peace for our people with the white settlement at Apache Tejo, New Mexico. It had been reported to us that the white men in this settlement were more friendly and more reliable than those in Arizona, that they would live up to their treaties and would not wrong the Indians.

Mangus-Colorado, with three other warriors, went to Apache Tejo and held a council with these citizens and soldiers. They told him that if he would come with his tribe and live near them, they would issue to him, from the Government, blankets, flour, provisions, beef, and all manner of supplies. Our chief promised to return to Apache Tejo within two weeks. When he came back to our settlement he assembled the whole tribe in council. I did not believe that the people at Apache Tejo would do as they said and therefore I opposed the plan, but it was decided that with part of the tribe Mangus-Colorado should return to Apache Tejo and receive an issue of rations and supplies. If they were as represented, and if these white men would keep the treaty faithfully, the remainder of the tribe would join him and we would make our permanent home at Apache Tejo. I was to remain in charge of that portion of the tribe which stayed in Arizona. We gave almost all of our arms and ammunition to the party going to Apache Tejo, so that in case there should be treachery they would be prepared for any surprise. Mangus-Colorado and about half of our people went to New Mexico, happy that now they had found white men who would be kind to them, and with whom they could live in peace and plenty.

No word ever came to us from them. From other sources, however, we heard that they had been treacherously captured and slain. In this dilemma we did not know just exactly what to do, but fearing that the troops who had captured them would attack us, we retreated into the mountains near Apache Pass.

During the weeks that followed the departure of our people we had been in suspense, and failing to provide more supplies, had exhausted all of our store of provisions. This was another reason for moving camp. On this retreat, while passing through the mountains, we discovered four men with a herd of cattle. Two of the men were in front in a buggy and two were behind on horseback. We killed all four, but did not scalp them; they were not warriors. We drove the cattle back into the mountains, made a camp, and began to kill the cattle and pack the meat.

Before we had finished this work we were surprised and

attacked by United States troops, who killed in all seven Indians—one warrior, three women, and three children. The Government troops were mounted and so were we, but we were poorly armed, having given most of our weapons to the division of our tribe that had gone to Apache Tejo, so we fought mainly with spears, bows, and arrows. At first I had a spear, a bow, and a few arrows; but in a short time my spear and all my arrows were gone. Once I was surrounded, but by dodging from side to side of my horse as he ran I escaped. It was necessary during this fight for many of the warriors to leave their horses and escape on foot. But my horse was trained to come at call, and as soon as I reached a safe place, if not too closely pursued, I would call him to me. During this fight we scattered in all directions and two days later reassembled at our appointed place of rendezvous, about fifty miles from the scene of this battle.

About ten days later the same United States troops attacked our new camp at sunrise. The fight lasted all day, but our arrows and spears were all gone before ten o'clock, and for the remainder of the day we had only rocks and clubs with which to fight. We could do little damage with these weapons, and at night we moved our camp about four miiles back into the mountains where it would be hard for the cavalry to follow us. The next day our scouts, who had been left behind to observe the movements of the soldiers, returned, saying that the troops had gone back toward San Carlos Reservation.

A few days after this we were again attacked by another company of United States troops. Just before this fight we had been joined by a band of Chokonen Indians under Cochise, who took command of both divisions. We were repulsed, and decided to disband.

After we had disbanded our tribe the Bedonkohe Apaches reassembled near their old camp vainly waiting for the return of Mangus-Colorado and our kinsmen. No tidings came save that they had all been treacherously slain. Then a council was held, and as it was believed that Mangus-Colorado was dead, I was elected Tribal Chief.

For a long time we had no trouble with anyone. It was

more than a year after I had been made Tribal Chief that United States troops surprised and attacked our camp. They killed seven children, five women, and four warriors, captured all our supplies, blankets, horses, and clothing, and destroyed our tepees. We had nothing left; winter was beginning, and it was the coldest winter I ever knew. After the soldiers withdrew I took three warriors and trailed them. Their trail led back toward San Carlos.

DOCUMENT B:

From Kansas State Historical Society *Collections*, Vol. 13, 1915

Cochise: The sun had been very hot on my head and made me as in a fire; my blood was on fire, but now I have come into this valley and drunk of these waters and washed myself in them and they have cooled me. Now that I am cool I have come with my hands open to you to live in peace with you. I speak straight and do not wish to deceive or be deceived. I want a good, strong and lasting peace. When God made the world he gave one part to the white man and another to the Apache. Why was it? Why did they come together? Now that I am to speak, the sun, the moon, the earth, the air, the waters, the birds and beasts, even the children unborn shall rejoice at my words. The white people have looked for me long. I am here! What do they want? They have looked for me long; why am I worth so much? If I am worth so much why not mark when I set my foot and look when I spit; The coyotes go about at night to rob and kill; I cannot see them; I am not God. I am no longer chief of all the Apaches. I am no longer rich; I am but a poor man. The world was not always this way. I cannot command the animals; if I would they would not obey me. God made us not as you; we were born like the animals, in the dry grass, not on beds like you. This is why we do as the animals, go about of a night and rob and steal. If I had such things as you have, I would not do as I do, for then I would not need to do so. There are Indians who go about killing and robbing. I do not command them. If I did, they would not do so. My warriors have been killed in Sonora. I came in here because God told me to do so. He said it was good to be at peace—so I came! I was going around the world with the clouds, and the air, when God spoke to my thought and told me to come in here and be at peace with all. He said the world was for us all; how was it? When I was young I walked all over this country, east and west, and saw no other people than the Apaches. After many summers I walked again and found another race of people had come to take it. How is it? Why is it that the Apaches wait to die—that they carry their lives on their finger nails? They roam over the hills and plains and want the heavens to fall on them. The Apaches were once a great nation; they are now but few, and because of this they want to die and so carry their lives on their finger nails. Many have been killed in battle. You must speak straight so that your words may go as sunlight to our hearts. *Tell me, if the Virgin Mary has walked throughout all the land, why has she never entered the wigwam of the Apache? Why have we never seen or heard her?*

I have no father nor mother; I am alone in the world. No one cares for Cochise; that is why I do not care to live, and wish the rocks to fall on me and cover me up. If I had a father and a mother like you, I would be with them and they with me. When I was going around the world, all were asking for Cochise. Now he is here—you see him and hear him—are you glad? If so, say so. Speak, Americans and Mexicans, I do not wish to hide anything from you nor have you hide anything from me; I will not lie to you; do not lie to me. I want to live in these mountains; I do not want to go to Tularosa. That is a long ways off. The flies on those mountains eat out the eyes of the horses. The bad spirits live there. I have drunk of these waters and they have cooled me; I do not want to leave here.

POSTSCRIPT TO THE DOCUMENTS:

It would be pleasant to record that after the United

States and the Apache agreed to live at peace the US for once respected their pledges. It didn't happen like that. The government arbitrarily shifted the reservations whenever they thought it would make their job easier or might produce profits for some new favorite town. Indian agents and traders were dishonest; a favorite story among the Indians described the agent's methods of distributing Indian goods, which was to throw them through a ladder. The Indians got whatever stuck to the rungs; the agent kept the rest. Such treatment resulted in the Apache breaking out of their reservations and resuming their guerrilla warfare in 1874 but without Cochise, who died that year. For another ten years the hostilities continued until simple attrition wore the Apache down. Unlike the Spaniards or the Mexicans the "Americans" seemed to have no end to the numbers of people with whom they could flood an area. One by one the war chiefs died until finally in 1885 Geronimo surrendered at the head of thirty-three Indians. The government promptly shipped them and 498 Chiricahuas to captivity in Florida. They were never allowed to return to their own lands. Instead, in 1894 they were transferred once again, this time to Oklahoma. Their exile ended in 1913—but even then they were not allowed back into Arizona. Some of the Chiricahua, however, were allowed to join another Apache band on their New Mexico reservation.

WOMEN AND CHILDREN FIRST

1864

A Half-Cheyenne at Sand Creek

Medicine Calf Beckwourth's Account

ABOUT THE DOCUMENTS:

It will be recalled that in 1851 a treaty was made with the Great Plains Indians to secure the safety of the Oregon Trail and to get the Indians to agree on their respective territorial boundaries. That treaty, agreed to at the council at Fort Laramie, did not involve any cession of Indian lands or any abridgement of their right to travel, hunt, or fish where they agreed the white men's roads might pass or where they said the white soldiers might build their posts. But with the roads came white men who stayed along its edges. Some stayed to trade with the Indians; some stayed to raise cattle and grow hay for sale to the endless streams of immigrants using the Oregon Trail. In 1858 there was the famous Pike's Peak gold rush with its flocks of miners and their villages and ultimately, Denver. The buffalo lands of the Cheyenne and Arapaho began to be taken up by white ranches. The government organized the Territory of Colorado and gave it a governor. The pressure began for Indian land cessions within the Indian Territory, guaranteed forever free of white men. In 1861 the Cheyenne and Arapaho were invited to sign a new treaty at a council held at Fort Wise. Though only six of the forty-four Cheyenne chiefs attended the council, the US commissioners did not feel that the Cheyenne's ability to sign a valid treaty was in any way impaired. The other chiefs, they said, could sign later. None of them ever did, but the US always insisted that the treaty was legally binding—for the Indians, that is.

The treaty process was the same old story. Indian chiefs were deceived as to what the treaty actually said. They agreed that they would live within an area bounded by Sand Creek and the Arkansas River but would retain full travel, hunting, and fishing rights to all their ancient territory. Without that freedom they could not hunt buffalo, and without buffalo they could not live. What the treaty said, however, was that they gave up ("ceded and relinquished") all the lands to which they had any claim, except for a small area bounded by the Arkansas River and Sand Creek. As for their hunting, the government had no intention of letting them continue. The idea was to make farmers of them, and for that purpose the treaty promised to purchase cattle, farming equipment, mills, and mechanics' tools for them. Further, they would receive thirty thousand dollars a year for fifteen years— unless the President decided they weren't making enough progress as farmers, in which case he would do for them whatever he and Congress "may judge to be suitable or proper."

Apart from larger issues of deception, bad faith, and illegality raised by the Fort Wise Treaty, the "Americans" were so petty as to renege even on the promise of farming implements—on whose "reasonable and satisfactory" use even the Indian's annuity depended.

Following the treaty, white settlers and soldiers alike felt justified in treating the Cheyenne in any way they liked whenever they came across them off the reservation. Incidents occurred—and though the Cheyenne continued to respect the Oregon Trail, they did not feel bound to swallow insult or injury from settlers squatting on their buffalo grounds or from soldiers roaming their territory along the Smokey Hill or Republican rivers. They did not swallow those insults, and their retaliations became fodder for atrocity stories told by white people who wanted the Army to remove the Cheyenne altogether. In addition to regular Army troops in the territory white settlers formed the Colorado Volunteers, whose soldiers were the settlers themselves and whose officers were often politically ambitious citizens of the territory. One such was Col. John M. Chivington, commanding officer of the Colorado Volunteers, who gave his men orders that they were to "kill Cheyennes whenever and wherever they may be found."

Another politically inclined man was governor of the Colorado territory, John Evans, who ordered all Cheyenne to report to Fort Lyon on their Sand Creek-Arkansas River reservation. All Indians found off the reservation would be considered at war with the whites. He followed this order with a proclamation to the citizens of Colorado, authorizing them to pursue and kill privately any Cheyenne found off the reservation.

While Cheyenne groups caught far from the reservation tried to reach safety or to join other bands fighting the white man, a group of Cheyenne chiefs led by Black Kettle, White Antelope, Bull Bear, and One Eye went to Denver with an Army escort to parley with Governor Evans and Colonel Chivington. Evans did not even want to talk with the Indians. "But what shall I do with the Third Colorado Regiment if I make peace?" Evans is reported to have asked. "They have been raised to kill Indians, and they must kill Indians." He had sworn to Washington that the regiment was necessary; if now he reported that the Indians were at peace, the Washington politicians would not think too highly of him. Nor would many of his own citizens—who might one day elect him governor of the new state of Colorado—if he disbanded the Colorado Volunteers. Those soldiers would then be subject to the Union draft and would have to face Confederate soldiers who were much better equipped and more numerous than the Cheyenne. No, Governor Evans didn't want peace. At the council meeting to which he finally agreed, he was so evasive that the Cheyenne left without knowing whether they had agreed to peace or not. In any event they returned to the reservation and camped on Sand Creek. There on the morning of November 28, 1864, Colonel Chivington led a column of more than seven hundred men with four mountain howitzers in an attack on the sleeping Cheyenne camp. The massacre that followed is infamous even in a history of infamy.

Whatever else Chivington's massacre of the peaceful Cheyenne meant, it signaled the war he and Governor Evans wanted. It raged along the Oregon Trail and across the Plains, and it split the Cheyenne into two factions: those who fought and then sought peace and those who fought and swore never to accept peace. The latter, the Northern Cheyenne, moved in large numbers into the lands of the Sioux, and for the years that the Plains Wars lasted they fought the white man. At Sand Creek the long struggle of the Plains Indians really began.

In the first of the two documents that follow, a half-Cheyenne named Robert Bent, whom Chivington had dragged out of bed on the morning of the Sand Creek Massacre to serve him as a guide, describes the events of that morning. At the Sand Creek camp that morning were two of Robert Bent's brothers, Charlie and George.

In the second document Medicine Calf Beckwourth, a Black man who had lived for fifty years among the Cheyenne, recounts the success of his mission to the Cheyenne chiefs following the massacre. Medicine Calf Beckwourth was also at Sand Creek; Chivington threatened to hang him unless he came along as a guide. Later Chivington became suspicious of the old man's guidance and forced Robert Bent to add his services.

DOCUMENT A:

From US Senate Report 156, 39th Congress, 2nd Session

ROBERT BENT: I am twenty-four years old; was born on the Arkansas River. I am pretty well acquainted with the Indians of the plains, having spent most of my life among them. I am employed as guide and imterpreter at Fort Lyon by Major Anthony. Colonel Chivington ordered me to accompany him on his way to Sand Creek. The command consisted of from nine hundred to one thousand men, principally Colorado volunteers. We left Fort Lyon

at eight o'clock in the evening, and came on to the Indian
camp at daylight the next morning. Colonel Chivington
surrounded the village with his troops. When we came in
sight of camp I saw the American flag waving and heard
Black Kettle tell the Indians to stand around the flag, and
there they were huddled—men, women, and children. This
was when we were within fifty yards of the Indians. I also
saw a white flag raised. These flags were in so conspicuous
a position that they must have been seen. When the troops
fired, the Indians ran, some of the men into their lodges,
probably to get their arms. They had time to get away if
they had wanted to. I remained on the field five hours,
and when I left there were shots being fired up the creek.
I think there were six hundred Indians in all. I think there
were thirty-five braves and some old men, about sixty in
all. All fought well. At the time the rest of the men were
away from the camp, hunting. I visited the battleground
one month afterwards; saw the remains of a great many;
counted sixty-nine, but a number had been eaten by the
wolves and dogs. After the firing the warriors put the
squaws and children together, and surrounded them to
protect them. I saw five squaws under a bank for shelter.
When the troops came up to them they ran out and
showed their person to let the soldiers know they were
squaws and begged for mercy, but the soldiers shot them
all. I saw one squaw lying on the bank whose leg had
been broken by a shell; a soldier came up to her with a
drawn saber; she raised her arm to protect herself, when
he struck, breaking her arm; she rolled over and raised
her other arm, when he struck, breaking it, and then left
her without killing her. There seemed to be indiscriminate
slaughter of men, women, and children. There were some
thirty or forty squaws collected in a hole for protection;
they sent out a little girl about six years old with a white
flag on a stick; she had not proceeded but a few steps
when she was shot and killed. All the squaws in that hole
were afterwards killed, and four or five bucks outside. The
squaws offered no resistance. Every one I saw dead was
scalped. I saw one squaw cut open with an unborn child,
as I thought, lying by her side. Captain Soule afterwards

told me that such was the fact. I saw the body of White Antelope with the privates cut off, and I heard a soldier say he was going to make a tobacco pouch out of them. I saw one squaw whose privates had been cut out. I heard Colonel Chivington say to the soldiers as they charged past him, "Remember our wives and children murdered on the Platte and Arkansas." He occupied a position where he could not have failed to have seen the American flag, which I think was a garrison flag, 6 x 12. He was within fifty yards when he planted his battery. I saw a little girl about five years of age who had been hid in the sand; two soldiers discovered her, drew their pistols and shot her, and then pulled her out of the sand by the arm. I saw quite a number of infants in arms killed with their mothers.

DOCUMENT B:

From US Senate Executive Doc. 26, 39th Congress, 2nd Session

I went into the lodge of Leg-in-the-Water. When I went in he raised up and he said, "Medicine Calf, what have you come here for; have you fetched the white man to finish killing our families again?" I told him I had come to talk to him; call in your council. They came in a short time afterwards, and wanted to know what I had come for. I told them I had come to persuade them to make peace with the whites, as there was not enough of them to fight the whites, as they were as numerous as the leaves of the trees. "We know it," was the general response of the council. "But what do we want to live for? The white man has taken our country, killed all of our game; was not satisfied with that, but killed our wives and children. Now no peace. We want to go and meet our families in the spirit land. We loved the whites until we found out they lied to us, and robbed us of what we had. We have raised the battle ax until death."

RED CLOUD'S WAR

1865

Spotted Tail Speaks

Red Cloud Speaks to the Dakotas

Red Cloud Parleys at Fort Laramie

ABOUT THE DOCUMENTS:

The Oregon Trail started just west of Independence, Missouri, and ran northwest through Cheyenne country across the Smokey Hill River and on to the Platte River, which it followed to the fork of the Platte and the North Platte. From there it followed the North Platte through Sioux country. White men were not long content with this single route. Soon they were pressing for passage through the Sioux' last great hunting ground to follow the newly defined Bozeman Trail that branched off from the Oregon Trail at Fort Fetterman to go north and then west to Virginia City, Montana.

The Sioux were determined to keep the white man off their lands—determined enough so that the various Sioux divisions willingly united in the fight to do so. After the Sand Creek Massacre many Cheyenne joined the Sioux.

Pressure to restrict the Sioux had begun even before Sand Creek, as the first of the following documents shows. It is interesting not because of the importance of the council from which it is taken but for the significance of the attitudes—both white and Indian—that were expressed. The document is from an account by Captain Ware of the Seventh Iowa Cavalry, a man who believed the Indian was an inferior being. Ware recorded a meeting between the "American" General Mitchell and Spotted Tail, chief of the Brule Sioux, at Cottonwood Springs in April, 1864.

The year following the Sand Creek Massacre and the very effective Cheyenne retaliation, four Army columns pushed into the Powder River country to force the opening of the Bozeman Trail. For the US it was one of the most disastrous campaigns of the Indian wars and one of their worst defeats at the hands of the Indians until that time. Sitting Bull of the Hunkpapa Sioux, Red Cloud and Crazy Horse of the Oglala Sioux, Two Moons and Dull Knife of the Cheyenne—these and many other names were well known to white soldiers by the time they drove the soldiers from the Powder River.

The next spring the commissioners came and invited the war chiefs to talk of peace. After showing a good deal of reluctance to trust white men in council, chiefs of the Sioux and Cheyenne met with Commissioner Taylor at Fort Laramie. During the council there was a slip-up; while the commissioner was assuring the Sioux of the white man's peaceful intentions and good will, an Army force arrived with orders to build forts along the Bozeman Trail, treaty or no treaty. Red Cloud, war chief of the Oglala, denounced the white man, denounced the commissioner, and led his people out, refusing the white man's gifts and promises. There followed a guerrilla war against the Bozeman Trail and against the forts protecting it—a war called Red Cloud's War, though many famous war chiefs took part in it. The most spectacular of the Indian successes was at Fort Phil Kearney, when Crazy Horse led a feint that drew the soldiers out from their fort into the open, where they were annihilated by the Sioux and Cheyenne. The Army decided to negotiate peace and for months made repeated attempts to get Red Cloud to come and parley. This he absolutely refused to do as long as the forts along the Bozeman Trail were manned. And finally, in the spring of 1868 the Army gave up. General Sherman, who had marched through Georgia but could not march through Sioux country, was prepared to agree to abandon the forts. Red Cloud would not even come to talk with him until the forts were actually abandoned. The order had to be given, and as the "American" troops pulled out, Indians came in and set fire to the forts. Then after keeping the treaty makers waiting a few more weeks, Red Cloud came into Fort Laramie and agreed to peace. It was one of a very few times that Indians were able to dictate the terms of peace.

The commissioners kept the last laugh for themselves by again misrepresenting the actual contents of the treaty.

Document B is a brief speech of Red Cloud's addressed to his followers not long before the attack on Fort Phil Kearney. Document C records Red Cloud's anger over the way the white man behaved following the Treaty of 1868 and his insistence on Indian rights.

DOCUMENT A:

From Captain Eugene F. Ware, The Indian War of 1864, Crane & Company, 1911

Spotted Tail, sitting quietly, said: "Why are we here? Why had the white brother asked us to come?"

Then General Mitchell said: "The object of this meeting is to have an understanding, and make a treaty, so each will know what he ought to do. We want you Sioux to stay off from the Platte Valley. You can come down to the hills on the edge of the valley while you are hunting, but you must not come down into the valley, for it scares the women and children that are living in the houses in the valley. If you wish to cross the road, and go north or south of the river, you must send in word during the daytime to one of the posts, and then you will be escorted across the valley from the hills on one side to the hills on the other, and then you can go where you will. But you musn't come down in the valley or allow spies, beggars, or bad Indians to come down into the valley. You must restrain your bad men; we will hold you responsible; this is an ultimatum. This we insist upon your doing. If it takes more to feed you, if it takes more bacon or blankets and corn, we will give you more, but you must stay out of the Platte Valley."

[Spotted Tail replied] "The Sioux nation is a great people, and we do not wish to be dictated to by the whites or anybody else. We do not care particularly about the Platte valley, because there is no game in it. Your young men and your freighters have driven all the game out, or killed it, so we find nothing in the Platte valley. But we want to come and trade in the Platte valley wherever we please. We want places where we can sell our beaver-skins and our buffalo-robes. The Platte valley is ours, and we do not intend to give it away. We have let the white man have it so that he could pass, but he has gone over it so often now that he claims it and thinks he owns it. But it is still ours, and always has been ours. It belonged to our forefathers, and their graves are along the hills overlooking the valley from the Missouri River to the mountains, and we do not expect to give it up. We are not afraid of the white man, nor are we afraid to fight him. We have not had in late years any very serious difficulties with the white men. Trouble has been brought about by "drunk-water." Bad whites have given it to bad Indians, and they have got both of us into trouble. The donations which the white men have been giving us are not sufficient; they are not adequate for the concessions which we have made. The goods that were brought us at Woc-co-pom'-any agency were neither as good as had been promised us, nor were they in amount as had been promised us. The Great Father through his army officers makes us great promises, but the agents, who are not army officers, cheat us, and do not carry out the treaty obligations. Last fall at the Woc-co-pom'-any agency, when the agent asked us to sign for our goods, we would not sign, because they were not what they should be in value or amount, and one of the army officers who was there told us not to sign, and he swore at the agent and told him he was a thief, and was cheating us. The army officers treat us well enough, but those who are not officers cheat us when they can, and we do not want to deal with any but the army officers. Besides this, we will not give up the Platte valley to you until we have a regular treaty, and until we have all agreed to it, and have been paid for it. It will soon be that you will want other roads to the west. If we give you this you will want another, and if we give you that you will want a third. Before we will agree to anything you must stop the surveyors that are going west at this very time on the river Niobrara. All of these things must be considered before we will make a treaty."

DOCUMENT B:

From *Indian Heroes and Great Chieftains*, Charles A. Eastman, 1918

RED CLOUD: Hear ye, Dakotas! When the Great Father at Washington sent us his chief soldier (General Harney) to ask for a path through our hunting grounds, a way for his iron road to the mountains and the western sea, we were told that they wished merely to pass through our country, not to tarry among us, but to seek for gold in the far west. Our old chiefs thought to show their friendship and good will, when they allowed this dangerous snake in our midst. They promised to protect the wayfarers.

Yet before the ashes of the council fire are cold, the Great Father is building his forts among us. You have heard the sound of the white soldier's ax upon the Little Piney. His presence here is an insult and a threat. It is an insult to the spirits of our ancestors. Are we then to give up their sacred graves to be plowed for corn? Dakotas, I am for war!

DOCUMENT C:

From US Senate Exec. Doc. 39, 41st Congress, 3rd Session

RED CLOUD: O Great Spirit, I pray you to look at us. We are your children, and you placed us first in this land. We pray you to look down on us, so nothing but the truth will be spoken in this council. We do not ask for anything but what is right and just. When you made your red children, O Great Spirit, you made them to have mercy upon them. Now, we are before you today, praying you to look down on us, and take pity on your poor red children. We pray you to have nothing but the truth spoken here. We hope these things will be settled up right. You are the Protector of the people who use the bow and arrow, as well as of the people who wear hats and garments, and I hope we do not pray to you in vain. We are poor and ignorant. Our forefathers told us we would not be in misery if we asked for your assistance. O Great Spirit, look down on your children and take pity on them.

You two [to the commissioners] are my friends; I want you to listen to what I say; I have nothing more to say now than I said to my Great Father; I want you to carry back what I say. We are all Ogallallas and friends, and that is why we are here. When at Washington we heard the Great Father's words; we saw a great many chiefs, and talked with them; what I then said, I repeat now; I have not since changed my mind. I then promised to stop war parties from going out, and have succeeded. It has been five months since I returned from Washington, and it now makes my heart glad that there has since been peace. At the treaty of 1852 the Great Father told me he would give me annuities for fifty-five years, but I only had annuities for ten years. In 1868 he promised that white men should not pass through my country, and I told my people so; I am not ashamed of my words. Why does General Flint here, the Major Chambers at Fort Fetterman, not stop these white men going on to my lands? They know that white men pass through our country; and lately a cattle herd passed through. . . . At all the councils before they never spoke about the roads through these lands. They spoke about the roads on the Missouri. As the Great Spirit is above me, that is the way that I understand what was said in those councils. I think you ought to be satisfied and let me live in peace on the lands that belong to me. I told my Great Father that he did not need any more of these lands. The Great Father's houses in Washington are full of money stolen from the proceeds of our lands. I want you to look at this from a good heart. I am now close to where the sun sets; my people were once where the sun rises. I have a good heart and good sense, and I want my rights. That is the way the whites make their money; they cheat those who are not smart, but I have sense and a heart, and they cannot cheat me. At the beginning of the war the whites shot each other down like dogs. They got into a war among themselves. My Great Father afterward sent his soldiers out here to spill blood. I did not first commence the spilling of blood. The Great Father did not look after us. That is the reason I went to Washington. I want the Great Father to quit the spilling of blood. When I was at the council in Washington I spoke these words, and have not since changed my mind. My friends, look all around this post, and you will see the bones of my people. I told my Great Father I wanted two traders here, to trade as they did before. I do not want my trading post across the river. I want it ten miles above here, at Mr. Ward's house. I want to know also what kind of presents you have brought me here, that you have come to see me with.

Mr. Brunot (in reference to the trading post): . . . when the treaty was made with General Sherman and General Harney in 1868, the Sioux agreed to go on the Missouri to live. Red Cloud signed that treaty, but he told the Great Father since then that it was too far, and he did not want to go there. The Great Father did not want him to come on this side of the river with his people, as they would meet bad whites who would sell the Indians whisky, and cause trouble. The Great Father listened to Red Cloud, and then told us when we came to see him here, that if Red Cloud would prefer it to going to the Missouri, he could have a trading post North of here where the whites would not trouble him, and that we might agree with Red Cloud about that. We were glad that the Great Father consented to let Red Cloud have his trading post near the Ogallallas' hunting country. We thought he would like to have it located at the Raw Hide Buttes, or somewhere around there.

RED CLOUD: We are all peaceable, and we intend to remain peaceable, as you may see by the way we have acted, and why can we not have our agency above here on the Platte where we want it?

MR. BRUNOT: The Great Father has told us that bad white people may make trouble, and that is the reason why he wanted the trading post in the Indians' own country, where none but such white men could go as the Great Father may send for the Indians' benefit.

RED CLOUD: I want my trading post on this side. The white people go on the other side of the river, and my Great Father has not done as he said. He told me that none should go on our land. A party went through with a cattle herd, and now another party is cutting hay across the river below the post.

MR. BRUNOT repeate   .hat the Great Father would let no one go and live in the Indians' country, and as commissioners they could say, that is what the Great Father means, but for his own purpose he claims the right to go there.

RED CLOUD: My Great Father has deceived me. He has made me and my young men ashamed. He told me he would let no one go across the river; now there are men cutting hay on that side. I learned when in the States that when a man cut hay or wood on another's land, he had to pay for it, and why can't I get payment for the same? . . . If the Great Father looked after my interest, and kept white men out of the country, peace would last forever; but if they disturb me there will be no peace. . . .

DEFENSE OF THE BLACK HILLS

1876

Two Moons' Account

Sitting Bull and His People Reply to the U.S. Commissioners

ABOUT THE DOCUMENTS:

The Treaty of 1868 banned all Indian trade on the Platte River and required the Indians to live on reservations west of the Missouri River, although the Black Hills, Powder River, and Big Horn country were still theirs and they were free to hunt there.

The peace of 1868 was an uneasy one. Though the treaty guaranteed that white men would stay out of the Indian country, the US did precious little to enforce the ban. In 1870 there were rumors of gold in the Big Horn Mountains; white men wanted it and began to demand that the government open the country to them. Red Cloud and Spotted Tail were invited to Washington to negotiate directly with President Grant, who was a rarity among presidents, as he had been among generals. Among other things President Grant appointed the first Indian to be Commissioner of Indian Affairs, an Iroquois named Donehogawa (Ely Samuel Parker among the "Americans"). In the world of venal politicians, favor seekers, and profiteers that had grown up around the Indian Office, Donehogawa was not popular. He had the notion that money appropriated for Indians should go into the designated Indians' pockets, rather than to white thieves or "bought" Indian chiefs who would connive to despoil their own people. In an effort to clean out the corruption in the Indian Office, Donehogawa fell into another trap; after removing the thieves he tried to insure honesty by appointing men recommended by religious groups. As many an "uncivilized" Indian could have told him, ministers and missionaries could be as destructive to Indians as the thieves were. This was a truth that Donehogawa was to learn himself and learn the hard way. In that same year, 1870, that Red Cloud and Spotted Tail traveled to Washington, Donehogawa's political enemies (who were developing into a strong club) managed to hold up congressional appropriation of the money due to reservation Indians. For some it was simply a way to embarrass Donehogawa. Others knew that if the reservation Indians got hungry enough, they would leave their reservations to hunt game. That, of course, would be an excuse to send soldiers after them, charge the Indians with making war, and provide a "legal" way to seize more Indian lands.

Donehogawa simply arranged for supplies to be purchased on credit and sent to the Indians. The supplies would be paid for when the money was finally appropriated. However, in doing so he broke a few of the financial regulations (he not delaying purchases while lobbying contractors furnished bids). Concerned also with the urgency of the problem, Donehogawa arranged for the goods to be transported double time and paid a slightly higher rate for the fast service.

Within months a merchant and part-time missionary to the Indians launched a public attack on Donehogawa for his handling of Indian affairs, charging him with fraud and mismanagement. William Welsh, his accuser, had been a member of a civilian watchdog Board of Indian Commissioners set up by President Grant and Donehogawa. Welsh resigned in outrage at Donehogawa's attitude toward Indian religions, saying that Donehogawa himself was only "a remove from barbarism." Welsh's attack in public newspapers naturally provided Donehogawa's political enemies with the excuse they needed, and he very shortly found himself answering to charges of misconduct before a House Committee on Appropriations. The charges were unfounded; Donehogawa proved them groundless; the board of inquiry exonerated him. But the publicity with which the charges were pressed was in no way matched by the publicity of his exoneration. Donehogawa's name had been blackened, and by 1871 he was convinced that he could not be of benefit to the Indians in his post. He resigned.

But his resignation was still in the future when Red Cloud and Spotted Tail came to Washington. At that time Donehogawa was investigating an Army massacre of Piegan Blackfeet (old enemies of the Plains Indians) who had been found camped peaceably on the Marias River in Montana. Maj. Eugene Baker, purportedly out searching for stolen horses, led a cavalry attack on the first Indian camp he came to. Most of the men were off from the camp hunting, and the 219 Piegans there were almost all old men, women, and children. Major Baker's troop killed thirty-three men, ninety women, and fifty children. The Army, sensitive to criticism, tried to cover up the massacre, and Donehogawa made few friends among the brass or their political supporters by demanding an investigation.

Donehogawa received Red Cloud and Spotted Tail with courtesy. Although aware of the Sioux chiefs' suspicion of the white man's government, he may not have realized as much the suspicion of Red Cloud and Spotted Tail that was growing among the Sioux people and leaders such as Crazy Horse. For Spotted Tail had accepted the government-urged move to the Dakota reservation with surprising ease, and it seemed that Red Cloud was finding it less and less difficult to talk to white men and listen to their arguments. For two centuries the Indians developed an awareness of the mechanics of the "American" divide-and-conquer technique; it could not be erased by simply appointing one Indian (who had learned to succeed in the white world) to a prominent position. So even though Red Cloud returned to his Oglala with a concession allowing them to continue to trade on the Platte, Crazy Horse and his followers no longer were so sure of Red Cloud's determination to resist white encroachment.

Even the trading post concession did not long survive Donehogawa. By 1873 Red Cloud's agency had been moved off the Platte and up to the banks of the White River. The move was accomplished while Red Cloud was away from the agency; on his return he was angry, but he did not react with his old vigor. It was not long before he was settled quietly at the new location.

Not so with the Sioux led by Crazy Horse, who were proved right in their fears that white men would immediately fill up Indian lands between the Platte and the White rivers. Almost immediately, an even worse thrust against Sioux country took place from another direction.

In 1873 Lt. Gen. George Armstrong Custer and his Seventh Cavalry were transferred up from the south, where he had fought the southern Cheyenne. In 1868 the massacre he led against Black Kettle and his people on the Washita River had earned him the name Squaw Killer— though white history books prefer the name later given him by the Sioux, Long Hair. Custer was a vain, glory-seeking butcher who sentenced his own men to death without trial. He seemed to think that Indians had been put on earth to provide human counters to keep score of his ability to kill. In 1873 he invaded Sioux territory, escorting a survey party for the Northern Pacific Railroad (neither he nor anyone else had asked if the Sioux would permit a railroad through their land). Crazy Horse fought several sharp engagements with Custer in August of that year, but his forces were unprepared for war and could not prevent the survey.

Squaw Killer Custer returned the next year at the head of a twelve-hundred-man expedition that included, besides the Seventh Cavalry, two infantry companies with Gatling guns and artillery, newspaper correspondents to report his exploits, scientists bent on exploring the Sioux' sacred Black Hills (or *Paha Sapa*), and gangs of white miners lured by the tales of gold Custer claimed he had found the previous year in the Black Hills.

This expedition of 1874 angered all the men of the Sioux Nation. The Black Hills, the *Paha Sapa*, were sacred. They were the center of the world, the dwelling place of gods, the holy place where warriors went to commune with the Great Spirit and to receive visions. Red Cloud protested the invasion, yet he counseled his young warriors to be patient and to seek peace, trusting the white man himself to end the invasion. When his warriors refused to allow soldiers to fly an "American" flag at their agency, Red Cloud's agency Indians protected the soldiers from the angry warriors' harassment. Many left Red Cloud and sought out Crazy Horse or Sitting Bull, neither of whom had ever lived on a reservation or accepted white handouts.

Red Cloud and Spotted Tail did protest to Washington against the Black Hills invasion. Washington's answer was to send a delegation authorized to buy the Black Hills. This commission represented political interests in the person of Senator W. B. Allison from Iowa; military concerns by General Terry; commercial interests by John Collins, a trader from Fort Laramie; and the missionary concern by Rev. Samuel Hinman, who had worked long to impose Christianity on the Santee Sioux. Neither Crazy Horse nor Sitting Bull would attend their council. Sitting Bull picked up a pinch of dust when he received the invitation and told the emissary to inform the Great Father that Sitting Bull would not sell any land—not so much as the dust he held in his fingers.

The importance of the white man's latest attempt to buy Sioux lands is shown by the fact that more than twenty thousand Sioux, Cheyenne, and Arapaho camped at the council site to keep an eye on their chiefs. Many of them knew that the 1868 treaty stipulated that any further cession could only be accomplished by the consent of three-quarters of all the male adult Indians. They were there to demonstrate that the commissioners could not again pretend they had arranged a deal with an Indian nation by simply suborning a few friendly chiefs. The move worked. Not even Spotted Tail—by then unquestionably a "good Indian"—dared accept the commissioners' proposals to sell the Black Hills. Next Senator Allison suggested that the Sioux might allow the white men to dig gold in the Black Hills if they would promise to go away after the gold was gone. This struck Spotted Tail as a suggestion that the Indians lend the Black Hills to the white man; a suggestion to which he replied by asking if the Senator would be willing to lend him a mule team on the same terms.

Eventually, the commissioners had to recognize the futility of their mission. They went away and recommended to Washington that Congress pay no attention to what the Indians wanted. It would be enough, they said, if the government decided by itself what the Indians should receive as payment for the Black Hills and present the purchase to them "as a finality." Ultimately, it was decided that the Army should subjugate the Indians.

The move began in 1875 with an order to General Sheridan from the War Department to commence operations against "hostile" Sioux, which meant those refusing to remain on the reservations. Foremost among these were the bands led by Crazy Horse and Sitting Bull, symbols of the Indian determination to resist. The orders were passed on down to Generals Crook and Terry. The required white man's sense of legality was satisfied by determining that the treaty of 1868 had already been broken, not by them but by the Indians. One of the treaty's stipulations—which almost certainly had never even been read to the Sioux—was that the Indians would give up hunting and take up farming. The Indians had not done so; therefore, the white man was under no obligation.

The campaign began in the winter of 1875-1876 with an order for all Indians to come in to the agencies. Some did so, preferring to spend the winter in comfort and so save their strength for the battles all felt were coming. Two Moons, leader of a Cheyenne band camped near Crazy Horse, decided to go in March, 1876. But before he could do so six companies of US cavalry found his village and attacked it in the best Army tradition—that is, at dawn while the Indian families were sleeping. Two Moons and his warriors recovered from their surprise, saw their women and children start for the safety of Crazy Horse's camp, and then counterattacked so fiercely that the white soldiers were driven from the village. The Army managed

to set it on fire first, though, and this angered not only the
Indians but General Crook as well, for he had hoped to
use the camp as a forward-area base for his own troops.
Two Moons and his men stayed with Crazy Horse, their
minds more firmly made up then ever to fight the white
man to the end.

Skirmishes continued through spring and early summer,
and ever larger numbers of Indians left the reservations
and joined with the "hostiles" to resist the white invaders.
The Sioux Nation was more closely united than it had
ever been before, and the unity bore fruits. At Two
Moons' Battle and later at the Rosebud engagement Indian resistance forced the white columns to abandon their
campaigns and withdraw, even though the white soldiers
claimed that the battles represented US victories. Then in
June, 1876, Indians and white soldiers met on the Little
Bighorn in the most famous battle of the Indian wars.
Hungry for glory and blind to all reason, Squaw Killer
Custer led a force of six hundred soldiers, over forty
Indian scouts, and his personal newspaper correspondent
up the Powder River in a two-prong attack ordered by his
superiors against the Indians camped on the Little
Bighorn. It was a large encampment; Sioux and Cheyenne
tepees stretched for three miles along the river's west
bank. Of the twelve to fifteen thousand Indians present,
probably five thousand were warriors.

Document A below is an account by Two Moons
of that fight. His vision was necessarily incomplete, since
he took active part in the battle, but not necessarily inac-
curate because of that. Crazy Horse, Gall, Black Moon,
and Sitting Bull all took active and effective part in the
fight that brought the US Army its greatest defeat in its
whole history of Indian fighting. The US defeat resulted
in white history books painting with romantic and
unearned glory the name of a crazy, self-seeking "American" military butcher described more accurately and more
simply by the Cheyenne as Squaw Killer. The name cannot be attributed to Indian prejudice or envy; Indians
were ever willing to give even to their enemies respect for
bravery, as can be clearly seen from Two Moons' ac-

count of the battle in which Custer stood for the last time.

DOCUMENT A:

From *McClure's* Magazine, Vol. 11, 1898

TWO MOONS: That spring [1876] I was camped on Powder River with fifty lodges of my people—Cheyennes. The place is near what is now Fort McKenney. One morning soldiers charged my camp. They were in command of Three Fingers [Colonel McKenzie]. We were surprised and scattered, leaving our ponies. The soldiers ran all our horses off. That night the soldiers slept, leaving the horses one side; so we crept up and stole them back again, and then we went away.

We traveled far, and one day we met a big camp of Sioux at Charcoal Butte. We camped with the Sioux, and had a good time, plenty grass, plenty game, good water. Crazy Horse was head chief of the camp. Sitting Bull was camped a little ways below, on the Little Missouri River.

Crazy Horse said to me, "I'm glad you are come. We are going to fight the white man again."

The camp was already full of wounded men, women, and children.

I said to Crazy Horse, "All right. I am ready to fight. I have fought already. My people have been killed, my horses stolen; I am satisfied to fight."

I believed at that time the Great Spirits had made Sioux, put them there, and white men and Cheyennes here, expecting them to fight. The Great Spirits I thought liked to see the fight; it was to them all the same like playing. So I thought then about fighting.

About May, when the grass was tall and the horses strong, we broke camp and started across the country to the mouth of the Tongue River. Then Sitting Bull and Crazy Horse and all went up the Rosebud. There we had a big fight with General Crook, and whipped him. Many soldiers were killed—few Indians. It was a great fight, much smoke and dust.

From there we all went over the divide, and camped in the valley of Little Horn. Everybody thought, "Now we are out of the white man's country. He can live there, we will live here." After a few days, one morning when I was in camp north of Sitting Bull, a Sioux messenger rode up and said, "Let everybody paint up, cook, and get ready for a big dance."

Cheyennes then went to work to cook, cut up tobacco, and get ready. We all thought to dance all day. We were very glad to think we were far away from the white man.

I went to water my horses at the creek, and washed them off with cool water, then took a swim myself. I came back to the camp afoot. When I got near my lodge, I looked up the Little Horn towards Sitting Bull's camp. I saw a great dust rising. It looked like a whirlwind. Soon Sioux horsemen came rushing into camp shouting: "Soldiers come! Plenty white soldiers."

I ran into my lodge, and said to my brother-in-law, "Get your horses; the white man is coming. Everybody run for horses."

Outside, far up the valley, I heard a battle cry, *Hay-ay, hay-ay!* I heard shooting, too, this way [clapping his hands very fast]. I couldn't see any Indians. Everybody was getting horses and saddles. After I had caught my horse, a Sioux warrior came again and said, "Many soldiers are coming."

Then he said to the women, "Get out of the way, we are going to have hard fight."

I said, "All right, I am ready."

I got on my horse, and rode out into my camp. I called out to the people all running about: "I am Two Moons, your chief. Don't run away. Stay here and fight. You must stay and fight the white soldiers. I shall stay even if I am to be killed."

I rode swiftly toward Sitting Bull's camp. There I saw the white soldiers fighting in a line [Reno's men]. Indians covered the flat. They began to drive the soldiers all mixed up—Sioux, then soldiers, then more Sioux, and all shooting. The air was full of smoke and dust. I saw the soldiers fall back and drop into the river-bed like buffalo fleeing.

They had no time to look for a crossing. The Sioux chased them up the hill, where they met more soldiers in wagons, and then messengers came saying more soldiers were going to kill the women, and the Sioux turned back. Chief Gall was there fighting, Crazy Horse also.

I then rode toward my camp, and stopped squaws from carrying off lodges. While I was sitting on my horse I saw flags come up over the hill to the east like that [he raised his finger tips]. Then the soldiers rose all at once, all on horses, like this [he put his fingers behind each other to indicate that Custer appeared marching in columns of fours]. They formed into three bunches [squadrons] with a little ways between. Then a bugle sounded, and they all got off horses, and some soldiers led the horses back over the hill.

Then the Sioux rode up the ridge on all sides, riding very fast. The Cheyennes went up the left way. Then the shooting was quick, quick. Pop—pop—pop very fast. Some of the soldiers were down on their knees, some standing. Officers all in front. The smoke was like a great cloud, and everywhere the Sioux went the dust rose like smoke. We circles all round him—swirling like water round a stone. We shoot, we ride fast, we shoot again. Soldiers drop, and horses fall on them. Soldiers in line drop, but one man rides up and down the line—all the time shouting. He rode a sorrel horse with white face and white fore-legs. I don't know who he was. He was a brave man.

Indians keep swirling round and round, and the soldiers killed only a few. Many soldiers fell. At last all horses killed but five. Once in a while some man would break out and run toward the river, but he would fall. At last about a hundred men and five horsemen stood on the hill all bunched together. All along the bugler kept blowing his commands. He was very brave too. Then a chief was killed. I hear it was Long Hair [Custer], I don't know; and then the five horsemen and the bunch of men, may be so forty, started toward the river. The man on the sorrel horse led them, shouting all the time [apparently a scout]. He wore a buckskin shirt, and had long black hair and mustache. He fought hard with a big knife. His men were all covered with white dust. I couldn't tell whether they were officers or not. One man all alone ran far down toward the river, then round up over the hill. I thought he was going to escape, but a Sioux fired and hit him in the head. He was the last man. He wore braid on his arms [a sergeant].

All the soldiers were now killed, and the bodies were stripped. After that no one could tell which were officers. The bodies were left where they fell. We had no dance that night. We were sorrowful.

Next day four Sioux chiefs and two Cheyennes and I, Two Moon, went upon the battlefield to count the dead. One man carried a little bundle of sticks. When we came to dead men, we took a little stick and gave it to another man, so we counted the dead. There were 388. There were thirty-nine Sioux and seven Cheyennes killed, and about a hundred wounded.

Some white soldiers were cut with knives, to make sure they were dead; and the war women had mangled some. Most of them were left just where they fell. We came to the man with big mustache; he lay down the hills towards the river [Custer fell up higher on the ridge]. The Indians did not take his buckskin shirt. The Sioux said, "That is a big chief. That is Long Hair." I don't know. I had never seen him. The man on the white-faced horse was the bravest man.

That day as the sun was getting low our young men came up the Little Horn riding hard. Many white soldiers were coming in a big boat, and when we looked we could see the smoke rising. I called my people together, and we hurried up the Little Horn, into Rotten Grass Valley. We camped there three days, and then rode swiftly back over our old trail to the east. Sitting Bull went back into the Rosebud and down the Yellowstone, and way to the north. I did not see him again.

POSTSCRIPT TO THE DOCUMENT:

Inevitably, although the Sioux and Cheyenne won bat-

tles in their defense of the Black Hills, they lost the war.
Pitted against an overwhelmingly superior force and with
no other source of supplies, they had no weapons available
to successfully defend themselves with against the white
man's lack of honor. And if the white man had had any
honor, no weapon would have been necessary. There were
more fights after the Little Bighorn, and the Indians won
more of them than the US military planners could account
for, but ultimately the Sioux lost their lands. Sitting Bull
led his band into exile in Canada and remained there,
refusing to compromise until 1881. Crazy Horse held out
with his warriors until 1877, when starvation forced them
to accept what was promised to be an "honorable" peace.
After his surrender, however, he was tricked into coming
to talk at Fort Robinson. He was led into a guard room,
and when he discovered that he was being jailed, he struggled to break free. One of the guards stuck his bayonet
twice into Crazy Horse's belly while other guards and
"good" Indians tried to hold him. He was thirty-five.

Three weeks later all the Sioux from the Red Cloud and
Spotted Tail agencies began their government-ordered removal to the Missouri River. During that march some two
thousand of Crazy Horse's people broke out of line and
escaped to join Sitting Bull in Canada.

Visions of Sitting Bull and his people still living in
freedom in Canada were galling to the US government.
They exerted every effort to get them back across the
border and safely under "American" control. Finally, late
in 1877 the US arranged with the Canadian government
for a special commission to visit Sitting Bull in Canada
and persuade him to return in exchange for a complete
"pardon" and land on the Great Sioux Reservation. The
following document recounts the replies of Sitting Bull
and of some of those with him on that occasion. They
expressed attitudes that Sitting Bull was able to maintain
until 1881 in spite of repeated reminders by the Canadi-
ans that he and his Indians were not subjects of Britain
and had no rights in Canada. Under those conditions life
grew increasingly difficult; one by one, bands slowly
slipped away from Sitting Bull and crossed the border.

Eventually, even Sitting Bull's most loyal chiefs, such as Gall and Crow King, gave up and went back. So ultimately, Sitting Bull too led the remnants of his people back into the United States, surrendering himself and 186 people at Fort Buford on July 19, 1881. It is unfortunately not even a surprise to learn that the "Americans" refused to honor even their promise of pardon; Sitting Bull was sent to Fort Randall and held as a military prisoner.

DOCUMENT B:

From the Report of the Commission of Indian Affairs to the Secretary of the Interior, 1876

SITTING BULL: For 64 years you have kept me and my people and treated us bad. What have we done that you should want us to stop? We have done nothing. It is all the people on your side that have started us to do all these depredations. We could not go anywhere else, and so we took refuge in this country. It was on this side of the country we learned to shoot, and that is the reason why I came back to it again. I would like to know why you came here. In the first place, I did not give you the country, but you followed me from one place to another, so I had to leave and come over to this country. I was born and raised in this country with the Red River Half-Breeds, and I intend to stop with them. I was raised hand in hand with the Red River Half-Breeds, and we are going over to that part of the country, and that is the reason why I have come over here. That is the way I was raised, in the hands of these people here, and that is the way I intend to be with them. You have got ears, and you have got eyes to see with them, and you see how I live with these people. You see me? Here I am! If you think I am a fool you are a bigger fool than I am. This house is a medicine-house. You come here to tell us lies, but we don't want to hear them. I don't wish any such language used to me; that is, to tell me such lies in my Great Mother's house. Don't you say two more words. Go back home where you came from. This country is mine, and I intend to stay here, and to raise this country full of grown people. See these people here. We were raised with them. That is enough; so no more. You see me shaking hands with these people.

The part of the country you gave me you ran me out of. I have now come here to stay with these people, and I intend to stay here. I wish you to go back, and to "take it easy" going back. These Santees—I was born and raised with them. He is going to tell you something about them.

THE-ONE-THAT-RUNS-THE-REE, a Santee Indian: Look at me. I was born and raised in this country. These people away north here, I was raised with my hands in their own. I have lived in peace with them. For the last 64 years we were over in your country, and you treated us badly. We have come over here now, and you want to try and get us back there again. You didn't treat us well, and I don't like you at all. I have been up and down these roads. We have been running up and down this country. I have been up and down there as often as these people have. I will be at peace with these people as long as I live. You come over here to tell us lies. I will shake hands with men here, and I have been in peace with them. I have come this far into this country. These are the people that learned me how to shoot the first time. This country is ours. We did not give it to you. You stole it away from us. You have come over here to our country to tell us lies, and I don't propose to talk much, and that is all I have to say. I want you to take it easy going back home. Don't go in a rush.

NINE, a Yankton Indian who joined the Santee band: I have shaken hands with everybody in the house. I don't wear the same clothes that these people do. You come over here to tell lies on one another. I want to tell you a few, but you have got more lies than I can say. Sixty-four years ago you got our country and you promised to take good care of us and keep us. You ran from one place to another killing us and fighting us, and I was born and raised with these people over here. I have come here to see the council and to shake hands with you all. I wanted to tell you what I think of this. There are seven different tribes of us. They live all over the country. You kept part of us over there, and part of us you kept on this side. You did not treat us right over there, so we came back over here. These people sitting around here, you promised to take good care of them when you had them over there, but you did not fulfill your promises. They have come over here to this side again, and here we are all together. I come in to these people here and they give me permission to trade with the traders; that is the way I make my living. Everything I get I buy from the traders. I don't steal anything. For fourteen years I have not fought with your people, and that is what I have lost by waiting in this country. I have come over here to these people, and these people, if they had a piece of tobacco, they gave me half; and that is why I live over here. I have a little powder in my powder-horn, and I gave you a little fourteen years ago. Since then I have been over in this country. We came over to this country, and I am going to live with these people here. This country over here is mine. The bullets I have over here I intend to kill something to eat with; not to kill anybody with them. That is what these people told me; to kill nothing but what I wanted to eat with the ammunition they gave me. I will do so.

A WOMAN NAMED THE-ONE-THAT-SPEAKS-ONCE: I was over to your country; I wanted to raise my children over there, but you did not give me any time. I came over to this country to raise my children and have a little peace. That is all I have to say to you. I want you to go back where you came from. These are the people that I am going to stay with, and raise my children with.

THE FLYING BIRD: These people here, God Almighty raised us together. We have a little sense and we ought to love one another. Sitting Bull here says that whenever you found us out, wherever his country was, why, you wanted to have it. It is Sitting Bull's country, this is. These people sitting all around me, what they committed I had nothing to do with it. I was not in it. The soldiers find out where we live, and they never think of anything good, it is always something bad.

[The interpreter was then directed to ask the following questions: Shall I say to the President that you refuse the offers that he has made to you? Are we to understand from what you have said that you refuse those offers?]

SITTING BULL: I could tell you more, but that is all I have to tell you. If we told you more—why, you would not pay any attention to it. That is all I have to say. This part of the country does not belong to your people. You belong on the other side; this side belongs to us.

THE CROW: This is the way I will live in this part of the country. That is the way I like them. When we came back from the other side you wanted to do something—to lie. You want us to go back to the other side; that is the reason why you stay here. What do you mean by coming over here and talking that way to us? All this country around here, I know, belongs to these people, and that is the reason why I came over here when I was driven out of the other country. I am afraid of God Almighty; that is the reason why I don't want to do anything bad. When I came over here I came to live with these people. My children, myself, and my women, they all live together. Those people that don't hide anything, they are all the people I like. I suppose you wanted to hear something; that is the reason you came over here. The people standing around here want to hear it also; that is the reason they stand around here. Sixty-four years ago we shook hands with the soldiers, and ever since that I have had hardships. I made peace with them, and ever since that I have been running from one place to another to keep out of their way. I was over across the line and stayed over there, and I thought you people would take good care of me. You did not do so, and these people over here gave me good care. I have waited here three days, and I have got plenty to eat and everybody respects me. I came from the other side of the line, and I expect to stay here. Going back, you can take it easy. Go to where you were born, and stay there.

I came over to this country, and my great mother knows all about it. She knows I came back over here, and she don't wish anything of me. We think, and all the women in the camp think, we are going to have the country full of people. When I shook hands before, there were lots of people here then. Now I have come back in this part of the country again to have plenty more people, to live in peace and raise children.

NO MORE FOREVER

1877

Chief Joseph's Account

ABOUT THE DOCUMENT:

By the end of the 1870s almost the entire Indian population within the United States had been forced onto reservations, and the days of Indian freedom fighting were almost numbered. Freedom fighting, that is, with its object as the preservation of freedom; soon the only possible object of resistance would be the regaining of freedoms already lost. But in 1877 there were still some few remnants: Sitting Bull was free though in exile in Canada, Geronimo was free but in exile in Mexico. And in the West, in the mountains of Oregon, a band of Nez Percé Indians still had not been forced onto the reservation planned for them.

The Nez Percé lived in eastern Oregon, divided into small bands living in scattered villages along the Clearwater and Salmon rivers and the Snake River and its tributaries. They called themselves Chute-pa-lu and were well known among other Indian nations as a traveling people who traded as far west as the Pacific Coast, raided their traditional enemies, the Shoshoni, in the south and hunted buffalo beyond the Bitterroot Mountains in Montana. They also became well known for the Appaloosa horse, a spotted war horse selectively bred and highly prized then as now. Their lands were not the first coveted by white men on the Pacific Coast, and pressures against them lagged, although they never ceased. But by 1877 the white man was unwilling to tolerate any Indian freedom, and it was determined to put the last Indian in his place on a reservation. So the Wallamwatkin band of the Nez Percé and their chief, Inmuttooyahlatlat (Joseph to the "Americans") became special objects of white attention. The story of Joseph's fight to escape white subjection is best told by himself, and that tale appears in the document that follows. There are a few factors, however, that Chief Joseph omits. First among these is an appreciation of the military brilliance exhibited by the Nez Percé, who in an extremely difficult trek of 1300 miles fought off attack after attack by at least four different Army groups. And this was done while accompanied by women, children, and the aged. Nor does Chief Joseph include in this account the brief speech with which he finally had to announce his surrender.

Tell General Howard that I know his heart. What he told me before I have in my heart. I am tired of fighting. Our chiefs are killed. Looking Glass is dead. Toohoolhoolzote is dead. The old men are all dead. It is the young men who say yes or no. He who led all the young men [Ollokot] is dead. It is cold and we have no blankets. The little children are freezing to death. My people, some of them, have run away to the hills, and have no blankets, no food; no one knows where they are—perhaps freezing to death. I want to have time to look for my children and see how many of them I can find. Maybe I shall find them among the dead. From where the sun now stands I will fight no more forever.
Hear me, my chiefs! I am tired; my heart is sick and sad.

Underscoring the bitterness of that final surrender on the strength of false promises is the fact that the Nez Percé' last battle found them only about thirty miles short of the Canadian line that was their goal.

THE DOCUMENT:

From a narrative by Chief Joseph, introduced by William H. Hare, missionary bishop of Niobrara, in "An Indian's Views of Indian Affairs," North American Review, Vol. 128, April, 1879

My friends, I have been asked to show you my heart. I am glad to have a chance to do so. I want the white people to understand my people. Some of you think an Indian is like a wild animal. This is a great mistake. I will tell you all about our people, and then you can judge whether an Indian is a man or not. I believe much trouble and blood would be saved if we opened our hearts more. I will tell you in my way how the Indian sees things. The white man has more words to tell you how they look to him, but it does not require many words to speak the truth. What I have to say will come from my heart, and I will speak with a straight tongue. Ah-cum-kin-i-ma-me-hut [the Great Spirit] is looking at me, and will hear me.

My name is In-mut-too-yah-lat-lat [Thunder traveling over the Mountains]. I am chief of the Wal-lam-wat-kin band of Chute-pa-lu, or Nez Percés [nose-pierced Indians]. I was born in eastern Oregon, thirty-eight winters ago. My father was chief before me. When a young man, he was called Joseph by Mr. Spaulding, a missionary. He died a few years ago. There was no stain on his hands of the blood of a white man. He left a good name on the earth. He advised me well for my people.

Our fathers gave us many laws, which they had learned from their fathers. These laws were good. They told us to treat all men as they treated us; that we should never be the first to break a bargain; that it was a disgrace to tell a lie; that we should speak only the truth; that it was a shame for one man to take from another his wife, or his property without paying for it. We were taught to believe that the Great Spirit sees and hears everything, and that he never forgets; that hereafter he will give every man a spirit-home according to his deserts: if he has been a good man, he will have a good home; if he has been a bad man, he will have a bad home. This I believe, and all my people believe the same.

We did not know there were other people besides the Indian until about one hundred winters ago, when some men with white faces came to our country. They brought many things with them to trade for furs and skins. They brought tobacco, which was new to us. They brought guns with flint stones on them, which frightened our women and children. Our people could not talk with these white-faced men, but they used signs which all people understand. These men were Frenchmen, and they called our people "Nez Percés," because they wore rings in their noses for ornaments. Although very few of our people wear them now, we are still called by the same name. These French trappers said a great many things to our fathers, which have been planted in our hearts. Some were good for us, but some were bad. Our people were divided in opinion about these men. Some thought they taught more bad than good. An Indian respects a brave man, but he despises a coward. He loves a straight tongue, but he hates a forked tongue. The French trappers told us some truths and some lies.

The first white men of your people who came to our country were named Lewis and Clarke. They also brought many things that our people had never seen. They talked straight, and our people gave them a great feast, as a proof that their hearts were friendly. These men were very kind. They made presents to our chiefs and our people made presents to them. We had a great many horses, of which we gave them what they needed, and they gave us guns and tobacco in return. All the Nez Percés made friends with Lewis and Clarke, and agreed to let them pass through their country, and never to make war on white men. This promise the Nez Percés have never broken. No white man can accuse them of bad faith, and speak with a straight tongue. It has always been the pride of the Nez Percés that they were the friends of the white men. When my father was a young man there came to our country a white man [Rev. Mr. Spaulding] who talked spirit law. He won the affections of our people because he spoke good things to them. At first he did not say anything about white men wanting to settle on our lands. Nothing was said about that until about twenty winters ago, when a number of white people came into our country and built houses and made farms. At first our people made no complaint. They thought there was room enough for all to live in peace, and they were learning many things from the white men that seemed to be good. But we soon found that the white men were growing rich very fast, and were greedy to possess everything the Indian had. My father was the first to see through the schemes of the white men, and he warned his tribe to be careful about trading with them. He had suspicion of men who seemed so anxious to make money. I was a boy then, but I remember well my father's caution. He had sharper eyes than the rest of our people.

Next there came a white officer [Governor Stevens], who invited all the Nez Percés to a treaty council. After the council was opened he made known his heart. He said there were a great many white people in the country, and many more would come; that he wanted the land marked out so that the Indians and white men could be separated. If they were to live in peace it was necessary, he said, that the Indians should have a country set apart for them, and in that country they must stay. My father, who represented his band, refused to have anything to do with the council, because he wished to be a free man. He claimed that no man owned any part of the earth, and a man could not sell what he did not own.

Mr. Spaulding took hold of my father's arm and said, "Come and sign the treaty." My father pushed him away, and said: "Why do you ask me to sign away my country? It is your business to talk to us about spirit matters, and not to talk to us about parting with our land." Governor Stevens urged my father to sign his treaty, but he refused.

"I will not sign your paper," he said; "you go where you please, so do I; you are not a child, I am no child; I can think for myself. No man can think for me. I have no other home than this. I will not give it up to any man. My people would have no home. Take away your paper. I will not touch it with my hand."

My father left the council. Some of the chiefs of the other bands of the Nez Percés signed the treaty, and then Governor Stevens gave them presents of blankets. My father cautioned his people to take no presents, for "after a while," he said, "they will claim that you have accepted pay for your country." Since that time four bands of the Nez Percés have received annuities from the United States. My father was invited to many councils, and they tried hard to make him sign the treaty, but he was firm as the rock, and would not sign away his home. His refusal caused a difference among the Nez Percés.

Eight years later [1863] was the next treaty council. A chief called Lawyer, because he was a great talker, took the lead in this council, and sold nearly all the Nez Percés country. My father was not there. He said to me: "When you go into council with the white man, always remember your country. Do not give it away. The white man will cheat you out of your home. I have taken no pay from the United States. I have never sold our land." In this treaty Lawyer acted without authority from our band. He had no right to sell the Wallowa (*winding water*) country. That had always belonged to my father's own people, and the other bands had never disputed our right to it. No other Indians ever claimed Wallowa.

In order to have all people understand how much land we owned, my father planted poles around it and said:

"Inside is the home of my people—the white man may take the land outside. Inside this boundary all our people were born. It circles around the graves of our fathers, and we will never give up these graves to any man."

The United States claimed they had bought all the Nez Percés country outside of Lapwai Reservation, from Lawyer and other chiefs, but we continued to live on this land in peace until eight years ago, when white men began to come inside the bounds my father had set. We warned them against this great wrong, but they would not leave our land, and some bad blood was raised. The white men represented that we were going upon the war-path. They reported many things that were false.

The United States Government again asked for a treaty council. My father had become blind and feeble. He could no longer speak for his people. It was then that I took my father's place as chief. In this council I made my first speech to white men. I said to the agent who held the council:

"I did not want to come to this council, but I came hoping that we could save blood. The white man has no right to come here and take our country. We have never accepted any presents from the Government. Neither Lawyer nor any other chief had authority to sell this land. It has always belonged to my people. It came unclouded to them from our fathers, and we will defend this land as long as a drop of Indian blood warms the hearts of our men."

The agent said he had orders, from the Great White Chief at Washington, for us to go upon the Lapwai Reservation, and that if we obeyed he would help us in many ways. "You *must* move to the agency," he said. I answered him: "I will not. I do not need your help; we have plenty, and we are contented and happy if the white man will let us alone. The reservation is too small for so many people with all their stock. You can keep your presents; we can go to your towns and pay for all we need; we have plenty of horses and cattle to sell, and we won't have any help from you; we are free now; we can go where we please. Our fathers were born here. Here they lived, here they died, here are their graves. We will never leave them." The agent went away, and we had peace for a little while.

Soon after this my father sent for me. I saw he was dying. I took his hand in mine. He said: "My son, my body is returning to my mother earth, and my spirit is going very soon to see the Great Spirit Chief. When I am gone, think of your country. You are the chief of these people. They look to you to guide them. Always remember that your father never sold his country. You must stop your ears whenever you are asked to sign a treaty selling your home. A few years more, and white men will be all around you. They have their eyes on this land. My son, never forget my dying words. This country holds your father's body. Never sell the bones of your father and your mother." I pressed my father's hand and told him I would protect his grave with my life. My father smiled and passed away to the spirit-land.

I buried him in that beautiful valley of winding waters. I love that land more than all the rest of the world. A man who would not love his father's grave is worse than a wild animal.

For a short time we lived quietly. But this could not last. White men had found gold in the mountains around the land of winding water. They stole a great many horses from us, and we could not get them back because we were Indians. The white men told lies for each other. They drove off a great many of our cattle. Some white men branded our young cattle so they could claim them. We had no friend who would plead our cause before the law councils. It seemed to me that some of the white men in Wallowa were doing these things on purpose to get up a war. They knew that we were not strong enough to fight them. I labored hard to avoid trouble and bloodshed. We gave up some of our country to the white men, thinking that then we could have peace. We were mistaken. The white man would not let us alone. We could have avenged our wrongs many times, but we did not. Whenever the Government has asked us to help them against other Indians, we have never refused. When the white men were few and we were strong we could have killed them all off, but the Nez Percés wished to live at peace.

If we have not done so, we have not been to blame. I believe that the old treaty has never been correctly reported. If we ever owned the land we own it still, for we never sold it. In the treaty councils the commissioners have claimed that our country had been sold to the Government. Suppose a white man should come to me and say,

"Joseph, I like your horses, and I want to buy them." I say to him, "No, my horses suit me, I will not sell them." Then he goes to my neighbor, and says to him: "Joseph has some good horses. I want to buy them, but he refuses to sell." My neighbor answers, "Pay me the money, and I will sell you Joseph's horses." The white man returns to me, and says, "Joseph, I have bought your horses, and you must let me have them." If we sold our lands to the Government, this is the way they were bought.

On account of the treaty made by the other bands of the Nez Percés, the white men claimed my lands. We were troubled greatly by white men crowding over the line. Some of these were good men, and we lived on peaceful terms with them, but they were not all good.

Nearly every year the agent came over from Lapwai and ordered us on to the reservation. We always replied that we were satisfied to live in Wallowa. We were careful to refuse the presents or annuities which he offered.

Through all the years since the white men came to Wallowa we have been threatened and taunted by them and the treaty Nez Percés. They have given us no rest. We have had a few good friends among white men, and they have always advised my people to bear these taunts without fighting. Our young men were quick-tempered, and I have had great trouble in keeping them from doing rash things. I have carried a heavy load on my back ever since I was a boy. I learned then that we were but few, while the white men were many, and that we could not hold our own with them. We were like deer. They were like grizzly bears. We had a small country. Their country was large. We were contented to let things remain as the Great Spirit Chief made them. They were not; and would change the rivers and mountains if they did not suit them.

Year after year we have been threatened, but no war was made upon my people until General Howard came to our country two years ago and told us that he was the white war-chief of all that country. He said: "I have a great many soldiers at my back. I am going to bring them up here, and then I will talk to you again. I will not let white men laugh at me the next time I come. The country belongs to the Government, and I intend to make you go upon the reservation."

I remonstrated with him against bringing more soldiers to the Nez Percés country. He had one house full of troops all the time at Fort Lapwai.

The next spring the agent at Umatilla agency sent an Indian runner to tell me to meet General Howard at Walla Walla. I could not go myself, but I sent my brother and five other head men to meet him, and they had a long talk.

General Howard said: "You have talked straight, and it is all right. You can stay in Wallowa." He insisted that my brother and his company should go with him to Fort Lapwai. When the party arrived there General Howard sent out runners and called all the Indians in to a grand council. I was in that council. I said to General Howard, "We are ready to listen." He answered that he would not talk then, but would hold a council next day, when he would talk plainly. I said to General Howard: "I am ready to talk to-day. I have been in a great many councils, but I am no wiser. We are all sprung from a woman, although we are unlike in many things. We can not be made over again. You are as you were made, and as you were made you can remain. We are just as we were made by the Great Spirit, and you can not change us; then why should children of one mother and one father quarrel—why should one try to cheat the other? I do not believe that the Great Spirit Chief gave one kind of men the right to tell another kind of men what they must do."

General Howard replied: "You deny my authority, do you? You want to dictate to me, do you?"

Then one of my chiefs—Too-hool-hool-suit—rose in the council and said to General Howard: "The Great Spirit Chief made the world as it is, and as he wanted it, and he made a part of it for us to live upon. I do not see where you get authority to say that we shall not live where he placed us."

General Howard lost his temper and said: "Shut up! I don't want to hear any more of such talk. The law says you shall go upon the reservation to live, and I want you to do so, but you persist in disobeying the law" [meaning the treaty]. "If you do not move, I will take the matter into my own hand, and make you suffer for your disobedience."

Too-hool-hool-suit answered: "Who are you, that you ask us to talk, and then tell me I sha'n't talk? Are you the Great Spirit? Did you make the world? Did you make the sun? Did you make the rivers to run for us to drink? Did you make the grass to grow? Did you make all these things, that you talk to us as though we were boys? If you did, then you have the right to talk as you do."

General Howard replied, "You are an impudent fellow, and I will put you in the guard-house," and then ordered a soldier to arrest him.

Too-hool-hool-suit made no resistance. He asked General Howard: "Is that your order? I don't care. I have expressed my heart to you. I have nothing to take back. I have spoken for my country. You can arrest me, but you can not change me or make me take back what I have said."

The soldiers came forward and seized my friend and took him to the guard-house. My men whispered among themselves whether they should let this thing be done. I counseled them to submit. I knew if we resisted that all the white men present, including General Howard would be killed in a moment, and we would be blamed. If I had said nothing, General Howard would never have given another unjust order against my men. I saw the danger, and, while they dragged Too-hool-hool-suit to prison, I arose and said: "*I am going to talk now*. I don't care whether you arrest me or not." I turned to my people and said: "The arrest of Too-hool-hool-suit was wrong, but we will not resent the insult. We were invited to this council to express our hearts, and we have done so." Too-hool-hool-suit was prisoner for five days before he was released.

The council broke up for that day. On the next morning General Howard came to my lodge, and invited me to go with him and White-Bird and Looking-Glass, to look for land for my people. As we rode along we came to some good land that was already occupied by Indians and white people. General Howard, pointing to this land, said: "If you will come on to the reservation, I will give you these lands and move these people off."

I replied: "No. It would be wrong to disturb these people. I have no right to take their homes. I have never taken what did not belong to me. I will not now."

We rode all day upon the reservation, and found no good land unoccupied. I have been informed by men who do not lie that General Howard sent a letter that night, telling the soldiers at Walla Walla to go to Wallowa Valley, and drive us out upon our return home.

In the council, next day, General Howard informed me, in a haughty spirit, that he would give my people *thirty days* to go back home, collect all their stock, and move on to the reservation, saying, "If you are not here in that time, I shall consider that you want to fight, and will send my soldiers to drive you on."

I said: "War can be avoided, and it ought to be avoided. I want no war. My people have always been the friends of the white man. Why are you in such a hurry? I can not get ready to move in thirty days. Our stock is scattered, and Snake River is very high. Let us wait until fall, then the river will be low. We want time to hunt up our stock and gather supplies for winter."

General Howard replied, "If you let the time run over one day, the soldiers will be there to drive you on to the reservation, and all your cattle and horses outside of the reservation at that time will fall into the hands of the white men."

I knew I had never sold my country, and that I had no land in Lapwai; but I did not want bloodshed. I did not want my people killed. I did not want anybody killed. Some of my people had been murdered by white men, and the white murderers were never punished for it. I told General Howard about this, and again said I wanted no war. I wanted the people who lived upon the lands I was to occupy at Lapwai to have time to gather their harvest.

I said in my heart that, rather than have war, I would give up my country. I would give up my father's grave. I would give up everything rather than have the blood of white men upon the hands of my people.

General Howard refused to allow me more than thirty days to move my people and their stock. I am sure that he began to prepare for war at once.

When I returned to Wallowa I found my people very much excited upon discovering that the soldiers were already in the Wallowa Valley. We held a council, and decided to move immediately, to avoid bloodshed.

Too-hool-hool-suit, who felt outraged by his imprisonment, talked for war, and made many of my young men willing to fight rather than be driven like dogs from the land where they were born. He declared that blood alone would wash out the disgrace General Howard had put upon him. It required a strong heart to stand up against such talk, but I urged my people to be quiet, and not to begin a war.

We gathered all the stock we could find, and made an attempt to move. We left many of our horses and cattle in Wallowa, and we lost several hundred in crossing the river. All of my people succeeded in getting across in safety. Many of the Nez Percés came together in Rocky Cañon to hold a grand council. I went with all my people. This council lasted ten days. There was a great deal of war-talk, and a great deal of excitement. There was one young brave present whose father had been killed by a white man five years before. This man's blood was bad against white men, and he left the council calling for revenge.

Again I counseled peace, and I thought the danger was past. We had not complied with General Howard's order because we could not, but we intended to do so as soon as possible. I was leaving the council to kill beef for my family, when news came that the young man whose father had been killed had gone out with several other hot-blooded young braves and killed four white men. He rode up to the council and shouted: "Why do you sit here like women? The war has begun already." I was deeply grieved. All the lodges were moved except my brother's and my own. I saw clearly that the war was upon us when I learned that my young men had been secretly buying

ammunition. I heard then that Too-hool-hool-suit, who
had been imprisoned by General Howard, had succeeded
in organizing a war-party. I knew that their acts would
involve all my people. I saw that the war could not then
be prevented. The time had passed. I counseled peace
from the beginning. I knew that we were too weak to fight
the United States. We had many grievances, but I knew
that war would bring more. We had good white friends,
who advised us against taking the war-path. My friend
and brother, Mr. Chapman, who has been with us since
the surrender, told us just how the war would end. Mr.
Chapman took sides against us, and helped General
Howard. I do not blame him for doing so. He tried hard
to prevent bloodshed. We hoped the white settlers would
not join the soldiers. Before the war commenced we had
discussed this matter all over, and many of my people
were in favor of warning them that if they took no part
against us they should not be molested in the event of war
being begun by General Howard. This plan was voted
down in the war-council.

There were bad men among my people who had quar-
reled with white men, and they talked of their wrongs
until they roused all the bad hearts in the council. Still I
could not believe that they would begin the war. I know
that my young men did a great wrong, but I ask, Who was
first to blame? They had been insulted a thousand times;
their fathers and brothers had been killed; their mothers
and wives had been disgraced; they had been driven to
madness by whisky sold to them by white men; they had
been told by General Howard that all their horses and
cattle which they had been unable to drive out of Wallowa
were to fall into the hands of white men; and, added to all
this, they were homeless and desperate.

I would have given my own life if I could have undone
the killing of white men by my people. I blame my young
men and I blame the white men. I blame General Howard
for not giving my people time to get their stock away from
Wallowa. I do not acknowledge that he had the right to
order me to leave Wallowa at any time. I deny that either
my father or myself ever sold that land. It is still our land.

It may never again be our home, but my father sleeps there, and I love it as I love my mother. I left there, hoping to avoid bloodshed.

If General Howard had given me plenty of time to gather up my stock, and treated Too-hool-hool-suit as a man should be treated, there *would have been no war*.

My friends among white men have blamed me for the war. I am not to blame. When my young men began the killing, my heart was hurt. Although I did not justify them, I remembered all the insults I had endured, and my blood was on fire. Still I would have taken my people to the buffalo country without fighting, if possible.

I could see no other way to avoid a war. We moved over to White Bird Creek, sixteen miles away, and there encamped, intending to collect our stock before leaving; but the soldiers attacked us, and the first battle was fought. We numbered in that battle sixty men, and the soldiers a hundred. The fight lasted but a few minutes, when the soldiers retreated before us for twelve miles. They lost thirty-three killed, and had seven wounded. When an Indian fights, he only shoots to kill; but the soldiers shoot a random. None of the soldiers were scalped. We do not believe in scalping, nor in killing wounded men. Soldiers do not kill many Indians unless they are wounded and left upon the battle-field. Then they kill Indians.

Seven days after the first battle, General Howard arrived in the Nez Percés country, bringing seven hundred more soldiers. It was now war in earnest. We crossed over Salmon River, hoping General Howard would follow. We were not disappointed. He did follow us, and we got back between him and his supplies, and cut him off for three days. He sent out two companies to open the way. We attacked them, killing one officer, two guides, and ten men.

We withdrew, hoping the soldiers would follow, but they had got fighting enough for that day. They intrenched themselves, and next day we attacked them again. The battle lasted all day, and was renewed next morning. We killed four and wounded seven or eight.

About this time General Howard found out that we were in his rear. Five days later he attacked us with three hundred and fifty soldiers and settlers. We had two hundred and fifty warriors. The fight lasted twenty-seven hours. We lost four killed and several wounded. General Howard's loss was twenty-nine men killed and sixty wounded.

The following day the soldiers charged upon us, and we retreated with our families and stock a few miles, leaving eighty lodges to fall into General Howard's hands.

Finding that we were outnumbered, we retreated to Bitter Root Valley. Here another body of soldiers came upon us and demanded our surrender. We refused. They said, "You can not get by us." We answered, "We are going by you without fighting if you will let us, but we are going by you anyhow." We then made a treaty with these soldiers. We agreed not to molest any one, and they agreed that we might pass through the Bitter Root country in peace. We bought provisions and traded stock with white men there.

We understood that there was to be no more war. We intended to go peaceably to the buffalo country, and leave the question of returning to our country to be settled afterward.

With this understanding we traveled on for four days, and thinking that the trouble was all over, we stopped and prepared tent-poles to take with us. We started again, and at the end of two days we saw three white men passing our camp. Thinking that peace had been made, we did not molest them. We could have killed or taken them prisoners, but we did not suspect them of being spies, which they were.

That night the soldiers surrounded our camp. About daybreak one of my men went out to look after his horses. The soldiers saw him and shot him down like a coyote. I have since learned that these soldiers were not those we had left behind. They had come upon us from another direction. The new white war-chief's name was Gibbon. He charged upon us while some of my people were still asleep. We had a hard fight. Some of my men crept around and attacked the soldiers from the rear. In this battle we lost nearly all our lodges, but we finally drove General Gibbon back.

Finding that he was not able to capture us, he sent to his camp a few miles away for his big guns [cannons], but my men had captured them and all the ammunition. We damaged the big guns all we could, and carried away the powder and lead. In the fight with General Gibbon we lost fifty women and children and thirty fighting men. We remained long enough to bury our dead. The Nez Percés never make war on women and children; we could have killed a great many women and children while the war lasted, but we would feel ashamed to do so cowardly an act.

We never scalp our enemies, but when General Howard came up and joined General Gibbon, their Indian scouts dug up our dead and scalped them. I have been told that General Howard did not order this great shame to be done.

We retreated as rapidly as we could toward the buffalo country. After six days General Howard came close to us, and we went out and attacked him, and captured nearly all his horses and mules [about two hundred and fifty head]. We then marched on to the Yellowstone Basin.

On the way we captured one white man and two white women. We released them at the end of three days. They were treated kindly. The women were not insulted. Can the white soldiers tell me of one time when Indian women were taken prisoners, and held three days and then released without being insulted? Were the Nez Percés women who fell into the hands of General Howard's soldiers treated with as much respect? I deny that a Nez Percé was ever guilty of such a crime.

A few days later we captured two more white men. One of them stole a horse and escaped. We gave the other a poor horse and told him he was free.

Nine days' march brought us to the mouth of Clarke's Fork of the Yellowstone. We did not know what had become of General Howard, but we supposed that he had sent for more horses and mules. He did not come up, but another new war-chief [General Sturgis] attacked us. We held him in check while we moved all our women and children and stock out of danger, leaving a few men to cover our retreat.

Several days passed, and we heard nothing of General Howard, or Gibbon, or Sturgis. We had repulsed each in turn, and began to feel secure, when another army, under General Miles, struck us. This was the fourth army, each of which outnumbered our fighting force, that we had encountered within sixty days.

We had no knowledge of General Miles's army until a short time before he made a charge upon us, cutting our camp in two, and capturing nearly all of our horses. About seventy men, myself among them, were cut off. My little daughter, twelve years of age, was with me. I gave her a rope, and told her to catch a horse and join the others who were cut off from the camp. I have not seen her since, but I have learned that she is alive and well.

I thought of my wife and children, who were now surrounded by soldiers, and I resolved to go to them or die. With a prayer in my mouth to the Great Spirit Chief who rules above, I dashed unarmed through the line of soldiers. It seemed to me that there were guns on every side, before and behind me. My clothes were cut to pieces and my horse was wounded, but I was not hurt. As I reached the door of my lodge, my wife handed me my rifle, saying: "Here's your gun. Fight!"

The soldiers kept up a continuous fire. Six of my men were killed in one spot near me. Ten or twelve soldiers charged into our camp and got possession of two lodges, killing three Nez Percés and losing three of their men, who fell inside our lines. I called my men to drive them back. We fought at close range, not more than twenty steps apart, and drove the soldiers back upon their main line, leaving their dead in our hands. We secured their arms and ammunition. We lost, the first day and night, eighteen men and three women. General Miles lost twenty-six killed and forty wounded. The following day General Miles sent a messenger into my camp under protection of a white flag. I sent my friend Yellow Bull to meet him.

Yellow Bull understood the messenger to say that General Miles wished me to consider the situation; that he did not want to kill my people unnecessarily. Yellow Bull understood this to be a demand for me to surrender and save blood. Upon reporting this message to me, Yellow Bull said he wondered whether General Miles was in earnest. I sent him back with my answer, that I had not made up my mind, but would think about it and send word soon. A little later he sent some Cheyenne scouts with another message. I went out to meet them. They said they believed that General Miles was sincere and really wanted peace. I walked on to General Miles's tent. He met me and we shook hands. He said, "Come, let us sit down by the fire and talk this matter over." I remained with him all night; next morning Yellow Bull came over to see if I was alive, and why I did not return.

General Miles would not let me leave the tent to see my friend alone.

Yellow Bull said to me: "They have got you in their power, and I am afraid they will never let you go again. I have an officer in our camp, and I will hold him until they let you go free."

I said: "I do not know what they mean to do with me, but if they kill me you must not kill the officer. It will do no good to avenge my death by killing him."

Yellow Bull returned to my camp. I did not make any agreement that day with General Miles. The battle was renewed while I was with him. I was very anxious about my people. I knew that we were near Sitting Bull's camp in King George's land, and I thought maybe the Nez Percés who had escaped would return with assistance. No great damage was done to either party during the night.

On the following morning I returned to my camp by agreement, meeting the officer who had been held prisoner in my camp at the flag of truce. My people were divided about surrendering. We could have escaped from Bear Paw Mountain if we had left our wounded, old women, and children behind. We were unwilling to do this. We had never heard of a wounded Indian recovering while in the hands of white men.

On the evening of the fourth day General Howard came in with a small escort, together with my friend Chapman. We could now talk understandingly. General Miles said to me in plain words, "If you will come out and give up your arms, I will spare your lives and send you to your reservation." I do not know what passed between General Miles and General Howard.

I could not bear to see my wounded men and women suffer any longer; we had lost enough already. General Miles had promised that we might return to our own country with what stock we had left. I thought we could start again. I believed General Miles, or *I never would have surrendered.* I have heard that he has been censured for making the promise to return us to Lapwai. He could not have made any other terms with me at that time. I would have held him in check until my friends came to my assistance, and then neither of the generals nor their soldiers would have ever left Bear Paw Mountain alive.

On the fifth day I went to General Miles and gave up my gun, and said, "From where the sun now stands I will fight no more." My people needed rest—we wanted peace.

I was told we could go with General Miles to Tongue River and stay there until spring, when we would be sent back to our country. Finally it was decided that we were to be taken to Tongue River. We had nothing to say about it. After our arrival at Tongue River, General Miles received orders to take us to Bismarck. The reason given was, that subsistence would be cheaper there.

General Miles was opposed to this order. He said: "You must not blame me. I have endeavored to keep my word, but the chief who is over me has given the order, and I must obey it or resign. That would do you no good. Some other officer would carry out the order."

I believe General Miles would have kept his word if he could have done so. I do not blame him for what we have suffered since the surrender. I do not know who is to blame. We gave up all our horses—over eleven hundred—

and all our saddles—over one hundred—and we have not heard from them since. Somebody has got our horses.

General Miles turned my people over to another soldier, and we were taken to Bismarck. Captain Johnson, who now had charge of us, received an order to take us to Fort Leavenworth. At Leavenworth we were placed on a low river bottom, with no water except river-water to drink and cook with. We had always lived in a healthy country, where the mountains were high and the water was cold and clear. Many of my people sickened and died, and we buried them in this strange land. I can not tell how much my heart suffered for my people while at Leavenworth. The Great Spirit Chief who rules above seemed to be looking some other way, and did not see what was being done to my people.

During the hot days [July, 1878] we received notice that we were to be moved farther away from our own country. We were not asked if we were willing to go. We were ordered to get into the railroad-cars. Three of my people died on the way to Baxter Springs. It was worse to die there than to die fighting in the mountains.

We were moved from Baxter Springs [Kansas] to the Indian Territory, and set down without our lodges. We had but little medicine, and we were nearly all sick. Seventy of my people have died since we moved there.

We have had a great many visitors who have talked many ways. Some of the chiefs [General Fish and Colonel Stickney] from Washington came to see us, and selected land for us to live upon. We have not moved to that land, for it is not a good place to live.

The Commissioner Chief [E. A. Hayt] came to see us. I told him, as I told every one, that I expected General Miles's word would be carried out. He said it "could not be done; that white men now lived in my country and all the land was taken up; that, if I returned to Wallowa, I could not live in peace; that law-papers were out against my young men who began the war, and that the Government could not protect my people." This talk fell like a heavy stone upon my heart. I saw that I could not gain anything by talking to him. Other law chiefs [Congressional Committee] came to see me and said they would help me to get a healthy country. I did not know who to believe. The white people have too many chiefs. They do not understand each other. They do not all talk alike.

The Commissioner Chief [Mr. Hayt] invited me to go with him and hunt for a better home than we have now. I like the land we found (west of the Osage reservation) better than any place I have seen in that country; but it is not a healthy land. There are no mountains and rivers. The water is warm. It is not a good country for stock. I do not believe my people can live there. I am afraid they will all die. The Indians who occupy that country are dying off. I promised Chief Hayt to go there, and do the best I could until the Government got ready to make good General Miles's word. I was not satisfied, but I could not help myself.

Then the Inspector Chief [General NcNiel] came to my camp and we had a long talk. He said I ought to have a home in the mountain country north, and that he would write a letter to the Great Chief at Washington. Again the hope of seeing the mountains of Idaho and Oregon grew up in my heart.

At last I was granted permission to come to Washington and bring my friend Yellow Bull and our interpreter with me. I am glad we came. I have shaken hands with a great many friends, but there are some things I want to know which no one seems able to explain. I can not understand how the Government sends a man out to fight us, as it did General Miles, and then breaks his word. Such a Government has something wrong about it. I can not understand why so many chiefs are allowed to talk so many different ways, and promise so many different things. I have seen the Great Father Chief [the President], the next Great Chief [Secretary of the Interior], the Commissioner Chief [Hayt], the Law Chief [General Butler], and many other law chiefs [Congressmen], and they all say they are my friends, and that I shall have justice, but while their mouths all talk right I do not understand why nothing is done for my people. I have heard talk and talk, but nothing is done. Good words do not last long unless they amount to something. Words do not pay for my dead people. They do not pay for my country, now overrun by white men. They do not protect my father's grave. They do not pay for all my horses and cattle. Good words will not give me back my children. Good words will not make good the promise of your War Chief General Miles. Good words will not give my people good health and stop them from dying. Good words will not get my people a home where they can live in peace and take care of themselves. I am tired of talk that comes to nothing. It makes my heart sick when I remember all the good words and all the broken promises. There has been too much talking by men who had no right to talk. Too many misrepresentations have been made, too many misunderstandings have come up between the white men about the Indians. If the white man wants to live in peace with the Indian he can live in peace. There need be no trouble. Treat all men alike. Give them all the same law. Give them all an even chance to live and grow. All men were made by the same Great Spirit Chief. They are all brothers. The earth is the mother of all people, and all people should have equal rights upon it. You might as well expect the rivers to run backward as that any man who was born a free man should be contented when penned up and denied liberty to go where he pleases. If you tie a horse to a stake, do you expect he will grow fat? If you pen an Indian up on a small spot of earth, and compel him to stay there, he will not be contented, nor will he grow and prosper. I have asked some of the great white chiefs where they get their authority to say to the Indian that he shall stay in one place, while he sees white men going where they please. They can not tell me.

I only ask of the Government to be treated as all other men are treated. If I can not go to my own home, let me have a home in some country where my people will not die so fast. I would like to go to Bitter Root Valley. There my people would be healthy; where they are now they are dying. Three have died since I left my camp to come to Washington.

When I think of our condition my heart is heavy. I see

men of my race treated as outlaws and driven from country to country, or shot down like animals.

I know that my race must change. We can not hold our own with the white men as we are. We only ask an even chance to live as other men live. We ask to be recognized as men. We ask that the same law shall work alike on all men. If the Indian breaks the law, punish him by the law. If the white man breaks the law, punish him also.

Let me be a free man—free to travel, free to stop, free to work, free to trade where I choose, free to choose my own teachers, free to follow the religion of my fathers, free to think and talk and act for myself—and I will obey every law, or submit to the penalty.

Whenever the white man treats the Indian as they treat each other, then we will have no more wars. We shall all be alike—brothers of one father and one mother, with one sky above us and one country around us, and one government for all. Then the Great Spirit Chief who rules above will smile upon this land, and send rain to wash out the bloody spots made by brothers' hands from the face of the earth. For this time the Indian race are waiting and praying. I hope that no more groans of wounded men and women will ever go to the ear of the Great Spirit Chief above, and that all people may be one people.

In-mut-too-yah-lat-lat has spoken for his people.

NO RESPECTER OF PERSONS

1879

Hairy Bear Describes the Death of Big Snake

ABOUT THE DOCUMENT:

Spokesmen for the "American" treatment of Indians alternated between painting the Indians first as bloodthirsty savages and then as innocents who would love the white man if they were not stirred up by a few "bad" Indians. In both pictures the white man appears as a brave and generous man who in the former case fought only to protect his children and his country's honor and in the second case dealt lovingly with Indians who had not had their minds poisoned against him.

Dealing with a single Indian living where the white man wanted him to live and asserting no more than his plain and simple right to the dignity of a man, the following document reveals the extent to which white men were capable of the most vicious response to any challenge of their superiority.

Big Snake, whose death is described in the document, was the brother of Standing Bear, chief of the Ponca Indians. These people were subjected to the standard kind of thievery, which by 1858 had reduced their lands to a fraction of what originally had been theirs. In 1868, however, the government added bureaucratic stupidity to its thievery and somehow included the Ponca lands among those it was assigning to the Sioux. It was a mistake the Ponca paid for by being shipped off to Oklahoma. Standing Bear refused to go, protesting so strongly that he was arrested and imprisoned at Fort Randall. A few days later he was released and he with the remaining Ponca left for Oklahoma at Army gunpoint.

Conditions in Oklahoma were bad. Many died; all grew homesick. When Standing Bear's last son lay sick and dying, he asked his father to be buried in the ancient Ponca burial ground back north along the Niobrara River. Standing Bear promised, and after his son's death, he and sixty members of his clan set out for their home grounds to bury the chief's dead son. They got as far as the Omaha reservation before being arrested by soldiers and jailed at Fort Omaha while arrangements were made to return them to Oklahoma.

This incident got into the press and attracted the attention and then the support of two white lawyers who persuaded Judge Dundy to issue a writ of *habeas corpus* to the Army general. The writ required the Army to produce the Ponca in court and show by what authority they were being held. The Army denied the Ponca's right to such a writ on the grounds that they were "not persons within the meaning of the law." The civil rights case of *Standing Bear vs. Crook* (General Crook) ended with a ruling that the Indians were "persons" and entitled to the protection of the law. This meant that Indians could not be compelled to go or refrain from going wherever they might choose. Standing Bear and the Ponca with him chose not to return to Oklahoma.

But a little later Standing Bear's brother Big Snake decided to test the law for himself. He left the Oklahoma reservation (whose agent, William H. Whiteman, described Standing Bear and his followers as troublemakers and renegades) to visit the Cheyenne reservation about a hundred miles away. Whiteman had already refused Big Snake's request for permission to visit his brother; now he telegraphed the Commissioner of Indian Affairs to request that Big Snake be arrested and returned to the reservation. This was done, for General Sherman decreed that the decision in the *Standing Bear vs. Crook* case did not apply to anyone else.

After Big Snake's return to the reservation Agent Whiteman went after him. By complaining that Big Snake was sullen and had refused to speak to him since returning—while at the same time alleging that Big Snake had threatened to kill him several times—Whiteman finally obtained authorization to put Big Snake under arrest and imprison him at the agency. To accomplish this, Whiteman asked for and received a squad of soldiers. Even then he resorted to treachery; he sent word among the Indians that those who had money due them for work they had done should report to the agency office. Among them was Big Snake; when he stepped into the office, Whiteman ordered the soldiers to make the arrest. What happened next was described by Hairy Bear, present on that occasion.

THE DOCUMENT:

From US Senate Exec. Doc. 14, 46th Congress, 3rd Session

I have heard what Big Bull said, and it is all right. I was present when the officer tried to arrest Big Snake. I stood by the door of the office, inside the door. The officer was in about the middle of the room. He told Big Snake, "I have come to arrest you." Big Snake said he did not want to go unless an interpreter went; then he would go along. Big Snake said, "If the interpreter doesn't go, I want to take one of my wives along." The officer said he could not do that; that he came to arrest only him. The agent told Big Snake he had better go, and said he would give him a blanket to sleep on. The officer told Big Snake to come along, to get up and come. Big Snake would not get up, and told the officer he wanted him to tell him what he had done. He said he had killed no one, stolen no horses, and that he had done nothing wrong. After Big Snake said that, the officer spoke to the agent, and then told Big Snake he had tried to kill two men, and had been pretty mean. Big Snake denied it. The agent then told him he had better go, and would then learn all about it down there. Big Snake said he had done nothing wrong, and that he would die before he would go. I then went up to Big Snake and told him this man [the officer] was not going to arrest him for nothing, and that he had better go along, and that perhaps he would come back all right; I coaxed all I could to get him to go; told him that he had a wife and children, and to remember them and not get killed. Big Snake then got up and told me that he did not want to go, and that if they wanted to kill him they could do it, right there. Big Snake was very cool. Then the officer told him to get up, and told him that if he did not go, there might something happen. He said there was no use in talking; I came to arrest you, and want you to go. The officer went for the handcuffs, which a soldier had, and brought them in. The officer and a soldier then tried to put them on, but Big

Snake pushed them both away. Then the officer spoke to the soldiers, and four of them tried to put them on, but Big Snake pushed them all off. One soldier, who had stripes on his arms, also tried to put them on, but Big Snake pushed them all off. They tried several times, all of them, to get hold of Big Snake and hold him. Big Snake was sitting down, when six soldiers got hold of him. He raised up and threw them off. Just then one of the soldiers, who was in front of him, struck Big Snake in the face with his gun, another soldier struck him alongside the head with the barrel of his gun. It knocked him back to the wall. He straightened up again. The blood was running down his face. I saw the gun pointed at him, and was scared, and did not want to see him killed. So I turned away. Then the gun was fired and Big Snake fell down dead on the floor.

INDIAN MESSIAH

1890

Masse Hadjo writes to the "Chicago Tribune"

ABOUT THE DOCUMENT:

Armed resistance became impossible for the Indians. But the resistance was there and had to have a form; in the last years of the nineteenth century it found its expression in a tremendous religious revival that swept through the Indian nations. The revival began with the teachings of a Paiute medicine man named Wovoka, who began to preach and describe a revelation that had come to him. Wovoka taught that spiritual regeneration of the Indians would result in the restoration of their world as it had been before the white man came to defile it. As earlier prophets had done, Wovoka, the Paiute Messiah, exhorted the Indians to avoid white ways and to seek communion with the spirits of the Indians. "You must hurt nobody and do harm to no one. You must not fight. Do right always." These were the teachings of the Paiute Messiah, and his promise was that the Great Spirit would cause a new mantle of earth to cover the ground, that the white man would disappear, and that the ghosts of the Indians' dead would return. The new religion's rituals involved special shirts and prayer dances; nervous Indian agents called these Ghost Dances, and this became the religion's common name.

White men did not like the Indians to have anything that was their own—except their misery. The Ghost Dance was felt to be subversive, and it was suppressed. First the government cut off food rations to the followers of the Paiute Messiah. When that proved insufficient, troops used physical violence and armed invasion of the reservations to suppress the Indians' religious freedom. Sitting Bull was suspected of plotting something; he was arrested and murdered in the process. After his death many of Sitting Bull's people, believers in Wovoka's teachings, fled to seek refuge on other reservations. Among those who fled was Big Foot, who camped at a place called Wounded Knee Creek with more than 350 of his people. Orders were out for Big Foot's arrest as a "fomenter of disturbances" because of his religious practices. It was December and cold, and Big Foot was suffering from pneumonia. At Wounded Knee the pursuing troops caught up to them. On the morning of December 29, 1890, Big Foot's Sioux were surrounded and ordered to surrender their arms. They did so, but the soldiers were not content with only firearms, and they searched tepees, bundles, and persons until they had collected all the knives, the axes, and even the tent stakes in a pile beside the guns. Then something happened—an uncertain scuffle —the sound of a gunshot. Whatever it was, it was enough to frighten the soldiers badly enough so that they shot down the disarmed Indians, killing about 350. And somehow, with bare hands, with knives seized from the pile, Indians killed twenty-five soldiers.

A blizzard moved in and the white men withdrew, leaving both the dead and wounded to freeze on the field. Later they were dumped together into a common grave.

White history books usually record the "battle" at Wounded Knee as the last between white soldiers and Indian warriors. It seems ironic that the last "battle" should have been fought by "Americans" bent on destroying a religion.

In 1890, the year of the Wounded Knee slaughter, the *Chicago Tribune* published an editorial hysterically critical of the Ghost Dancers. Prompt reply to this editorial came in the form of a letter to the editor written by a Sioux named Masse Hadjo. His response is given in the document that follows.

THE DOCUMENT:

Letter to the Editor, Chicago Tribune, 1890.

You say, "If the United States army would kill a thousand or so of the dancing Indians there would be no trouble." I judge by the above language you are a "Christian," and are disposed to do all in your power to advance the cause of Christ. You are doubtless a worshiper of the white man's Saviour, but are unwilling that the Indians should have a "Messiah" of their own.

The Indians have never taken kindly to the Christian religion as preached and practiced by the whites. Do you know why this is the case? Because the Good Father of all has given us a better religion—a religion that is all good and no bad, a religion that is adapted to our wants. You say if we are good, obey the Ten Commandments and never sin any more, we may be permitted eventually to sit upon a white rock and sing praises to God forevermore, and look down upon our heathen fathers, mothers, brothers and sisters who are howling in hell.

It won't do. The code of morals as practiced by the white race will not compare with the morals of the Indians. We pay no lawyers or preachers, but we have not one-tenth part of the crime that you do. If our Messiah does come we shall not try to force you into our belief. We will never burn innocent women at the stake or pull men to pieces with horses because they refuse to join in our ghost dances. You white people had a Messiah, and if history is to be believed nearly every nation has had one. You had twelve Apostles; we have only eleven, and some of those are already in the military guard-house. We also had a Virgin Mary and she is in the guard-house. You are anxious to get hold of our Messiah, so you can put him in irons. This you may do—in fact, you may crucify him as you did that other one, but you cannot convert the Indians to the Christian religion until you contaminate them with the blood of the white man. The white man's heaven is repulsive to the Indian nature, and if the white man's hell suits you, why, you keep it. I think there will be white rogues enough to fill it.

AFTER THE CONQUEST

1933–1953

Standing Bear Refutes the American Way

The Navajo and the New Deal

The Death of Ira Hayes

ABOUT THE DOCUMENTS:

With the ending of the nineteenth century the "American" conquest of the Indian seemed to have been completed; what was still left to be accomplished was the destruction of Indian culture and Indian life. That goal was given the more respectable names of "assimilation" or "acculturation," rather than that of genocide. An elaborate rationale based on the "superiority" of white economy, culture, and religion made a program of destruction and exploitation of Indians seem one of philanthropy and assistance.

The contradiction between the "American's" stated goals and their real ones could not be hidden. As with the Cherokee Nation prior to removal, the US government and the white culture continued to demonstrate that they did not really want Indians to be equal to white people, and they would not respect proof that Indians could use the tools of white "civilization" as well as white people could. Even after the conquest was accomplished, the US government continued a policy of aggression against the Indian.

An important phase of that aggression began even before the final conquest. In 1887 the General Allotment Act, or the Dawes Act, was passed to destroy the reservation system and to end tribal relations based on the shared use of land. The Dawes Act provided that Indians on the reservations would be allotted land individually: 160 acres per head of family, 80 acres per single adult, and 40 acres per minor. Reservation lands left over after the allotment would be sold to whites. According to the "assimilation" rationale, the Dawes Act would be good for the Indian because it would encourage him "to take his land in severalty and in the sweat of his brow and by the toil of his hands to carve out, as his white brother had done, a home for himself and his family." It rarely worked that way. First of all, the land was not allotted to Indians directly but was given in trust to the Bureau of Indian Affairs—the government agency with almost total power over all things Indian.

It was the BIA that had to approve any Indian's plan to lease or sell his allotted land or to pass it on in his will or even to make use of it in some specific way. Most often the decisions that the BIA encouraged or allowed an Indian to make about his land contradicted the supposed intention of helping him to become a prosperous, self-sufficient farmer. For example, an Indian with land but without tools might well be advised to lease it to a white man, instead of being helped to obtain capital credit even from his own tribe or nation's funds (which the BIA also held in trust). Rarely would the lease price be enough to live on. Then if the Indian applied for assistance, he might find that he was ineligible because he owned land. So the BIA agent could approve a sale of the land to a white man. Even then the Indian would not receive the price of his land in a lump sum—which might let him make a reasonable economic start again. Instead, the BIA would collect the sale price of the land and dole it out to the Indian in small amounts. Only after that money was gone would the Indian be finally eligible for assistance, and by then he would have completely used up his resources, effectively insuring that he would remain dependent on assistance. By this and similar devices the BIA helped reduce the approximately 138 million acres owned by Indians in 1877 to a little more than 50 million acres in 1966. Along with the loss of land went greatly increased poverty and disease, loss of tribal unity and culture, loss of language, and loss of self-determination.

In 1924, the US government passed the Citizenship Act, which conferred citizenship on all Indians. This was in "recognition of services" rendered in the armed forces by Indians during the First World War. Among other things it meant that much Indian land could now be taxed locally. Many Indians were too poor to pay taxes, and so their lands were seized and sold by local governments.

Land ownership was not the only tool of "assimilation." The BIA also provided "white man's" education to Indian children in both day schools and boarding schools. Whichever type of school an Indian child attended, however, he soon discovered that his teachers were concerned more with destroying his attachment to Indian life than with teaching him anything useful. Children were beaten for using their Indian language; their customs and crafts were degraded; their religions were dismissed as "savage" superstitions. It was made clear to them that white employees of the BIA did not expect them to succeed at anything more than menial jobs in the service of whites.

The Great Depression that was so disastrous for "American" society in general brought about the New Deal era of the 1930s, which marked an apparent change in government attitude toward the Indians. In 1934 the Indian Reorganization Act put an end to the allotment policy and recognized that the Indians wanted education, medical services, and a voice in the decisions that affected their lives. The BIA was left as the agency responsible for making necessary changes; how it went about it is illustrated in the "model constitution" it drew up and distributed to the tribes and nations. Under the "model constitution" the BIA was given the right to pass final judgment on any matters decided by an Indian government. It was the BIA of course that approved or disapproved the constitutions drawn up by the tribes and nations.

The first two documents which follow are from the 1930s. In the first the Sioux Chief, Standing Bear, examines the Indian attitude toward white culture and "assimilation." In the second the Navajo experience with the BIA agricultural assistance program is described.

Final recovery from the Great Depression was made possible by the Second World War, which provided an answer to unemployment via either military service or defense employment. Since Indians were now citizens, they were also subject to military draft. Some Indians rejected the US government's right to compel military service. Some, like the Iroquois Ernie Benedict, went to prison rather than submit to forced military service—and then enlisted in the Army after finishing their prison sentence. Others simply went into the service and proved themselves as warriors. The same government that discriminated against Indians was (and not for the first time) more than willing to accept Indian support in battle: twenty-five thousand Indian soldiers served during the Second World War. In individual cases, too, the War Department was ready enough to capitalize on the heroism of the Indians. It was to its advantage to make such use of the Pima, Ira Hayes, a volunteer Marine and veteran of the Pacific theater, who became one of the best known soldiers of the Second World War.

Ira Hayes enlisted in the Marine Corps in 1942 and became a parachutist. In the Pacific he fought on Vella Lavella, Bougainville, and Iwo Jima. On Iwo Jima his fame began when he was one of a group of Marines photographed raising the US flag atop Mount Suribachi during the heat of battle. The photograph became the most famous war photo ever made; and the military public relations department hit on the idea of bringing the flag raisers back to the US for a bond-raising tour. Ira Hayes and the other surviving soldier were returned to the states, honored, decorated, and made famous. Then the war ended. Ira Hayes returned to his people's reservation. The recognition and honors that had been given him had not changed the government's attitudes toward the Pima however. When Ira Hayes went to Washington to petition for Pima rights, saying that they "want to manage their own affairs and cease being wards of the government," he could accomplish nothing. The government did not forget him; when the Iwo Jima photograph was transformed into a bronze statue for Arlington National Cemetery, Ira Hayes was sent for once more and honored as a symbol of "American" democracy and heroism. Then after the ceremony he went back again to being just another Indian.

Ira Hayes became a symbol of something else, too: the demoralization produced by the contradictions of being an Indian in the US. Ira Hayes was arrested fifty times for drunkenness after the war—and once for escaping from an Arizona work gang. In January, 1955, he was picking cotton for three dollars per hundred pounds; one night he passed out drunk in a field. Some say he froze to death; some say he drowned in three inches of water at the bottom of an irrigation ditch.

Ira Hayes was given a hero's military funeral in Washington, D.C. The state of Arizona named a legislative bill to treat alcoholics after him; Hollywood made a feature film of his war experiences (in which he was portrayed by a white actor); and veterans' organizations passed the hat so that his family could attend his funeral.

The third document that follows contains Ira Hayes's reply to one-too-many requests from white people (on this occasion, the Phoenix radio station KOY) to speak in celebration of "America" (for Flag Day, 1953). Ira Hayes was in Chicago at the time; his refusal to return to Arizona for the occasion was expressed briefly but clearly. His statement is followed by a poem in which Simon J. Ortiz remembers Ira Hayes and says some of the things Arizona would rather not hear.

DOCUMENT A:

From Land of the Spotted Eagle, the autobiography of Chief Luther Standing Bear, Boston, 1933

The Indian was a natural conservationist. He destroyed nothing, great or small. Destruction was not a part of Indian thought and action; if it had been, and had the man been the ruthless savage he has been acredited with being, he would have long ago preceded the European in the labor of destroying the natural life of this continent. The Indian was frugal in the midst of plenty. When the buffalo roamed the plains in multitudes he slaughtered only what he could eat and these he used to the hair and bones. Early one spring the Lakotas were camped on the Missouri river when the ice was beginning to break up. One day a buffalo floated by and it was hauled ashore. The animal proved to have been freshly killed and in good condition, a welcome occurrence at the time since the meat supply was getting low. Soon another came floating downstream, and it was no more than ashore when others came into view. Everybody was busy saving meat and hides, but in a short while the buffalo were so thick on the water that they were allowed to float away. Just why so many buffalo had been drowned was never known, but I relate the instance as a boyhood memory.

I know of no species of plant, bird, or animal that were

exterminated until the coming of the white man. For some years after the buffalo disappeared there still remained huge herds of antelope, but the hunter's work was no sooner done in the destruction of the buffalo than his attention was attracted toward the deer. They are plentiful now only where protected. The white man considered natural animal life just as he did the natural man life upon this continent, as 'pests.' Plants which the Indian found beneficial were also 'pests.' There is no word in the Lakota vocabulary with the English meaning of this word.

There was a great difference in the attitude taken by the Indian and the Caucasian toward nature, and this difference made of one a conservationist and of the other a non-conservationist of life. The Indian, as well as all other creatures that were given birth and grew, were sustained by the common mother—earth. He was therefore kin to all living things and he gave to all creatures equal rights with himself. Everything of earth was loved and reverenced. The philosophy of the Caucasian was, 'Things of the earth, earthy'—to be belittled and despised. Bestowing upon himself the position and title of a superior creature, others in the scheme were, in the natural order of things, of inferior position and title; and this attitude dominated his actions toward all things. The worth and right to live were his, thus he heartlessly destroyed. Forests were mowed down, the buffalo exterminated, the beaver driven to extinction and his wonderfully constructed dams dynamited, allowing flood waters to wreak further havoc, and the very birds of the air silenced. Great grassy plains that sweetened the air have been upturned; springs, streams, and lakes that lived no longer ago than my boyhood have dried, and a whole people harassed to degradation and death. The white man has come to be the symbol of extinction for all things natural to this continent. Between him and the animal there is no rapport and they have learned to flee from his approach, for they cannot live on the same ground. . . .

The feathered and blanketed figure of the American Indian has come to symbolize the American continent. He is the man who through centuries has been moulded and sculped by the same hand that shaped its mountains, forests, and plains, and marked the course of its rivers.

The American Indian is of the soil, whether it be the region of forests, plains, pueblos, or mesas. He fits into the landscape, for the hand that fashioned the continent also fashioned the man for his surroundings. He once grew as naturally as the wild sunflowers; he belongs just as the buffalo belonged.

With a physique that fitted, the man developed fitting skills—crafts which today are called American. And the body had a soul, also formed and moulded by the same master hand of harmony. Out of the Indian approach to existence there came a great freedom—an intense and absorbing love for nature; a respect for life; enriching faith in a Supreme Power; and principles of truth, honesty, generosity, equity, and brotherhood as a guide to mundane relations.

Becoming possessed of a fitting philosophy and art, it was by them that native man perpetuated his identity; stamped it into the history and soul of this country—made land and man one.

By living—struggling, losing, meditating, imbibing, aspiring, achieving—he wrote himself into ineraceable evidence—an evidence that can be and often has been ignored, but never totally destroyed. Living—and all the intangible forces that constitute that phenomenon—are brought into being by Spirit, that which no man can alter. Only the hand of the Supreme Power can transform man; only Wakan Tanka can transform the Indian. But of such deep and infinite graces finite man has little comprehension. He has, therefore, no weapons with which to slay the unassailable. He can only foolishly trample.

The white man does not understand the Indian for the reason that he does not understand America. He is too far removed from its formative processes. The roots of the tree of his life have not yet grasped the rock and soil. The white man is still troubled with primitive fears; he still has in his consciousness the perils of this frontier continent, some of its fastnesses not yet having yielded to his questing footsteps and inquiring eyes. He shudders still with the memory of the loss of his forefathers upon its scorching deserts and forbidding mountain-tops. The man from Europe is still a foreigner and an alien. And he still hates the man who questioned his path across the continent.

But in the Indian the spirit of the land is still vested; it will be until other men are able to divine and meet its rhythm. Men must be born and reborn to belong. Their bodies must be formed of the dust of their forefathers' bones.

The attempted transformation of the Indian by the white man and the chaos that has resulted are but the fruits of the white man's disobedience of a fundamental and spiritual law. The pressure that has been brought to bear upon the native people, since the cessation of armed conflict, in the attempt to force conformity of custom and habit has caused a reaction more destructive than war, and the injury has not only affected the Indian, but has extended to the white population as well. Tyranny, stupidity, and lack of vision have brought about the situation now alluded to as the 'Indian Problem.'

There is, I insist, no Indian problem as created by the Indian himself. Every problem that exists today in regard to the native population is due to the white man's cast of mind, which is unable, at least reluctant, to seek understanding and achieve adjustment in a new and a significant environment into which it has so recently come.

The white man excused his presence here by saying that he had been guided by the will of his God; and in so saying absolved himself of all responsibility for his appearance in a land occupied by other men.

Then, too, his law was a written law; his divine decalogue reposed in a book. And what better proof that his advent into this country and his subsequent acts were the result of divine will! He brought the Word! There ensued a blind worship of written history, of books, of the written word, that has denuded the spoken word of its power and sacredness. The written word became established as a criterion of the superior man—a symbol of emotional fineness. The man who could write his name on a piece of paper, whether or not he possessed the spiritual fineness to honor those words in speech, was by some miraculous formula a more highly developed and sensitized person than the one who had never had a pen in hand, but whose spoken word was inviolable and whose sense of honor and truth was paramount. With false reasoning was the quality of human character measured by man's ability to make with an implement a mark upon paper. But granting this mode of reasoning be correct and just, then where are to be placed the thousands of illiterate whites who are unable to read and write? Are they, too, 'savages'? Is not humanness a matter of heart and mind, and is it not evident in the form of relationship with men? Is not kindness more powerful than arrogance; and truth more powerful than the sword?

True, the white man brought great change. But the varied fruits of his civilization, though highly colored and inviting, are sickening and deadening. And if it be the part of civilization to maim, rob, and thwart, then what is progress?

I am going to venture that the man who sat on the ground in his tipi meditating on life and its meaning, accepting the kinship of all creatures, and acknowledging unity with the universe of things was infusing into his being the true essence of civilization. And when native man left off this form of development, his humanization was retarded in growth. . . .

After subjugation, after dispossession, there was cast the last abuse upon the people who so entirely resented their wrongs and punishments, and that was the stamping and the labeling of them as savages. To make this label stick has been the task of the white race and the greatest salve that it has been able to apply to its sore and troubled conscience now hardened through the habitual practice of injustice.

But all the years of calling the Indian a savage has never made him one; all the denial of his virtues has never taken them from him; and the very resistance he has made to save the things inalienably his has been his saving strength—that which will stand him in need when justice does make its belated appearance and he undertakes rehabilitation.

All sorts of feeble excuses are heard for the continued subjection of the Indian. One of the most common is that he is not yet ready to accept the society of the white man—that he is not yet ready to mingle as a social entity.

This, I maintain, is beside the question. The matter is not one of making-over the external Indian into the likeness of the white race—a process detrimental to both races. Who can say that the white man's way is better for the Indian? Where resides the human judgment with the competence to weigh and value Indian ideals and spiritual concepts; or substitute for them other values?

Then, has the white man's social order been so harmonious and ideal as to merit the respect of the Indian, and for that matter the thinking class of the white race? Is it wise to urge upon the Indian a foreign social form? Let none but the Indian answer!

Rather, let the white brother face about and cast his mental eye upon a new angle of vision. Let him look upon the Indian world as a human world; then let him see to it that human rights be accorded to the Indians. And this for the purpose of retaining for his own order of society a measure of humanity. . . .

When the Indian has forgotten the music of his forefathers, when the sound of the tomtom is no more, when noisy jazz has drowned the melody of the flute, he will be a dead Indian. When the memory of his heroes are no longer told in story, and he forsakes the beautiful white buckskin for factory shoddy, he will be dead. When from him has been taken all that is his, all that he has visioned in nature, all that has come to him from infinite sources, he then, truly, will be a dead Indian. His spirit will be gone, and though he walk crowded streets, he will, in truth, be—*dead!*

But all this must not perish; it must live, to the end that America shall be educated no longer to regard native production of whatever tribe—folk-story, basketry, pottery, dance, song, poetry—as curios, and native artists as curiosities. For who but the man indigenous to the soil could produce its song, story, and folk-tale; who but the man who loved the dust beneath his feet could shape it and put it into undying, ceramic form; who but he who loved the reeds that grew beside still waters, and the damp roots of shrub and tree, could save it from seasonal death, and with almost superhuman patience weave it into enduring objects of beauty—into timeless art!

Regarding the 'civilization' that has been thrust upon me since the days of reservation, it has not added one whit to my sense of justice; to my reverence for the rights of life; to my love for truth, honesty, and generosity; nor to my faith in Wakan Tanka—God of the Lakotas. For after all the great religions have been preached and expounded, or have been revealed by brilliant scholars, or have been written in books and embellished in fine language with finer covers, man—all man—is still confronted with the Great Mystery.

So if today I had a young mind to direct, to start on the journey of life, and I was faced with the duty of choosing between the natural way of my forefathers and that of the white man's present way of civilization, I would, for its welfare, unhesitatingly set that child's feet in the path of my forefathers. I would raise him to be an Indian!

DOCUMENT B:

The Navajo and the New Deal, from the New York Times, November 11, 1941

GREASEWOOD SPRINGS, ARIZ.

The New Dealers, having taken over the Indian, in 1934, started first by reorganizing his education system. Then they proceeded to overhaul his economic life. And thereby hangs a tale.

As far as the Navajo Indian is concerned, his tribe has always been the only self-supporting tribe in the Southwest. In all, there are about 50,000 Navajos on the reservation here, and there also used to be over 1,000,000 head of cattle, too. The heart of the Navajo's economy is grazing, and sheep and goats comprise the Navajo's major source of wealth.

For such an economy, an abundance of grass is necessary, but part of the Navajo reservation falls in the Dust Bowl, hence the Navajo herder must always keep on the move to find the best grazing grounds for his flocks.

The soil erosion problem in the Dust Bowl is well known. Overgrazing and plowing up of grass means that the soil doesn't hold but sails away on the winds. To some extent this is true of the Navajo reservation.

But when you've said all that, what follows? It means that you must explain the problem to the Navajo, perhaps make some arrangements to ship his flocks to other areas, temporarily, while his overgrazed land in the central part of the reservation, gets a start again. It means that you must instruct the Indian that if he wants corn in semi-arid soil, he must plant some feterita in every other row to help hold the soil and the moisture. Sounds simple, doesn't it?

Yet the New Dealers bungled the business so badly that this and probably the next generation of Navajos will never forget the invasion of 1935-36, when the Washington planners took the field in an endeavor to remake the Navajo Indian.

After carloads of college boy "experts" surveyed the reservation, the Navajo was told that he must reduce his flocks. *Must reduce!* Those were orders not requests.

The Navajo Tribal Council, forced to accept the Government decree, begged that no reduction would be made in flocks of fewer than one hundred head, for an Indian could scarcely live and support his family the year round with less cattle than that. But the Indian Bureau wasn't bound by any Navajo tribal wishes. The New Dealers tagged about 400,000 sheep and goats—almost forty per cent of the entire Navajo holdings—and after paying their owners $1 a head, slaughtered the cattle right then and there.

As one Indian Bureau field man proudly told this correspondent:

"There isn't much cattle in here now. Back in '36 and

thereabouts, the Government came in and bought about 19,000 head in this section alone. Paid a dollar a head and we killed them. That was my first job out here. Killing cattle. This rifle here," he said pointing to one he carried in the back end of his auto, "has shot about 5,000 sheep alone. Now I use it for prairie dogs."

The Navajo also discovered that the Government men had not left the small, one hundred-head flocks alone, but had concentrated here because the large holder had managed to split up his flocks and drive some of them into box canyons where the Indian Bureau men couldn't find them. Then, too, Indian employees of the Indian Bureau, having received the regulations, proceeded to carry them out to the letter. They rode into villages and arbitrarily reduced this man's flock from one hundred to fifty, that man's fifty to twenty-five, another's twenty to ten, and so on. The Navajos were powerless to stop the slaughter (at $1 per head), since the Government badge is all-powerful on the reservation. The upshot of it was actual hunger.

To meet this problem, the Indian Bureau ordered two things: First, grazing permits were in order for all Indians, and second, irrigation projects were to be started so that the dispossessed Indians (dispossessed from their flocks) might earn some kind of a living by working on these Government jobs.

What the Indian Bureau was aiming at all along was turning the Navajo Indians from herding to subsistence farming. Of course, the Bureau of Indian Affairs never asked the Navajos whether they wanted to go into farming. Washington had drawn the plan, and since the Indian was a ward of the Government, he had nothing to say over his fate.

But something went wrong. Many of the Navajos knew nothing of grazing permits, and anxiously tended their flocks to build them up again, only to be faced by angry Government field men. So, many of the herders took to the canyons off the beaten paths in the hopes that the field men would not find them.

Then, Congress, which had not been consulted on the

large-scale plan to refashion the Navajo into a farmer, refused to appropriate the money for the huge irrigation projects and the large proposed lakes. The result was that after about a year and a half, most of the irrigation work was halted, dams went uncompleted, the Indians laid off, and the situation returned to its former status—except, of course, that now the Indians had no flocks to fall back upon.

When the 1939 drought came along, the bitterest grumbling arose throughout the reservation, the Navajo crying that if the Indian Bureau hadn't been in such a rush to cut down the number of goats and sheep, they would be eating them now. So Indian relief became more widespread, and the Navajo, unaccustomed to the mendicant philosophy of the New Deal, bitterly accepted the handouts, and returned to his *hogan* cursing the Indian Bureau.

Even the traditional form of protest has been denied to the Navajo. Formerly, the reservation was divided into six independent districts, so that every Navajo knew his own supervisor and could ride in and discuss his difficulties with him—and get something done if need be. These supervisors were located at Crownpoint and Shiprock, N. M., and at Leupp, Tuba City, Keams Canyon and Fort Defiance, Ariz. But the New Deal tendency to centralize and multiply jobs led to the abolition of the six districts, and in their place eighteen superintendencies were set up. These, however, while they are closer to the Indian, have no power to do anything, but serve merely as field offices. All power now resides at Window Rock, and all talk goes one way: From Window Rock to the Indian.

Even the Navajos' eighty chapter organizations, subsidiaries of the Tribal Council, have been discouraged by the Indian Bureau.

The current plight of the Navajo is instanced by the tale of a Navajo woman. Visiting a Navajo *hogan* (which reminds you of a croquette with the top cut off), we found a woman who knew the trader accompanying us. She was neatly dressed in a worn waist of calico and a flowing skirt which covered a multitude of petticoats. She was typical of the district, and her story was typical of the reservation.

"We have thirty sheep and fourteen goats," she told the trader who translated. "Once we have more than one hundred sheep alone. Then policeman come from Indian agency and read law and we must sell. We hide some, they shoot others. Then policeman come, read law for grazing permits. I am frightened. All around Indians work on tree planting, but soon stop. Then we get hungry. We try pick pinon nuts to sell, but policeman from agency come and read law and take them away.

"All around Indians are hungry and traders don't give credit any more. They know we have few sheep, few goats, no wool. Policeman read law and they can't sell. Indian agency bring food in cans, if not Indian must beg from white man who visits. Even my children now cough too much, not enough goat milk or goat meat. Indian agency has lots men on reservation now, but Indians have no work, no coffee, no flour, no meat. Next they take *hogans* and we live under pinon tree."

Of such are the fruits of a planned economy.

DOCUMENT C:

From a Statement by Ira Hayes, Chicago, Illinois, Flag Day, 1953

I was out in Arizona for eight years and nobody paid any attention to me. They might ask me what I think of the way they treat Indians out there, compared to how we are treated in Chicago. I'd tell them the truth and Arizona would not like it.

AND THE LAND IS JUST AS DRY

line from song by Peter LaFarge

the horizons are still mine

the ragged peaks
the cactus the brush the hard brittle plants
these are mine yours
we must be humble with them

the green fields
a few a very few
Interstate highway 10 to tucson
sacaton, bapchule,
my home is right there
off the road to tucson
before the junction
on the map it is yellow
and dry, very dry
breathe tough swallow
look for rain and rain

used to know ira he said
his tongue slow spit on his lips
in mesa used to chop cotton
coming into phoenix from north
you pass by john jacobs farm
many of the people there
they live in one room shacks
they're provided for by john jacobs
pays them about $5 per day in sun
enough for quart of wine on friday
ira got his water alright
used to know him in mesa in the sun
my home is brown adobe
and tin roof and lots of children
broken down cars the pink ford
up on those railroad ties
still paying for it
and it's been two years since
it ran motor burned out
had to pull it back from phoenix

gila river the sign states
at the bridge full of brush

and sand and where's the water
the water which you think about
sometimes in empty desperation
it's in those green very green fields
which are not mine

you call me a drunk indian go ahead

Simon J. Ortiz

SURVIVAL IN WASHINGTON

1968–1969

The Nisqually Diary

Sid Mills: A Choice of Allegiance

ABOUT THE DOCUMENTS:

When Isaac Ingalls Stevens was appointed governor of the new Washington Territory in 1853 and began his drive for wholesale "settlements" with the Indian peoples there (see "From Sea to Shining Sea"), among the many treaties he concluded on behalf of the US were those at Medicine Creek (1854) and Point Elliott (1855). Among the tribes and bands affected by the first treaty were the Nisqually and the Puyallup; ancestors of the Muckleshoot lost their lands by the terms of the second treaty. Both treaties, after describing the lands being ceded to the United States government, contained articles guaranteeing the Indians' rights to fish both on and off the reservation. Article V of the Point Elliott treaty stated:

The right of taking fish at usual and accustomed grounds and stations is further secured to said Indians in common with all citizens of the Territory, and of erecting temporary houses for the purpose of curing, together with the privilege of hunting and gathering roots and berries on open and unclaimed lands; provided, however, that they shall not take shell fish from any beds staked or cultivated by the citizens.

An almost identical article in the Medicine Creek Treaty (Article III) added only that "they shall alter all stallions not intended for breeding horses, and shall keep up and confine the latter."

Governor Stevens was well pleased with his success in "settling" with the Indians; he felt, and rightly, that the US had driven very favorable bargains for itself. But times change; by the 1950s the white population of Washington had increased enormously and even these vestigial fishing rights became the objects of white encroachment. In the mid-1950s the Washington authorities tried to control Indian fishing on the Puyallup River. The Indians protested, and white courts upheld their right to fish. Only a few years later, however, Indian fishing beyond the confines of the reservation began to be limited. And so began a contest that continues until today. Washington Indians have continued to exercise their treaty rights to fish; white sportsmen, Washington state police, and game officials harass and arrest the Indians; state and federal courts hand down conflicting and inconsistent decisions that avoid a clear resolution of the problem; the BIA equivocates. Below are some of the principal events of this struggle.

1963: The United States Court of Appeals upheld the decision recognizing the Indians' fishing rights referred to above. Nevertheless, state courts granted injunctions closing the entire Green River to Indian net fishing.

1964: State courts granted an injunction closing the Nisqually River to Indian fishermen below the Nisqually Reservation.

In the same year the Survival of American Indians Association was founded to assert and preserve off-reservation fishing rights. Protest fish-ins were held at Frank's Landing on the Nisqually River; fishermen were arrested; petitions were filed demanding court investigations of brutality by law enforcement officers.

1965: Judge Cochran ruled that the Puyallup Tribe does not exist and issued a permanent injunction against its members fishing the Puyallup River.

A large force of state and local officers raided Frank's Landing, smashing boats and fishing gear, slashing nets, and manhandling people. Two observers of the American Friends Service Committee reported that two white state officials had been drinking. Seven Indians were arrested; charges that officers used undue force were ignored. Further demonstrations were carried out by Muckleshoot on the Green River. (Earlier a judge had decided that the Muckleshoot Tribe does not exist, either.)

1966: The Department of Justice announced that it would honor an Indian request for a defense of Indian fishing rights; it entered the case as Friend of the Court.

1967: A State Superior Court ruled that the Muckleshoot really are a tribe—but denied their right to fish off the reservation.

1968: The US Supreme Court confirmed Indian fishing rights under the treaty but said that the state had the right to regulate all fishing "provided the regulation meets appropriate standards and does not discriminate against Indians." The state courts then granted a new injunction against the Puyallup that was almost the same as the original one protested.

1969: The Indians arrested at Frank's Landing in 1965 were brought to trial and acquitted. Washington's Department of Fisheries allowed the Nisqually to fish off the reservation—but prohibited the customary fishing of the Indians involved in the Frank's Landing protest.

1970: Another police raid at Frank's Landing resulted in the arrest of sixty persons. Indians once again charged unnecessary use of force by the police.

1971: Hank Adams, a member of the Survival of American Indians Association, was shot in the abdomen. Adams accused two white sport fishermen of the attack, and his story was confirmed by an Indian companion.

Tacoma police called off an investigation of the shooting, implying they believed Adams had shot himself.

The first of the two following documents is an account of events around Frank's Landing, from January to May, 1969. The account was prepared by the communications section of the Survival of American Indians Association.

The second document is a statement by Sid Mills, an Indian soldier who refused to continue in military service, choosing instead to support the Frank's Landing Indians in their struggle to force white respect for their treaty rights. The statement was made by Sid Mills on October 13, 1968, and published by the communications section of the SAIA in 1969.

DOCUMENT A:

Nisqually Diary. From the Communications section of the Survival of the American Indians Association

EVENTS FROM JANUARY TO MAY, 1969

Jan. 2—Other State raids have occurred: around Christmas and prior to New Years. A bench warrant is issued for Rick Hoy to begin serving a 30 day sentence and additional time for a $100 fine imposed after a conviction of illegal fishing on October 21 at a trial December 16. Later it's learned, when the State attempts to execute the 6 months sentence on Mounts, Quinones and Laducer, that the Court's rules on appeals and procedures are changed, with changes effective on January 1. Superior Court Judge Wright refuses to execute sentences on the three later cases; but it's too late to help Rick on his appeal action. His conviction was based upon Sandy Miller's "positive identification and observations" that Rick handled a net before his arrest. The observations and positive identification occurred by binoculars in near-total darkness at a distance of 200 yards. The judge pro tem Gerry Alexander could not believe the verdict of the jury, but said he was powerless to impose his private view and judgement in place of the juries. But, his sentencing was light and the appeal bond was set at only $500.

Jan. 9.—The Dog (Chum) salmon are running real heavy, and the nets fill up within 20 minutes after they're set. Al Bridges is fishing at the Trestle. A small "Warning Security" is on shore. Maiselle Bridges takes lunch to the trestle. The salmon are being put in the trunk of a car. About 3:30 in the afternoon, sport fishermen are along the river. Half a dozen carloads of Game agents, led by Walter Neubrech, come speeding into the area.

Al takes one net from its tie-up and pulls it into the boat while in the river, Jerry Powless (Oneida) runs to the other net. It is cut loose, but hangs up because of all the fish in it and the State grabs it. Jerry Powless is arrested for "illegal fishing" ($250 bail), and police surround the car of Gene Allan (Quinault) and demand that he open the trunk. He refuses and Maiselle tells them he doesn't have to open it. She takes the trunk key and runs about a mile to the Landing to alert the others there. Neubrech is hysterically shouting at Al Bridges; jumping up and down, as in childish tantrum. When a KING-TV program producer arrives at the trestle, all State officers are gone, but a reserve contingent of three Sheriff's cars and a State Patrol car are parked at the local grocery store. The limited Armed Guard position is re-established at Frank's Landing in anticipation that the area will be overrun to arrest Al, and SAIA calls the Governor's Office to tell Jim Dolliver that officers of the State will not be permitted to kidnap Indian Persons from the Landing. No officers show up.

Jan. 13—An 8-member film crew arrive from London, England to begin a television documentary for the Independent Thames Television commercial station. Ross Devenish is producer-director; and the company is in the area for two weeks to film activities around Frank's Landing for a feature on the fishing rights struggle; and additionally films on the Quinault Reservation, before traveling to South Dakota.

Jan. 15—Sid Mills is arrested when going to the County Courthouse for the trial of Al and Maiselle Bridges, Suzanne Saticum, Don and Janet McCloud, Nugent Kautz and Don George for their arrests on "obstructing justice or officers" during the skirmish at Frank's Landing on October 13, 1965. Sid is returned to Fort Lewis Post Stockade. The Sheriff's Office refuses to accept a complaint of assault against Sheriff's Officer Tony Sexton for threatening Hank Adams in an unwarrented rage before arresting Sid.

The trial lasts two days, with the State presenting the evidence most damaging to itself; particularly films that showed big men in uniform pushing little children around, and getting pretty rough with both men and women Indian adults. The trial was heard in Judge Franklin K. Thorpe's Justice Court with ACLU's Al Ziontz representing all 7 Indians in their defense. The State provided some detailed information of their methods of operation at that time, when officers were mobilized from enforcement districts throughout the State in preparation for the planned demonstration. Officer after officer testified that the State force was totally unarmed during the skirmish and the State's case was hurt critically by the appearance for the defense of an officer who identified a leather-encased steel "sap" as his own (his identification was on it) and who recalled preparations for the raid. The women on the jury seemed turned-off from the State because of the treatment of women and children during the attack. Defense motions for dismissal were denied or not acted upon, and the question of who had jurisdiction at Frank's Landing was apparently lost without any answers being given. One tense moment in the trial occurred when Mrs. Don McCloud was tearfully testifying about the events of 39 months previous; the deputy prosecutor offered to get her a drink, left the room and returned with a cup of water and handed it to her. Some off-the-wall spectator and cult leader from California suddenly shouted, "Janet, don't drink that water—you don't know what the prosecutor put in it!" The judge ordered the guy from the courtroom and Mrs. McCloud drank the water.

The jury found all seven defendants not guilty. The verdict was good in freeing the defendants from the long-endured worry of going to jail, or of continuing it through appeal processes. Otherwise the trial was not particularly significant in relation to the fishing rights issue—resolving none and changing nothing. Al Bridges had already been convicted for "illegal salmon fishing" on October 13, 1965, the incident precipitated the other arrests. And of the seven defendants, only Suzanne Satiacum, Al and Maiselle Bridges—and sometimes Don George and Nugent Kautz—remain actively involved with the fishing rights fight ... either as fishermen or acting in support of off-reservation fishermen. However, it was the first such case that ACLU handled totally by itself with its resources—but this was initially justified on basis of its involving "civil rights and civil liberties" rather than involving a pure Indian rights or Treaty Rights question. (ACLU has however recently enacted a new policy position respecting these rights Statewide.)

Jan. 17—On the morning of the second day of the trial (Jan. 16), or a day after Sid Mills was arrested, 11 carloads of State officers made a raid on Frank's Landing from the military side of the river; ASSISTED BY TWO MILITARY (U.S. ARMY) VEHICLES AND ARMY PERSONNEL in setting up roadblocks to keep sport fishermen, newsmen, or Indians from approaching from the rear. The State officers traveled upriver and onto the Nisqually Indian Reservation to seize nets, informing some non-Indians that they would not be bothered if they removed their nets. On the evening of January 16 and continuing into the morning of January 17 (the trial verdict was rendered around midnight), a number of State Department of Game Enforcement Officers were observed at the Tyee Motel south of Olympia engaged in a party. In fact, a room had been reserved for a "Victory Celebration" that night; but the celebration was aborted by the jury's verdict.

Nevertheless the party did go on until shortly after 2 a.m. when the bars close and the liquor is shut down. At a little past 2:30 a.m. the celebrants arrived at the "public access" area to Fort Lewis Military Reservation directly across the river from Frank's Landing with a force of 7 State Game Patrol cars with 6 men per car; all fully uniformed with all items of equipment. They launched two boats and traveled the river only in the vicinity of the Landing. They motored right into the boat docking area below the Grandfather's house—Bill Frank, Sr. is 90 years old, and his wife, Angeline is 75—moving to within 20 ft. of the house, shining high-powered spotlights on the house and into the house and all around the house. Then they traveled around the pilings from the area washed away by high waters (which had done considerably more damage during the first week of January) to shine their light on other buildings and equipment in the yard. When their spotlight finally settled upon the 2 boats that had been carried out of the water and into the yard, they left and returned to the ARMY PROPERTY on the other side of the river. When the boats hit the launching area officers could be seen coming from all parts of the public access area, apparently dispersed for some reason. The Peace Officers then spent the next hour talking and taking turns hollering across the river, swearing, and cussing out Indians, "Hippies", and making gratuitous statements about "Black Panthers" ... as well as challenging and daring Hank Adams and Al Bridges to "Come over here, if you are there," "Is Hank Adams over there?" At about 4 a.m. their cars started leaving and headed toward the trestle. Two cars left Frank's Landing for the trestle to make certain that Indians weren't getting caught alone at the trestle, if any were there. Mike Watson drove one car with four Persons in it, and Gene Allan drove the other with five Persons in it including Al and Alison Bridges and Hank Adams.

When the 2 cars drove into the area of the trestle, Game Patrol cars immediately pulled into the narrow, humped exit covering a culvert, blocking entry or exit. 17 public servants jumped out of the three cars, each swinging either a riot club or flashlight—and some handling both. Only one person remained in the "road block" cars.

only one not wearing a uniform; it being Ellsworth "Buzz" Sawyer, an administrative chief for the Game Patrol State wide, (whereas the uniformed officers are assigned to particular districts). Groups of officers surrounded each car from the Landing and began asking them to get out and start something. Several officers sapped the cars with their clubs, Officer; "Why don't you have your People get out here, Adams?" Officer to another officer; "Che (sic) Guevere, at least he had style, I bet he'd get his People out here." Officer; "Adams, what you trying to be—another Martin Luther Coon?"

Hank got out of the car and walked over to Mike Watson's car and instructed them to stay in their car, that they had to see if they'd be allowed to leave; not to start anything with anyone, that there were another 4 Patrol Cars somewhere and it appeared to be a "trap". At that time Billie Louise McCloud drove up in her car and ran past the "road block" cars to Gene's car to talk with Alison and Al. Not knowing yet whether Sawyer and Dougherty would permit exit. Billie Louise left to bring back some more Indians. Hank then instructed Gene to try to leave the area. The "road block" cars stayed in position for about five minutes and Adams asked Officer Daugherty if they were going to permit them to leave. A couple more minutes, and after discussing with Sawyer, Sawyer's car was pulled back out of the way. Adams decided his group shouldn't leave since Billie Louise might come back and get caught there alone with her car (others with her). So they backed up to their previous position, leaving the exit clear. Adams then walked over to Watson's car, where a young officer was ridiculing Mike about his hair and asking him if he was "queer." At this point, a driver was in each Patrol Car with all motors running. Hank told George Meskuotis that they should delay the officers there until the others came back, 'cause if they left first "they" might raid Frank's Landing itself while their 2 cars waited at the trestle. He said that probably the best way to keep them there would be for him to walk by himself down by the river—but when he got back into Gene's car they should drive to the other side of the hump, so "we don't get blocked in here again." When lights turned in at the end of the road a quarter mile away, Hank got into the car, and Gene followed Mike to the other side of the narrow exit and both pulled to the side of the road. Billie Louise said the only People she could find were the others at the Landing mostly women: Maiselle Bridges, Suzette Mills, Valerie Bridges, Marcie Hall, Carmen Laducer, and Joe Barosa and Chiefy John (on crutches). With Billie Louise were Danny McGee, Babe John, Russell McCloud and Sherri Anderson. Hank instructed all vehicles to return to Frank's Landing. As the cars started leaving, 3 other Game Patrol cars holding at least another 18 agents pulled into the road from off the highway. Their carefully planned trap had not worked. Within 2 hours, "Survival" had secured all information about their prior party at the Tyee Motel.

Two days later, Walter Neubrech, top State enforcement officer for the Game Department stopped his car by Russell McCloud and Joe Barosa, walking on the road, to tell them Indians were going to see just how rough HIS department could get with their clubs and other weapons.

Jan. 22—George Meskuot defends himself on his "illegal fishing charge" quite competently, but is found guilty in a five minute deliberation. A veteran of Vietnam, and sometime student from Detroit, Ohio. The judge decides to delay sentencing until after the "3rd degree assault" trial scheduled for January 24—suggesting that he would probably allow for a probation arrangement similar to that allowed for Roger Crowley. George becomes ill and is not able to attend trial on January 24—and when the court refuses to believe him and says it will arrest him if a County Doctor dispatched to the Landing and doesn't confirm his illness. The Court is told to "forget it" and George instead participates in fishing demonstration for filming by the British television crew. During the action, no arrests are made—although Sandy Miller keeps yelling at Al Bridges that he is under arrest and orders him to bring his boat into shore, which he doesn't. George then leaves for California with Bill Hess.

Feb. 23—Jamie Sanchez, 15-year old Nisqually Indian is shot in the Yelm City Hall by one of 3 deputy sheriffs who have had him in custody for an hour.

Officers say Jamie lunged with a switchblade knife at Bill McClusky, who shot the 135-pound, 5'3" youth with his .38-caliber service revolver. Jamie lays on floor for 30 minutes while ambulance comes from 15 miles away and another ambulance sets 75 feet away for lack of driver. Jamie had the knife out for some time while sitting in a chair, then for several minutes while standing up. All officers had revolvers—one, Deputy Bill Triggs, had a can of MACE, but bullets are more effective. Blade is 3½ feet from McClusky when shot fired: Jamie less than five feet away when sitting down. Jamie is a great lunger. Sheriff's Office arranges for investigation which takes deputies' statement. Deputies refuse to give account of shooting to U.S. Civil Rights Commission. Local FBI conducts no investigations; liberal giving conclusion and Jamie charged with assault.

Mar. 1—Learn BIA has enacted new regulations to move Indians off from Cook's Landing and other "in lieu fishing sites" on Columbia River in name of sanitation and health—prohibit permanent dwellings or residences. BIA action illegal—not provided for by law.

Mar. 7—Begin campaign to secure release from Marine Corps of Charles Cantrell, Puyallup Indian.

Mar. 14—Sid Mills ordered released from Post Stockade by Commanding General William W. Beverley at Fort Lewis—and ordered discharged immediately.

DOCUMENT B:

The Statement of Sid Mills
Frank's Landing on the Nisqually River, Washington, October 13, 1968

I am a Yakima and Cherokee Indian, and a man. For two years and four months, I've been a soldier in the United States Army. I served in combat in Vietnam—until critically wounded. I recently made a decision and publicly declare it today—a decision of conscience, of commitment and allegiance.

I owe and swear first allegiance to Indian People in the sovereign rights of our many Tribes. Owing to this allegiance and the commitment it now draws me to, I hereby renounce further obligation in service or duty to the United States Army.

My first obligation now lies with the Indian People fighting for the lawful Treaty Rights to fish in usual and accustomed waters of the Nisqually, Columbia and other rivers of the Pacific Northwest, and in serving them in this fight in any way possible.

This fight is real—as is the threat to Indian existence under the enforced policy objectives of the State of Washington, as permitted by the compromised position and abdication of responsibilities by the U.S. Government.

The defense of Indian People and a chosen way of life in this fight for unrelinquished fishing rights is more compelling and more demanding of my time and commitment than any duty to the U.S. military. I renounce, and no longer consider myself under, the authorities and jurisdiction of the U.S. Army.

I have served the United States in a less compelling struggle in Vietnam and will not be restricted from doing less for my People within the United States.

The U.S. would have accepted sacrifice of my life in Vietnam in a less legitimate cause—in fact, nearly secured such sacrifice and would have honored such death. Yet I have my life and am now prepared to stand in another battle, a cause to which the United States owes its protection—a fight for People who the United States has instead abandoned. My action is taken with the knowledge that the nation that would have accepted and "honored death" by its requirement may now offer only severe consequence and punishment because I now choose to commit myself to Indian People.

I have given enough to the U.S. Army—I choose now to serve my People.

My decision is influenced by the fact that we have already buried Indian fishermen returned dead from Vietnam, while Indian fishermen live here without protection and under steady attack from the power processes of this Nation and the States of Washington and Oregon. I note that less than a month ago, we counted the death of another Indian fisherman, Jimmy Alexander, because of conditions imposed upon our People to secure a livelihood while avoiding arrest. These conditions continued off Cook's Landing on the Columbia River, where Jimmy drowned, largely because the President of the United States ignored a direct appeal to intervene in the arrest case of Army Sergeant Richard Sohappy, a friend and fellow fisherman of Jimmy Alexander.

Sergeant Sohappy is back in Vietnam on this third tour of duty there [as of May, 1969 Sgt. Sohappy had been returned to San Francisco, California; to the hospital to be exact. Ed.] He was arrested three times in June for illegal net fishing, while home on recuperative furlough, recovering from his fourth series of combat wounds, and while attempting to secure income for his large family.

For his stand in Vietnam, this Nation awarded him Silver and Bronze Stars, among other awards. For fighting for his family and People, this Nation permitted a professional barber acting as Justice of the Peace to interpret his Treaty, to ignore his rights, and to impose punishment and record under criminal conviction. His Commander-in-Chief, Lyndon Johnson, routinely referred the appeal for intervention to the Department of Interior, which routinely refused to act on basis of false information and facts—and on basis of a presumption of guilt on the part of Sergeant Sohappy.

He now continues to fight for this Nation in Vietnam. His fellow Yakima tribesman Jimmy Alexander is dead, and the United States stands indifferent while his People and their rights are destroyed.

Equally, I have been influenced by the fact that many Indian women and children have become obligated by conditions and necessity to sustain a major burden in this fight. These women and children have sustained some of the most brutal and mercenary attacks upon their lives and persons that have been suffered by any Indian People since prior Indian wars.

Just three years ago today, on October 13, 1965, 19 women and children were brutalized by more than 45 armed agents of the State of Washington at Frank's Landing on the Nisqually River in a vicious, unwarranted attack.

It is not that this is the aniversary of that occasion that brings us here or which prompts my declaration on this day—but rather the fact such actions have gained in frequency and have come to be an everyday expectation in their lives. As recently as last night we witnessed the beating or injury of women simply because they are among the limited numbers who will not surrender our limited rights.

This consideration, as much as any, gives immediacy to my decision and prompts me to act upon it now. I will not be among those who draw pride from a past in which I had no part nor from a proud heritage I will not uphold.

We must give of ourselves today—and I will not be content to have women and children fighting in my stead. At the least, I will be among them—at the least they will not be alone [and that my brother, is Ghost Dance talk. Ed.].

The disturbing question is, "Why must our People fight?"

Is it because the U.S. Constitution, which declares all Treaties made to be the Supreme Law of the Land and contradictory state laws void, is almost 200 years old? But treaties are still being made under force of that document. Or, is it because the Indian Treaties involved here are slightly more than one hundred? Or is it because the non-Indian population in this area has increased in that century from 3,900 to more than 3,000,000?

We do not believe that either antiquity in years or numerical superiority in population act to diminish legitimate rights not granted by this Nation, but rights retained in valid agreement and guaranteed the protection of the United States in their continued existence and exercise.

The Treaties define the extent of these fishing rights, as well as their limitation. The Indian "right of taking fish" exists only in the traditional waters of each respective Tribe and do not extend beyond these geographical boundaries.

State laws act to permit commercial fishing of salmon almost exclusively in areas where the Indian rights to fish do not exist. There are no State laws or regulations which would specifically permit Indian commercial fishing on the Nisqually River where several Tribes or bands of Indians hold co-existing rights. In no way do state laws and regulations account for the existence of Indian fishing rights in the waters where these rights exist.

The greatest impact upon the salmon resource, or 80% of the total catch, is made by non-Indians permitted to fish commercially by all types of gear and equipment in areas where Indian fishing rights do not exist. Roughly 15% of the salmon catch is annually taken by sport fishermen.

Indian fishermen have shown the utmost regard for conservation, but have maintained that the question of conservation must involve all elements which or who have impact upon the salmon resources. All adult salmon caught are returning to spawning grounds to engage in reproduction processes—whether they be among an 11,-000,000 salmon caught by non-Indians or among the few hundred thousand caught by Indians.

The State must deal with conservation issues at the point where adult salmon return to its territorial waters. Conservation must draw its validity in force from consideration of the total resource, irrespective of its being salt water or freshwater fisheries, and of being on or off reservations.

The State claims it seeks only to give equal application of law to all persons. Yet their equal application of law would permit non-Indians to catch up to 11 million salmon in all waters—yet can and does prohibit Indians from catching any in areas where the Supreme Law and their rights exist. The State claims that any other situation would give superior status to Indian "citizens", not recognizing under law that a separate and distinct status or legal dimension of the Indian exists.

Citizenship of the Indian has too frequently been used as a convenience of government for deprivation of rights or property held owing to our being Indians.

We did not generally become citizens of this nation nor lawful residents of its states until June 2, 1924—and not when all other people gained nationality and citizenship under the Fourteenth Amendment since it was immediately held in the U.S. Supreme Court that Indians were born unto the allegiance of their Tribes and not unto the allegiance of the United States. The granting of citizenship was not to act negatively upon Indian allegiance nor rights.

It is such first allegiance that I now declare and embrace in making total commitment to the Indian Cause and the immediate fight for undiminished Fishing Rights.

There is no legitimate reason why this nation and the State of Washington can not respect the equitable interests and rights of Indian People and be responsive to our needs.

Interestingly, the oldest human skeletal remains ever found in the Western Hemisphere were recently uncovered on the banks of the Columbia River—the remains of Indian fishermen. What kind of government or society would spend millions of dollars to pick upon our bones, restore our ancestral life patterns, and protect our ancient remains from damage—while at the same time eating upon the flesh of our living People with power processes that hate our existence as Indians, and which would now destroy us and the way of life we now choose—and by all rights are entitled to live?

We will fight for our rights.

INDIANS IN REVOLT

1969–1970

Indians in Revolt—1970
Alcatraz Reclaimed
Statements on Cultural Survival
The Suppressed Speech of Frank James, Wampanoag

ABOUT THE DOCUMENTS:

The first document, "Indians in Revolt—1970," serves as an introduction to modern Indian protest. It was selected for its objectivity—and also because of the innovative and nonprofit approach of its publishers, the Race Relations Information Center, Nashville, Tennessee.

In keeping with the Indian concept that puts principle above profit, the Race Relations Information Center published this report—and several others on racism in the US —without benefit of copyright, automatically making it available for republication by all interested groups.

DOCUMENT A:

From "Indians in Revolt—1970," by the Race Relations Information Center, December, 1970. The problems and examples cited in the report are all amplified below in additional documents published in contemporary Indian newspapers and journals, none of which claims copyright. Their addresses appear in the back of this book.

"Beginning with the most pitiful and primitive Indians found by explorers, the Digger Indians of Nevada and Utah, Mr. Farb shows that even they are much above the highest non-human primates."

—Elman R. Service, 1968, in an introduction to *Man's Rise to Civilization As Shown by the Indians of North America from Primeval Times to the Coming of the Industrial State.*

"Thank you, Mr. Farb, we were pretty worried about that."

—Vine Deloria, Jr., 1969, in a reaction to *Man's Rise to Civilization As Shown by the Indians of North America From Primeval Times to the Com-Coming of the Industrial State*

There is a widespread assumption that armed Indian uprisings are a thing of the past in the United States. It is not true. The days of Sitting Bull and Geronimo and Crazy Horse may be gone, but there *is* an Indian revolt and the 20th Century warriors are deadly serious.

In the State of Washington, peaceful fishermen from the Muckleshoot, Puyallop and Nisqually tribes—determined to preserve a way of life guaranteed by 19th Century treaties—took up arms earlier this year and clashed with police. The issue—the right to fish in the rivers of Western Washington—may sound frivolous to many Anglo-Saxon anglers, but to the tribes involved the stakes are nothing less than their identity as a people.

They don't intend to lose.

Probably, however, modern Indians will not resort to a widespread use of guns, even in self-defense. Their ancestors have already tried it, and the results were disastrous. And besides, Indians are, and for the most part they always have been, a peaceful people.

But they are angry, and the reason lies partly in a set of statistics now becoming familiar to a large number of Americans. For example:

• Indian life expectancy on reservations is 44 years, compared to the national average of 64 years.

• Suicide among young Indians is the second leading cause of death—three times higher than the national average.

• Infant mortality among Indians is four times higher than the rate among whites and twice the rate among blacks.

• The average educational level for federally supervised Indians (those having a historical treaty relationship with the United States) is only slightly more than five school years—although education is so highly valued among Indians that it was one of the highest priorities in nearly every treaty signed between the United States and the tribes.

Bad as they are, however, such facts are not the whole story. The Indian struggle today transcends poverty and civil rights, and the goal is not assimilation into what is called the American mainstream. What is really at issue, says Gerald Wilkinson of the National Indian Youth Council, is "not simply our survival, but our survival as Indians."

The Indian way of life apparently will not die of its own accord. It has been preserved through a very long and unsatisfying relationship with transplanted Europeans. But whites may yet kill it. A case in point is the story of the Pueblos of New Mexico—an Indian culture dating back thousands of years.

Congress made headlines late in 1970 by passing a bill guaranteeing the Taos Pueblos ownership of 48,000 acres of land which the tribe regards as holy. The bill, one part of President Nixon's 7-part legislative package concerning Indians, came after a long and bitter struggle by the Pueblos and other Indian groups such as the National Congress of American Indians.

But there have been few headlines about the other 18 Pueblo tribes in New Mexico, some of which may cease to exist in the not too distant future. Perhaps the most seriously threatened is Cochiti Pueblo, where, if the developers have their way, the "Land of the 7-Day Weekend" will spring from the blueprints and burst full-blown onto the ancient reservation. A giant corporation known as Great Western United (most famous for its Shakey's Pizza chain) is building from scratch a resort city of 50,000 people on 7,500 acres of Cochiti land.

The project delights businessmen in nearby Albuquerque, N.M., but for many of the Cochiti Indians, the development scheme would end their way of life. For thousands of years they have lived a slow-paced, harmonious existence in a dusty cluster of adobe homes between Albuquerque and Santa Fe. Their land is rugged, arid, mountainous, and largely unspoiled. It is also at the heart of the spirituality that has always infused the tribal lifestyle.

Several weeks ago, one of the Pueblo's two holy men announced that as far as he was concerned, the tribe had ceased to exist. The bulldozers had killed it. He took the sacred objects which symbolize the Cochitis' identity, and transported them to the neighboring Santo Domingo Pueblo. "It was like some cosmic disaster," Gerald Wilkinson of the National Indian Youth Council remarked later, "like a star going out after thousands of years."

The unfolding story of the development scheme was pieced together by the Race Relations Information Center with considerable help from the *New Mexico Review,* a monthly newspaper published in Albuquerque. What emerges is a seizure of Indian lands involving the Bureau of Indian Affairs, the U.S. Corps of Engineers, the U.S. Congress, powerful business interests in Albuquerque, and several of the nation's large corporations. In the face of such a vast array of power, the Indians were intimidated and prevented from exercising any real choice about their future.

The story began in the 1950's when Albuquerque grew from a town of 35,000 into a city of nearly 200,000. Businessmen in the area became optimistic about their economic future, but they recognized one critical deficiency: the shortage of water that has long plagued the entire state of New Mexico.

To secure more water for the Albuquerque area, the various interests involved began to push for a dam on the Rio Grande mainstream as it flowed through Cochiti Pueblo. A hearing was held in 1957 to allow interested parties to testify on the desirability of the proposed dam. Cochiti leaders say they were never told of the hearing, and there is no record of Indian testimony. A BIA official, however, assured all those present that such a dam "would greatly benefit the Pueblos in the Middle Rio Grande Valley."

Thus, in 1960, legislation was introduced in Congress to allow the construction of the dam. Texas and Colorado objected, however, that any dam on the Rio Grande mainstream would jeopardize their own water supplies, and they demanded changes in the bills. To meet such objections, a compromise was worked out whereby a dam could be built on the river as long as the Rio Grande was diverted only to the extent required for effective flood control.

The result was that the proponents of urbanization had their dam but no water. They set out to rectify the situation.

Two years later, a bill was introduced to allow the diversion of water from the San Juan River on the western side of the continental divide, back through the divide and ultimately into the Rio Grande river near Espanola, N.M. The additional water could then be dammed at Cochiti. The bill passed, despite Navajo Indian contentions that their water supply would be jeopardized, and the Cochiti reservoir came a giant step closer to reality.

The final step came in 1964 when a bill was passed allowing the water to be pooled, provided the Indians approved. And the powers that mattered were correctly convinced that securing such approval would not be a problem.

The Indians were told that bills had been passed to allow the building of the dam, the creation of a reservoir, and the development of the area for recreation purposes. The U.S. Corps of Engineers, which was to build the

dam, offered to pay the tribe for an easement. The Bureau
of Indian Affairs, meanwhile, warned Cochiti leaders that
if they did not take the offer, the Engineers might simply
condemn the land under a 1926 law granting the government eminent domain over Indian land.

"We thought about not allowing the dam and the reservoir," recalls one tribal leader. "But it didn't seem like a
real choice. As it was presented to us, we could either lose
our lands and get paid for them, or lose our lands and not
get paid for them."

A resolution passed by the tribal council in 1964 reveals the hopeless Cochiti mood at the time:

> Whereas, the Pueblo of Cochiti . . . has been advised by
> the Corps of Engineers and the United States Department
> of Defense . . . that it is proposing to construct . . . a flood-
> control structure on the Rio Grande near Cochiti Pueblo
> designated as Cochiti Dam and Reservoir; and
>
> Whereas, legislation has been adopted which will . . .
> make water available for a permanent pool for recreational
> purposes; and
>
> Whereas, the proposed dam and reservoir, when con-
> structed, will occupy and flood a large portion of the Pueblo
> lands; and
>
> Whereas, certain of the Pueblo lands to be so occupied
> and flooded are sacred areas of great spiritual, moral and
> emotional significance to members of the Pueblo; and
>
> Whereas, the Pueblo lands to be so occupied and inun-
> dated comprise a substantial portion of the irrigated and
> grazing land of the Pueblo and taking of these lands will
> have a disastrous effect upon the subsistence economy of
> the Pueblo members . . .

There follows a resolution agreeing to accept money as
compensation for the hardships. From then on, the tribe
set out to maximize their economic gain from the loss of
their lands.

In 1967, the Cochitis—reconciled to the building of the
recreation area—were searching for a developer. Four oil
companies and the California City Development Corporation offered their services. In 1969, following the recommendation of the BIA, the tribe signed a 99-year lease

with California City Development, granting the company control of approximately one-third of the reservation.

What many of the tribal leaders say they did not know was that the company was being sued and investigated for alleged fraud in connection with a development project in California. Pat Wehling, the BIA official closest to the negotiation of the lease, claims the Indians *were* fully informed, while the then BIA commissioner, Robert Bennett, told the *New Mexico Review* only that he gave California City Development a clean bill of health on the grounds that "anybody can sue anybody." Bennett, according to the *Review,* never told the Cochitis of the suit.

Soon after the lease was signed, Great Western United bought out California Development, inheriting both the Cochiti contract and the California lawsuit. And that is where the situation stands today.

Phillip Ashby, the attorney for the Cochiti Pueblo, says Great Western has honored the terms of the lease, and Great Western's 31-year-old president, William White, has estimated that the Indians will receive up to a million dollars a year from the contract once the development plans get rolling. "We know some of the Cochiti people are hostile to the contract," said Great Western Vice-president Tom Rondell. "We know we have a problem there. But when you have a problem, what you do is solve it. We are going to make this a project that will benefit the Cochitis. We are out to get a return on our investments, but we are not out to rape anybody."

But the cost, in human rather than economic terms, will be high. One former governor of the tribe stared out at the untamed beauty of the tribal lands recently and remarked: "This new city will destroy our culture, our way of life, what we believe in, our traditions, and it will take away 7,500 acres of our land. Our Pueblo will become a suburb. It may end our identity as a people. I just don't know. I feel very guilty about my part in it."

The Cochiti project is not isolated. It is one more in a series of development projects that William Veeder, a water expert for the Department of the Interior, feels may destroy the water supplies of all 19 Pueblo tribes in New

Mexico. If that happens, one of the oldest cultures in the western hemisphere will come to an end.

In addition, numerous other tribes face similar problems. For example:

• The Cherokee Nation, at one time one of the most stable and prosperous of Indian societies, once maintained a constitutional form of government patterned after that of the United States. The tribe instituted a progressive system of taxation and an extraordinarily effective school system. The literacy rate among the Cherokees was more than 90 per cent in their own language, and it was not uncommon for Cherokee young people to go on to eastern colleges. But the nation was systematically dismantled in 1907 when Oklahoma became a state, and Cherokee affairs were placed under the control of the U.S. government.

Today the average Cherokee adult has only five years of schooling, and the average income for a Cherokee family is $500 a year. Some 10,000 full-bloods cling to their language and traditions in the Oklahoma hills, while their tribal government is in the hands of W. W. Keeler, the chairman of the board of Phillips Petroleum and a man who is only one-sixteenth Cherokee. Keeler was appointed to his post by President Truman—an act that dramatized the tribe's lack of control over its own affairs.

• Many Navajo children are shipped 400 miles from their reservation to attend the BIA's Intermountain school in Brigham City, Utah. Students and Indian employees at the school claim that Navajo language, religion and culture are systematically repressed by routine head-shaving and handcuffing of students, and by other forms of severe corporal punishment. When the National Indian Youth Council led a protest against conditions at the school last spring, the BIA promoted Intermountain's superintendent, Wilma Victor, to acting director of all Indian education within the BIA. Miss Victor served in that capacity for three months before being transferred in late November to her current post in the Phoenix, Ariz., BIA office.

• Extensive strip-mining, the kind that has ravished Appalachia, is now under way on the Navajo and Hopi reservations, decimating their holy lands. The principal company involved is the Peabody Coal Company.

• Alaska is probably the only area in the country with sufficient untainted space for native Americans to pursue their way of life freely. But that situation appears likely to change with the entrance into the area of oil companies and other powerful interest groups. That the Alaskan Indians, Eskimos, and Aleuts will have to part with much of their land now appears to be a foregone conclusion. The remaining question is how unsatisfactory the final settlement will be.

Basic to all these situations is the implicit assumption among many powerful whites that Indian culture is, at best, a quaint anachronism that has no place in the 20th Century. "Let's face it," said Tom Rondell of Great Western United. "The Cochiti Pueblo people are just now coming out of the stone ages." Indians reply that their culture has a right to exist regardless of what non-Indians may think of it—because Indians should be allowed to live as they choose and because there is no justification for cultural genocide. They add that whites should reconsider their assumptions of superiority.

Even before Gen. Philip Sheridan began equating good Indians with dead Indians, and before George Armstrong Custer was writing college term papers about impending Indian extinction, the assumption of the red man's inferiority has pervaded official and unofficial U.S. policy. The policy in the beginning was administered very effectively by the War Department along with a large number of self-appointed Indian fighters. Those were the days when theories of manifest destiny were most unsettling to the tribes and when they still had the power to resist.

But gradually the continent became settled by whites, and benevolence began to set in. The authorities in Washington came slowly to the conclusion that it was enough merely to destroy the Indians' way of life—though not the people themselves—and the result was the Dawes Act of 1887.

The act granted each Indian a plot of ground, in the

hope that red men would learn to become civilized farmers. The policy failed dismally, not because of Indian savagery, but because the tribes had no tradition of individual ownership of land, and because it became even easier for white speculators to acquire title to Indian holdings. While the Dawes Act was in effect, Indian landholdings were reduced by 80 million acres.

The allotment era lasted until the New Deal, when in an uncharacteristic burst of humanity, the government made an attempt to rectify its previous errors. Congress passed the Indian Reorganization Act of 1934, which had the effect of repealing the Dawes law and allowing the Indians to regroup their shattered tribal holdings.

Soon, however, the country became engulfed in World War II, and the problems of the Indians were relegated to a decidedly minor spot in the nation's list of priorities. When the war ended, the errors of the past began to resurface.

The decade of the 1950's was characterized by a policy known as termination. The Termination Act was passed under the pretext of granting first-class citizenship to Indians and breaking their dependence upon the government. In practice, however, the only thing that was terminated was government service to the tribes. Indian dependency on the Bureau of Indian Affairs, if anything, became more pronounced. The termination laws are still on the books (although President Nixon has disavowed the policy and called instead for "self-determination without termination."), and the pending Congressional bills affecting Alaskan natives are shot through with what many Indian leaders see as terminationist overtones.

As a result, Indians are nearly unanimous in calling for radically altered policies towards native Americans. And even more strikingly, perhaps, some Indians are now urging whites to adopt radically different policies toward themselves before everyone is destroyed.

The Example of the Red Man

In the opulent banquet hall of a Tulsa hotel, a stout,

matronly Indian woman peered over a podium that was nearly as tall as she was. Mrs. Martha Grass, a Ponca, stared out at a sea of non-Indian faces before her, and when she began talking she minced no words. "We got along fine before you people came to this continent," she told the assemblage of human rights workers. "You could learn a beautiful culture from Indians. We still have a lot to teach you."

Buffalo Tiger, the chairman of the very traditional Miccosukee tribe, amplified on Mrs. Grass' point in a recent interview. "I am one of those people who believe the Indian way is superior to the white man's way," he said. "White men need to learn the simple things from Indians, such as how to live in harmony with what God has given them."

To many whites, Buffalo Tiger's view is patently false. How, they ask, can a man whose people hunt frogs and small game for a living, refuse to live in houses, frequently refuse to send their children to public schools, and reject urban living in favor of a subsistence existence in the Everglades—how can such a man contend that his way of life is superior?

The answer, according to many Indians is this: Indian culture does not necessarily imply a complete rejection of technological advances. The Miccosukees, one of the most conservative of all tribes, are willing to adopt modern methods with regard to health care, sanitation, even transportation (they now use airboats instead of canoes), and a few other limited areas. Other tribes go much further in that direction. "There are things we have learned from the white man, that's true," says John Olguin, an Isletta Pueblo who heads the Indian program at Dartmouth. "But there is strength in the Indian culture. Learning needs to be a two-way process."

What Indians say they have to teach is a kind of spiritual/philosophical view of other people, other forms of life, and man's physical environment. "The white man," says Charles Cambridge, a young leader among the Navajos, "simply has not developed the philosophical and cultural sophistication to control the technology he has

created. Now that technology controls him, and if something isn't done, it may destroy everybody."

Perhaps the most systematic presentation of Cambridge's point has been the book *We Talk, You Listen,* by
Vine Deloria, Jr., a Standing Rock Sioux who gained fame
from another book called *Custer Died for Your Sins.* In
the introductory section to *We Talk, You Listen,* Deloria
writes:

> Every now and then I am impressed with the thinking of
> the non-Indian. I was in Cleveland last year and got to talk-
> ing with a non-Indian about American history. He said that
> he was really sorry about what had happened to Indians,
> but that there was a good reason for it. The continent had
> to be developed and he felt that Indians had stood in the
> way and thus had had to be removed. "After all," he re-
> marked, "what did you do with the land when you had it?"
> I didn't understand him until later when I discovered that
> the Cuyahoga River running through Cleveland is inflam-
> mable. So many combustible pollutants are dumped into
> the river that the inhabitants have to take special precau-
> tions during the summer to avoid accidentally setting it on
> fire. After reviewing the argument of my non-Indian friend
> I decided that he was probably correct. Whites had made
> better use of the land. How many Indians could have
> thought of creating an inflammable river?

Beyond such biting witticisms, however, Deloria makes
a number of serious points: first that non-Indian America
is shaped by philosophical suppositions that rob people of
their identity; second, that America's religion has failed
and that a new one is needed; and third, that radical steps
must be taken to gain control of technology before the
planet becomes uninhabitable.

Concerning the first point, Deloria (whose thought
mixes heavy doses of Marshall McLuhan and Sitting Bull)
contends that there are at least two primary flaws in
America's philosophical outlook. The first is the country's
long-standing adulation of the economic individual; the
second is the melting-pot dogma.

Individuals, in Deloria's view, do not exist in isolation,

and he sees in America a negation of the importance of the group. While Anglo-Saxon America glorifies individual struggle in the economic jungle, the Indian individual (according to Deloria) derives his identity, purpose and sense of self from cooperative participation within a group.

But he believes whites may be changing. "People are becoming more aware of their isolation even while they continue to worship the rugged individualist who needs no one. The self-sufficient man is casting about for a community to call his own. The glittering generalities and mythologies of American society no longer satisfy the need and desire to belong."

A belief in the importance of the group is tied up with Deloria's denial of the desirability, as well as the possibility, of America becoming a great melting pot in which individuals of diverse backgrounds take on a common culture and a uniform way of life. In a paper presented last month at a Smithsonian Institute symposium, Deloria maintained that Americans are beginning to leave "the comfortable land of assimilation and have been thrust into the outer darkness of ethnicity, and every tool we have to gather information to find our way was designed for a world of assimilation and integration. Our government, our economic system and the basic documents of our society are built on other premises than those which we are coming to recognize today."

Deloria also sees major problems with America's religion—among them, what he regards as the Christian assumption that God gave men dominion over the creatures and the elements. Indian religion teaches exactly the opposite, says Deloria. Man, he contends, has no divinely ordained dominion over anything except himself. He is, or should be, simply one more part of the earth's on-going cycle, coexisting unobtrusively with other forms of life, and respecting the spiritual significance and limited life-giving resources of the earth.

But white men, according to Deloria, generally don't see it that way, and as Stella Leach, a leader in the Alcatraz takeover, put it, "they have raped our Earth

Mother." Too many white Americans, lacking any spiritual reverence for the land, have regarded it as something to use, or to exploit. The result, says Deloria, has been the creation of an "artificial universe," which may prove incapable of sustaining life.[1]

He takes seriously the findings of a group of European scientists who concluded that life on earth may end in 35 years because available oxygen may be used up. To prevent that from happening, Deloria contends, a number of radical changes are necessary. He proposes, among other things, that all available land—particularly unused farmland—be replanted with its natural growth; that such lands be restocked with game; that large numbers of people be taught and encouraged to live by hunting and fishing; and that such powerful forces as government and industry redefine their conceptions of growth and progress.

Similar points have been made recently by such non-Indian writers as Charles Reich, author of *The Greening of America*. But there is a difference. Reich is essentially optimistic, while Deloria and many Indian leaders are pessimists. "I don't think the people in power are capable of changing as radically as they need to," Deloria maintained in a recent interview. "I don't hold out much hope for this country; I just think there may be some small clusters of survivors who have adopted social forms and philosophical concepts that are essentially non-Western European." Deloria expects Indians to be among those survivors.

Inspired in part by the growing militancy of blacks and other minorities, the Indian movement has gained strength in the last five years, and it has provided whites with further evidence of their racism. But it does not stop there. Indians are also confronting white America with the contention that the Anglo-Saxon heritage may be suicide;

[1] A number of Indians interviewed by RRIC find the ecology movement mildly encouraging, but with major qualifications. Many of them seem to view it as a panicked reaction to a bad situation, rather than a movement grounded in the kind of spiritual appreciation of the land that could give it the strength to succeed.

that blind reliance on technology may be deadly; that the concept of radically improving on what nature has provided may be foolish; and that the arrogant assumption of a manifest destiny may yet catch up with the most powerful nation on earth.

DOCUMENT B:

Alcatraz Reclaimed. From the Newsletter of the Indian Tribes of All Nations, January, 1970

On November 9, 1969, seventy-eight American Indians made a predawn landing on Alcatraz Island in San Francisco Bay. The takeover was extraordinarily dramatic and focused world attention on Indian protest. By November 30 nearly six hundred Indians, representing more than fifty tribes, were living on the island. Their numbers decreased drastically in later months, as the US government cut off telephones, electricity, and water in the hope that they would have to leave altogether. But the Indians were unyielding. They incorporated themselves as Indians of All Tribes and remained until they were forcefully removed a year and a half later. Document B consists of two proclamations, the first made at the time of the original Alcatraz landing; the second, to commemorate the one-year anniversary of the takeover.

PROCLAMATION:

To the Great White Father and All His People

We, the native Americans, re-claim the land known as Alcatraz Island in the name of all American Indians by right of discovery.

We wish to be fair and honorable in our dealings with the Caucasian inhabitants of this land, and hereby offer the following treaty:

We will purchase said Alcatraz Island for twenty-four dollars (24) in glass beads and red cloth, a precedent set by the white man's purchase of a similar island about 300 years ago. We know that $24 in trade goods for these 16 acres is more than was paid when Manhattan Island was sold, but we know that land values have risen over the years. Our offer of $1.24 per acre is greater than the 47 cents per acre the white men are now paying the California Indians for their land.

We will give to the inhabitants of this island a portion of the land for their own to be held in trust by the American Indian Affairs and by the bureau of Caucasian Affairs to hold in perpetuity—for as long as the sun shall rise and the rivers go down to the sea. We will further guide the inhabitants in the proper way of living. We will offer them our religion, our education, our life-ways, in order to help them achieve our level of civilization and thus raise them and all their white brothers up from their savage and unhappy state. We offer this treaty in good faith and wish to be fair and honorable in our dealings with all white men.

We feel that this so-called Alcatraz Island is more then suitable for an Indian reservation, as determined by the white man's own standards. By this we mean that this place resembles most Indian reservations in that:

1. It is isolated from modern facilities, and without adequate means of transportation.

2. It has no fresh running water.

3. It has inadequate sanitation facilities.

4. There are no oil or mineral rights.

5. There is no industry and so unemployment is very great.

6. There are no health care facilities.

7. The soil is rocky and non-productive; and the land does not support game.

8. There are no educational facilities.

9. The population has always exceeded the land base.

10. The population has always been held as prisoners and kept dependent upon others.

Further, it would be fitting and symbolic that ships from all over the world, entering the Golden Gate, would first see Indian land, and thus be reminded of the true history of this nation. This tiny island would be a symbol

of the great lands once ruled by free and noble Indians.
What use will we make of this land?

Since the San Francisco Indian Center burned down,
there is no place for Indians to assemble and carry on
tribal life here in the white man's city. Therefore, we plan
to develop on this island several Indian institutions:

1. A CENTER FOR NATIVE AMERICAN
STUDIES will be developed which will educate them to
the skills and knowledge relevant to improve the lives and
spirits of all Indian peoples. Attached to this center will be
traveling universities, managed by Indians, which will go
to the Indian Reservations, learning those necessary and
relevant materials to know about.

2. AN AMERICAN INDIAN SPIRITUAL CEN-
TER which will practice our ancient tribal religious and
sacred healing ceremonies. Our cultural arts will be
featured and our young people trained in music, dance,
and healing rituals.

3. AN INDIAN CENTER OF ECOLOGY which will
train and support our young people in scientific research
and practice to restore our lands and waters to their pure
and natural state. We will work to de-pollute the air and
waters of the Bay Area. We will seek to restore fish and
animal life to the area and to revitalize sea life which has
been threatened by the white man's way. We will set up
facilities to desalt sea water for human benefit.

4. A GREAT INDIAN TRAINING SCHOOL will be
developed to teach our people how to make a living in the
world, improve our standard of living, and to end hunger
and unemployment among all our people. This training
school will include a center for Indian arts and crafts, and
an Indian restaurant serving native foods, which will
restore Indian culinary arts. This center will display Indian arts and offer Indian foods to the public, so that all
may know of the beauty and spirit of the traditional
INDIAN ways.

Some of the present buildings will be taken over to
develop an AMERICAN INDIAN MUSEUM which will
depict our native food & other cultural contributions we
have given to the world. Another part of the museum will

present some of the things the white man has given to the Indians in return for the land and life he took: disease, alcohol, poverty and cultural decimation (as symbolized by old tin cans, barbed wire, rubber tires, plastic containers, etc.). Part of the museum will remain a dungeon to symbolize both those Indian captives who were incarcerated for challenging white authority, and those who were imprisoned on reservations. The museum will show the noble and the tragic events of Indian history, including the broken treaties, the documentary of the Trail of Tears, the Massacre of Wounded Knee, as well as the victory over Yellow Hair Custer and his army.

In the name of all Indians, therefore, we re-claim this island for our Indian nations, for all these reasons, We feel this claim is just and proper, and that this land should rightfully be granted to us for as long as the rivers shall run and the sun shall shine.

Signed,

Indians Of All Tribes
November 1969
San Francisco, California

American Anniversary Proclamation, November, 1970

Indians Of All Tribes greet our brothers and sisters of all races and tongues upon our Earth Mother. We here on Alcatraz Island, San Francisco Bay, California represent many tribes of the United States as well as Canada, Alaska, and Central and South America.

We are still holding the Island of Alcatraz in the true names of Freedom, Justice and Equality, because you, our brothers and sisters of this earth, have lent support to our just cause. We reach out our hands and hearts and send spirit messages to each and every one of you—WE HOLD THE ROCK!

Our anger at the many injustices forced upon us since the first whitemen landed on these sacred shores has been transformed into a hope that we be allowed the long-suppressed right of all men to plan and to live their own

lives in harmony and co-operation with all fellow creatures and with Nature. We have learned that violence
breeds only more violence and we therefore have carried
on our occupation of Alcatraz in a peaceful manner,
hoping that the government of these United States will
also act accordingly.

Be it known, however, that we are quite serious in our
demand to be given ownership of this island in the name
of Indians Of All Tribes. We are here to stay, men,
women and children. We feel that this request is but little
to ask from a government which has systematically stolen
our lands, destroyed a once-beautiful and natural landscape, killed-off the creatures of nature, polluted air and
water, ripped open the very bowels of our earth in sense-
less greed; and instituted a program to annihilate the
many Indian Tribes of this land by outright murder which
even now continues by the methods of theft, suppression,
prejudice, termination, and so-called re-location and assimilation.

We are a proud people! We are Indians! We have
observed and rejected much of what so-called civilization
offers. We are Indians! We will preserve our traditions and
ways of life by educating our own children. We are Indians! We will join hands in a unity never before put into
practice. We are Indians! Our Earth Mother awaits our
voices.

We are Indians Of All Tribes! WE HOLD THE
ROCK!

DOCUMENT C:

*Statements on the Alcatraz action. From the newspaper
El Grito, an interview with Richard Oakes, the 27-year-
old Mohawk leader and with Carol Williams, a Yurok
Indian and mother of four.*

RICHARD OAKES: There's a sad neglect of all the
different tribal cultures. Ten years from now, there may
not be anybody out on the reservation to retain our cul-

ture and to be able to relate it. So this is actually a move, not so much to liberate the island, but to liberate ourselves for the sake of cultural survival . . .

For the most part, you find that the people coming here are here for the knowledge they can acquire. We hope we've been instrumental in bringing about an awareness in young people, an awareness that there is something good in the traditional aspect of Indian life. And we hope that the young people begin to respond to the old people, not coming from the high schools, which are white oriented, and trying to teach the old people, when in fact the old people can teach them much more . . .

One of the basic tenets of Indian life is humbleness, though, it's true, for instance, that the Chicano people don't identify with the Indian part of their life. It's the invisible side for them; or it's the pagan side for them; or it's the side of them that's very savage. They rationalize, so far away from the Indian part of their lives; and I think all their lives try to believe in something they're not, trying to be more and more American . . .

The sad fact about the non-Indian world is that most of it is not based on the truth, and that's why it's going to fall, to crumble. It's crumbling now, it's falling apart . . .

Here on this island, we've got so much more. It has so much more in the way of promise, hope, for our own people. Our people are slow to react to something of this nature, and they want to find out how much truth there is in it. It's hard to live a lie.

I speak as a youth, and I speak as a spokesman for the people on the island here, and we are ready to start listening to the old people. Leave the land that has caused so much trouble and heartbreak and come to a neutral area; and leave with us the knowledge so we can go back and teach your children.

CAROL WILLIAMS: When we claimed Alcatraz island for Indians of all tribes, we meant exactly that. It's so very important for the Indian people to realize that we're never going to get the island unless the Indian people are going to come here, and represent the Indians of all tribes.

We need to have Indian people that know the Indian culture, to begin now teaching it to the younger people here on Alcatraz.

This is why we want a cultural center and a college that represents young people learning the forgotten culture they left to learn the white man's culture. The young Indians want to come back. They want to learn. Because out there in the white man's culture, you learn that we no longer need the white man's culture. The white man's culture needs our culture . . .

I have four children of my own. I want them to learn what the Indian people represented on this whole earth. What their heritage is—not just of their tribe, but of all tribes.

And what we want to accomplish on Alcatraz Island is only symbolic of what we hope, in the future, will be the way that all mankind will live in harmony, without the prison . . .

We need more people. We need people with Indian ways to teach. We need people to teach languages, to tell what the different dances mean. The standards of how the college will be set up will not be white man's standards. It'll be by the standards that the Indians had before the white man came . . .

I think throughout the years the older people began to be slighted because the younger people were going into a modern world and the older people didn't want to hold them back. And I think now that the younger people have come back and said, "I want my culture." We want to come back. We see out there in the world many, many people. Lost people; unhappy people; people that are wandering around lost and homeless and needing spiritual guidance. We can give it to them, if they want it. We have to go home. We have to learn . . .

POSTSCRIPT TO THE DOCUMENT:

Richard Oakes later became involved with the Pit

River people's occupation of their ancestral lands in California. On September 21, 1972, at the age of 31, he was shot and killed by a white man who was known to have strong feelings against Indians. The man was charged with involuntary manslaughter.

DOCUMENT D:

Three hundred and fifty years after the Pilgrims landed on the shores of Massachusetts and began to colonize the lands of the Wampanoag, their "American" descendants planned an anniversary celebration. Still clinging to the white schoolbook myth of friendly relations between their forefathers and the Wampanoag, the anniversary planners thought it would be nice to have an Indian make an appreciative and complimentary speech. After 350 years of "civilization" it was not easy to find a Wampanoag, but it was done: Frank James was asked to speak at the celebration. He accepted. The planners, however, asked to see his speech in advance of the occasion, and it turned out that Frank James' views— based on history rather than on mythology—were not what the Pilgrims' descendants wanted to hear. Frank James refused to deliver a speech written by a public relations man. Frank James did not speak at the anniversary celebration. If he had spoken, this is what he would have said.

Suppressed Speech to have been delivered at Plymouth, Massachusetts, 1970

I speak to you as a Man—a Wampanoag Man. I am a proud man, proud of my ancestry, my accomplishments won by a strict parental direction—(you must succeed—

your face is a different color in this small Cape Cod
Community!")—I am a product of poverty and discrimination from these two social and economic diseases. I, and
my brothers and sisters have painfully overcome, and to
an extent earned the respect of our community. We are
Indians first—but we are termed "good citizens".—
Sometimes we are arrogant but only because society has
pressured us to be so.

It is with mixed emotions that I stand here to share my
thoughts. This is a time of celebration for you—
celebrating an anniversary of a beginning for the white
man in America. A time of looking back—of reflection. It
is with heavy heart that I look back upon what happened
to my People.

Even before the Pilgrims landed it was common practice for explorers to capture Indians, take them to Europe
and sell them as slaves for 220 shillings apiece. The
Pilgrims had hardly explored the shores of Cape Cod four
days before they had robbed the graves of my ancestors,
and stolen their corn, wheat, and beans. Mourt's Relation
describes a searching party of sixteen men—he goes on to
say that this party took as much of the Indian's winter
provisions as they were able to carry.

Massasoit, the great Sachem of the Wampanoag knew
these facts, yet he and his People welcomed and befriended the settlers of the Plymouth Plantation. Perhaps he did
this because his Tribe had been depleted by an epidemic,
or his knowledge of the harsh on-coming winter was the
reason for his peaceful acceptance of these acts. This
action by Massasoit was probably our greatest mistake.
We, the Wampanoags, welcomed you, the white man with
open arms, little knowing that it was the beginning of the
end; that before 50 years were to pass, the Wampanoags
would no longer be a Tribe.

What happened in those short 50 years? What has
happened in the last 300 years? History gives us facts and
there were atrocities; there were broken promises—and
most of these centered around land ownership. Among
ourselves we understood that there were boundaries—but

never before had we had to deal with fences and stone walls, with the white man's need to prove his worth by the amount of land that he owned. Only ten years later, when the Puritans came, they treated the Wampanoag with even less kindness in converting the soul of the so-called savages. Although they were harsh to members of their own society, the Indian was pressed between stone slabs and hanged as quickly as any other "witch."

And so down through the years there is record after record of Indian lands taken, and in token, reservations set up for him upon which to live. The Indian, having been stripped of his power, could but only stand by and watch—while the whiteman took his lands and used it for his personal gain. This the Indian couldn't understand; for to him, land was survival, to farm, to hunt, to be enjoyed. It wasn't to be abused. We see incident after incident, where the white man sought to tame the savage and to convert him to the Christian ways of life. The early settlers led the Indians to believe that if he didn't behave, they would dig up the ground and unleash the great epidemic again.

The whiteman used the Indian's nautical skills and abilities. They let him be only a seaman—but never a Captain. Time and time again, in the whiteman's society, we Indians have been termed, "low man on the Totem Pole."

Has the Wampanoag really disappeared? There is still an aura of mystery. We know there was an epidemic that took many Indian lives—some Wampanoags moved west and joined the Cherokee and Cheyenne. They were forced to move. Some even went north to Canada! Many Wampagnoag put aside their Indian heritage and accepted the white man's way for their own survival. There are some Wampanoag who do not wish it known they are Indian for social or economic reasons.

What happened to those Wampanoags who chose to remain and lived among the early settlers? What kind of existence did they live as civilized people? True, living was not as complex as life today—but they dealt with the confusion and the change. Honesty, trust, concern, pride, and politics wove themselves in and out of their daily living. Hence he was termed crafty, cunning, rapacious and dirty.

History wants us to believe that the Indian was a savage, illiterate uncivilized animal. A history that was written by an organized, disciplined people, to expose us as an unorganized and undisciplined entity. Two distinctly different cultures met. One thought they must control life —the other believed life was to be enjoyed, because nature decreed it. Let us remember, the Indian is and was just as human as the whiteman. The Indian feels pain, gets hurt and becomes defensive, has dreams, bears tragedy and failure, suffers from loneliness, needs to cry as well as laugh. He, too, is often misunderstood.

The white man in the presence of the Indian is still mystified by his uncanny ability to make him feel uncomfortable. This may be the image that the whiteman created of the Indian; "his savageness" has boomeranged and isn't mystery; it is fear; fear of the Indian's temperament!

High on a hill, overlooking the famed Plymouth Rock stands the statue of our great Sachem, Massasoit. Massasoit has stood there many years in silence. We the descendants of this great sachem have been a silent People. The necessity of making a living in this materialistic society of the white man caused us to be silent. Today, I and many of my People are choosing to face the truth. We ARE Indians!

Although time has drained our culture, and our language is almost extinct, we the Wampanoags still walk the lands of Massachusetts. We may be fragmented, we may be confused. Many years have passed since we have been a People together. Our lands were invaded. We fought as hard to keep our land as you the white did to take our land away from us. We were conquered, we became the American Prisoners of War in many cases, and wards of the United States Government, until only recently.

Our spirit refuses to die. Yesterday we walked the woodland paths and sandy trails. Today we must walk the macadam highways and roads. We are uniting. We're standing not in our wigwams but in your concrete tent.

We stand tall and proud and before too many moons pass we'll right the wrongs we have allowed to happen to us.

We forefited our country. Our lands have fallen into the hands of the aggressor. We have allowed the white man to keep us on our knees. What has happened cannot be changed but today we work towards a more humane America, a more Indian America where men and nature once again are important; where the Indian values of honor, truth and brotherhood prevail.

You the white man are celebrating an anniversary. We the Wampanoags will help you celebrate in the concept of a beginning. It was the beginning of a new life for the Pilgrims. Now, 350 years later it is a beginning of a new determination for the original American—The American Indian.

There are some factors involved concerning the Wampanoags and other Indians across this vast nation. We now have 350 years of experience living amongst the whiteman. We can now speak his language. We can now think as a white man thinks. We can now compete with him for the top jobs. We're being heard; we are now being listened to. The important point is that along with these necessities of everyday living, we still have the spirit, we still have a unique culture, we still have the will and most important of all, the determination to remain as Indians. We are determined and our presence here this evening is living testimony that this is only a beginning of the American Indian, particularly the Wampanoag, to regain the position in this country that is rightfully ours.

THE STRUGGLE ESCALATES
1972—1978

Trail of Broken Treaties

Wounded Knee

Declaration of Continuing Independence

Red Paper

Denial of Legal Remedies under U.S. Law

Geneva Conference

Human Rights

Land Claims Cases and Trust Responsibility

Women of All Red Nations

The Longest Walk

ABOUT THE DOCUMENTS:

The 1970s have been a time of escalating struggle, as Native people have faced intensive exploitation of their lands and resources by multinational corporations and continued acts of genocide from U.S. society. In turn, their resistance to these realities has led to widespread repression by the U.S. government. Throughout this period, however, the Indian movement has progressed organizationally, theoretically and in terms of developing awareness and support among non-Indians in the U.S. and world-wide.

The documents that follow cover only a few of the many significant events of the 1970s. But from them emerges a dominant theme, the demand that has held constant since the first treaties were signed between Native nations and European colonial powers—recognition of the sovereignty and treaty rights of Indian nations. The chronology highlights as well the evolving focus of the contemporary movement—away from seeking redress from the U.S. government and towards gaining international recognition of, and solidarity with, the Indian struggle for sovereignty, independence and self-determination. This focus reflects the fact that treaties are not domestic legal documents but international legal documents, signed between sovereign nations. It reflects as well the painful lessons of U.S./Indian history—that to seek redress from the very nation that colonizes Inidan nations is futile. This focus follows earlier approaches to the League of Nations, in 1926, and to the United Nations, in 1947.

As with the struggles of nations in the Third World against colonialism and for independence, the Native struggle has been a long one. Given the reality of U.S. economic and military power, it will be a struggle which will continue for many years. But the lesson of history, as demonstrated in Asia and Africa in the last two decades, is that the fight against colonial domination will ultimately be successful. The documents that follow present information on a crucial decade of that fight.

DOCUMENT A:

On October 26, 1972, caravans left Seattle, Los Angeles, and San Francisco, headed for Washington, D.C. Another caravan left Oklahoma on October 23, retracing the "Trail of Tears" of the 1830s. "The Trail of Broken Treaties" caravans were going to Washington to demand revisions in U.S./Indian affairs and to draw public attention to Native concerns and issues. They carried "Twenty Points" they wanted to discuss with federal officials.

When housing problems arose the "Trail" group went to the Bureau of Indian Affairs in D.C. to seek assistance. As leaders negotiated a tentative agreement with BIA officials and the rest of the group rested downstairs, government guards suddenly tried to clear the building. Some of the "Trail" group were clubbed and bloodied and panic spread.

The guards were evicted and the Native people secured the building against further assaults. Thus, a spontaneous, seven-day occupation of the BIA began, accompanied by constant threat of government attack and vows from the "Trail" group to hold the building at all cost. Although much press coverage was given to the occupation and to damage done to the building, little attention was paid to the "Twenty Points," excerpts of which follow.

1 RESTORATION OF CONSTITUTIONAL TREATY-MAKING AUTHORITY: . . . repeal the provision in the 1871 Indian Appropriations Act, which withdrew federal recognition from Indian Tribes and Nations as political entities which could be contracted by treaties with the U.S. . . .

2 ESTABLISHMENT OF TREATY COMMISSION TO MAKE NEW TREATIES: . . . establish . . . a Treaty Commission to contract a security and assistance treaty, or treaties, with Indian people to negotiate a national commitment to the future of Indian people for the last quarter of the Twentieth Century. . . .

3 AN ADDRESS TO THE AMERICAN PEOPLE AND JOINT SESSION OF CONGRESS: . . . arrange for four Native Americans . . . to address a joint session of Congress and the American people through national communications media, regarding the Indian future within the American Nation, and relationships between

the Federal Government and Indian Nations. . . .

4 COMMISSION TO REVIEW TREATY COMMIT-
MENTS AND VIOLATIONS: . . . create a multilateral,
Indian and non-Indian, Commission to review domestic
treaty commitments and complaints of chronic violations, and to recommend or act for corrective actions. . . .

5 RESUBMISSION OF UNRATIFIED TREATIES TO
SENATE FOR CONFIRMATION: . . . resubmit to the
U.S. Senate . . . those treaties negotiated with Indian
nations or their representatives, but never heretofore
ratified nor rendered moot by subsequent treaty contract. . . .

6 ALL INDIANS TO BE GOVERNED BY TREATY
RELATIONS: . . . enact Joint Resolution declaring that
. . . all Indian people in the U.S. shall be considered to be
in treaty relations with the Federal Government and
governed by doctrines of such relationship.

7 MANDATORY   RELIEF   AGAINST   TREATY
RIGHTS VIOLATIONS: . . . provide for the judicial
enforcement and protection of Indian Treaty Rights. . . .

8 JUDICIAL RECOGNITION OF INDIAN RIGHT
TO INTERPRET TREATIES: . . . provide for a new
system of federal court jurisdiction and procedure, when
Indian treaty or governmental rights are at issue, and
when there are non-Indian parties involved in the controversy. . . .

9 CREATION OF CONGRESSIONAL JOINT COM-
MITTEE ON RECONSTRUCTION OF INDIAN RELA-
TIONS: . . . withdraw jurisdiction over Indian Affairs
and Indian-related program authorizations from all
existing Committees, except Appropriations of the House
and Senate and create a Joint House/Senate "Committee
on Reconstruction of Indian Relations and Programs" to

assume such jurisdiction and responsibilities for recommending new legislation and program authorizations to both houses of Congress. . . .

10 LAND REFORM AND RESTORATION OF A 100-MILLION-ACRE NATIVE LAND BASE: . . . restore a permanent non-diminishing Native American land-base of not less than 110-million acres by July 4, 1976. This land base and its separate parts should be . . . perpetually non-taxable, except by autonomous and sovereign Indian authority, and should never again be permitted to be alienated from Native American or Indian ownership and control.

10a PRIORITIES IN RESTORATION OF THE NATIVE AMERICAN LAND BASE: . . . priorities in restorations of land bases be granted to those Indian Nations who are landless by fault of unratified or unfulfilled treaty provisions; Indian Nations, landless because of congressional and administrative actions reflective of criminal abuse of trust responsibilities; and other groupings of landless Indians. . . .

10b CONSOLIDATION OF INDIANS' LAND, WATER, NATURAL AND ECONOMIC RESOURCES: . . . restoration [of the land base] should be accompanied by enlightened revision in the present character of alleged "trust relationships" and by reaffirmation of the creative and positive characters of Indian sovereignty and sovereign rights . . . usable land, water, forests, fisheries, and other exploitable and renewable natural resources [should be consolidated] into productive economic, cultural, and other community-purpose units, benefiting both individual and tribal interests in direct forms under autonomous control of properly-defined, appropriate levels of Indian government. . . .

10c TERMINATION OF LEASES AND CONDEMNATION OF NON-INDIAN LAND TITLE: . . . A large-scale, if selective, program of lease cancellations and non-renewals should be instituted. . . . Indian Tribes should be authorized to re-secure Indian ownership of alienated lands within reservation boundaries under a system of condemnation . . . with the Federal Government bearing the basic costs of "just compensation" as burden for unjustified betrayals of its trust responsibilities to Indian people. . . .

10d REPEAL OF THE MENOMINEE, KLAMATH AND OTHER TERMINATION ACTS: . . . repeal the Termination Acts of the 1950s and 1960s, and restore ownership of the several million acres of land to the Indian people involved, perpetually non-alienable and tax-exempt. The Indians' rights to autonomous self-government and sovereign control of their resources and development should be reinstated. . . .

11 REVISION OF 25 U.S.C. 163; RESTORATION OF RIGHTS TO INDIANS TERMINATED BY ENROLL-MENT AND REVOCATION OF PROHIBITION AGAINST DUAL BENEFITS: . . . enact measures fully in support of the doctrine that an Indian Nation has complete power to govern and control its own member-ship, but eradicating the . . . coercive devices in federal policy . . . which have subverted and denied the natural human relationships and natural development of Indian communities, and committed countless injuries upon Indian families and individuals [such as] blood quantum criteria, closed and restrictive enrollment, and "dual benefits prohibitions." . . .

12 REPEAL OF STATE LAWS ENACTED UNDER PUBLIC LAW 280 (1953): State enactments under the authority conferred by the Congress in Public Law 280 [which gave states legal jurisdiction over certain crimes committed on reservations] has posed the most serious threat to Indian sovereignty and local self-government of any measure in recent decades. Congress must now nullify those State statutes.

13 RESUME FEDERAL PROTECTIVE JURISDIC-
TION FOR OFFENSES AGAINST INDIANS: . . . enact
. . . new provisions under Titles 18 and 25 of the U.S.
Code, which shall extend the protective jurisdiction of the
U.S. over Indian persons wherever situated in its territory . . . outside of Indian reservations or country, and
provide the prescribed offenses of violence against Indian
persons shall be federal crimes. . . .

13a ESTABLISHMENT OF A NATIONAL FEDERAL
INDIAN GRAND JURY: . . . a special national grand
jury, consisting solely of Indian members . . . be granted
jurisdiction to act in the bringing of indictments . . .
within any federal judicial district where a crime of
violence has been committed against an Indian . . .
when finding reason to be not satisfied with handling or
disposition of a case or incident by local authorities. . . .
the grand jury should be granted broad authority to
monitor the enforcements of law . . . respecting Indian
jurisdiction and civil rights protections . . . and issue
special reports bringing indictments when war-
ranted. . . .

13b JURISDICTION OVER NON-INDIANS ON RES-
ERVATIONS: . . . Title 18 of the U.S. Code should be
amended to clarify and compel that all persons within
the originally-established boundaries of an Indian Reservation are subject to the laws of the sovereign Indian
Nation in the exercise of its autonomous governing
authority. . . .

13c ACCELERATED REHABILITATION AND RE-
LEASE PROGRAMS FOR STATE AND FEDERAL
PRISONS: . . . contract an appropriately staffed Commission of Review on Rehabilitation of Indian Prisoners
in federal and state institutions . . . consisting of Indian
membership. . . . The commission would act to provide
forms by which Indian people may assume the largest
measures of responsibility in reversing the rapidly-

increasing crime rates on Indian reservations, and re-approaching situations where needs for jails and prisoner institutions may again be virtually eliminated.

14   ABOLITION OF THE BUREAU OF INDIAN AF-FAIRS BY 1976: . . . direct that the Bureau of Indian Affairs shall be abolished as an agency on or before July 4, 1976 [and] provide for an alternative structure of government for sustaining and revitalizing the Indian-federal relationship between the President and the Congress of the U.S., respectively, and the respective Indian Nations and Indian people at last consistent with constitutional criteria, national treaty commitments, and Indian sovereignty. . . .

15   CREATION OF AN "OFFICE OF FEDERAL IN-DIAN RELATIONS AND COMMUNITY RECON-STRUCTION": The Bureau of Indian Affairs should be replaced by a new unit in the Federal Government which represents an equality of responsibility among and between the President, the Congress, and the governments of the separate Indian Nations (or their respective people collectively), and equal standing in the control of relations between the Federal Government and Indian Nations. . . .

16   PRIORITIES AND PURPOSE OF THE PROPOSED NEW OFFICE: The central purpose of the proposed "Office of Federal Indian Relations and Community Reconstruction" is to remedy the break-down in constitutionally-prescribed relationships between the U.S. and Indian Nations and people and to alleviate the destructive impact that distortion in those relationships has rendered upon the lives of Indian people. . . .

17   INDIAN COMMERCE AND TAX IMMUNITIES: . . . enact a statute or Joint Resolution certifying that trade, commerce, and transportation of Indians remain wholly outside the authority, control, and regulation of the several States. . . . provide that complete taxing

authority . . . and business activities within the exterior boundaries of Indian reservations, as well as commerce between reservations and Indian Nations, shall be vested with the respective or related tribal governments . . . or . . . that total Indian immunity to taxing authority of states is reaffirmed and extended with uniformity to all Indian Nations as a matter-established or vested right. . . . (The Congress should remove any obstacles to the rights of Indian people to travel freely between Indian Nations without being blocked in movement, commerce, or trade, by barriers of borders, customs, duties, or tax.)

18 PROTECTION OF INDIANS' RELIGIOUS FREEDOM AND CULTURAL INTEGRITY: . . . the religious freedom and cultural integrity of Indian people shall be respected and protected throughout the U.S. . . .

19 NATIONAL REFERENDUMS, LOCAL OPTIONS, AND FORMS OF INDIAN ORGANIZATION: The Indian population is small enough to be amenable to voting and elective processes of national referendums, local option referendums, and other elections for rendering decisions, approvals, or disapprovals on many issues and matters. The steady proliferation of Indian and Indian-interest organizations and Indian advisory boards and the like, the multiplication of Indian officials, and the emergence of countless Indian "leaders," represent a less-preferable form for decision-making, a state of disorganization, and a clear reflection of deterioration in the relations between the U.S. and Indian people as contracting sovereigns holding a high standard of accountability and responsibility. . . .

20 HEALTH, HOUSING, EMPLOYMENT, ECONOMIC DEVELOPMENT AND EDUCATION: The Congress and Administration and proposed Indian Community Reconstruction Office must allow for the most creative, if demanding and disciplined, forms of community development and purposeful initiatives. The proposed

$15,000,000,000 budget for the 1970s remainder could provide for completed construction of 100,000 new housing units; create more than 100,000 new permanent, income and tribal revenue-producing jobs on reservations and lay foundation for as many more in years following; meet all the economic and industrial development needs of numerous communities; and make education at all levels and provide health services or medical care to all Indians as a matter of entitlement and fulfilled right. . . .

POSTSCRIPT TO THE DOCUMENT:

Two months after the occupation, the White House responded to the "Twenty Points," ignoring the substantive issues of treaties and sovereignty.

ABOUT THE DOCUMENTS:
Wounded Knee

In 1890, U.S. troops massacred 300 Lakota (Sioux) people, mainly women, children and old men, at Wounded Knee. On February 27, 1973, after repeated attempts to get the U.S. to respect provisions of the 1868 Fort Laramie Treaty and to force changes in the corrupt and autocratic BIA controlled "tribal government," several hundred Oglala Lakota and other Native people returned to Wounded Knee. At the request of traditional Oglala leaders, they were joined by members of the American Indian Movement (AIM).

The village of Wounded Knee was immediately surrounded by government forces. Pine Ridge reservation was already occupied by a paramilitary force consisting of U.S. marshalls, FBI agents, BIA and State police, because of an impeachment hearing against the BIA "tribal chairman" based on charges brought by the Oglala Civil Rights Organization. Government reinforcements were brought in, armed with M-16 machine guns, armored personnel carriers, helicopters, and other sophisticated weapons supplied by the Pentagon.

The liberation of Wounded Knee continued for 71 days. During that time, the U.S. tried to starve the people out, as well as firing thousands of rounds of ammunition into the village. Two people—Frank Clearwater and Buddy Lamont—were killed by government fire. Worldwide attention was focused on Wounded Knee.

Finally, the U.S. agreed to negotiate. Document *B* presents a part of the Oglala 10-point negotiating proposal. U.S. negotiators agreed to certain aspects of the demands, a stand-down was arranged and on May 8, the people left Wounded Knee.

Document *C* provides a sense of the spirit, determination and goals of the people inside the Independent Oglala Nation during the siege. Document *D* contains excerpts of a March 9, 1973 message from the Haudenosaunee (Six Nations of the Iroquois Confederacy) in support of the liberation of Wounded Knee. Document *E*—"AIM Three-Point Program"—was issued after Wounded Knee and reiterates some of the demands made there.

DOCUMENT B:
Portion of Oglala Negotiating Proposals

The Fort Laramie Treaty of 1868 between the U.S. and the Sioux Nation of Indians provided that the Sioux should always live in a state of independence, if not an independent State, but never be forced to live in a condition of dependency. The Treaty recognized the sovereignty of the Sioux, that being our capacity to govern ourselves consistent with our traditions, heritage, values and beliefs, and to maintain our relationships with our universe and among our people. . . . Those promises and purposes of the 1868 Treaty have long been betrayed—and those constant, countless betrayals have returned us to Wounded Knee.

The 1868 Treaty is basic to our lives. Our armed defense at Wounded Knee is then both defense of life and defense of Treaty. However, it is not a protest born of the hates and hurts of history as, more immediately, it was made necessary because the present experience of hundreds of Sioux Indian families is too frequently that of fear—while our country and our communities have fallen under a reign of terror. . . .

An end to the armed defense of Wounded Knee can be achieved, if the Fort Laramie Treaty of 1868 is restored in substance to the lives of the Sioux people, and if its standing as being the law of the American land is no longer denied.

To initiate such a settlement, we propose that certain actions, processes, and commitments be undertaken for completion, or that the appropriate machinery and systems be set in motion to effect the desired or just results. *We Demand:*

Establishment of a Presidential Treaty Commission for the time needed to examine, review, and negotiate Articles and provisions of the 1868 Sioux Treaty and other agreements with the traditional headsmen and chiefs of all the Sioux tribes, bands, or different reservations under the Treaty. . . .

Statement by Lakota Woman Who Participated in Liberation of Wounded Knee

The longest war that the U.S. government has ever waged has been against the American Indians. The war has never ceased. In the year 1973, from February 27 to May 8, there was the Independent Oglala Nation, established within the boundaries of the State of South Dakota, U.S.A. No U.S. officials had any power within the borders of this new nation. No taxes were paid to any level of the U.S. government. This tiny piece of land was surrounded by U.S. troops, armored personnel carriers, helicopters, a daily barrage of bullets, a blockage of all medical and food supplies. No services were supplied by any governmental agency other than that created by the Oglala people in their own independent nation.

For the first time in many years, the Oglala people could organize themselves according to their ancient spiritual values and ways of life—the Indian Way. The life of the Indian people is their spirituality. We were free! It was the first time that we had ever known freedom. We ran a hospital, a school for our children, we had a common commissary, we ran our own security force to enforce our borders. People got married, babies were born in a free land. For 71 days there was power in the hands of the Indian people. Men and women stood side by side in the kitchen, in the bunkers, on patrol, in the hospital and in the schools, and at the constant negotiations with the U.S. government. The governing body of the Oglala Independent Nation consisted of every resident.

DOCUMENT D:
Six Nations' Statement

The Six Nations Iroquois Confederacy stands in support of our brothers at Wounded Knee.

We find it deplorable that the Native Americans have to risk their very lives to focus attention on the terrible conditions of our people in this country. We cite the poor health conditions, education, welfare, illegal drafting of our people, and the utter disregard for the treaties that we have paid for with our lives as examples of these conditions. . . .

The people at Wounded Knee are making a statement. The question is not what damage or destruction of property has occurred, but why it becomes necessary for our people to have to resort to such extremes to gain some recognition of our desperate situation.

We are a free people. The very dust of our ancestors is steeped in our tradition. This is the greatest gift we gave to you, the concept of freedom. You did not have this. Now that you have taken it and built a constitution and country around it, you deny freedom to us. There must be some one among you who is concerned for us, and if not for us, at least for the honor of your country. In 1976, you are going to have a birthday party proclaiming 200 years of democracy, a hypocritical action. The people of the world would find this laughable.

The solution is simple: be honest, be fair, honor the commitments made by the founding fathers of your country. We are an honorable people—can you say the same? You are concerned for the destruction of property at the BIA building and at Wounded Knee. Where is your concern for the destruction of our people, for human lives? Thousands of Pequots, Narragansetts, Mohicans, thousands of Cherokees on the Trail of Tears, Black Hawk's people, Chief Joseph's people, Captain Jack's people, the Navajos, the Apaches, Sand Creek Massacre (huddled under an American flag seeking the protection of a promise), Big Foot's people at Wounded Knee. When will you cease your violence against our people? Where is your concern for us?

What about the destruction of our properties? The thousands of acres of land, inundated by dams built on our properties, the raping of the Hopi and Navajo territories by the Peabody strip mining operations, timber cutting, power companies, water pollution, and on and on. Where is your concern for these properties?

The balance of the ledger is up to you. Compare the property damage of the BIA and Wounded Knee against the terrible record and tell us that we are wrong for wanting redress. We ask for justice, and not from the muzzle of an M-16 rifle. . . .

Put your energies and money now being expended for the suppression of Indian people at Wounded Knee into a real effort to understand why they are there. And begin here in the capital through an investigation of the BIA, and of the government policies dealing with our most urgent needs.

Reaffirm and respect the treaties entered into between our two peoples. . . .

> We have not asked you to give up your religions and beliefs for ours.
> We have not asked you to give up your language for ours.
> We have not asked you to give up your ways of life for ours.

We have not asked you to give up your government
for ours.
We have not asked that you give up your territories to
us.

Why can you not accord us the same respect? For your
children learn from watching their elders, and if you
want your children to do what is right, then it is up to
you to set the example.

DOCUMENT E:
AIM three point program—1973

. . . Wounded Knee raised three important issues for
the Pine Ridge Reservation and all other Indians. The
people who went to Wounded Knee asked that the
government enforce their land rights under the Treaty of
1868; they asked for an independent investigation of the
Bureau of Indian Affairs' mishandling of Indians' rights
and interests, and that new tribal elections, free from
violence and fraud, be held.

POINT 1: A Senate Treaty Commission should examine the 371 treaties the U.S. has made (and broken) with
Indians. All treaty rights should be enforced.
The land rights involved here for reservations are very
large. The 1972 "Trail" [of Broken Treaties] proposal
called, at a minimum, for restoration to Indian control of
at least 110 million acres of land. Presently, the federal
government holds "in trust" about 40 million tribal acres
(much of it used for mineral, park, and other interests),
with an additional 10 million acres held "in trust" for
individual tribal members. Much of this land is leased
out, advantageously to white interests. On Pine Ridge
Reservation (South Dakota), Indian range land is leased
for 80 cents an acre; this land is exactly like land owned
by whites, which brings $15 an acre.
One response to the efforts to enforce the rights of this
treaty (re. the 1868 Sioux/U.S. treaty) has been a government "offer" to settle a 50-year-old claim based on it. The

U.S. National Indian Claims Commission finds about $102 million (or $2000 per person for about 60,000 Sioux) a fair settlement for 7.5 million acres of land—including the Homestake Mine, largest gold producing mine in the Western Hemisphere, and the sacred Paha Sapa—the beautiful Black Hills. However, old habits of cheating Indians die hard. By the time the U.S. government has finished taking deductions for "money spent on the Sioux," only about $4 million is left. We don't want little bits of cash; we want a land base which is ours by right and could support meaningful lives. . . .

We need a Treaty Commission, and it should get to work quickly. The sort of litigation which goes on forever is all too familiar. . . . From Washington to New York, there have been many such incidents and cases; it should not be necessary for Indians to go to court to win rights they (supposedly) already have by treaty.

POINT 2: Repeal the Indian Reorganization Act of 1934 (Wheeler-Howard Act); it has been a major weapon used in robbing Indians of their land, setting white-controlled governments on many reservations, and establishing tribal constitutions which offer no real protection against sale and wholesale lease-out of tribal lands.

POINT 3: Remove the Bureau of Indian Affairs from the Department of the Interior, restructure it as an independent agency, controlled by and accountable to, Indian people; audit the BIA records and make reparations for the many crooked land deals; cancel BIA-sanctioned non-Indian leasing of Indian land.

The BIA should never have been located in the Department of the Interior. (Maybe that's better than its original location—the Department of War—but not much.) The Department of the Interior serves oil, mineral, land trusts, transportation, shipping, wood forestry, and energy interests; these usually conflict with Indian rights.

The BIA has a long history of corruption and mismanagement of our affairs. A tough, independent audit of

BIA books and land rent records should be supported by all. Forced land sales and lease rentals arranged by the BIA should be examined, with returns and reparations made.

Pine Ridge data show part of the reason why this needs to be done. As of 1969, the federal government was spending, through the BIA, about $8040 a year per family, to "help the Oglala Sioux out of poverty." But median family income from all sources (employment, land rental, and federal) was only $1910 per family— supporting many children and old people. Where did the rest of it go? The fact that there was about one well-paid bureaucrat per family gives part of the answer; kickbacks and corruption give another part. All Indians would benefit if this inept and corrupt agency were accountable to us. . . .

This Three Point Program provides a strategy for a nationally coordinated attack on powerful financial and political interests, which have used the U.S. government to take advantage of Native Americans for more than a century. It will require strong commitment and wide support to win against these interests. Indian rights of sovereignty, self-government, and a decent means of living in accordance with traditions and beliefs will not come easily. Without massive public pressure, the government will simply continue its present treatment of Indians, a continuing shame to all, and a continuing profit source to a few. . . .

POSTSCRIPT TO THE DOCUMENTS:

The U.S. reneged on most of what it had agreed to once the people left Wounded Knee and began a judicial assault against the people who had been in the village. Of 147 indictments, the U.S. obtained only 15 convictions. But the Wounded Knee trials tied up leaders and supporters in court and forced them to spend huge amounts of money, time and talent to keep people out of jail. Additionally, what has been described as a "reign of terror" spread over Pine Ridge reservation, as the FBI and the so-called "goon squad" of the BIA "tribal

chairman" harassed, intimidated and assaulted supporters of AIM and the traditional government. Violence and
death have stalked the reservation since that time, and
the list of AIM members and supporters who have been
killed or injured is long.

DOCUMENT F:

*In June 1974, 4,000 representatives from 97 Native
nations met on the Standing Rock Lakota (Sioux) Reservation at the First International Indian Treaty Conference to consider action on the 371 treaties signed with the
U.S. Participants issued a "Declaration of Continuing
Independence"—Document F—which set forth issues of
concern and calls for action.*

We, the sovereign Native Peoples, recognize that all
lands belonging to the various Native Nations now
situated within the boundaries of the U.S. are clearly
defined by the sacred treaties solemnly entered into
between the Native Nations and the government of the
U.S.A.

We, the sovereign Native Peoples charge the U.S. with
gross violations of our International Treaties. [The docu-
ment cites the taking of the sacred Black Hills from the
Great Sioux Nation in 1877 in violation of the Fort
Laramie Treaty of 1868 and the forced march of the
Cherokee people from their national lands in what is now
the State of Georgia to the then "Indian Territory" of
Oklahoma as examples.]

The Council further realizes that securing U.S. recognition of treaties signed with Native Nations requires a
committed and unified struggle, using every available
legal and political resource. Treaties between sovereign
nations explicitly entail agreements which represent "the
supreme law of the land" binding each party to an
inviolate international relationship.

We acknowledge the historical fact that the struggle for
Independence of the Peoples of our sacred Mother Earth
has always been over sovereignty of land. These historical freedom efforts have always involved the highest
human sacrifice.

We recognize that all Native Nations wish to avoid violence, but we also recognize that the U.S. government has always used force and violence to deny Native Nations basic human and treaty rights.

We adopt this Declaration of Continuing Independence, recognizing that struggle lies ahead—a struggle certain to be won—and that the human and treaty rights of all Native Nations will be honored. In this understanding the International Indian Treaty Council declares:

The U.S. Government in its Constitution, Article VI, recognizes treaties as part of the Supreme Law of the U.S. We will peacefully pursue all legal and political avenues to demand U.S. recognition of its own Constitution in this regard, and thus to honor its own treaties with the Native Nations. We will seek the support of all world communities in the struggle for the continuing independence of Native Nations.

We, the representatives of sovereign Native Nations unite in forming a council to be known as the International Indian Treaty Council to implement these declarations.

The International Indian Treaty Council will establish offices in Washington, D.C. and New York City to approach the international forces necessary to obtain the recognition of our treaties. These offices will establish an initial system of communications among Native Nations to disseminate information, getting a general consensus concerning issues, developments and any legislative attempt affecting Native Nations by the U.S.A.

The International Indian Treaty Council recognizes the sovereignty of all Native Nations and will stand in unity to support our Native and international brothers and sisters in their respective and collective struggles concerning international treaties and agreements violated by the U.S. and other governments.

All treaties between the Sovereign Native Nations and the U.S. Government must be interpreted according to the traditional and spiritual ways of the signatory Native Nations. . . .

We call upon the conscionable nations of the world to

join us in charging and prosecuting the U.S.A. for its genocidal practices against the sovereign Native Nations, most recently illustrated by Wounded Knee 1973 and the continued refusal to sign the United Nations 1948 Treaty on Genocide.

We reject all executive orders, legislative acts and judicial decisions of the U.S. related to Native Nations since 1871, when the U.S. unilaterally suspended treaty-making relations with the Native Nations. This includes, but is not limited to, the Major Crimes Act, the General Allotment Act, the Citizenship Act of 1924, the Indian Reorganization Act of 1934, the Indian Claims Commission Act, Public Law 280 and the Termination Act. All treaties made between Native Nations and the U.S. prior to 1871 shall be recognized without further need of interpretation.

We hereby ally ourselves with the colonized Puerto Rican People in their struggle for Independence from the same U.S.A.

We recognize that there is only one color of Mankind in the world who are not represented in the United Nations; that is the indigenous Redman of the Western Hemisphere. We recognize this lack of representation in the United Nations comes from the genocidal policies of the colonial power of the U.S.

The International Indian Treaty Council established by this conference is directed to make the application to the United Nations for recognition and membership of the sovereign Native Nations. We pledge our support to any similar application by an aboriginal people.

This conference directs the Treaty Council to open negotiations with the government of the U.S. through its Department of State. We seek these negotiations in order to establish diplomatic relations with the U.S. When these diplomatic relations have been established, the first order of business shall be to deal with U.S. violations of treaties with Native Indian Nations, and violations of the rights of those Native Indian Nations who have refused to sign treaties with the U.S.

We, the People of the International Indian Treaty

Council, following the guidance of our elders through instructions from the Great Spirit, and out of respect for our sacred Mother Earth, all her children, and those yet unborn, offer our lives for our International Treaty Rights.

POSTSCRIPT TO THE DOCUMENT:

The Treaty Council office was established in New York City in the fall of 1974 and on February 10, 1977, the International Indian Treaty Council was recognized by the United Nations and given consultative status as a Non-Governmental Organization (NGO).

DOCUMENT G:
Red Paper
The Second International Indian Treaty Conference was held from June 13-20, 1976 on the Yankton Lakota (Sioux) Reservation in South Dakota. The document produced is entitled "The Red Paper." The following excerpts deal with natural resources and sovereignty.

The assembled Indian people resolved to take action on an international level to combat the continuing violation by the U.S. government of our right to sovereignty and self-determination. We submit the following statement for world attention and action.

American Indians belong to separate sovereign nations in North America. Collectively and individually we have a nationality of our own which is separate from that of the U.S. Our history, culture, customs, traditions, values, and interests are totally different from those of the imperialist U.S.

The people of American Indian nations have a long history of struggle for self-determination and independence. . . . When natural resources have been discovered on Indian land the U.S. has proceeded to completely exploit them. In the case of the Black Hills of South Dakota the U.S. stole the lands and extracted the gold. Presently on the Cheyenne Indian and Crow Indian reservations in Montana, the collusion of the BIA and major coal producers such as Peabody Coal, AMEX, Standard Oil, Shell Oil, Gulf Oil, etc., resulted in contracts in which the Indians would receive only one-third of the market price for their resources. Indians are not free to contract for themselves or to hire a lawyer without BIA (U.S.) approval so they are unable to achieve restitution. The use of government "front companies" with so-called Indians as administrators of said companies, is another government policy used to exploit Indian natural resources.

We have, therefore, resolved to initiate the following plan of action to maintain and develop our natural resources:

1 Policy of Development:
We declare that as nations of Indian people we have exclusive control of our natural resources. We will use these resources to provide food and livelihood for our people, for trade and economic development in non-capitalist, non-exploitative or ecologically destructive methods pursuant to our traditional values. The U.S. through its Federal Power Commission and contrary to tribal desires licenses tribal lands for flooding and other ecological destruction to support power projects.

2 Determine and Document What Resources We Have, and Where, by Seeking All Possible Technical Assistance.

3 Methods of Defeating Present Colonial Situations:
a) Exposing the fraudulent and corrupt lawyers, tribal chairmen, and BIA officials who serve as instruments in the theft and destruction of our natural resources, including land, petroleum, coal, natural gas, copper, uranium, gold, timber, water, electrical power, fish, and other food sources, air, and human resources such as the labor force

and skilled and educated people.

b) Educate people, including our own children according to our traditional methods, values, and including people of other nations, as to what resources actually exist.

c) Bring international pressure to bear in our effort to maintain all of our resources.

d) Expose corporate and government collusion in the theft of our resources, especially by the large multinational corporations, by exchanging data and information with other Third World countries which have been exploited by those corporations and the U.S. government.

. . . What has happened has not been a loss of sovereignty by the Indian Nations. Discovery gave no legal authority to the U.S. The tribes for the most part had not been conquered, certainly not in a just war. Cession of sovereignty by international agreement cannot be claimed. The treaties reaffirmed sovereignty of the Indian Nations. In no manner did they constitute the relinquishment of such. What has happened is that the U.S. has unilaterally determined that it has the prerogative of abrogating, repealing, changing and nullifying treaties. What has happened is that the U.S. has unilaterally, through its own legislation, purported to limit the sovereign expression of the Indian nations. . . .

Through design of tribal structure and limitation of the exercise of the normal sovereign prerogative the U.S. has been seeking to turn Indian lands into mere colonies. Exploitation of Indian lands and resources has been as fierce as from any colonial empire. All pretense of respect for our tribal entities has been abandoned with the termination policy expressed congressionally in 1953 (House Concurrent Resolution 108) and since retreated from as an official policy. The truth is that our termination has always been the policy of the U.S. Each act abrogating a treaty has been an expression of this policy. Other expressions of the genocidal policy of the U.S. toward the native peoples of this land abound throughout American history. Examples include the Indian Removal

Act which transported Indian peoples from their homelands; the Major Crimes Act which substituted U.S.
criminal standards and arbitrary enforcement for tribal
jurisdiction; the General Allotment Act which carved up
and distributed the reservation lands guaranteed to us;
the Homestead Acts which opened Indian lands for white
settlement; the Citizenship Act which imposed the obligations and stigma of U.S. citizenship upon our peoples,
without consent; the Indian Reorganization Act which
restructured tribal government; Public Law 280 which
adds state infringement of the Indian nations to that of
the Federal Government. The list goes on and on. Even
the Indian Claims Commission Act which purports to
adjust past illegalities is only a way of solidifying U.S.
claims on Indian lands at a cheap price. . . .

The extinguishment of our sovereignty cannot be
legislated. Sovereignty is an expression of national
consciousness of identity, of tradition, and of the spirit.
Despite massive assault our Indian Nations remain
sovereign. The understanding and expression of this
sovereignty is not diminishing; it is on the upswing,
bringing all Indian people together and unifying support
of the world's people. We seek the support of all people of
goodwill.

DOCUMENT H:

Denial of Legal Remedies

*The evolving focus on seeking international support for
Native struggles was further developed by Robert T.
Coulter in a paper published by the Institute for the
Development of Indian Law in July 1977. The excerpts in
Document H summarize the arguments made.*

The horrible wrongs to Indian nations committed by
the U.S. and its citizens, both historically and presently,
are well-established and copiously documented. The
question of greatest concern to other nations, to non-
governmental organizations and to other observers is

whether the U.S. and its legal system provide a legal and effective means for redressing these wrongs. Under well-accepted principles of international law, national governments, arguably including Indian governments, are not obliged to resort to municipal law remedies for national wrongs. Nevertheless if such remedies were available, the need for international attention and action would be lessened. The U.S. legal system does not, however, offer such legal procedures for determination of the most fundamental Indian claims and controversies.

The law of the U.S. does not permit the legal redress of the most serious wrongs to Indian nations and Indian peoples because 1) the fundamental legal issues are not subject to judicial review [Political Question Doctrine]; 2) U.S. law through the legislature and the courts has conclusively resolved the most crucial legal issues in favor of the U.S. and contrary to Indian interests; and 3) no real remedy is provided for some classes of cases such as claims against the U.S. To be sure, there are restricted legal remedies available for certain wrongs to individual Indian people and, to a very limited extent, for wrongs to Indian nations or "tribes." However, it can be stated with certainty that no remedy is available and no legal relief is possible under U.S. law with respect to any of the following fundamental issues of Indian rights and Indian relations with the U.S.: the status of Indian governments; the title to Indian lands; the validity and operation of Indian treaties and purported or alleged treaties; the power of Congress to legislate over Indian people and territory; and historic Indian claims against the U.S. . . .

Indian nations and Indian peoples cannot expect a legal resolution of their conflicts with the U.S. by resorting to the U.S. legal system. The absence of legal remedies in the U.S. law is not, however, a terrible condition, if Indian governments are recognized as true sovereigns and subjects of international law. Certain Indian peoples have now tragically lost their governments, and for them, the absence of legal remedies in the U.S. was and is a cruel injustice. For many Indian nations, resort to the remedies of international law may be the most appropriate answer for future controversies, especially if other nations of the world heed and act upon the call of Indian nations for support and assistance.

In any event, it is or ought to be clear that the relations between Indians and the U.S. are not merely domestic affairs. The U.S. cannot continue to subject Indian peoples to all the legal disadvantages of foreign nationhood and yet insist that Indian affairs are not a matter for international concern and that Indian nations are not subjects of international law.

ABOUT THE DOCUMENTS:
Geneva Conference

The International Non-Governmental Organization (NGO) Conference on "Discrimination Against Indigenous Populations in the Americas" was held at the Palais des Nations in Geneva, Switzerland from September 20-23, 1977. The Conference was sponsored by the Sub-Committee on Racism, Racial Discrimination, Apartheid, and Decolonialism of the Special Committee on Human Rights, which is part of the Economic and Social Council of the United Nations. Sixty NGOs and other international organizations attended, as well as U.N. agencies such as the Human Rights Commission and UNESCO. Forty nations of the U.N. sent observers.

The International Indian Treaty Council, a recognized NGO, organized the Indian delegation and documentation. Over 100 delegates and participants, representing more than 60 Indian nations and peoples from 15 countries in North, Central and South America, attended.

Document *I* contains excerpts of speeches by representatives from the Americas. Document *J* contains information on the economic status of Native people in the U.S., discussions of treaty and water rights, and of resource exploitation on reservations. Document *K*—"A Question of Genocide"—is from a paper produced by Native women during the Third International Indian Treaty Conference and presented to the Geneva Conference.

DOCUMENT I:
Statements to the Geneva Conference from Representatives of North, Central and South America

RUSSELL MEANS, *Opening Plenary Session, September 20:* We've come to you once again to tell you that for centuries since the invaders came to our shores we have shown the world mutual respect. We have come to show that respect. We are people who live in the belly of the monster. The monster being the U.S.A. Every country in the Western Hemisphere follows the lead of the monster. I come not to turn the other cheek. We have turned it now for almost 500 years, and we realize that here in Geneva, this is our first small step into the international community. . . . the President of the U.S.— to show you what a racist he is—[talks] about human rights while my people are suffering genocide. Not only in the U.S. but in the entire Hemisphere—planned genocide by the governments. We have brought documents to Geneva that support this charge.

We are approaching the international community this first time for support and assistance to stop not only this rape of our sacred mother earth, but also to stop the genocide of a whole people. A people with international rights backed up especially in North America by treaties between the U.S. and Indian Nations. The U.S., the monster, and its multinational corporations have dictated foreign policy in this world. They no longer care about the future as witnessed by the Dene, by my people, by Central and South America. . . .

You see, there is only one color of mankind that is not allowed to participate in the international community, and that color is red. The black, the white, the brown, the yellow—all participate in one form or another. We no longer, until this day, have had a voice within the international community.

Someone once said you can tell the power of a country

by the oppression its people will tolerate. No longer are we going to tolerate the monster.

OREN LYONS, *Onondaga, Six Nations Iroquois Confederacy, Opening Plenary:* The President of the U.S.A. has brought forth into the forum of the international world the issue of human rights. It affords us the opportunity at this time to present our position on the issue of human rights. It is strange indeed that we have to travel this far to the east, to the European continent, to turn and face the President of the U.S. and ask him about our human rights.

It is the future of not only our people, the Red People of the Western Hemisphere, but it is the future of yourselves that is at stake. We have been given principles by which to live, mutual respect, the understanding of creation. If we continue to ignore the methods by which we exist and we continue to destroy the source of our life, then our children will suffer. . . . We were told in the beginning that we were not human. There are great arguments in many histories as to the humanness of the red peoples of the Western Hemisphere. The equality of all life is what you must understand and the principle by which you must continue the future of this world. Economics and technology may assist you, but they will also destroy you if you do not use the principles of equality. Profit and loss will mean nothing to your future generations. . . .

The Six Nations were here 53 years ago to say the very same thing, the unity of spirit and brotherhood. United Nations is nothing new to us. Our confederacy is 1000 years old. . . . And so for this short time I would ask that you open your ears, that you open your hearts, that you open your minds and that you consider very seriously the future of the generations, of our children to come.

MARIE SANCHEZ, *Northern Cheyenne Tribal Judge, at the Opening Plenary:* I come with greetings from the women of the Western Hemisphere . . . we are the target for the total final extermination of us as people. . . . The only positive thing that I feel should come out of this conference, is to include us as part of the international family. . . . Only with that can we continue to live as completely sovereign people. There are other concerns of the Native American women. They do not stop at the concern of being sterilized. They go beyond that because of our relationship to Mother Earth. The raping, plundering, because of the greed of the U.S.A. for our natural resources is still yet a form of sterilization, because we depend on Mother Earth for life. And you also, because you are part of the family of this world, you should also be very concerned, because the common enemy is your enemy too, and that enemy dictates policy to your governments also. I warn you not to be so dependent on the country that we are under, on the government that we are under. We have demonstrated to you how many hundreds of years we have survived, but only because we are still united, we can only still be together in struggle.

ED BERNSTICK, *Cree Nation, Canada, American Indian Movement—statement to Economic Commission:*
. . . The situation that exists for Native people in Canada is that we have been categorized by Canada as Eastern or Western or Northern Canadian Indians, and treaty and non-treaty Indians, registered and non-registered, status Indians and non-status Indians, Metis, half-breed. Economically each category is affected differently. The responsibility of the Canadian government lies in the control they have gained over all Indian peoples. . . . Indian people have not had a say in the economic situation of their communities. . . . there was a new economic development program set up called the Mid-Canada Corridor. This is the Northern Development Plan. This was a plan to take all economic basis away from Indian people. It involves the Department of Northern Saskatchewan and Northlands in Alberta, the Department of Northern Manitoba where there is a huge hydrodevelopment project going on, and the development programs in Northern Ontario, Quebec, British Columbia and the Territories.

These programs are developed without consultation with the native people, who are extremely isolated and out of touch. This adds up to genocide against the native people of Canada—culturally and physically. . . . Each province and territory exerts control of the native people within its claimed boundaries. We are affected by such laws as the Migratory Bird Act, and yet in our treaties we have fishing and hunting rights. We have court cases where our people have been put in court for shooting a duck to feed their family because it infringed on the Migratory Bird Act. In many areas, there are no jobs, and people must rely on hunting and fishing to survive.

A lot of our land areas have been subject to manipulation. For years, the ranchers have cleared land around the reservations with the cheap labor of native people. Today most of our reserves are faced with dealing with timber mills, paper mills around the reserves. There are power plants which destroy the fish around reserves.

The Government uses "legal" tactics to keep Indian people in poverty. They try to assimilate entire reserves, and have succeeded on some in destroying the language, education and livelihood of the people. . . . The corporations are looking for resources and look more and more to Indian land. We need protection. The death rate has climbed three fold in the last 10 years. Our elders tell us from their oral history, that land that was ceded through treaties included only one foot down, and does not include water and most minerals. The timber and water that exists would be enough for all if shared equally. The world community should think of the human rights of Indian people. We are not saying we do not want to share our resources, but we are saying that we must think of a future where everyone can survive.

JOSE MENDOZA ACOSTA, *Representacion de Autoridad y Pueblo Indigena de Panama:* Before this Conference, we have shown that there is discrimination in our countries. Through facts, we have shown and proven the loss of our territories and the constant physical aggression against our nations. . . . We have come here, however, not to claim our rights but to demand those rights be respected because we have already acquired those rights since we have begun our existence in those territories. . . . We should like once more to ask that no compromise be made with our people with the genocide that has been committed, that is committed daily against our peoples. . . . We do not know whether we shall come here again next year or perhaps in a hundred or two hundred years. But what I do know is that our people will maintain the unity we have here maintained in defense of our territories.

Meantime, representatives of all nations of the world, remember one thing and do not forget it. We will not give up our territories. . . . We are going to defend our territories through all possible means because that territory, recognized as a nation or not, has been ours and it will continue to be ours.

ANTONIO MILLAPE, *Mapuche Confederation, Chile [in exile] in the Economic Commission:* I am president of the Confederation of Mapuche. I was selected by the leadership of the Confederation, before the coup in Chile in 1973. The Confederation is composed of 63 regional associations of Mapuches, which includes 3,098 indigenous communities. It represents a population of 900,000 Mapuches. I have to say that many years ago there were many more Mapuches. . . .

Economic aspects of the situation: From 1800 on, there was a massive establishment of haciendas and farms in Chile, taking the best lands, and the useless lands were left to the Mapuches, reducing the lands of the Mapuches more than just in area. The farms were tactically surrounded by a cheap indigenous labor force, which was forced to work without salaries as farm labor. It is not bad to cultivate the land, but it is inhuman to torture a whole population to achieve this. The treatment of the Indians came from "civilized" societies. The Mapuche was described by one Spanish poet as proud, strong, enduring, but were reduced to bad health and misery.

In 1973 when the coup took place in Chile, . . . a

massive extermination of the Mapuche occurred. In some places a hen or two only exists. People are . . . dying of starvation and extreme malnutrition. That is the form of extermination today under Pinochet. The goal is to totally wipe out the indigenous population of Chile. More than 70% suffer this misery . . . No banks or corporations will take my people out of this misery. I beg my brothers from North America to go and see. All these realities in Chile are taking place in other countries of the Americas, except not so extreme. Millions and millions of children at this moment are crying, and their parents do not have enough to feed them.

All regional associations have been banned. It is difficult to organize now. Our most immediate goal is to stop starvation, this extermination. We cannot allow this to continue. Dictatorships will not provide the solutions, only us.

DOCUMENT J:
Economic Situation of American Indian People in U.S.

There are almost three hundred reservations in the United States that are under the control of the Bureau of Indian Affairs (BIA), which claims to be the "trustee" of Indian land. Under this trusteeship, most of our land is leased to white ranchers or to corporations, so that we do not have the use of it. For the past ten years we have been losing our remaining land at the rate of 45,000 acres a year.

These conditions cause extreme poverty and alienation. More than 75% of all Indians in the U.S. suffer from malnutrition and related diseases. One of every three Indian infants dies in the first six months after birth. The average life span of an Indian male is 44 years of age, compared to the United States national average of 67 years of age.

Ninety percent of all the uranium in the U.S. is on Indian Land. 30% of the petroleum is on Indian land, 30% of the coal is on Indian land. We also have copper and other minerals, timber, grazing and farm land. Obviously, colonialism is the only reason for our desperate situation.

Most Indians in the U.S. are unskilled laborers, and many work for less than one-half the legal minimum wage under government subsidized "trainee" programs. As soon as their "training" is over they are fired and new "trainees" are hired.

Average education for Indian people is five years. Most schools on reservations are directly controlled by the U.S. government or by the churches. In all cases these schools are extremely sub-standard.

In 1972 the average annual income of an American citizen was $4000. In 1975 it was almost $6000. But for Indians in the same country, the average income in 1972 was less than $1000, in other words, about 5 times less than the national average. In 1975 the Indian average annual income had not yet reached $2000. Indian unemployment ranges from an average of 70% up to 90% in winter months.

This, of course, causes in its turn severe alienation and frequently alcoholism.

According to the U.S. Senate American Indian Policy Review Commission report of 1976: "The rate of increase of American Indian per capita income has not kept pace with either the rate of inflation or the rate of increase in the average U.S. per capita income, with the result of disparity between Indian and non-Indian per capita income, with the result that more rather than fewer American Indians are living below the poverty level . . . the rate of increase in employment has not yet kept pace with the increase of the American Indian labor force, with the result being increasingly higher rates of unemployment among American Indians."

In 1969 the report of the Bureau of Indian Affairs stated that Indian unemployment at that time was 74%. If indeed unemployment is increasing as the government states and as we know to be true from first hand experience, what is being done to alleviate the situation? The U.S. government has come up with a plan called

"Operation Bootstrap" wherein the government loans a reservation some of its own (the reservations') money with which it builds a plant or factory which is then leased at a very low price to outside corporations such as Fairchild Electronics. The government works in collusion with the corporations by providing work and "trainee" programs. Indians in these factories work at one-half the U.S. minimum wage. When they complete their training they are fired.

When AIM protested such abuses on the Navajo Reservation in 1975, Fairchild Electronics moved its entire plant to South Korea, leaving the people with an empty plant that they had paid for and several people charged with criminal acts.

The poverty and unemployment of Indian people must be seen as a deliberate act on the part of the U.S. government and the large corporations. For example, the Pine Ridge Reservation is one of the poorest (and also one of the largest) in the country, yet millions of dollars are made each year by white ranchers on the reservation to whom the government has leased 90% of the available land. The Indians themselves could be raising cattle on their land, but the government does not allow it. Moreover, there is a gold mine on the reservation which is legally part of the reservation which has mined literally billions of dollars of gold over the years. The mine is "owned" by the William Randolph Hearst Corporation, which has never paid a cent to the Sioux people (according to the Treaty of 1868, one half of the minerals mined goes to the tribe). Instead, Indians who are serving time in prison are made to work in the mine. Even on small reservations, most of the land is leased to white ranchers or to mining and oil companies.

Indian reservations are rich in natural resources which are being stolen. According to a report made by a Federal Energy Administration in 1975, "over 2.7 billion dollars of oil and gas; 187 million dollars of coal; 349 million dollars of uranium have been produced from Indian lands" in recent years, and also "over 434 million dollars of . . . lead, zinc, phosphate, copper and limestone."

Indian Treaties and Treaty Rights

It is important to recognize that Indian Treaty Rights are not "gifts" or "grants" made by the U.S. They are legal rights already possessed by Indian people that are specifically protected by written treaty wording.

History reveals that a number of treaties between Indian Nations and the U.S. have involved the transfer of lands or other rights from the Native people to the U.S. Several important rules of interpretation have been used over the years in determining how specific wording in those treaties is to be understood. One such rule of interpretation of Indian treaties states that all rights which are not expressly ceded to the U.S. by treaty are considered to be reserved by the Indian Nations. . . .

This rule is applied by the U.S. Supreme Court in *United States v. Winans,* a case decided in 1905:

> The right to resort to the fishing places in controversy was part of larger rights possessed by the Indians, upon the exercise of which there is not the shadow of impediment, and which were not much less necessary to the existence of the Indians than the atmosphere they breathed. . . . In other words, the treaty was not a grant of rights to the Indians, but a grant of rights from them—a reservation of those not granted.

Another rule of interpretation that has been applied states that treaty wording is to be interpreted as the Native people understood it. A third rule requires that doubtful or vague wording in a treaty is to be interpreted in a way that would be beneficial to Indians. . . .

How a treaty is to be interpreted is an important question. Properly ratified treaties between Indians and the U.S. have the force of law. Treaties with Indians have consistently been held to be equal in status and dignity to those negotiated by the U.S. with other foreign Nations. Under Article VI, section 2 of the U.S. Constitution, treaties, like the Constitution itself and acts of Congress, are declared to be the "supreme law of the land." . . .

Indian Water Rights

Before the coming of European immigrants, Indian people had full control over the use and protection of the water that flowed across their territories; no competing governmental agencies were around to interfere. With the arrival of large numbers of immigrants, Native people gave up some lands to make room for newcomers. Other lands were reserved under treaty as homeland for the Native people.

Almost always, however, the treaties that guaranteed Native rights to the reserved lands did not specifically mention water or Native water rights. What did this mean? Were these treaties to be understood as giving up all rights to water and reserving only the land itself? Water was essential to the Native people if they were to survive on their lands, particularly in the dry regions, such as the Missouri River Basin.

The treaties did not say that the Native people had the rights to water for their lands, yet they also did not say that the water was given up. Applying the first rule, that what is not specifically given up through treaty is reserved and kept, the U.S. Supreme Court in *Winters v. United States* ruled that the Assiniboine and Gros Ventre Nations reserved rights to enough water from the Milk River to meet their needs in living on their reserved lands. The Court explained:

> The lands were arid, and, without irrigation, were practically valueless. And yet, it is contended, the means of irrigation were deliberately given up by the Indians and deliberately accepted by the government. . . . The Indians had command of the lands and the waters,—command of all their beneficial use, whether kept for hunting, "and grazing roving herds of stock," or turned to agriculture and the arts of civilization. Did they give up all this? Did they

reduce the area of their occupancy and give up waters which made it valuable or adequate?

The Court said no. Under the treaty and agreement in question the Native people had reserved the rights to enough water to meet their own needs, though these rights were not specifically mentioned in the wording of the documents themselves. From this initial decision, the courts of the U.S. have developed what is called the "Winters Doctrine." The "Winters Doctrine" can be stated simply: under treaty that creates a reservation land base for a Native Nation or group, that Nation has a superior right to enough water to meet its needs.

Judicial decisions in the later cases have held that Indian "Winters Doctrine" rights include not only enough water to meet the needs of the Nation at the time the treaty was ratified, but include the Indians' future needs as well. The *Winters* case and those that followed it do not limit the kind of use to which the water may be applied. . . . The U.S. courts have developed a formula for determining how much water an Indian Nation has the right to use, based on the amount of land within the reservation that can be irrigated. They have not dealt with the question of the amount in the case of the Native group which realistically needs more water than would be used to irrigate the available lands on its reservation.

The water rights of Native American Nations recognized by treaty under the "Winters Doctrine" can be interpreted to apply to potentially large amounts of water. What makes these rights particularly important to Indians and non-Indians alike is that Indian water rights, as recognized by the courts, are superior to the rights of all other water users, including the U.S. Native nations possessed these rights long before the U.S. came into being, and can continue to exercise these rights to meet their continued needs. In the arid West, where water is always scarce, the fulfillment and protection of Native rights might often prevent development of competing non-Indian uses. . . .

Coal Gasification on Navajo Lands: The Impact

The Navajo Indians are the largest Indian tribe in the country. . . . The reservation that they live on is also the largest in the country, roughly the size of West Virginia. . . . The land is basically dry and mostly desert, yet the Navajos have managed to live off it through raising sheep and subsistence farming. Water is precious, but scarce.

Two large energy corporations (El Paso Natural Gas and Western Gasification Company) are planning to build six large coal gasification plants on the Navajo reservation. . . . Each plant will produce 250 million cubic feet of gas a day or 1.8 billion altogether. But in order to do that, the two companies must strip mine approximately 57,000 acres of former Navajo grazing land to get the coal. . . . Approximately 1.7 billion tons of coal will be strip mined during the 25-year life span of the plants' operation. All of this synthetic natural gas will go off the reservation to mushrooming urban centers in the Southwest and Southern California.

The Navajos will only get a 15 to 25 cent royalty on each ton of coal that is mined while the coal companies sell it for $4.50 a ton. Navajo land is leased for one to two dollars an acre per year. The Navajo Tribe is contractually forbidden from taxing these plants in exchange for Navajo jobs. Yet the U.S. Bureau of Reclamation estimates that 45% of the construction jobs will have to come from *outside* the reservation and 95% of the so-called permanent jobs will also have to come from *outside* the reservation. . . .

Last year the National Academy of Sciences . . . concluded that successful reclamation of [strip mined land in the Southwest] is virtually impossible due to the low level of rainfall received there annually. . . . The study also quoted the U.S. government as referring to the Navajo reservation as a "national sacrifice area" because it would be too expensive to reclaim the land for future productive use after strip mining.

Furthermore, these six gasification plants will be in addition to several other existing power plants on and near the reservation. The notorious Four Corners Power Plant is only 25 miles northeast of the proposed gasification sites. In fact, the pollution from the Four Corners plant was the only man-made object seen from space by astronauts during the Gemini expeditions of the 60's. Since then, the plant has almost doubled in size. . . . Several years ago, it was reliably estimated that its coal ash and other impurities . . . spewed out more pollution in a day than New York City and Los Angeles combined. . . .

The proposed gasification plants will also be built right next to the developing Navajo Indian Irrigation Project. The project will eventually be a 100,000 acre agricultural project to be owned and operated by the Navajo Tribe. It will grow a variety of crops for both human consumption and animal grazing. It will also benefit approximately 30,000 Navajos through direct employment and in secondary food processing industries such as canneries, co-op stores, and a food marketing and distribution system. Unlike gasification or strip mining, the project will not destroy the land or deplete its resources. . . . The successful completion of the project is the number one priority of the Navajo Tribe and offers a unique opportunity in which Indian resources can be independently developed and utilized by Indian people for the primary benefit and use of Indian people. When the Navajo people were forced to give up almost one half of their ancestral homeland, they were promised an agricultural project by the U.S. government. This promise was specifically stated in the Treaty of 1868 signed between the Navajo Nation and the federal government.

Yet the proposed gasification plants pose a serious threat to all of this. There will be at least two deadly toxic air pollutants (lead and mercury) emitted from these plants in uncontrolled quantities that will inflict permanent damage to all animal, plant, and human life in the vicinity of the plants. . . . all people living within a thirteen mile radius from the plants will have to be evacuated. . . . . Another toxic emission (boron) is greatly feared by the planners of the Navajo Indian Irrigation Project because it can easily wipe out all of the crops to be grown there. . . .

The huge influx of non-Indians (construction workers, technicians, etc.) will pose a massive threat to the future of Indian sovereignty. . . . A boom town of over 50,000 is expected to spring up overnight in the gasification area, increasing already serious social problems such as alcoholism and suicide. . . . Coal gasification will consume an enormous amount of water annually. One gasification plant will require at least 10,000 acre feet of water a year. One acre foot is equivalent to 326,000 gallons of water. . . . If gasification requires more water [than now estimated] then it will surely have to come from the Navajo Indian Irrigation Project's share. . . . there is simply not enough water in the San Juan River for both. . . .

At present, outside corporations are coming on Indian lands and exploiting resources for the profit and benefit of outsiders. In their wake, these corporations leave destroyed land, depleted resources, polluted air and water, and devastated Native culture. . . . On the Navajo reservation, a sacred mountain (Black Mesa in Arizona) is now being strip mined by the world's largest coal producer, Peabody Coal Company. Almost half the Crow and Northern Cheyenne reservation in eastern Montana may soon be strip mined away.

In order for this to change, it is necessary that the Indian people begin to organize and unite toward positively developing and utilizing their own land and resources in alternative ways, such as more diversified agricultural development and live stock raising. There is much potential in the Navajo Irrigation Project which may begin a totally Indian owned and controlled economic base, the possibility of an expanded agricultural project to help alleviate world hunger, and the opportunity for Indian people to contribute to the world crisis in a direct and meaningful way, instead of having to sacrifice their lands and resources.

*Northern Cheyenne: Coal Strip Mining and the
Environmental Effects*

The Cheyenne people, as well as the Lakota, are
signatories of the Treaty of April 29, 1868 (Fort Laramie).
Article 17 in this treaty defines certain lands as "unceded
Indian territory." . . . The Article 17 lands, including the
Cheyenne Reservation, contain perhaps the richest de-
posits of low sulphur content coal within the U.S. It has
been estimated that 90% of the surface strippable coal
within the U.S. lies in this area. . . . it is cheaper to
surface strip it than to deep mine coal from the eastern
U.S. The low sulphur content of this coal also makes it
more valuable, because it can more easily be used to meet
air quality control standards in cities. In 1971, a group of
energy corporations . . . under the support of the U.S.
government . . . laid out a plan for building more than 40
coal-fired electrical power generating plants—almost all
of them located on the Article 17 lands, and several on or
near the Northern Cheyenne reservation. Meanwhile,
large portions of the reservation's land were leased or
optioned to the energy corporations, for strip mining of
the coal. Other strip mines have been opened and
developed nearby, but off the reservation land. The
Bureau of Reclamation (a part of the Department of
Interior) leased or promised large quantities of water to
the corporations, to use in processing the coal and
running the electric plants. All of this was done with no
thought for Indian rights in the matter, for the bad
effects on land, water, vegetation, animal life, and the
lives of Indian people.

. . . The Fort Union coal formation, which underlies
our reservation, also extends north, east, west and south
of us. Outside the boundaries of our reservation, strip
mining is already going on, and the construction of
several large electrical generation plants—with all the
pollution, destruction, and medical damage they will
cause—have been approved. Damage done to us by such
development not on our land is damage which presently
we can do little about. We have attempted to have the

U.S. classify our reservation for an air quality control standard which might halt such development, or force the corporations to operate in nonpolluting ways. . . .

All of these developments are violating our human, religious, and cultural rights. Physically, we may be threatened with disease and death by the industrial pollution. If our land and water are destroyed, we could not physically survive that and remain on our reservation, which is our only home, and *final* homeland. Even if the Cheyenne people survive as individuals, our culture could not survive the attack on land, air, water, and vegetation, so that we as a people, with unique values and way of life would be no more.

Sovereignty and recognition of our rights under our treaties is the real solution to these matters, because there can be no real solution which is not determined by ourselves. If the 1868 Treaty were acknowledged as valid international law, binding upon the U.S. and followed by it, almost all the coal lands that concern us would be under Indian control. With recognized sovereignty, we would also be able to deal on a nation-to-nation basis with activities taking place outside our territory which have effects on our land, air, or water that might threaten our well-being or our cultural survival.

DOCUMENT K:
"A Question of Genocide," a report by Native women.

Our people have lived on this continent for tens of thousands of years. We have lived in harmony with nature, and have developed our cultures which place respect for all life, respect for persons, and respect for communities foremost in our values. Our way of living is communal and co-operative. Our societies and nations ("tribes") are founded on the family structure. We do not have "nuclear" families, but include in our immediate family, grandparents, aunts and uncles and first cousins. The extended family includes second cousins, etc. From the immediate family our societies are structured into what are called in English clans, then bands, and finally the nation ("tribe") itself. It may be seen then that our families are the basic, key element and foundation of our existence. We have found that this system works for us, with no conflict with other peoples, and in balance with our mother the earth. We also find that other, imposed systems do not work for us. The U.S. government, through its various agencies such as the Bureau of Indian Affairs, the Bureau of Land Management, the Department of Health, Education and Welfare, the Indian Health Service, the Department of Justice, state and county welfare offices, courts, and in collusion with churches and other private organizations, has maintained a continuous policy of destroying our cultural values and systems. Today this unstated policy is most often carried out by attempts to destroy our families, primarily through sterilization and removal of our children. This must be seen as deliberate genocide, and we appeal to all people who love justice that international attention be focused on this urgent situation here in the U.S. and in Bolivia, where Indian women are also being sterilized. . . .

Sterilization: 24% of Native women [in the U.S.] have been sterilized. 19% are of child bearing age. For every 7 babies born, one Indian woman is sterilized. The Indian birth rate has been steadily declining since 1965. In 1973 in Claremore, Oklahoma, of 132 women sterilized only 32 of these were for therapeutic reasons (medically required). In Oklahoma City, of 15,000 women of child bearing age, 1,761 were sterilized within 46 months. In the Aberdeen area, of 9,000 Native women, 740 were sterilized in a 46 month period. In Phoenix, Arizona, of 8,000 women, 784 were sterilized.

In 1973, as it was becoming clear that sterilization was increasing at an alarming rate, Senator Abourezk of South Dakota asked for the General Accounting Office to perform a study on sterilization abuse in the Indian Health Service (IHS) areas. In April of 1974, the HEW had passed a series of regulations in response to a U.S. District Court order, including a moratorium on sterilization of persons under 21 years of age, or mentally incompetent.

The GAO Report: Between 1973 and 1976, in four out of twelve IHS areas, 3,406 sterilizations were performed on Native women. Of these, 3,000 were between the ages of 13 and 44. In the GAO Report (B-164031-5), it was concluded that consent forms used by IHS were not in compliance with regulations, and that the moratorium was being violated. Several different consent forms were being used. The most widely used form did not:

    1) indicate that basic informed consent had been orally presented;

    2) contain written summaries of oral presentations;

    3) contain a statement notifying subjects of their right to withdraw consent.

The GAO Report, although an important exposé of sterilization abuse of Native American women, has one major weakness. When doing the study, the government investigators failed to interview patients to determine if they were adequately informed before consenting to sterilization. Instead, they relied totally on documents found in the medical records of the institutions performing the sterilizations. . . .

Child Stealing: The mass removal of one nation's children from their homes and cultural heritage by another nation—to be reared in the homes of the second nation—is genocide, as defined by the United Nations Convention on Genocide. The U.S., which conspicuously did not endorse this convention, pursues a systematic policy of child stealing against Native American Nations.

This child stealing is mainly carried out in two ways: removing Native children from their homes and putting them up for adoption or in foster homes; and by placing them in white run boarding schools removed from their communities.

Adoption: Surveys by the Association of American Indian Affairs show that from 25-35% of all Indian children under 18 are removed from their homes by child welfare officials; 85% of these children are placed in non-Indian homes. In most cases, the parents and family of these children do not understand the document and legal proceedings involved, and are not represented by an attorney.

The reasons given for the separation of Native children from their homes almost always reflect the racism of the welfare worker as well as the poverty of the Native family; thus the oppression of Native people is used to justify further oppression. For example, homes are called "unfit" because there is no running water, or because two or more children are sharing one bed. "It isn't necessary for Indian children to have one bed apiece" said one Native mother. "Our children learn sharing right from the start." This lack of respect for Indian ways means that Native families are prevented from being adoptive parents even if they are relatives of the children involved; yet non-Indian parents receive governmental subsidies for caring for the children that their parents were "too poor" to keep. . . .

BIA Boarding Schools: Another means by which Native children are removed from their homes and families is by placing them in white run boarding schools. According to the BIA annual school census for 1973, 68% of all Indian children attended public school; 26% attended federal boarding schools; and 6% attended mission and other "private" schools. In that year the BIA operated 195 schools with an enrollment of 51,180 Indian, Aleut and Eskimo children and 19 "dormitories" for 3,871 children in public schools. Of all Indian children in federal schools, over two-thirds (33,672) were in boarding schools.

The purpose of these schools is to assimilate Native children into the culture of their oppressor, and to downgrade and destroy their own culture. The curriculum of BIA schools is designed to meet the standards of the state in which they are located and to provide for the "special needs" of the children. These include enrichment courses in English (none in Native languages), and "courses designed to overcome educational and other cultural deficits that result from isolation and deprivation."

This education is compulsory and thorough. Indian children in federal boarding schools are encouraged to attend Christian church services; and those in day schools are given "released time" for Christian religious instruction. Meanwhile, the teachers and textbooks conspire to downgrade the importance and viability of Native religions. . . .

As a result of this child stealing policy, implemented through the foster homes and adoptive agencies and the boarding schools, one-half of Native American children are removed from their own culture, traditions and nations at an early age.

The U.N. Convention on Genocide states that imposing measures intended to prevent births within a group of people and forcibly transferring the children of one group to another group are acts of genocide. Stealing children and sterilization of women are direct attacks on nationhood. Sterilization must continue as a birth control choice for women, but for Native people it should be seen in the context of national identity. If an Indian woman is a member of a 3,000 member nation, sterilization has serious consequences for the survival of the people as a whole.

DOCUMENT L:
Declaration of Principles for Defense of the Indigenous Nations and Peoples of the Western Hemisphere.

PREAMBLE

Having considered the problems relating to the activities of the United Nations for the promotion and encouragement of respect for human rights and fundamental freedoms,

Noting that the Universal Declaration of Human Rights and related international covenants have the individual as their primary concern, and

Recognizing that individuals are the foundation of cultures, societies, and nations, and

Whereas, it is a fundamental right of any individual to practice and perpetuate the cultures, societies and nations into which they are born, and

Recognizing that conditions are imposed upon peoples that suppress, deny or destroy the culture, societies or nations in which they believe or of which they are members,

Be it affirmed that,

1. RECOGNITION OF INDIGENOUS NATIONS: Indigenous peoples shall be accorded recognition as nations, and proper subjects of international law, provided the people concerned desire to be recognized as a nation and meet the fundamental requirements of nationhood, namely:

    a. Having a permanent population
    b. Having a defined territory
    c. Having a government
    d. Having the ability to enter into relations with other states

2. SUBJECTS OF INTERNATIONAL LAW: Indigenous groups not meeting the requirements of nationhood are hereby declared to be subjects of international law and are entitled to the protection of this Declaration, provided they are identifiable groups having bonds of language, heritage, tradition, or other common identity.

3. GUARANTEE OF RIGHTS: No indigenous nation or group shall be deemed to have fewer rights, or lesser status for the sole reason that the nation or group has not entered into recorded treaties or agreements with any state.

4. ACCORDANCE OF INDEPENDENCE: Indigenous nations or groups shall be accorded such degree of independence as they may desire in accordance with international law.

5. TREATIES AND AGREEMENTS: Treaties and other agreements entered into by indigenous nations or groups with other states, whether denominated as treaties or otherwise, shall be recognized and applied in the same manner and according to the same international laws and principles as the treaties and agreements entered into by other states.

6. ABROGATION OF TREATIES AND OTHER RIGHTS: Treaties and agreements made with indigenous nations or groups shall not be subject to unilateral abrogation. In no event may the municipal laws of any state serve as a defense to the failure to adhere to and perform the terms of treaties and agreements made with indigenous nations or groups. Nor shall any state refuse to recognize and adhere to treaties or other agreements due to changed circumstances where the change in circumstances has been substantially caused by the state asserting that such change has occurred.

7. JURISDICTION: No state shall assert or claim to exercise any right of jurisdiction over any indigenous nation or group or the territory of such indigenous nation or group unless pursuant to a valid treaty or other agreement freely made with the lawful representatives of the indigenous nation or group concerned. All actions on the part of any state which derogate from the indigenous nations' or groups' right to exercise self-determination shall be the proper concern of existing international bodies.

8. CLAIMS TO TERRITORY: No state shall claim or retain, by right of discovery or otherwise, the territories of an indigenous nation or group, except such lands as may have been lawfully acquired by valid treaty or other cessation freely made.

9. SETTLEMENT OF DISPUTES: All states in the Western Hemisphere shall establish through negotiations or other appropriate means a procedure for the binding settlement of disputes, claims, or other matters relating to indigenous nations or groups. Such procedures shall be mutually acceptable to the parties, fundamentally fair, and consistent with international law. All procedures presently in existence which do not have the endorsement of the indigenous nations or groups concerned, shall be ended, and new procedures shall be instituted consistent with this Declaration.

10. NATIONAL AND CULTURAL INTEGRITY: It shall be unlawful for any state to take or permit any action or course of conduct with respect to an indigenous nation or group which will directly or indirectly result in the destruction or disintegration of such indigenous nation or group or otherwise threaten the national or cultural integrity of such nation or group, including, but not limited to, the imposition and support of illegitimate governments and the introduction of non-indigenous religions to indigenous peoples by non-indigenous missionaries.

11. ENVIRONMENTAL PROTECTION: It shall be unlawful for any state to make or permit any action or course of conduct with respect to the territories of an indigenous nation or group which will directly or indirectly result in the destruction or deterioration of an indigenous nation or group through the effects of pollution of earth, air, water, or which in any way depletes, displaces or destroys any natural resource or other resources under the dominion of, or vital to the livelihood of an indigenous nation or group.

12. INDIGENOUS MEMBERSHIP: No state, through legislation, regulation, or other means, shall take actions that interfere with the sovereign power of an indigenous nation or group to determine its own membership.

13. CONCLUSION: All of the rights and obligations declared herein shall be in addition to all rights and obligations existing under international law.

POSTSCRIPT TO THE DOCUMENTS:

The Final Resolution of the Geneva Conference contained a number of recommendations including: "to observe October 12, the day of so-called 'discovery' of America, as International Day of Solidarity with the Indigenous Peoples of the Americas." The "Declaration of Principles" was recommended in the Final Resolution and, as the Legal Commission (one of three Commissions that heard testimony during the Conference) stated, "the Declaration of Principles reflects a consensus among the indigenous delegates and represents a united call for justice which cannot be ignored by the international community." The Conference also recommended that the U.N. Special Committee on Decolonization investigate the situation of Native peoples in the Americas and that the U.N. Committee on Trans-National Corporations investigate "the role of multinational corporations in the plunder and exploitation of Native lands, resources, and peoples in the Americas." The Conference resolutions were formally presented to the President of the U.N. General Assembly on November 17, 1977. (A report on the Geneva Conference is available for $1.00 from the American Indian Treaty Council Information Center listed on page 391.)

ABOUT THE DOCUMENTS:
Human Rights

The latter half of the 1970s was a time of much discussion of "human rights" and political prisoners," a discussion generated by U.S. President Carter but focusing on "human rights" and "political prisoners" in other countries. Major U.S. news media said little or nothing about these issues within the U.S.

Native peoples' efforts to fight the exploitation of their lands and resources and the genocide practiced against them have been met by increased U.S. government repression, using the FBI, BIA, state and local police. The Native struggle, like the Black liberation struggle, was a target of the infamous COINTELPRO program, which sought to disrupt and destroy those movements. Large numbers of American Indian Movement (AIM) members and supporters have been killed, jailed or tied up in long, expensive court battles.

Document *M* includes excerpts from a speech to the Human Rights Commission in Geneva in March, 1978 by Jimmie Durham of the International Indian Treaty Council. Document *N* contains information about six AIM members or supporters who have been killed or imprisoned. The cases presented here serve merely as examples of a much greater number of similar cases about which documentation is available.

DOCUMENT M:

Testimony to the Commission on Human Rights in Geneva—March 1978

. . . The Carter administration has stated its willingness to be open to real and responsible charges of human rights violations in the U.S. Therefore, the Treaty Council respectfully suggests that the U.S. might provide to the Commission on Human Rights, thorough and statistical documentation on the situation Black, Indian and Spanish-speaking prisoners in its federal and state prisons, for the purpose of realistic discussion on ways to implement a body of principles for protection of prisoners. . . .

For example, Indians in the U.S. are the poorest sector of the population. Their arrest rate is three times higher than that of American Blacks and ten times that of whites. Unless we assume that Indians are racially more prone to criminal acts, we must concede that the situation has political and economic causes. . . .

American Indians are given longer sentences for the

same crimes than either Blacks or whites and, once in prison, they are parolled less often than either Blacks or whites. Studies show that that situation has grown more severe since the Wounded Knee occupation in 1973. Indians in prison suffer more cultural deprivation and alienation than other prisoners, but special programs are not provided, and in most prisons are denied when Indian prisoners attempt to set up programs on their own. In one prison in Oklahoma the government has reacted to Indian demands to the right to cultural and religious expression by removing even the health services.

In all U.S. prisons health services are inadequate and sometimes non-existent. This is especially serious to Indian prisoners, who often suffer diseases caused by the poverty on the reservations. . . . It has been said many times, and is no exaggeration, that it is impossible for an Indian to obtain a fair trial in the U.S. He is never tried by a jury of his peers, usually has no money to hire a lawyer, and racism affects the judges, juries, and the legal system itself. But many Indians, especially members of AIM and the Treaty Council, are in prison for strictly political reasons. . . .

We believe that it would be an important advance in the area of human rights of prisoners, for the U.S. to provide detailed information on its prison policies and conditions to the Human Rights Commission.

DOCUMENT N:

Information on and statements from individuals mentioned in the testimony to Commission on Human Rights—March 1978

Pedro Bissonette, Oglala Lakota, was a leader in the liberation of Wounded Knee and was vice-president of the Oglala Civil Rights Organization. During the occupation he said in an interview:

At one time, I thought all I could ever be is a drunk. When I found out I could fight for my people, I became a man. I wasn't here [a few years ago]—I was working on high structural steel, making plenty of money—but I was tired of what's happening here, the way Indians have been pushed around, and I have been for my Indian people all the time. I wanted to come home to work for my people, getting something done, and without getting pay for it. Something that would be good for every district out here, for the kids and the older generation.

He later said:

I will stand with my brothers and sisters. I will tell the truth about them and about why we went to Wounded Knee. I will fight for my people. I will live for them, and if it is necessary to stop the terrible things that happen to Indians on the Pine Ridge Reservation, I am ready to die for them.

On October 17, 1973, Pedro Bissonette, 33 years old, was shot and killed by a BIA police officer.

John Waubanascum was a member of the Menominee Warrior Society, a group that for 34 days occupied the Alexian Brothers' abandoned novitiate near Gresham, Wisconsin, in 1975. The novitiate was on Menominee land illegally taken in 1848. The Warrior Society wanted the abbey buildings and land deeded back to the Menominee people for use as a badly needed hospital. They also wanted to raise issues about the illegal treaty of 1848, the effects of Public Law 280, and the termination of the Menominee by the U.S. government in the 1950's. Waubanascum had been involved in the liberation of Wounded Knee. In a letter written from jail, he said:

. . . I was talked into joining the Marine Corps. I was rushed through boot camp and my mind programmed with one thought: to kill. They rushed me to Vietnam and I participated in many operations while there.

Being wounded three times really shook me up and I realized what crimes I was committing. These crimes

came from the top—orders to kill anything that didn't
have roots. . . . I wanted to return to my people and my
peaceful reservation to live out the rest of my life among
Indians.

I returned and found my people hurting also. Hurt by
the same White government I was fighting for. The same
government I was sent by to annihilate this foreign
country. The same government that ripped off my people.
I realized how much they had brainwashed me—they had
made me think like them. So I started fighting for my
people and now they are labelling me as "criminal."

Earlier he had said:

I don't care what happens to me. As long as we have
made our point, it will be a start. They may put us away,
but others will follow. Things have to get better.

*John Waubanascum was shot and killed on February
3, 1976 by the Menominee County Sheriff. Also killed was
Arlin Pamanet, 27, a Menominee worker for the Menominee Legal Defense/Offense Committee, which was organizing for the trials resulting from the takeover.*

*Anna Mae Pictou Aquash was born and raised on a
Micmac reserve in Nova Scotia. After becoming involved
with the Boston Indian Center, she participated in the
Trail of Broken Treaties/BIA takeover, the liberation of
Wounded Knee and other protests. On November 14, 1975
she and other activists were arrested in Oregon on
explosives and firearms charges (which were later
thrown out of court after police claimed to have lost the
explosives). After being arrested, Aquash and KaMook
Banks, another passenger in the vehicle, issued the
following statement:*

We are proud of being born Indian, and we will never
be ashamed of our heritage or our decisions. . . . When
we decided to join our husbands and sons, we knew that
we would have to carry the struggle if they were killed

along the way, and we accepted that challenge. And we will carry ourselves in a manner that will be remembered with pride.

We stand today because we are tired of watching our people die of broken hearts, brutal slayings and other injustices of this country. We pledge our lives that we will never tolerate that abuse anymore. And even though we may be killed in struggle, we will die with pride knowing that our children are that much closer to victory.

On February 24, 1976, Anna Mae Aquash's body was found along a highway on the Pine Ridge Reservation. She was 31 years old. The coroner contracted by the BIA declared that death was caused by exposure. FBI agents, who had occupied the reservation since 1973 and knew Aquash well, severed the hands from her body and sent them to Washington for identification. Her body was buried in an unmarked grave. Relatives and friends later demanded an independent autopsy, which found a bullet wound in the back of Aquash's head. No one has been charged with her murder.

Leonard Crow Dog is a Lakota holy man and a spiritual leader of the American Indian Movement. He participated in the liberation of Wounded Knee. He has been imprisoned a number of times by the U.S. government. He has said:

A reservation Indian is already well-prepared to go to the penitentiary. Before he gets there he has already practiced being in prison. And even off the reservation, many Indians are still having a barbed-wire attitude—I try to teach my children and my people to get rid of the barbed-wire mind. We want sovereignty.

Do you want to know what my crime is? I said: *"Listen, White America!"* and that is my main crime. White people tell me, "No, Crow Dog, don't blame me. It's my ancestors who have done wrong. Don't blame me—I'm not involved." But you are. You should be involved—you are living on our land now. Indians are living now, suffering, in jail. You should take some responsibility.

Not for what was, but for what is!

*Russell Means has been involved in the Indian struggle
for many years, founding an Indian Center in Cleveland
before joining the American Indian Movement. He has
been involved in most of the major AIM-related events
since the late 1960s. A special target of the U.S. government, he has been arrested 13 times, charged with 37
felonies and 3 misdemeanors. All these charges have
ended in only one felony conviction, and that for a crime
which was later repealed by the South Dakota legislature
(i.e., riot and injury to a public building). Of the potential
330 years, 90 days plus life imprisonment he has faced,
he is presently serving a four-year sentence in the South
Dakota penitentiary. Before his federal trial on 11 indictments stemming from the liberation of Wounded Knee, he
said:*

Wounded Knee happened because traditional chiefs
and holy men of the Oglala people directed and supported
our attempt to ascertain the treaty rights of the Lakota
people based on an 1868 Sioux treaty. We did not break
any laws, but in fact we went into Wounded Knee to
uphold laws. The statement put forth by the Independent
Oglala Nation inside Wounded Knee is that we were
trying to force the U.S.A. to live up to its own laws. They
made those laws, we didn't.

We are going to attempt, for the first time in history,
through the federal judiciary system, in front of a jury, to
prove we, the American Indian do have treaty rights. If
the U.S. is going to live up to its Constitution and idea of
democracy, if it is going to honor its sacred trust, made
with American Indian people, it will have to honor the
1868 Treaty—and find us not guilty. They have no
recourse because treaties are on par with, and equal to,
the Constitution, the law of the land. Therefore, treaties
made by the U.S., ratified by Congress and proclaimed
by the President, supercede federal statements and local
laws.

Before Means had an opportunity to find out if the

arguments were persuasive, the federal judge dismissed the charges, stating that the U.S. had used illegal wiretaps, paid witnesses and FBI informers, submitted altered evidence, lied under oath, and illegally used U.S. troops disguised as civilians during Wounded Knee, 1973.

Leonard Peltier. In June 1976, a shootout occurred on Pine Ridge Reservation, leaving three people dead—two FBI agents, part of the FBI force that has been occupying the reservation since 1973, and Joe Stuntz, a Native American. Although the firefight involved a large number of people, four AIM activists were indicted. Two were tried and acquitted, in part because of evidence of the reign of terror on the reservation and their argument that the firefight was an act of self-defense. The case against the third defendant was dismissed. The fourth, Leonard Peltier, Turtle Mountain Chippewa, fled to Canada to seek political asylum. He was extradited to the U.S. on the basis of affidavits signed by a woman who later testified she had been coerced by FBI agents. While in prison awaiting trial, Peltier wrote the following poem:

I am the Indian Voice.
I long to be heard across our land.

I have been a prisoner of war for more than two hundred
    years on my very own soil!
I am a captive of hate, greed, lies, prejudice, indifference,
    ignorance, injustice
by men who outnumber me and my people
since they have landed on my shores
and have overrun my homeland. They have wrought on
    me
their society, their religion, and their laws,
all of which have caused the number of my people
to be less today than when he first came
with his false promises to our shores.

I am the collective Indian Voice

and I cry out from a million graves of unresting souls
and another million cries that ask the questions:
where does my future belong and to whom:
Does it belong to my people?
Is it to prosper on the land that is rightfully mine?
Yes, it does and it shall.
For my voice shall not be stilled
nor my spirit stopped from soaring
to the heights of greatness
which my people have known and shall know again.

I am the Indian Voice—
I shall be heard and my people shall see
the coming of a new day.

The Mother Earth provides and the Great Spirit guides
so that truth is known from shore to shore
by the voice of a proud Indian Race.

*Peltier's trial in June 1977 was marked by rulings from
the bench which prevented the defense from entering
evidence of FBI misconduct, the situation on Pine Ridge
at the time of the shootout, and the political nature of the
trial. On the other hand, the judge allowed the prosecution to present evidence irrelevant to the case but prejudi-
cial to the defendant. Before he was sentenced, Peltier
spoke eloquently about the nature of his trial:*

. . . I stand before you as a proud man; I have no guilt. I
have done nothing to feel guilty about. I have no regrets
of being a Native American activist—thousands of people
in the United States, Canada, and around the world have
and will continue to support me to expose the injustices
that have occurred in this courtroom. I do feel pity for
your people that they must live under such an ugly
system. Under your system, you are taught greed, racism
and corruption—and most serious of all, the destruction
of Mother Earth. Under the Native American system, we

are taught all people are Brothers and Sisters; to share the wealth with the poor and needy. But the most important of all is to respect and preserve the Earth, who we consider to be our Mother. We feed from her breast; our Mother gives us life from birth and when it's time to leave this world, she again takes us back into her womb. But the main thing we are taught is to preserve her for our children and our grandchildren, because they are the next who will live upon her.

No, I'm not the guilty one here. I'm not the one who should be called a criminal—white racist America is the criminal for the destruction of our lands and my people; to hide your guilt from the decent human beings in America and around the world, you will sentence me to two consecutive life terms without any hesitation.

The judge sentenced Leonard Peltier to two consecutive life terms.

DOCUMENT O:
Land Claims Cases and Trust Responsibility

The latter half of the 1970s saw a number of lawsuits in U.S. courts over land claims in the East brought by Native nations, many of which had no treaties with the U.S. and thus had never legally ceded any of their lands. The lands were taken by states—in some instances through treaties—but never ratified by the Federal Government. According to a U.S. law of 1790—the Indian Trade and Non-Intercourse Act—any such transaction not approved by the U.S. government was null and void.

The most publicized case was in Maine, where the Passamaquoddy and Penobscot nations, with legal assistance from the Native American Rights Fund (NARF), sued for return of their lands, which comprise over half of the present State of Maine. Most of the claimed land is "owned" by seven large multinational paper corpora-

tions. The two nations won a ruling from a federal court requiring the U.S. to recognize the Passamaquoddy and Penobscot, to give them trust status and to sue in court for the return of their lands—since it was a U.S. law that was broken in the taking of the lands. Any lands thus returned would fall under the control of the B.I.A. When this book went to press the U.S. was attempting to reach an out-of-court settlement.

In a 1978 interview, Robert T. Coulter, Director of the Indian Law Resource Center, discussed the Maine land claims case and the trust responsibility doctrine from the perspective of international law and the sovereign status of Native nations. Document O contains excerpts from that interview which appeared in Akwesasne Notes *(Vol. 10, No. 3).*

I don't see any hope in the domestic law setting for the vindication of Indian rights. Indian rights didn't originate in domestic law and they won't be upheld there. And Indian rights are not truly upheld under the so-called federal trust responsibility. There isn't much that is important about Indian rights except their rights as nations. . . .

The Passamaquoddy and Penobscot people [in Maine] have stated in past years that they are sovereign nations. But their rights as sovereign nations only exist in international law. The [Maine land] claim is not put forward in that way. The claim is presented in such a way that they are forced to admit that their rights are subject to U.S. law. . . .

Since the Indians clearly were the original owners of the land they now have, and since there is no proof that the Indians ever sold that land or gave away the title to that land, the question naturally arose concerning the theory by which the U.S. could claim title to it. The answer to that question has been, quite cynically, that the U.S. has become the "trustee" of the Indian land because the Indians, like children, are incompetent to take care of their own property. Because of this incompetence, the theory goes, the U.S. has assumed a responsibility to "hold" it "for the benefit" of the Indian people. . . .

I simply don't understand all the efforts to use the trust relationship as the basis for the protection of Indian rights. I don't see why intelligent lawyers try to insist that Indian treaties are not like other international treaties. They seem to assert that the U.S. law is wonderful and favorable toward Indian people, and that the route to survival is to improve the internal law of the U.S.

They say that Indian treaties aren't like international treaties because Congress can abrogate them. But that's circular. They are not like international treaties because the U.S. doesn't abide by international law! That doesn't prove that the Indian treaties are not like international treaties—it proves that the U.S. is violating international law! One thing is as true as another.

Well, they say the trust responsibility is something that you need in U.S. law. But the trust responsibility is an invention of people who thought that there was something wrong with the notion that the U.S. could simply steal Indian land. The U.S. claims, in fact, to own all Indian land, with the exception of some Indian land in the original thirteen colonies.

The Maine land claim is an example of the problems associated with reliance on the trust responsibility theory. The Maine claim is vulnerable the way [Native American Rights Fund] lawyers have presented the claim. Penobscot and Passamaquoddy people may have rights under international law which the U.S. could not validly extinguish. On the other hand, they have virtually no rights under U.S. law which cannot be destroyed by Congress.

DOCUMENT P:
Women of All Red Nations

In September, 1978, over 200 Native women gathered in

Rapid City, South Dakota for the founding of W.A.R.N.—
Women of All Red Nations. The delegates discussed
issues related to health, education and judicial needs,
national/international affairs and strategies, and eco-
nomic independence. Document P is the Founding Decla-
ration of W.A.R.N.

In following the Declaration of Continuing Independence in the 1st International Indian Treaty Council of
Standing Rock, 1974, we, Women of All Red Nations,
continue to realize that our struggle in this hemisphere is
unique. Our land base is guaranteed through international treaties. Our culture and way of life has survived
through resistance to foreign domination. Our fight
today is to survive as a people. Indian women have
always been in the front lines in the defense of our
nations. Today we are targets of the colonial governments of the Western Hemisphere. Our young are being
attacked through the racist educational system of governments and churches. Our unborn are attacked through
programs of genocide called sterilization. We value our
young for they are the very foundation of our future
generations. Only by throwing off the yoke of coloniza-
tion with the strength of our spirituality will we survive
as Peoples and Nations. We will work on local, national
and international levels to obtain our goals of true
liberation and freedom.

We, the Women of All Red Nations will take our place
and stand proudly with our sisters in the world in the
common struggle for all basic rights.

DOCUMENT Q:
  The Longest Walk

In February 1978, people set out from San Francisco for
a cross-country walk to Washington, D.C. "The Longest
Walk" was designed to draw public attention to a number

of bills in the U.S. Congress that would, if passed, abrogate Indian treaties, take away fishing and water rights, and open up lands for further exploitation. In mid-July, 1978, "The Longest Walk" reached Washington, D.C. On that occasion, three traditional governments— the Dine (Navajo), the Lakota (Sioux) and the Haudenosaunee (Six Nations of the Iroquois Confederacy)—issued a joint position paper. This paper—"Statement to the People of the U.S. and the World"—follows.

For countless thousands of years our people have lived on this continent in peace and tranquility, coexisting with all Natural Life. In the beginning we were told that the human beings who walk upon the Earth have been provided with all the things necessary for life. We were instructed to carry a love for one another, and to show a great respect for all beings of this Earth. We were shown that our life exists with the tree life, that our well-being depends on the well-being of the vegetable life, that we are close relatives of the four-leggeds. In our way, Spiritual consciousness is the highest form of politics.

Our roots are deep in the lands where we live. We have a great love for our country, for our birthplace is here. The soil is rich from the bones of thousands of our generations. Each of us was created in these lands and it is our duty to take great care of them, because from these lands will spring the future generations of our peoples. We walk about with great respect, for the Earth is a very Sacred Place.

Our traditional governments are truly governments "of the people, by the people, and for the people." All power of authority at all levels comes from the people and can be withdrawn at any time if the power is abused or responsibilities not met.

Our traditional governments cannot be adequately compared to the different forms of government that exist around us today. As with all aspects of Native life, our governments have their roots in the religious systems. Leaders are chosen for, among other things, the way they live their lives according to the four main virtues of bravery, fortitude, generosity, and wisdom. They are men who have proven themselves and show commitment to uphold and enforce the Spiritual and Natural Law, and also the laws of the people.

We are peoples who strongly believe in the cycles of the Universe. Everything is based on concepts of harmony and balance. With the coming of the peoples from the East, this hemisphere has experienced a 486-year conflict between Western Civilization and the Natural World Peoples.

The Western culture has been horribly exploitative and destructive of the Natural World. Over 140 species of birds and animals were utterly destroyed since the European arrival in the Americas, largely because they were unusable in the eyes of the invaders. The forests were levelled, the waters are polluted, our people subjected to genocide. The vast herds of herbivores are reduced to mere handfuls, the Buffalo nearly became extinct. Western technology and the people who employ it have been and continue to be the most amazingly destructive forces in all human history. No natural disaster has ever destroyed as much. Not even the Ice Ages counted as many victims.

Many would like to believe that all of these injustices have ended. This couldn't be further from the truth. Our Native nations entered into hundreds of treaties with the European colonists and the U.S. These treaties recognized the sovereignty of our nations, and guaranteed the lands and resources which belong to our nations.

Our people are the most abused of all peoples in North America. The extreme wrongs which are committed against our people today affect our everyday lives. Under the laws and policies of the U.S. we do not possess recognition of even the most fundamental rights necessary to our survival. We have no real rights in our lands, no rights to determine our Way of Life, no rights to our economic development. We are not even allowed to protect our communities against unfair actions by any people who choose to invade our homelands. Our lands are leased "for us" by the Bureau of Indian Affairs. Our governments are frequently controlled or hindered by the Interior Department. Our rights to exist as communities and nations are not protected, and are often denied by the courts. We are a horribly oppressed people in our own land. The most basic justice is denied to our peoples, and only to our peoples!

We are the only peoples in North America who own land and resources and who must worry that these things can be taken away from us. No one else who owns resources is subjected to an unrelenting fear that the U.S. government will take those things away. . . .

We are the only people who have formal legal agreements with the U.S. government, which the U.S. freely violates without legal liability. The Constitution of the U.S. does not allow this to happen to other peoples. Yet, the U.S. claims the legal right to violate and ignore legal treaties made with our nations. . . .

Our people are often subjected to such extensive bureaucratic control and manipulation that the process amounts to the denial of even the slightest amount of real self-government. Although there are laws and policies that give the appearance of participation in the processes that affect our land and peoples, the reality is that we have no power over the bureaucracies or laws and policies which affect our lives. Indeed, the practices of the U.S. have the impact of foreign control over our affairs. The official U.S. position states that there exists on our lands a significant measure of self-determination. This is an illusion created to confuse the people of the U.S. and the world. Our peoples possess the least self-determination of any communities in North America.

Only the Native People can be subjected to acts of theft and fraud with no possibility of justice under law. What other people are told that even if a fraudulent, or other illegal act can be proven beyond any doubt, that the courts have no power to correct the wrongs which are committed? Yet, that is the actual practice of the courts.

The Political Question Doctrine applied by the courts prevents the courts from questioning fraudulent treaties, prevents the courts from correcting many treaty violations, and prevents the courts from questioning or correcting the abusive acts of government relating to our peoples.

What other communities have no right, under law, to pass ordinances to protect their members from the acts of violent and destructive outsiders? What other communities of people in the whole world are denied the right to control the acts of companies and individuals operating on their lands? Yet this is exactly the situation suffered by our peoples in the U.S. today, right now!

Only our peoples can be driven from their lands without due process of law. Under the U.S. Supreme Court decision in the case of the Tee-Hit-Ton Indians, the U.S. can, and does, take lands which have been forever the lands of our peoples. They not only take the land, but they assert the power to do so without any compensation, and without due process, and there is no law which protects our peoples from these obvious thefts.

The struggles of our peoples have brought our leaders before the Judicial, Legislative, and Executive branches of the U.S. government time after time in futile attempts to find Justice.

The real issues of Sovereignty and Treaty Rights have been consistently submerged to the processes of bureaucratic white-tape. Time after time we have been referred to the Interior Department which has neither the competency nor the power to effectively deal with these issues. We cannot allow these acts to continue if we are to survive as a People.

It seems the basic attitude of the American people and the government towards our peoples is yet one of extreme apathy.

Presently the Human Rights, Rights of Nationhood, Right of Self-Determination, and the basic right of existence of our peoples are being actively denied in the U.S.

We challenge the President of the U.S. to take the first step in correcting these wrongs by meeting with the Traditional and Spiritual leaders of our peoples to begin serious negotiations.

The basic issue of Human Rights raised by the President of the U.S. is hypocrisy and an outrage when viewed in the context of the history and present conditions of our peoples.

The definition of Genocide as stated in Article II of the International Convention on Genocide provides the basis of our peoples' charge of Genocide made at the United Nations in Geneva, Switzerland, in September, 1977.

Article II states: "In the present Convention, genocide means any of the following acts committed with intent to destroy, in whole or in part, a national, ethnical, racial, or religious group, such as:

    (a) Killing members of the group;
    (b) Causing serious bodily or mental harm to members of the group;
    (c) Deliberately inflicting on the group conditions of life calculated to bring about its physical destruction in whole or in part;
    (d) Imposing measures intended to prevent births within the group."

Many of our young people went across the seas and never returned. We were told that we went to war to fight for our country. Our war casualties under the U.S. flag are greater than any other sector of the North American population. Yet today, our country is threatened by the U.S.

U.S. police and intelligence agencies have directed illegal military operations against our peoples, such as COINTELPRO. These actions have resulted in the violent deaths of a number of our leaders. The process has not stopped, and we have no protection against these actions. As a result of these actions there are in many U.S. prisons patriotic Native People who only advocate peace and freedom for their nations.

According to a GAO report issued last year, 24% of our women were forcibly or illegally sterilized during the period 1971-1975.

Nearly one out of three of our children are being placed in non-Indian foster homes daily by various county, state and federal agencies.

The Indian Reorganization Act of 1934 continues to destroy the traditional governments of our people, causing widespread disruption of a tranquil Way of Life, and literally putting brother against brother.

The clearcut policy of genocide of the last century continues in more sophisticated forms in this century.

Our religions have been attacked, and degraded. Our children continue to be processed through various forms of Western educational programs. The Spiritual leaders of our nations are now being subjected to the destructive nature of government program moneys. Taxpayers' moneys are being used to regulate the practice of our natural religions. There are even efforts to certify our medicine peoples and to despiritualize the nature of our healing culture. That practice is a policy that is destroying our natural healing practices. It is a policy which is an outrageous attempt to interfere with, and ultimately destroy our natural religion.

Finally, the bills currently before Congress which call for the abrogation of Indian treaties, and termination of our lands, resources, and water, present a clear signal that the threat of genocide to the existence of our peoples is alive and well. The fact that the present Congress of the U.S., in the year 1978, can consider such legislation should alarm the people of the U.S. When a government denies the human rights of one people, it is only a matter of time before those rights will be denied to all of its peoples.

We call upon the voting public of the U.S. to seriously consider and question the ethics and morality of their representative leadership in Congress who are responsible for the introduction of dangerous and racist legislation against our peoples.

We call upon the U.S. to acknowledge its responsibilities under international law to respect Indian treaties, to insure genuine self-determination for our nations, and to correct past wrongs in an honorable and equitable manner.

The traditional people recognize that the injustices perpetuated upon our people, and indeed upon many of the peoples of the world, are the major factors destroying the Spirituality of the Human Race. Peace and Unity are the foundations of the Spiritual Way of Life of our peoples. But Peace and Unity are not companions to injustice.

We call upon all the peoples of the world to join with us in seeking peace, and in seeking to insure survival and justice for all indigenous peoples, for all the Earth's creatures, and all nations of the Earth.

We will take whatever steps necessary in the protection of our Sacred Mother Earth, and the rights and well-being of our peoples.

We will continue our efforts before the World Community to regain our inherent Human and Sovereign Rights.

PUBLICATIONS

Below is a listing of some Native American newspapers and journals.

ABC, Americans Before Columbus, a monthly publication of the National Indian Youth Council, 201 Hermosa, N.E., Albuquerque, New Mexico 87108.

Akwesasne Notes, a monthly collection of articles and reprints reflecting various aspects of Indian oppression and struggle. A contribution of at least $10 is suggested, though there is no set rate. *Akwesasne Notes,* Mohawk Nation, via Rooseveltown, N.Y. 13683.

American Indian Journal, a monthly publication of the Institute for the Development of Indian Law, 927 15th Street, N.W., Suite 200, Washington, D.C. 20005. Subscription $15 indiv., $25 instit.

NCAI Sentinel is published quarterly by the National Congress of American Indians, 1346 Connecticut Ave., N.W., Washington, D.C. 20036.

Wassaja, a monthly publication of the American Indian Historical Society, 1451 Masonic Ave., San Francisco, California 94177.

ORGANIZATIONS

The following organizations are committed to the interests of Native Americans. Organizations that are run by Native people are indicated with an asterisk.

*American Indian Movement (AIM)
  643 Virginia St.
  St. Paul, Minnesota 55103

*American Indian Treaty Council Information Center
  870 Market St.
  San Francisco, California 94102
  (Serves as communications and publication center for the International Indian Treaty Council)

Association on American Indian Affairs, Inc.
432 Park Ave. South
New York, New York 10010

*Indian Law Resource Center
1101 Vermont Ave., N.W.
Washington, D.C. 20005

*International Indian Treaty Council
777 U.N. Plaza, Suite 10F
New York, New York 10017

*National Congress of American Indians (NCAI)
1346 Connecticut Ave., N.W.
Washington, D.C. 20036

*National Indian Youth Council, Inc.
201 Hermosa, N.E.
Albuquerque, New Mexico 87108

Native American Solidarity Committee
P.O. Box 3426
St. Paul, Minnesota 55165